Language Te

Language Pedagogy

Language Teaching Research & Language Pedagogy

Rod Ellis

WILEY-BLACKWELL

A John Wiley & Sons, Ltd., Publication

This edition first published 2012
© 2012 John Wiley & Sons, Inc

Wiley-Blackwell is an imprint of John Wiley & Sons, formed by the merger of Wiley's global Scientific, Technical and Medical business with Blackwell Publishing.

Registered Office
John Wiley & Sons Ltd, The Atrium, Southern Gate, Chichester, West Sussex, PO19 8SQ, UK

Editorial Offices
350 Main Street, Malden, MA 02148-5020, USA
9600 Garsington Road, Oxford, OX4 2DQ, UK
The Atrium, Southern Gate, Chichester, West Sussex, PO19 8SQ, UK

For details of our global editorial offices, for customer services, and for information about how to apply for permission to reuse the copyright material in this book please see our website at www.wiley.com/wiley-blackwell.

The right of Rod Ellis to be identified as the author of this work has been asserted in accordance with the UK Copyright, Designs and Patents Act 1988.

Wiley also publishes its books in a variety of electronic formats. Some content that appears in print may not be available in electronic books.

Designations used by companies to distinguish their products are often claimed as trademarks. All brand names and product names used in this book are trade names, service marks, trademarks or registered trademarks of their respective owners. The publisher is not associated with any product or vendor mentioned in this book. This publication is designed to provide accurate and authoritative information in regard to the subject matter covered. It is sold on the understanding that the publisher is not engaged in rendering professional services. If professional advice or other expert assistance is required, the services of a competent professional should be sought.

Library of Congress Cataloging-in-Publication Data

Ellis, Rod.
    Language teaching research & language pedagogy / by Rod Ellis.
        p. cm.
    Includes bibliographical references and index.
    ISBN 978-1-4443-3610-8 (cloth) – ISBN 978-1-4443-3611-5 (pbk.)
    1. Language and languages–Study and teaching.   2. Language and languages–Research.
3. Second language acquisition research.   4. Language teachers–Training of.   I. Title.
    P118.2.E38 2012
    418.0071–dc23

                                                                        2011036327

A catalogue record for this book is available from the British Library.

Set in 10.5/13pt Minion by Aptara Inc., New Delhi, India

1   2012

Contents

List of Figures   vi

List of Tables   vii

Preface   ix

Acknowledgements   xiii

1   Introduction: Developments in Language Teaching Research   1

2   Methods for Researching the Second Language Classroom   21

3   Comparative Method Studies   51

4   Second Language Classroom Discourse   75

5   Focus on the Teacher   115

6   Focus on the Learner   151

7   Investigating the Performance of Tasks   195

8   Interaction and L2 Learning in the Classroom   237

9   Form-Focused Instruction and Second Language Learning   271

10 Instruction, Individual Differences and L2 Learning   307

11 Conclusion: Research and Language Teaching   337

References   349

Index   385

List of Figures

8.1   The relationships between focus on form, uptake and acquisition   249
9.1   Key FFI methodological options   277
9.2   Input-based FFI options   285
10.1 The mediating role of individual learner factors in instructed
       L2 learning   308
10.2 Design of an aptitude-treatment-interaction study   312
10.3 Structural model of willingness to communicate in English in the
       Chinese EFL classroom (Peng and Woodrow, 2010: 853; simplified)   324

List of Tables

1.1	Major journals publishing articles on language teaching research	5
2.1	Summary of Ellis and He's experimental study (1999)	22
2.2	Summary of Lyster and Ranta's study of corrective feedback (1997)	24
2.3	Summary of an action research study (based on Penner, 1998)	28
2.4	Summary of Bloom's (2007) exploratory study	32
2.5	Summary of Guilloteaux and Dörnyei's (2008) correlational study	38
2.6	Examples of data collection methods used in experimental research	40
2.7	Summary of Harklau's (1994) ethnographic study	44
3.1	Experiential and analytic features in language pedagogy (based on Stern, 1990)	63
3.2	Summary of the comparative method studies presented	66
4.1	Coded extract illustrating Fanselow's FOCUS system	80
4.2	Summary of different dimensions of interaction analysis systems (based on Long, 1980)	81
4.3	COLT Part A (based on Allen, Frohlich, and Spada, 1984)	83
4.4	Aspects of turn-taking mechanisms in four different instructional contexts (based on Seedhouse, 2004)	99
5.1	Ten features of discourse in the EFL classroom (Walsh, 2002)	116
5.2	A teacher-educator's perspective on teacher-talk (based on O'Neill, 1994)	119
5.3	Long and Sato's (1984) taxonomy of teacher questions (based on Kearsley, 1976)	122
5.4	Functions of teachers' L1 use (based on Polio and Duff, 1994)	130
5.5	Taxonomy of teachers' corrective strategies (Lyster and Ranta, 1997: 46–49)	138
5.6	Two dimensions of corrective feedback strategies	139
5.7	Regulatory scale – implicit to explicit (Aljaafreh and Lantolf, 1994: 471)	140

5.8	Focus on the teacher – cognitive and social perspectives	147
6.1	Summary of Lightbown's (1983) study	154
6.2	Examples of creative and modelled speech in the speech of ESL learners	168
6.3	Selected studies of L2 learners' metalingual knowledge	172
6.4	Types of metalanguage used by learners in a dictogloss task (Fortune, 2005)	175
6.5	Types of uptake move (Lyster and Ranta, 1997)	179
6.6	Observable characteristics of language play as 'fun' and as 'rehearsal' (based on Broner and Tarone, 2001)	182
7.1	A comparison of three approaches to TBLT (based on Ellis, 2009)	197
7.2	Selected measures of fluency, accuracy and complexity	207
7.3	Three types of input in a listen-and-do task	213
7.4	Task design and implementation variables investigated in interaction studies (based on Ellis, 2003)	214
7.5	Simple and complex tasks in Kim (2009)	217
7.6	Task design and implementation variables investigated in L2 production studies (based on Ellis, 2003)	219
7.7	Classroom-based studies of the effects of strategic planning	220
7.8	Selected studies of structure-based production tasks	225
7.9	Principal focus-on-form options (Ellis, Basturkmen and Loewen, 2002)	228
8.1	Types of 'development' in sociocultural theory	239
8.2	Operationalizing 'acquisition' in interactionist-cognitive theories	240
8.3	Design of study by Swain et al. (2009)	246
8.4	Effects of different kinds of input on L2 acquisition	254
8.5	Selected studies investigating the effects of recasts and prompts on L2 acquisition	260
9.1	Focus on form versus focus on forms	272
9.2	Implicit and explicit forms of form-focused instruction (de Graaf and Housen, 2009: 737)	276
9.3	Simple and complex features (Spada and Tomita, 2010: 273)	300
10.1	Key individual difference factors mediating instructed L2 learning	309
10.2	Role of language aptitude in L2 acquisition (based on Skehan, 2002)	313
10.3	Factors influencing two L2 learners' WTC (based on Cao, 2009)	323
10.4	Summary of main demotivating factors	327
11.1	Example of a teacher education unit designed to raise awareness about a critical issue in language pedagogy	346

Preface

In 1988 Craig Chaudron published a book entitled *Second Language Classroom*. In it, Craig reviewed the research that had investigated the L2 classroom up to that date. Since then, there has been an enormous body of research investigating different aspects of the second language (L2) classroom. I was a great admirer of Craig's book. Sadly, he is no longer with us. Otherwise, he would have been the ideal person to survey the more recent research. Thus, I have tried to undertake the task myself.

There are two ways of viewing 'language teaching'. One is what I refer to as the 'external view'. This conceptualizes language teaching in terms of methods, approaches, materials and techniques. It is evident in books about the L2 curriculum (e.g. White, 1988) and in handbooks written for language teachers (e.g. Ur, 1996). Such a view can assist teachers in planning their lessons. I refer to the other way of conceptualizing teaching as the 'internal view'. This sees language teaching as a 'process'. It entails a consideration of the classroom interactions that occur when teachers implement their lesson plans in different participatory structures (e.g. teacher-class versus small group work). It addresses such matters as turn-taking, how meaning is negotiated, scaffolding, the questions that teachers ask, the use made of the learners' first language (L1) and metalanguage, and corrective feedback.

This distinction allows us to consider the different ways in which researchers go about investigating language teaching:

1. They can examine the effect of externally defined instructional devices on language learning. For example, they might ask whether one method is more effective than another in promoting language proficiency or whether some specific way of teaching grammar is more effective than another.

2. They can examine the general processes that arise in language lessons. This requires observing or recording lessons and then analyzing the interactions that occur in them.
3. They can examine which classroom processes arise as a result of the teacher selecting some specific externally defined device. For example, they might investigate the uses of language that result from selecting different types of tasks.
4. They can examine the relationship between classroom processes and L2 learning. For example, they can investigate how learners attend to form while performing a communicative task and whether such attention promotes learning.

All the studies discussed in this book can be classified in terms of this simple typology of L2 classroom research. Of course, process-product studies, which are arguably the most informative, combine more than one approach. For example, studies investigating some specific way of teaching grammar might examine both the classroom processes that arise in the instruction and the learning that takes place, thus combining approaches (1), (3) and (4).

L2 classroom researchers draw on a variety of research tools and theoretical paradigms. Broadly speaking, there are two principal research paradigms:

1. The normative paradigm: this seeks to test hypotheses drawn from an explicit theory of L2 teaching or learning and typically involves some form of experiment. Cognitive-interactionist theories of L2 acquisition have served as the basis for a number of such experiments. They view instruction as triggering the internal mechanisms responsible for acquisition. They employ quantitative ways of measuring instruction and learning.
2. The interpretative paradigm: this seeks to describe and understand some aspect of teaching by identifying key variables and examining how they interrelate. The sociocultural theory of L2 learning has informed research in this paradigm. This treats learning not as something that happens *as a result of* instruction but rather as occurring *within the interactions* that instruction gives rise to. Conversational analysis is the preferred tool for investigating this.

In this book I have endeavoured to include research belonging to both paradigms as my aim is not to enter the debate regarding which paradigm and which supporting theories are best suited to researching language teaching. Rather, I have tried to show that both can provide valuable information about teaching and its relationship to learning.

This is a book intended for both teachers and researchers. Teachers can familiarize themselves with the results of current language teaching research. Hopefully, this will assist them in conducting research in their own classrooms. Researchers can use the book to identify the key issues that have figured in language teaching research over the last sixty years or so, the research methods employed and the limitations of these.

The book provides teachers and researchers with 'technical' knowledge. How this knowledge can best be used in actual teaching or in teacher education programmes is a matter for debate. I conclude the book (see Chapter 11) with a discussion of this issue.

Rod Ellis
Auckland, May 2011

Acknowledgements

Special acknowledgements go to Natsuko Shintani for both her support while I was writing the book and her painstaking work in checking and compiling the references. I am also grateful to the University of Auckland for providing me with the research time needed and to Julia Kirk and Louise Ennis for all their editorial help.

1

Introduction: Developments in Language Teaching Research

What is 'Language Teaching Research'?

The journal that I currently edit is called *Language Teaching Research*. It provides this guidance to authors:

> Language Teaching Research will publish articles related to qualitative or quantitative research in the fields of second and foreign language teaching. Articles dealing with the teaching of languages other than English will be welcome. Articles reporting studies of language learning without a clear reference to the role of teaching will not be considered.

This definition recognizes that language teaching research can focus on teaching that takes place in different contexts and different languages. It also seeks to make a distinction between research that focuses on teaching, and research that focuses only on learning, excluding the latter. This distinction, however, is not always clear cut. What if the research focuses on the learning that results when learners perform some instructional task? Is this research on 'teaching' or on 'learning'? The answer depends on whether the 'task' is viewed as 'teaching'. In fact, I think a case can be made for this. 'Teaching' is a complex phenomenon that can be operationalized in many different ways. Ultimately, language teaching research (as opposed to language learning research) entails the systematic investigation of some instructional artifact (e.g. a 'task') or some instructional procedure (e.g. small group work). This can be carried out descriptively in which case it simply documents what happens when the artifact or procedure is used or by investigating the link between what is taught and what is learned. In this book, I will base my selection of the research to be examined on this definition.

Language Teaching Research & Language Pedagogy, First Edition. Rod Ellis.
© 2012 John Wiley & Sons, Ltd. Published 2012 by John Wiley & Sons, Ltd.

Another somewhat problematic distinction is between 'language teaching re-search' and 'second language classroom research'. Allwright (1983: 191) distinguished 'research centred on the classroom' and 'research that concentrates on the inputs to the classroom (the syllabus, the teaching materials) and the outputs from the classroom (learner achievement scores)'. The problem here lies in the difficulty of distinguishing what is an 'input' from what actually transpires when an input is implemented in the language classroom. For example, is research that focuses on the kind of language that arises when learners perform a specific task (e.g. a Spot-the-Difference task) in groups 'research centred on the classroom' or 'research that concentrates on the input to the classroom'? It is clearly both. I have elected to focus on 'language teaching research' because this term encompasses both research centred on the classroom and research on the inputs to the classroom. However, I will not con-sider research that has examined inputs in isolation from their actual use. In short, my concern is to document what has been discovered when language teaching takes place.

Language teaching research covers an enormous range of issues making it neces-sary for me to restrict the research I will cover in another way. I will limit my coverage to research that has focused on teaching directed at increasing learners' knowledge of a second language. I will address the central question 'How does teaching promote interlanguage development'? The term 'interlanguage', coined initially by Selinker (1972), refers to the systematic knowledge of a second language (L2) that learners construct at different stages of development through their experiences of the L2. Thus, I will examine how classrooms provide contexts in which learners can develop their interlanguages. This means that I will exclude the vast body of research that has investigated how teaching assists the development of language skills – for exam-ple, how teaching helps learners become proficient readers and writers in an L2. To include such research would make this book unwieldy and it would lose its essential focus on the language classroom as a site where learners build their knowledge of language as a system.

This raises another definitional problem – what is meant by 'language classroom'? Stereotypically, this consists of a teacher and a number of students who meet face-to-face in a confined space. But this definition raises questions. Is a 'content' or 'immersion' classroom also a language classroom? In such classrooms, there may not be any planned attempt to teach language directly, but they nevertheless constitute sites in which many L2 learners find themselves and they afford opportunities for language learning as well as content learning. Such classrooms have generally been viewed as 'language classrooms'. Another issue is whether one-on-one academic advising sessions between an instructor/tutor and a language learner constitute a 'language classroom'. A number of often-cited studies (e.g. Aljaafreh and Lantolf, 1994) have examined this kind of setting. Finally, there is the question of computer-mediated instruction, which itself can take a number of different forms (for example, learners working in small groups on a computer-delivered activity or in teacher-centred online lessons). These take place in cyber 'classrooms'. In this book, I will draw on research that has investigated all these types of language classrooms but, in general, I will focus on teaching that takes place in face-to-face classrooms.

There is still one further definitional issue. Nunan (1991) drew a distinction between 'classroom research' and 'classroom-orientated research'. The former consists of studies that investigated learners inside actual classrooms, while the latter consists of studies that were motivated by issues of clear relevance to classroom teaching and learning but which were conducted outside the classroom in a laboratory setting. A number of studies (e.g. Foster, 1998; Gass, Mackey, and Ross-Feldman, 2005) have sought to compare whether what transpires in a laboratory and a classroom setting is similar or different. The results are somewhat mixed. However, as Spada and Lightbown (2009) pointed out, 'classroom studies are more likely to lead to a better understanding about the kind of interaction that occurs in classrooms where the teacher is the only proficient speaker and interacts with a large number of learners' (p. 159). For this reason, I have elected to consider mainly research that has taken place inside classrooms in this book.

Why Investigate L2 Classrooms?

There are two very different reasons. Some researchers use the classroom as a convenient site to collect data in order to test hypotheses based on some theory of language learning. For example, Trahey and White (1993) conducted a classroom-based study in order to investigate to what extent positive evidence helped French learners of English to eradicate an error involving adverb placement (e.g. * Mary hugged passionately John). Their study was framed within a particular theory of language learning which claims that positive evidence is sufficient for learning to occur (i.e. learners do not require negative evidence in the form of explicit instruction or corrective feedback). This study is an example of 'pure research' conducted in a classroom.

Other researchers conduct classroom-based studies because they are interested in collecting data relating to specific instructional practices and, often, the impact of these practices on language learning. Their aim is to gain a better understanding of how instruction works and how it facilitates learning. For example, Bitchener and Knoch (2008) conducted a study to investigate the effect of different types of written corrective feedback on the writing produced by two different groups of English as a second language (ESL) learners – migrants (i.e. learners who were resident in the country) and international students (i.e. students living temporarily in the country for the purposes of improving their proficiency). They framed their study not in terms of theory but in terms of the debate that has raged regarding the value of written corrective feedback in helping learners achieve greater accuracy in their writing and also the need to investigate such issues on different populations of instructed learners. The results they provide, therefore, speak directly to the kinds of questions teachers are likely to ask (i.e. Should I correct my students' written errors and if so how?). Of course, studies such as those by Bitchener and Knoch are not atheoretical and the results they provide can be used to support or refute theoretical propositions. But they constitute 'applied research' because they have as their starting point a pedagogic rather than a theoretical issue.

The purpose of this book is to examine how language teaching research can inform language pedagogy. It is a book intended for teachers, especially those engaged in some form of post-service training who are interested in theorizing about language teaching and who wish to base their enquiry not just on their own experience of language classrooms but also on what research has shown about language teaching and its contribution to language learning. For this reason, I will focus mainly on 'applied' rather than 'pure' classroom-based research. So doing allows for a more direct link between research and pedagogy. Arguably, a teacher informed about what research has shown about language teaching is better placed to reflect on instructional materials and practices and the theory that underscores them. However, it must be acknowledged from the outset that applied research does not solve pedagogic problems – the results of such research cannot be simply 'applied' to teaching. Rather the value of such research lies in its ability to identify problems that otherwise might go unnoticed and, sometimes, to provide evidence as to how these problems might be solved in specific teaching contexts. As Widdowson (2003) noted, applied linguists fall into the same category as methodologists and teacher trainers – 'they are in no position to recommend particular courses of action' but can only 'point out possibilities it might be profitable to explore' (p. 15). In other words, applied research can only offer what Stenhouse (1975) called 'provisional specifications' and it is up to teachers themselves to decide whether these are relevant to their own teaching context. This is the perspective that informs this book.

A Brief History of Language Teaching Research

In the introduction to her impressive and compendious *Handbook of Research in Second Language Teaching and Learning*, Hinkel (2005) commented 'systematic research into language teaching is a relatively new enterprise' and then noted that, in contrast, 'for thousands of years in the actual practice of L2 teaching and learning, development and refinement of methods has been carried out experientially, experimentally, and intuitively' (p. xix-xx). Hinkel makes an important distinction between the informal research that takes place when teachers subject their own teaching to critical scrutiny and 'systematic research' by which she means research carried out in a principled manner and (usually) reported explicitly. This is an important distinction. It raises questions as to the value of these two kinds of enquiry – experiential and systematic – to the language teaching profession. It also invites an enquiry into whether these two approaches are as distinct as Hinkel suggests and whether it is possible to combine them. In Chapter 2, I will consider Allwright's (2003) proposals for 'exploratory practice', which aims to merge the 'systematic' and the 'experiential'. For the time being, however, I will accept Hinkel's distinction, and focus on providing a brief history of 'systematic' language teaching research. However, I will show that this is not quite the 'relatively new enterprise' that Hinkel claims it is. My definition of 'systematic research' is research where a question or problem has been identified, relevant data for addressing this problem collected, appropriate analysis and interpretation undertaken and, except in the case of practitioner research, a report of the study published in a form that makes it available for public scrutiny.

One of the commonest ways of publishing research is in a journal. Table 1.1 gives the titles of some major journals that publish research on language teaching, the date of the first issue of each journal and the name of the publisher. There are of course many other regional journals that publish research on language teaching including in languages other than English.

It is revealing to trace how these journals have evolved. The editorial of the first issue of *TESOL Quarterly*, for example, announced that 'the content of the journal will be varied' and then went on to say that although the major emphasis would be on 'practical matters' linguistic theory would also be addressed. Interestingly, there is no mention in this editorial of research on language teaching. Nor does the list of contents of this first issue include a research article. The early issues of *TESOL Quarterly* are dominated by articles on 'practical issues' and reports of particular instructional programmes. However, by the fourth issue of the second volume (December, 1968), the journal acknowledges the importance of research by introducing a section called 'Recent Research in TESOL' with the aim of publishing 'critical evaluations of selected reports' (Spolsky, 1968). This paved the way for a gradual increase in research-based articles. Today, the majority of articles published in *TESOL Quarterly* are research-based. All the main articles in Volume 42, issue 2 (the current issue at the time I am writing this chapter) report empirical studies of some aspect of teaching. The evolution of *TESOL Quarterly* – from a primary

Table 1.1 Major journals publishing articles on language teaching research

Journal	Date of first issue	Publisher
The Modern Language Journal	1916	Published initially by the National Association of Modern Language Teachers Associations and currently by Wiley-Blackwell
English Language Teaching Journal	1946	Published initially by the British Council and in later years by Oxford University Press
TESOL Quarterly	1967	Published by The Teachers of English as a Second or Other Language (TESOL) from its inception to now
Foreign Language Annals	1967	Published by the American Council on the Teaching of Foreign Languages
System	1973	Elsevier Publications
Language Teaching Research	1987	Published initially by Edward Arnold and later by Sage Publications

concern for 'practical matters' to an overriding preference for reports of empirical studies is reflected to a very large extent in those journals listed in Table 1.1 that predated 1970.

Chaudron (2001) undertook a review of articles reporting L2 classroom research published in one of these journals – *The Modern Language Journal* (*MLJ*) – which was first published in 1916 and thus has the longest history. Chaudron's review provides a snapshot of what counted as language teaching research from that date up to today. Chaudron offered the following synoptic picture of classroom research.

Chaudron notes that classroom research throughout the past century has principally documented the nature of programmes, methods, techniques, and other processes of interaction in classrooms, in association with their outcomes in learners' behaviours and attitudes (p. 57). He distinguished four broad research trends: (1) quasi-experimental method comparisons directed at identifying the relative effect of different teaching methods on L2 achievement, (2) observational studies of the oral interactions that take place in a language classroom, (3) discussions of research methodology for classrooms and (4) investigations of the teacher-student interactions that occur when performing specific instructional tasks. After electing to limit his review mainly to post-secondary foreign language classroom research and after eliminating studies of language laboratory use and computer-assisted language learning, studies that focused exclusively on learner characteristics and psycholinguistic experiments not oriented towards teaching, Chaudron identified more than 100 studies which he saw as affording 'a fascinating profile of many of the major tendencies and evolving concerns in modern language teaching' (p. 59), which he then proceeded to document.

The early period (1916–1935) was characterized primarily by method–comparison research. Bennett (1917), for example, compared two approaches to the use of translation as a teaching technique – first language (L1) to second language (L2) and L2 to L1. In the 1920s method comparisons focused on the effects of grammar translation as opposed to the Reading Method or Direct Method. These method comparisons carried on into the 1930s in studies that grew increasingly rigorous in their methodology.

In the war years (1936–1950) few classroom research studies meeting his selection criteria appeared. Chaudron speculated that this might be because of an editorial preference for articles with a political slant. Even in the 1950s, relatively few research studies appeared and those that did involved more method comparisons (e.g. Beck's (1951) study comparing the audiolingual and reading methods). The 1950s was a period during which attention switched to the linguistic and psychological underpinnings of audiolingualism with little attention given to the empirical investigation of the claims made on behalf of this method. An interesting exception to this generalization, however, was Grew's (1958) diary study that documented his teaching experience in an elementary grade French class on a daily basis over an entire school year. As Chaudron noted, this study was the first to report direct observation of actual teaching and was unique. No replication of Grew's approach appeared in the subsequent years.

The 1960s saw a number of classroom studies published in the journal, which in part reflected the innovatory nature of teaching in this decade. Moskowitz and Amidon (1962) for example compared the effects of the use of television as opposed to live audiolingual classes on children's attitudes to their French classes. Method comparisons of one kind or another continued to dominate, however, although these were now conducted with better designs, with attention given to collecting information about students' attitudes to the different kinds of instruction that were being compared, as for example in Blickenstaff and Woerdehoff (1967). Interestingly, the research in this decade was still characterized by a lack of attention to the actual instructional behaviours that arise when a method is implemented in the classroom. An article towards the end of the decade, however, paved the way for such research. Jarvis (1968) described a classroom observation scheme that could be used to record teacher and learner behaviours and provided an illustration of its use.

The method comparison studies continued into the 1970s. The focus of these comparisons, however, shifted to an examination of individualized instruction in comparison to more traditional, whole class instruction. Boyd-Bowman et al. (1973), for example, investigated the relative effects of individualized instruction, traditional classroom instruction and team-taught lessons on Spanish achievement.

A natural development of this interest in individualized instruction was the increased focus on the classroom learner. Interest in the learner was also motivated by the growing body of research into L2 acquisition which showed that instructed learners seemed to follow a similar acquisitional path to naturalistic learners (e.g. Dulay and Burt, 1973). However, the research articles published in the *MLJ* during the 1980s were focused more on individual difference factors such as attitudes, anxiety, personality, cognitive styles and beliefs than on acquisitional orders and sequences. It was left to other journals – in particular *TESOL Quarterly* and *Language Learning* – to publish articles that addressed the latter. Other *MLJ* articles in the 1980s focused on the verification of actual teaching practices by asking teachers to self-report their classroom practices, as in Swaffar, Arens and Morgan (1982), and actual observation of their behaviours in the classroom, as in Nerenz and Kopf (1982). In addition to these new developments, the method comparisons continued, although Chaudron noted that this line of research was weakening.

The 1990s saw a real break from method comparisons. Classroom research was now more clearly influenced by L2 acquisition research, as evidenced in the studies that examined the effects of task-based interaction on L2 performance and learning, the experimental studies that examined the effects of specific types of form-focused instruction on the acquisition of grammatical features, and the interest in documenting the characteristics of teacher-talk and learner contributions to classroom interaction, with both viewed as shaping opportunities for language acquisition. Chaudron noted:

> After more than 80 years of research on classrooms, it is noteworthy to finally encounter in the journal such revealing evidence of the real processes of teaching and learning (p. 65).

In fact, the *MLJ* was a little late on the scene in this respect, as articles examining 'the real processes of teaching and learning' had begun to appear in other academic journals, notably *Applied Linguistics* and *Language Learning*, in the previous decade (see, for example, my 1984b article 'Can Syntax be Taught? A study of the effects of formal instruction on the acquisition of WH questions by children'). The 1990s also witnessed another significant development in classroom research. In this decade, the *MLJ* began publishing articles that drew on a particular theoretical view of teaching and learning – sociocultural theory – which was gaining the attention of both L2 acquisition researchers and teacher educators. In 1994, the *MLJ* published a collection of papers based on this theoretical perspective, including a number that examined language instruction. Most notable is Aljaafreh and Lantolf's detailed study of corrective feedback episodes based on one-on-one interactions between a student and their tutor. Overall, then, the 1990s witnessed a notable broadening and deepening of focus on actual teaching-learning behaviours.

A number of points stand out in this brief history of the changing research trends that Chaudron identified in his review. The first is that method comparisons of one kind or another have been pervasive. The second is that the main focus of research has shifted somewhat from one period to another (for example, individualized instruction was the focus of the 70s, individual learner factors figured in the 1980s, and classroom processes featured in the 1990s). It should be noted, however, that there is considerably more to L2 classroom research than that reported in the *MLJ*. Chaudron's review, therefore, is only an incomplete reflection of trends in this domain. A final point, emphasized by Chaudron, is that the research improved notably in methodological sophistication and rigour over the years.

Chaudron reviewed research up to 2000 but we are now well into the twenty-first century. What developments have taken place in classroom-based research into L2 teaching in the first decade of this century? I will undertake my own brief review of the *MLJ* to answer this question. Of immediate note is that in this decade there are two special issues of the *MLJ* devoted to classroom research. Volume 88, issue 4, entitled 'Classroom Talks' reports studies that employed a variety of methods to document the oral interactions that take place in classrooms. Volume 89, issue 3 on 'Methodology, Epistemology, and Ethics in Instructed SLA Research' demonstrates classroom researchers' increasing need to address both methodological issues and the wider moral issues involved in investigating classrooms. These two volumes are a testimony to the centrality of classroom-based research in the *MLJ* during this decade. Indeed, the majority of articles now report empirical studies of some aspect of the L2 classroom. There is also a relatively new area of interest – the role of information and communication technologies (ICT) in language learning. However, many of the research themes apparent in the 1990s are still evident.

Overall, one is struck by the sheer range of research topics and research methodologies that figure in this decade of the *MLJ*. There are survey studies that examine teachers' and learners' perceptions of and beliefs about different instructional practices (such as corrective feedback). There are studies that examine the impact of such individual difference variables as anxiety and willingness to communicate on learners' responsiveness to instruction. There are studies investigating the effects of learner strategy training. There are numerous descriptive studies documenting 'processes' such as attention to form and code switching that arise in classroom interaction. There are product-oriented studies that investigate the effects of some specific instructional practice on learning. There are experimental process-product studies that examine the relationship between specific instructional processes and learning outcomes. There are studies that look at whole programmes (such as study abroad) in terms of how they are implemented or how effective they are. These studies address all aspects of the L2 – phonology, vocabulary, grammar, discourse – and also all the language skills – listening, speaking, reading and writing – in a variety of L2s. The studies investigate very different instructional contexts – foreign language, second language, heritage language and immersion – and from a variety of theoretical perspectives – cognitive, interactionist, sociocultural and sociocognitive. In addition there are one or two studies that report the effects of teacher education/training programmes on teachers' actual teaching. There are also other avenues of research not represented in this decade of *MLJ* articles. For example, researchers have become interested in teachers' non-verbal behaviour in the classroom, as illustrated by Lazaraton's (2004) microanalytic study in *Language Learning*, which investigated one teacher's speech and use of gesture when explaining vocabulary to students in an intensive English language programme. It also possible to see a shift in the choice of research methodology in this decade, with an increasing number of studies utilizing qualitative methods of data collection and analysis.

The variety and scope of current research is truly remarkable and poses a challenge to anyone – such as myself – seeking to synthesize its findings. In the following sections of this Chapter I will begin my attempt at this synthesis. The main challenge facing me is how best to organize my review of the language teaching research. Chaudron in his 1988 review of the research identified four main topics: teacher-talk, learner behaviour, teacher-student interaction and learning outcomes. I have included these topics in my own synthesis but expanded on them by including separate chapters on comparative method studies (reflecting the prevalence of this type of research early on), on task-based teaching (given the current interest in this form of instruction), on form-focused instruction (given the large number of studies that have investigated this) and the current interest in the role played by individual difference factors such as language aptitude and motivation in mediating the effects of instruction. Here I provide a brief introduction to the key issues that will be examined in greater detail in subsequent chapters.

Comparative Method Studies

As we have seen, much of the earliest research investigating the effects of teaching was 'method' oriented; that is, it consisted of comparisons of language teaching methods that differed in their conceptualizations of how to teach language and investigated their effects on learning in terms of general proficiency. Such studies began in the early 1900s and have continued up to today, although their popularity has diminished in recent years as language teaching moved into the 'post-method' era (Kumaradivelu, 1994). I examine a number of key comparative method studies in Chapter 3.

The aim of comparative method studies is to establish which of two or more methods or general approaches to language teaching is the most effective in terms of the actual learning (the 'product') that is achieved after a given period of time. Many of the earlier studies were 'global' in nature, conducted over weeks, months, and even years. Later ones were more 'local'; that is they examined differences resulting from shorter periods of exposure with more narrowly defined methods and measured learning outcomes in terms of the acquisition of specific linguistic features rather than general language proficiency. The design of these studies typically was experimental, with one group of learners taught by one method and a second group by another method. At the end of the specified period the learners completed a battery of tests. The two groups' scores on these tests were then compared.

Perhaps the heyday of the method comparison studies was in the 1960s. However the studies reported in Scherer and Wertheimer (1964), Smith (1970) and Levin (1972) failed to produce clear-cut results and this led to a questioning of the value of such method studies. Gradually, the focus of research shifted away from method comparisons in favour of process studies that documented classroom behaviours.

Comparative method studies were not abandoned, however. For example, when communicative language teaching (CLT) appeared in the 1970s and 1980s, attempts were made to compare this with 'traditional' instruction (e.g. Beretta and Davies, 1985; Palmer, 1979). But, once again, the results of these studies were mixed with many failing to demonstrate any differences in the learning outcomes that resulted from the different methods. A problem underlying all the studies was the difficulty in controlling the presage and process variables that potentially impact on learning.

However, the tradition of comparing different ways of teaching has not disappeared. Rather than such comparisons being carried out on a global scale (e.g. over a whole course), they are now conducted in short-term experimental studies that investigate the effects of highly specific instructional strategies on L2 learning. Increasingly, the instructional strategies chosen for study are derived not from 'methods' but from theories of language learning. A good example of these later studies can be found in the investigations of different types of form-focused instruction (see Chapter 9).

Second Language Classroom Discourse

Disenchantment with the global method studies following the large scale studies conducted in the 1960s and 1970s led to a growth in research that sought to provide descriptions of the teaching and learning behaviours that arose in the L2 classroom.

The key characteristic of the studies emanating from this new form of enquiry was that they were 'descriptive'; that is they focused on the 'process' features of L2 classrooms. Under this general heading, however, the studies have drawn on a variety of different research methods. The earlier studies (i.e. those in the 1960s and 1970s) employed 'interactional analysis' (i.e. they used observational systems consisting of a set of categories for coding specific classroom behaviours). A limitation of such systems is that information is lost about 'the sequential flow of classroom activities' (McLaughlin, 1985: 149) because the behaviours of the teacher and the learners are treated separately. Later approaches sought to describe the structure of the interactions that occur, using the methods involved in 'discourse analysis' (e.g. Sinclair and Coulthard, 1975), 'conversational analysis' (e.g. Markee, 2000; Seedhouse, 2004), the 'ethnography of communication' (e.g. Zuenglar and Cole, 2005) and in research based on sociocultural theory (e.g. Ohta, 2001). Chapter 2 examines these different descriptive methods in detail.

This research illuminated a number of key aspects of L2 classroom discourse. It showed, for example, that many classroom interactions were characterized by a particular type of structure known as (IRF), where the teacher initiates an exchange, a student responds and the teacher then follows up. The extent to which this structure inhibits or promotes opportunities for language learning has been the subject of considerable debate (see, for example, Gourlay, 2005). Other studies (e.g. Ellis, 1984a; Johnson, 1995; Van Lier, 1988) showed that the nature of the discourse that arises varies according to the particular type of language use involved. In a similar mode, Seedhouse (2004) used conversational analysis to show how classroom turn-taking mechanisms vary according to whether the context is 'form and accuracy' or 'meaning and fluency'. Major foci of ethnographic studies are the 'participant structures' (e.g. teacher–class versus teacher–student versus student–student) found in the classroom and how learners are socialized into the norms of classroom behaviour. Researchers who draw on sociocultural theory have focused on how specific types of classroom interaction (for example, interactional routines) 'scaffold' learners' L2 production and acquisition. Underlying much of this research has been the assumption that the discourse that results when the focus is on trying to learn a language, is different from that which results when the focus is on trying to communicate. This comparison was motivated by the assumption that the general characteristics of classroom discourse are so far removed from those of naturalistic discourse that they are unlikely to promote the communicative competence needed for everyday communication.

Chapter 4 examines research that has looked at the general characteristics of L2 classroom discourse. However, it is also possible to examine the nature of the teacher's and the learners' contributions separately.

Focus on the Teacher

In Chapter 5, I examine a number of the key characteristics of the teacher's use of language in the L2 classroom. These are:

1. Teacher-talk: Studies of teacher-talk were common in the 1970s and 1980s (see Chaudron 1988 for a review) but they have gradually lost popularity. They sought

to describe the phonological, lexical, grammatical, and discoursal properties of the teacher's language, motivated by the felt need to document the nature of the 'input' that learners are exposed to in classroom environments.

2. Teacher questions: Teachers typically ask a lot of questions (see, for example, Long and Sato, 1984). Much of the research has been taxonomic and quantitative in nature. It has shown that teachers typically ask 'display' questions (i.e. questions that 'test' the learner by eliciting already known information). Some researchers have seen such questions as limiting opportunities for learning. However, other researchers (e.g. McCormick and Donato, 2000) have been critical of the taxonomic approach to investigating teacher questions, arguing that they are better viewed as 'dynamic discursive tools' that serve 'to build collaboration and to scaffold comprehension and comprehensibility'.

3. Use of the L1: This remains a complex and controversial issue. It is complex because clearly the potential of the L1 to assist learning depends on the instructional context. It is controversial because different theories of L2 acquisition afford very different hypotheses about the value of L1 use in the classroom. Reviewing research that had investigated the teacher's use of the L1, Turnbull and Arnett (2002) argued that 'since teachers are often the primary source of linguistic input in the target language (TL), it is therefore reasonable to argue that maximizing the TL in the classroom is a favourable practice' (p. 205). Other researchers, however, have seen merit in some uses of the L1.

4. Metalanguage: The teachers' use of metalanguage has attracted less attention. It is likely to vary considerably depending on whether or not they believe that learning grammar explicitly is important for language learning and on their assessment of their students' ability to handle technical terms (see Borg, 1999).

5. Corrective feedback: The study of how teachers correct their students' errors spans several decades. Some studies have adopted a taxonomic approach, identifying and quantifying the different strategies that teachers use to correct learner errors (see, for example, Lyster and Ranta, 1997). Other studies have made use of the techniques of conversational analysis to describe how teachers 'repair' learner errors. It is clear that corrective feedback is an enormously complex process that varies from teacher to teacher depending on such factors as the broader instructional context, the kind of instructional activity they are engaged in, and the teachers' assessment of the relevance of correction to the particular learners they are teaching.

6. Teacher cognitions: Teachers hold beliefs about teaching and construct their own personal theories of teaching (Woods, 1996) which potentially influence how they act. One of the findings of research that has examined the relationship between teachers' beliefs and their actual use of language is that there is often a mismatch between beliefs and practice due to the fact that teachers' beliefs are sometimes in conflict – creating what Woods (1996) called 'hotspots'. Faced with a specific situation in the classroom, teachers may act in accordance with one belief knowing that in so doing they are ignoring another. In time, such hotspots may be resolved as teachers gain in experience and expertise.

Focus on the Learner

Chapter 6 examines learners' use of language in the L2 classroom.

Longitudinal studies of classroom learners are based on the speech they produce in a classroom context. Early studies (Ellis, 1984a; Felix, 1981; Lightbown, 1983) investigated the route of learners' grammatical development, comparing this to the order and sequence of acquisition reported for naturalistic learners. They showed that the process of classroom learners' acquisition is very similar to that of naturalistic learners. Later studies have focused on classroom learners' pragmatic development (e.g. Belz and Kinginger, 2003; Ellis, 1992). Also a number of ethnographic studies (e.g. Morita, 2004) have viewed L2 classrooms as social contexts that require learners to behave in specific ways, often limiting their opportunities to participate actively in the discourse. The longitudinal studies provide valuable information about how learner participation and L2 acquisition take place in a classroom context.

Descriptive studies have addressed different aspects of learners' classroom language:

1. *Silent period.* Some learners (especially young children) manifest a silent period in the beginning stage unless they are required to produce. However, when this occurs they may also engage in private speech, which seems to prepare them for later production.
2. *Formulaic speech.* Studies (e.g. Myles, Hooper and Mitchell, 1988) have shown that learners make extensive use of formulaic sequences such as 'I don't know' and 'Can I have a —?' in order to cope with their basic communicative needs in both second and foreign language classrooms. There is some evidence that these sequences are subsequently broken down and their components fed into their developing rule systems.
3. *Learner initiation.* Other studies have investigated learners' use of the L1, the extent to which they possess L2 metalanguage and the uses they make of this when performing different instructional activities, learner questions, the role played by repetition of the teacher's or other learners' speech, the extent to which they repair their errors following corrective feedback (i.e. their 'uptake'), and language play. A key theme in these studies is the importance of learner initiation. Van Lier (1988) argued that learners need opportunities to self-select because these cater for experimentation with language at the cutting edge of their linguistic development. Self-selection depends to a large extent on the opportunities afforded the learner to control topic development, which in turn depends on the nature of the instructional activity.

One of the most obvious ways of encouraging learner participation in the classroom is through small group work. A number of studies have reported that students working in small groups produce a greater quantity of language and also better quality language than students in a teacher-fronted, lockstep classroom setting.

Group work also affords learners the opportunity to negotiate for meaning when a communication problem arises, especially if the task the learners are performing requires a two-way flow of information (see Pica and Doughty, 1985a). These studies suggest that group work can provide the interactional conditions that have been hypothesized to facilitate acquisition more readily than interaction involving teachers. However, some educators and researchers (e.g. Prabhu, 1987) have argued that group work may be less effective than is often claimed as it exposes learners to 'interlanguage talk' (i.e. input that is non- target-like) and thus may stunt their development.

Investigating Tasks

The study of group work is closely associated with research that has investigated 'tasks' as much of this has examined how learners perform different kinds of tasks when working together in pairs or small groups. The investigation of 'tasks' constitutes a major focus in language teaching research since the mid 1980s, stimulated to a large degree by growing interest in task-based language teaching (Ellis, 2003; Samuda and Bygate, 2008). In Chapter 7 I consider the research that has investigated the language use that results from performing tasks in the classroom.

A number of studies (e.g. Ellis, Tanaka, and Yamazaki, 1994; Loschky, 1994) have investigated input-based tasks. These tasks often take the form of listen-and-do tasks where learners are required to demonstrate their comprehension of the teacher's instructions or descriptions either non-verbally or by means of minimal verbal responses. Other studies have investigated interactive tasks (i.e. information-gap or opinion-gap tasks) performed in pairs or small groups in terms of whether they create contexts where communication problems and subsequent 'negotiation of meaning' occurs (Long, 1983c; 1996). Still other studies (e.g. Foster and Skehan, 1996) have investigated the impact of various task-design variables (e.g. topic familiarity) and implementation variables (e.g. pre-task planning) on learner production, measured in terms of fluency, accuracy and complexity. Another strand of research has investigated 'focused tasks' (i.e. tasks that have been designed to elicit the use of some specific linguistic feature such as a grammatical structure).

Underlying much of this research is the importance of 'focus on form'. Long (1991) defines 'focus on form' as interactional behaviour that 'overtly draws students' attention to linguistic elements as they arise incidentally in lessons whose overriding focus is on meaning or communication' (pp. 45–46). Researchers have explored the different ways in which this takes place – pre-emptively when a learner asks a question about a form or the teacher explicitly draws attention to it and reactively through corrective feedback. Focus on form is hypothesized to play an important role in language acquisition because it induces learners to pay conscious attention to form while they are engaged in trying to communicate.

Other researchers have examined tasks from the perspective of sociocultural theory, focusing on how the interactants jointly construct their performance of a task.

One of the points that researchers in this tradition emphasize is the distinction between 'task' (i.e. the actual task materials that are given to the learners) and 'activity' (i.e. the actual performance of the task). They stress that the 'task' cannot determine the 'activity' as learners will approach tasks with different goals, motives and strategies and that these influence how they perform it. The emic perspective adopted by socioculturally oriented researchers has helped to enrich our understanding of constructs such as pre-task planning, negotiation of meaning, and task engagement.

Finally, some researchers (e.g. Carless, 2004) have conducted evaluations of task-based teaching to investigate the extent to which tasks are successful in achieving their goals and the kinds of problems that teachers experience when trying to implement task-based teaching. The aim of such evaluations has been to establish to what extent tasks constitute effective devices for planning and teaching a language course.

Interaction and L2 Learning

If, as Allwright (1984) suggested, interaction is the fundamental fact of the L2 classroom (in the sense that whatever learners learn must be derived from the interactions they experience), then the key question becomes 'In what ways does interaction in the classroom facilitate L2 acquisition?' By and large this question has been addressed by speculating, on the basis of a variety of theories of L2 acquisition, the likelihood of different aspects of interaction creating the conditions needed for acquisition to occur. This is the approach that has been applied to the study of classroom discourse, teacher-talk, learner participation and the choice of tasks, which I consider in Chapter 4, Chapter 5, and Chapter 6. Clearly, though, there is also a need for studies that go beyond theory-based hypothesizing to investigate how interaction actually contributes to learning. Chapter 8 examines the research that has attempted this.

One branch of research has investigated whether the kinds of interaction that arise in the 'communicative classroom' promote acquisition. There is some evidence that they do. Two studies (Beretta and Davies, 1985; Lightbown, 1992) demonstrated that classrooms where the focus is placed on meaning rather than on form are effective in promoting L2 acquisition. However, other studies (e.g. Ellis, 1992; Spada and Lightbown, 1989) suggest there may be limitations to what can be achieved in communicative classrooms.

Other studies have investigated the role that interaction plays in classroom language learning more directly by exploring the extent to which (1) learners attend to linguistic form and (2) the impact this has on acquisition. In other words they have explored these relationships:

$$\text{Interaction} \overset{(1)}{\to} \text{attention to form} \overset{(2)}{\to} \text{acquisition}$$

Two different approaches have been used to investigate these relationships. One draws on sociocultural theory to examine how tasks that elicit 'language-related episodes' (i.e. sequences of talk directed at addressing specific linguistic problems that arise in communication) assist language acquisition. Studies by Aljaafreh and Lantolf (1994) and Swain and Lapkin (2007), among others, have shown that when language problems are resolved through collaborative interaction, learning takes place. The second approach draws on interactionist-cognitive theories to investigate the effects of 'focus on form' on learning. Loewen (2005), for example, administered tailor-made tests to students who had participated in form-focused episodes that occurred in task-based ESL lessons. He found that learning did result especially when the students self-corrected or demonstrated understanding of the meaning of the forms addressed in the episodes.

Other interactionist-cognitive studies have been experimental in design. They employed what are known as 'focused tasks'. These allow for a pre-test – treatment – post-test design as they make it possible to investigate what effect the performance of the task has on the acquisition of the specific feature targetted by the task. A good example of this approach can be found in studies that have investigated the effects of different kinds of corrective feedback. Ellis, Loewen and Erlam (2006), for example, investigated the effects of different kinds of corrective feedback in communicative lessons. They found that explicit feedback (e.g. when the teacher corrects a learner error directly and/or provides a brief metalinguistic explanation) is more effective than more implicit feedback by means of recasts (e.g. when the teacher responds to a learner utterance containing an error by reformulating it).

All of these studies investigated incidental acquisition (i.e. the learning that occurs without any deliberate intention to learn). In so doing they address what is one of the main claims of task-based teaching – namely, that learners do not have to be explicitly taught a linguistic feature in order to acquire it. It is in this sense that 'focus on form' contributes to acquisition.

Form-Focused Instruction

In Ellis (2001a) I defined form-focused instruction (FFI) as 'any planned or incidental instructional activity that is intended to induce language learners to pay attention to linguistic form' (pp. 1-2). Defined in this way many of the studies considered in the previous chapter would have to be considered examples of form-focused instruction research. The key distinction, however, is whether the instruction is directed at incidental as opposed to intentional language learning. I have elected to address studies of incidental focus on form under the heading of 'Interaction and L2 Learning', leaving research that has investigated deliberate attempts to teach specific linguistic forms to Chapter 9. Thus, the definition of form-focused instruction that informs Chapter 9 is 'any planned instructional activity that is designed to induce intentional language learning'.

I use the term 'instructional activity' to refer to both materials (i.e. texts, exercises and tasks) and procedures for using the materials (e.g. metalinguistic explanations and corrective feedback). These can be usefully considered in terms of four macro-options:

1. *Input-based options* (i.e. instruction that involves the manipulation of the input that learners are exposed to, or are required to process). They include enhanced input (i.e. input with the target feature made salient to the learners, for example, by means of emphatic stress or bolding), and structured input (i.e. input that has been contrived to induce conscious processing of the target feature). These options are all comprehension-based.
2. *Explicit options* (i.e. instruction directed at helping learners develop explicit knowledge of the target structure). They include both direct explicit instruction (i.e. learners are provided with metalinguistic descriptions of the target feature) and indirect explicit instruction (i.e. learners are provided with data illustrating the target feature and are required to 'discover' the rule for themselves).
3. *Production options* (i.e. instruction directed at enabling/inducing learners to produce utterances containing the target structure). Production options can be distinguished in terms of whether they involve text manipulation (for example, fill-in-the-blank exercises) or text creation (for example, situational grammar exercises that involve learners in producing their own sentences). They can also be distinguished in terms of whether they are error-avoiding or error-inducing.
4. *Corrective feedback options*. Corrective feedback can be implicit (for example, recasts) or explicit (for example, overt indication that an error has been committed). It can also be input-providing (for example, recasts or metalinguistic explanations) or output-prompting (for example, requests for clarification or elicitations).

Cutting across these options is the distinction between 'focus on forms' and 'focus on form'. This distinction is not without its problems but broadly speaking it concerns the extent to which the instruction is based on a structural syllabus and employs traditional type exercises or is based on a task-based syllabus containing focused tasks that induce attention to the target forms while the learners are primarily meaning-oriented.

The research investigating FFI has employed a number of different approaches. Early research (e.g. Pica, 1983) sought to compare the order of acquisition in instructed and naturalistic learners. Other studies (e.g. Pienemann, 1984) investigated whether instruction could enable learners to bypass early stages in the sequence of acquisition of specific structures. In the 1990s studies of FFI became more theory-driven, seeking to test specific hypotheses drawn from some theory of L2 acquisition such as VanPatten's (1996) information-processing theory. This theory claimed that FFI would be effective if learners were induced to process features that normally they would overlook in the input they were exposed to.

It is not easy to arrive at clear conclusions about what all the research has shown about the effects of FFI. It is clear that instruction does not work well if it focuses purely on linguistic form (as opposed to form-meaning mapping). It is also clear that FFI is often more effective when it is directed at helping learners to use features that they have already partially acquired with greater accuracy rather than entirely new forms. What is less clear is what type of instruction is the most effective. Controversy exists, for example, regarding the relative benefits of input-based as opposed to output-based instruction and of focus on form as opposed to focus on forms. A key issue is whether FFI (of any kind) is effective in helping learners acquire implicit knowledge (i.e. the kind of procedural knowledge needed to engage in fluent communication) or whether it only results in explicit knowledge (i.e. declarative knowledge of L2 rules).

Ultimately if FFI works it does so through the classroom interactions which arise when it is implemented. For this reason, it is important for researchers to examine the 'process' features of the instruction, not just the 'product'. Only a few studies have attempted this.

The Mediating Role of Individual Difference Factors

It is self-evident that although there may be universal aspects to the way instruction unfolds in L2 classrooms and of the effects that different kinds of instruction have on language learning, there will also be differences in how individual learners respond to instruction and what they learn from it. However, there are still relatively few studies that have explored how individual difference factors influence learners' response to instruction in actual classrooms. Chapter 10 examines these studies.

Three major sets of learner factors can be identified (Dörnyei, 2009): cognitive factors such as language aptitude and working memory, affective factors such as language anxiety and willingness to communicate, and motivational factors. There are studies that have investigated how these individual difference factors mediate the effects of instruction. For example, Mackey et al. (2010) investigated the role played by working memory. Studies that have investigated learners' motivation indicate that this influences how they respond to instruction (e.g. Takahashi, 2005), how instruction can lead to demotivation (Ushioda, 1998) and how it affects the way in which individual students respond to a specific task (Dörnyei and Csizér, 1998).

It is unlikely that teachers will be able to systematically adjust their instruction to cater for these differences in learners. An alternative approach, therefore, might be to equip students with the learner strategies they need to benefit from whatever instruction they provide. A number of studies (e.g. Holunga, 1995) have investigated the effects of learner training by identifying specific strategies that are seen as likely to foster learning and then assisting students to use these when performing instructional activities.

In another approach, researchers have tried to identify learner 'types' in order to match different types of learners to different types of instruction. However, such an approach is problematic for two reasons. First, it is virtually impossible to distinguish 'types' that take account of all the individual difference factors. As a result, researchers are obliged to select a single factor (e.g. language aptitude) as the basis for distinguishing learners but this may or may not be the crucial factor for a given learner in a particular instructional context. Second, this approach ignores the essential fact that the role played by individual difference factors is a dynamic one. That is, the various factors interact with the social and cognitive processes involved in learning in different ways, at different times, and in different kinds of instructional activities. The most promising approaches, therefore, are those that (1) explore how individual difference factors affect the interactional and learning processes that take place as learners grapple with different kinds of instructional activities and (2) provide rich case studies of how individual learners respond to instruction.

Conclusion

Language teaching has been the object of intense enquiry over the years and, not surprisingly, there has been an enormous amount of research that has investigated various aspects of it – much of it completed since Chaudron's (1988) book. While some of this research has been driven by theoretical issues in second language acquisition research (SLA), much (perhaps most) of it has had a pedagogical motivation – that is, it was carried out with a view to gaining a better understanding of the practice of language teaching and how it can be improved. The question arises therefore 'What value does language teaching research have for teachers?'

   SLA researchers have expressed reservations about applying their theories and research to language teaching (see, for example, Lightbown, 1985a and 2000). Classroom researchers have expressed greater confidence. Chaudron (1988), for example, concluded his book with the claim that L2 classroom research has 'an important role' to play in both language teaching and language teacher education. However, the problems of applying research to language teaching remain even when the research is classroom-based. The essential problem is the extent to which the findings derived from the study of *one* instructional context can be generalized to *other* instructional contexts. It is now acknowledged that what works in one context may not work in another. This is not just a problem for descriptive studies of specific classrooms but also for experimental studies that employ inferential statistics in order to claim generalizability. Such studies are still sited in specific instructional contexts and thus cannot claim to inform instruction in general. What is needed, then, is a principled way of making use of the research – one that takes account of the fact that the findings of any one study (or even several taken together) can never be more than 'provisional specifications' (Stenhouse, 1975). I conclude the book, in Chapter 11, with a discussion of ways in which the language teaching research reviewed in the rest of the book can inform language teaching.

2

Methods for Researching the Second Language Classroom

Introduction

It is useful to make a broad distinction between formal and practitioner research. By formal research I mean research that is conducted by an external researcher drawing on one or more of the established research traditions. Formal classroom research can be motivated by theoretical issues (e.g. whether opportunities to negotiate for meaning facilitate second language – L2 – learning) or by pedagogic issues (e.g. how and to what extent teachers implement a particular approach to language teaching). In many cases, the issues investigated are of both theoretical and pedagogical significance. Practitioner research is research conducted by teachers in their own classrooms drawing on the principles of action research (for example, Wallace, 1998; Burns, 2009) or exploratory practice (Allwright, 2003). It is invariably motivated by pedagogic concerns and is directed at enabling teachers to solve problems they are experiencing with their teaching or develop a deeper understanding of some aspect of the quality of life in the L2 classroom. It should be noted, however, that both types of research have in common the general features of research – that is, there is a problem or question to be addressed, data is collected and analyzed and an interpretation of the findings provided.

This chapter begins with a discussion of formal and practitioner research. It will then move on to examine the main research traditions (i.e. descriptive research and confirmatory research). Both of these traditions can figure in both formal and practitioner research and, increasingly, are combined in the same study. These traditions will be considered in terms of their theoretical underpinnings, their research design, the data collection methods they employ, and methods for analyzing the data.

Language Teaching Research & Language Pedagogy, First Edition. Rod Ellis.
© 2012 John Wiley & Sons, Ltd. Published 2012 by John Wiley & Sons, Ltd.

Table 2.1 Summary of Ellis and He's experimental study (1999)

Participants	Research questions	Design	Materials	Results
50 learners enrolled in intermediate-level classes in an Intensive English Language Programme in the USA	The questions addressed the effects of premodified input, interactionally modified input, and modified output on: - comprehension - receptive knowledge of new words - ability to produce the new words	Quasi-experimental – three groups: group (1) received premodified input containing new words; group (2) received interactionally modified input; group (3) had the opportunity to produce the new words in interaction with a partner	A listen-and-do task (learners had to locate items of furniture in a plan of an apartment). Performance on this task provided a measure of comprehension Pre-test – designed to establish which words were new to the learners Post-tests – measured both receptive and productive knowledge of the new words	Group (3) outperformed groups (1) and (2) on the measure of comprehension and in the receptive and productive tests of vocabulary acquisition

The intention of this chapter is to provide a general account of the methods used to research the L2 classroom rather than to offer guidelines about how to carry out research. Readers interested in the details of the different research methods should consult a relevant book on research methodology (e.g. Brown and Rodgers, 2002; Dörnyei, 2007; Mackey and Gass, 2005; Nunan and Bailey, 2009).

Formal L2 Classroom Research

It is helpful to begin with some examples of formal classroom research. I will draw on a series of classroom-based studies that my fellow researchers and I conducted in the 1990s, all of which were informed by Long's (1983a) Interaction Hypothesis. This hypothesis claims that L2 acquisition is facilitated when a communication problem arises that causes learners to try to resolve it through the negotiation of meaning. Negotiation potentially aids acquisition in a number of ways – by helping to make input comprehensible, by prompting learners to notice the difference between their own erroneous output and the correct target language form through feedback, and by pushing learners to self-correct. Numerous studies have investigated the Interaction Hypothesis (see, for example, the list in Table 1 in Mackey, 2007). However, many of these were laboratory studies. My own studies, which sought to investigate the effect that negotiation had on comprehension and the acquisition of vocabulary, all took place in a classroom context.

The studies were all experimental in nature. That is, there were one or more experimental groups that received a 'treatment' (consisting of either input that had been premodified to facilitate comprehension or input that the students had the opportunity to modify through interaction or an opportunity to use the target items in production). In all the studies there was a pre-test to establish which of the target vocabulary the students already knew, a post-test more or less immediately following the treatment, and a delayed post-test to establish whether any learning that had taken place was durable. Table 2.1 summarizes one of the studies I carried out (Ellis and He, 1999).

The formal nature of my research is evident in a number of ways. First, as already stated, it was theoretically motivated. I wanted to test the claims of the Interaction Hypothesis. At the time, although a number of studies had shown that modified interaction assisted comprehension, there were few studies that had investigated whether it facilitated acquisition. Thus, there was a conspicuous 'gap' between what the Interaction Hypothesis claimed and the supporting evidence. My intention was to try to fill that gap. Second, I wanted to demonstrate a cause-effect relationship (i.e. the relationship between interactionally modified input and output and L2 acquisition). For this reason, I elected to use an experimental design rather than carry out a purely descriptive study. Third, as a university professor I was keen to conduct a study that would lead to publications in academic journals. The articles that resulted from the research were published in *Language Learning*, *Applied Linguistics* and *Studies in Second Language Acquisition*, all leading journals in my field. Nevertheless, even

Table 2.2 Summary of Lyster and Ranta's study of corrective feedback (1997)

Participants	Research questions (RQs)	Design	Materials and analysis	Results
Teachers and students in four Grade 4/5 classes in French immersion classrooms in Canada	The RQs addressed: - the different types of corrective feedback - the distribution of learner uptake following corrective feedback - the relationship between different types of corrective feedback and students repairing their errors	Descriptive – 100 hours of classroom interaction were audio-recorded. Data analysis was based on transcripts of 18.3 hours of transcripts	- Transcripts of the 100 hours of audio-recorded lessons - All student turns coded as containing an error or not - Each instance of corrective feedback identified and coded - Student uptake coded as 'repair' or 'no repair'	- Six types of corrective feedback identified, with recasts accounting for 55 per cent. Uptake was least likely following recasts - Output-prompting types of feedback (e.g. clarification requests) most likely to result in students repairing their errors

though my research was clearly theoretical in nature, it was also of potential practical significance. If it could be shown that learners could successfully learn vocabulary by performing listen-and-do tasks then I would be in a position to propose that such tasks had a place in language pedagogy. Indeed, I chose to investigate the Interaction Hypothesis precisely because of its pedagogic relevance.

Not all formal research is driven by theory. Much of the L2 classroom research has been descriptive in nature, aimed at understanding a specific aspect of teaching or learning and also at providing information that can ultimately be used to shape a theory. A good example of such research is Lyster and Ranta's (1997) study of how teachers in French immersion classrooms correct students' linguistic errors when interacting with them. A summary of this study is provided in Table 2.2. Such studies can also be considered formal in that they are carried out by researchers (Lyster and Ranta are both university professors) rather than by teachers and were conducted with a view to publishing an article in an academic journal (Lyster and Ranta's study was published in *Studies in Second Language Acquisition*). Also, like my experimental studies, this study was intended to contribute to theory. Indeed, Lyster followed up this descriptive research with a number of experimental studies (see Lyster, 2004; Lyster and Mori, 2006) which were informed by the findings of the earlier descriptive study and which sought to investigate theoretically based hypotheses about the relative effectiveness of different types of corrective feedback. Finally, also like my studies, Lyster and Ranta's study aimed to contribute to language pedagogy.

Formal L2 classroom research, then, whether experimental or descriptive, aims to contribute to research-based language pedagogy. That is, it seeks to provide teachers with information that they can use to decide what and how to teach. Its characteristics are as follows:

1. The phenomenon investigated is determined by the researcher.
2. The researcher 'borrows' a classroom in order to carry out the study.
3. The researcher may also solicit the help of a classroom teacher to conduct the research.
4. The research is either theoretically driven (as in experimental research) or carried out with a view to developing theory (as in descriptive research).
5. The results of the research are written up in accordance with the requirements of academic articles and with a view to publishing them in academic journals.
6. In many cases the research is intended to contribute to research-based language pedagogy.

Such research is of undoubted value – both for testing and developing theory and for language pedagogy. A limitation, however, is that it may not address the kinds of issues that preoccupy teachers and, in fact, may never reach teachers as they are unlikely to read the journals in which it is published. Thus, if it does have an impact on teachers it will do so in a top-down fashion – that is, through the mediation of teacher educators who draw implications for teaching from the research and convey these to teachers. In the view of some researchers and teacher educators, teachers would do better to engage in their own practitioner research.

Practitioner Research

Practitioner research is research conducted by practitioners (usually teachers) in their own classrooms either acting independently or in collaboration with others. Stewart (2006), citing Thesen and Kuzel (1999: 27) notes that it is 'oriented towards reform rather than simply toward description or meaning'. Practitioner research, then, is directed at enabling teachers to become 'expert knowers about their own students and classrooms' (Cochran-Smith and Lytle, 1999: 16). In this way it aims to make a direct connection between research and practice. To this end, the research topics are not derived from theory but from teachers' desire to experiment with some innovation in their classroom, to seek a solution to some problem they have identified with their teaching or their students, or simply to develop a fuller understanding of some aspect of life in their classrooms. Practitioner research, then, is inherently local. It is focused on a specific group of learners in a specific classroom where the teacher teaches. It follows that it should be evaluated not in terms of whether it contributes to our general understanding of some issue of theoretical significance but in terms of the contribution it can make to teachers' practice of teaching and, through the reflection that it can promote, to teacher development.

Arguably, then, the value of practitioner research lies more in the process of conducting it than in the product of the research. Indeed, it can be questioned whether teachers engaging in practitioner research need to produce a product – in the form of a report or a public presentation of their research. However, Freeman (1996: 105) has argued that 'the knowledge that teachers articulate through the process of disciplined enquiry must become public'. Borg (2009a) too has emphasized the importance of teachers 'making their research public' while acknowledging that teachers themselves express uncertainty about the need for this. There are obvious advantages in teachers sharing the results of their research – both for themselves (in terms of the feedback they will receive in a public forum) and for other teachers (who can benefit from the insights the research provides). There are a number of outlets available for the publication of practitioner research – teacher conferences and a number of journals (e.g. *Language Teaching Research* has a section entitled 'Practitioner Research'). Practitioner research, however, is not likely to be published in the same academic journals as formal research, which raises the question of its status in the field of L2 classroom research as a whole – a point I will revisit in the final chapter of the book.

A key point that emerges in discussions of practitioner research conducted by practitioners is the need for a model (in a way, a theory) for how to conduct it. Such models have originated from teacher educators who promote teacher research as a way of both helping to solve local problems they are experiencing and of developing themselves as members of the teaching profession. I will consider two of the most widely promoted models – action research and exploratory practice.

Action research

Action research is 'a form of self-reflective enquiry undertaken by participants in social situations to improve the rationality and justice of their own practices, and the situations in which those practices are carried out' (Carr and Kemmis, 1986: 162). As so defined, it applies to a wide range of professional activities. Indeed, its origin lies in the work of Kurt Lewin (1948), who conducted research that showed that the highest level of output by factory apprentices was by those who had the opportunity to formulate their own 'action plan'. Action research is a form of self-reflective enquiry undertaken by practitioners in their own contexts of action. It is intended to lead to improvement in the practice of some professional activity – in our case, in language teaching. It can be undertaken by individual teachers or collaboratively involving a team of teachers. Readers interested in the historical development of action research in the field of language teaching should refer to Burns (2005).

The model for conducting action research for teachers emphasizes a number of features: (1) it is context-specific, (2) it is practical, (3) it is systematic, (4) it is reflective, and (5) it is cyclical. The model proposes a number of iterative phases:

1. Identifying an issue or problem relevant to a specific instructional context (the initial idea).
2. Obtaining information relevant to the problem/issue (fact finding).
3. Working out a possible solution to this problem and devising ways of trying this out (the action plan).
4. Trying out the solution in the specific instructional context (implementation).
5. Collecting data to investigate whether the solution is effective (monitoring).
6. If necessary, revising the action plan and proceeding through steps (4) and (5) again or alternatively identifying a new issue thrown up by the initial study.

Such a procedure is context-specific in that the problems are identified by teachers and are located in their own teaching. It is practical in that it is directed at improving teaching. It is systematic in that it offers a set of clearly delineated steps for conducting an action research study. These steps, it should be noted involve more than just teaching (i.e. they involve the collection and analysis of data). It is reflective in that it requires teachers to examine problems in their own teaching, identify possible solutions and evaluate their effectiveness. It is cyclical in that it recognizes the importance of continuous research to find solutions and the possibility of new problems arising out of teachers' attempts to find solutions to initial problems.

Table 2.3 summarizes a small-scale action research study conducted by a teacher in her own classroom to address the problem of her students' use of the first language (L1) – Japanese. This is a problem that arises in many monolingual language

Table 2.3 Summary of an action research study (based on Penner, 1998)

Context	Problems	Solutions	Monitoring
A five-week course for a group of 'high-beginning' Japanese university students from Japan on a study abroad programme in Canada	1. Use of L1 in order to understand task instructions during pair work 2. Responding to teacher questions in Japanese 3. Students translating words for others and consulting a bilingual dictionary 4. Using Japanese for social purposes	1. Teacher repeats instructions in English 2. Teacher provided students with ways of saying 'I don't know' in English 3. Teacher attempted to explain words in English 4. Teacher unsure how to address this problem	The teacher's experience of trying out solutions to the various problems associated with L1 finally led her to administer a short questionnaire asking students to rate 10 reasons for why they used Japanese during English class time

classrooms. Penner's study is not a classic action research study but has clear elements of action research. That is she identified a general problem and then narrowed this down to more specific problems she was having with the students' using their L1. She tried out solutions to these specific problems but did not systematically investigate their effectiveness. This ultimately led her to collect data to help develop a better understanding of the problem. The questionnaire she administered helped her to see more clearly why her students used Japanese. In particular, she came to understand that it was motivated by the social need to establish a relationship/rapport with their fellow classmates. In this study, therefore, the action research did not result in a clear solution regarding the use of the L1 (as Penner admits) but did stimulate reflection about the problem and a fuller understanding of its causes. At the end of it, Penner was better placed to work out new strategies for dealing with it.

Penner's study serves as a good example of the importance of the first step in an action research study – specifying the problem or issue to be investigated. Indeed, undertaking this can constitute a study in its own right. Wallace points out that problem areas can cover a number of possibilities:

Problems with classroom management
Problems of appropriate materials
Problems related to particular teaching areas (e.g. reading, oral skills)
Problems relating to student behaviour, achievement or motivation
Problems relating to personal management issues (e.g. time management and
   relationships with colleagues/higher management) (1998: 19).

But he then notes that 'the topics given are probably too broad' and recommends that teachers be more specific. Barkhuizen (2009) investigated the problems identified by a group of Chinese teachers of English working in universities. He asked them to complete the following sentence: 'I remember once in my classroom I had a very difficult time trying to . . .'.

His analysis of their responses found that the three most commonly identified problem areas were (1) students' unwillingness to speak in class (reported by 29 per cent of the sample), (2) students' lack of motivation (19 per cent), and (3) teaching materials (18 per cent). Barkhuizen also considered the reasons that these teachers gave for their problems. For example, reasons given for (1) included the students' lack of proficiency, their insufficient knowledge about a topic, shyness, fear of being laughed at by others, lacking confidence, and focus on examinations. Clearly, it is not sufficient to simply identify a problem; it is also important to consider the reasons for why the problem exists, as only then is it possible to formulate a research question that can guide the study.

The precise specification of a problem is not something that teachers always find easy. Nunan (1990b) reported that teachers' proposals tended to be rather grand and unmanageable because they had failed to identify specific research questions. It was with this in mind that I have proposed a different starting point for action research. In Ellis (1998b) I outlined a procedure for conducting the micro-evaluation of classroom activities. The starting point for such research is not a problem but rather some 'task' that the teacher is interested in using with the students. The idea behind my proposal is that teachers would benefit exploring empirically whether the task 'worked' and that this would stimulate reflection on the choice of task and the manner in which it was implemented. I outlined a five step procedure for conducting a micro-evaluation: (1) description of the task, (2) planning the evaluation, (3) collecting information, (4) analyzing the information, and (5) reaching conclusions and making recommendations (e.g. for changes that were needed to the task materials or implementation). I distinguished three types of micro-evaluation: (1) student-based (involving eliciting the views of the students about the task, (2) response-based (collecting data to see if the performance of the task accorded with its pedagogic aims), and (3) learning-based (investigating whether any language learning resulted from the performance). Many micro-evaluations involve more than one of these types.

However, action research – whether conducted in the traditional way or as a micro-evaluation of a task – is not without its problems. Barkhuizen's teachers expressed a number of these – it is very time-consuming, they lacked the expertise to conduct research and their students might not be willing to participate. Doubts have also been expressed about its lack of rigour and therefore its lack of status in academic circles. Brumfit and Mitchell (1990), for example, argued 'there is no good argument for action research producing less care and rigour unless it is less concerned with clear understanding, which it is not' (p. 9). While I think Brumfit and Mitchell have partly missed the point of action research (namely, that it constitutes a process that can stimulate reflection on teaching and, therefore, does not need to conform to academic criteria for research), it does raise the important question of what standards should be used to judge it. The key issue, however, concerns its feasibility. It was his belief that teachers could not be expected to engage in action research without 'burnout' that led Allwright (2003) to propose an alternative form of practitioner research for teachers.

Exploratory practice

Allwright (2005) has argued strongly in favour of 'exploratory-practice'. He explains that this developed out of two ethical concerns – 'the damaging split between researchers and teachers and the high risk of burnout associated with current proposals for teacher-based classroom research' (p. 27). Allwright (2003) formulated a number of general principles to guide the practice of exploratory research. At the centre of these is the notion of 'classroom life', which Allwright suggests should be considered in terms of the 'quality of the learning', the 'quality of education' and, finally, the 'quality of life' with the latter involving factors that lie outside the classroom itself. Allwright's principles were:

1. Put the 'quality of life' first (i.e. 'practical problems' are best considered in context and will involve a holistic understanding of the 'lives' of the participants involved).
2. Work primarily to understand the language classroom life. Allwright emphasizes that 'only a serious effort to understand life in a particular setting will enable you to decide if practical change is necessary, desirable and/or possible' (p.128). This requires converting a 'practical problem' into a 'puzzle'.
3. Involve everybody. Allwright sees exploratory research as a collaborative endeavour, involving learners as 'co-researchers'.
4. Work to bring people together. The need for social harmony requires that exploratory research be directed at achieving collegiality.
5. Work also for mutual development. Participants in the research should work for each other's development.
6. Integrate the work for understanding into classroom practice. Allwright argues that 'practitioner research must not become parasitic upon the life it is trying to understand' (p. 129). This implies that any investigative tool used should be part of the instructional activities that are a natural part of a lesson.
7. Make the work a continuous enterprise. Exploratory research needs to be seen as 'a continuous, indefinitely sustainable enterprise' (p. 130). A corollary of this is that teachers should avoid time-limited funding as this will compromise the whole enterprise.

Exploratory practice, then, aims to make the time that teachers and learners spend together 'pleasant and productive' and, in so doing, create the conditions for pedagogic change. For Allwright, teacher research needs to be feasible: he argues that if teachers see classroom research as too demanding, they will not engage in it. It is for this reason that exploratory practice needs to integrate enquiry into classroom practice. He sees the role of academic researchers as 'consultants' rather than 'directors'; they should advise on the conduct of investigations but not attempt to control them. Above, all exploratory research needs to be a collegial enterprise; the investigations should involve learners as well as teachers and should focus on 'puzzles' rather than on 'problems'.

The special issue of *Language Teaching Research* (Volume 7, Issue 2) provides a number of reports of exploratory practice in action. Subsequently, this journal introduced a section called 'Practitioner Research' which provides an outlet for teacher research based on the principles of exploratory practice. The study reported in Table 2.4 was published in this section.

Bloom's (2007) study of the tensions that arose in a Spanish course for university-level health professionals reflects the seven principles of exploratory research. She was primarily concerned with the 'quality of life' of her classroom, this being the driving force behind her wish to understand why tensions arose and to find ways of addressing them. Bloom treated these tensions as a 'puzzle' rather than as problems. She involved the students and herself in exploring the tensions and ways of relieving them. She was constantly concerned with 'bringing people together', recognizing that the tensions arose because of differences between her own and the students' expectations (e.g. some of her students were focused on achieving accurate products in Spanish where she was more concerned with engaging them in a communicative process). She constantly worked for mutual development – both the students' development as effective learners and her development as a teacher. She was very careful to integrate her investigative tools into the practice of her own teaching: the students were not asked to perform any tasks purely for the purpose of data collection. Her work was truly a continuous enterprise, covering the duration of the semester-long course. Commenting on Bloom's article, Allwright (2007) emphasizes that what lay at the centre of her study was the search for the 'human issues' that arose in her classroom and the importance of 'dialogue' as a means of understanding and resolving these issues.

There are a number of differences between action research and exploratory research. One is the starting point – a 'problem' or, perhaps, a 'task' in the case of action research and a 'puzzle' in the case of exploratory research. Another difference lies in the methodology for the two approaches. Action research employs similar methods of data collection to those found in formal research and involves going beyond the materials used for teaching; exploratory research embeds data collection into the actual practice of teaching. What they have in common is an emphasis on the continuous nature of the enquiry. Action research is 'cyclical' (although to what extent this is actually achieved by many teachers is doubtful); exploratory research is a long-term enterprise and, because it is part of teaching is potentially more sustainable.

Table 2.4 Summary of Bloom's (2007) exploratory study

Context	Participants	Purpose	Methodology	Understandings
The semester-long study took place in an elective introductory Spanish course for health-care professionals in a university in the USA. The course involved a negotiation of the curriculum with an emphasis on the process rather than product of learning.	Bloom herself as the teacher and 13 students (undergraduates and graduates), who were enrolled in the course. Their previous study of Spanish ranged from 0 to 6 years.	Bloom set out to investigate the experiences of herself (the teacher) and her students as she negotiated the instruction. Subsequently, she switched to examining the sources of tension that arose as a result of the non-traditional form of instruction.	The data consisted of Bloom's notes taken during and after class; video-taped lessons; informal interviews with students; informal and formal feedback sessions; student- and teacher-generated documents.	Bloom identified a number of themes where tensions arose: (1) student- vs. teacher-centred learning, (2) self-efficacy vs. laissez faire, (3) communication vs. accuracy, (4) process vs. product orientation. Bloom saw these tensions as productive as they caused her to renegotiate the class with the students.

Practitioner research: concluding comments

Practitioner research is research carried out by teachers working in their own class-rooms with a view to improving practice (in the case of action research) or under-standing the 'life of the classroom' (in the case of exploratory research). Where such research is published, it typically takes the form of narrative accounts. Both Penner's action research study and Bloom's exploratory research study were presented as 'sto-ries' about these two teachers' experiences of how they investigated their classrooms and what they discovered through these investigations. They reflect Crookes' (1993) call for new discourses and genres that can represent what teachers find from their research. The question arises as to the contribution that such 'stories' can make to our knowledge of how language learning takes place in a classroom. If such research is to be judged by the standard criteria of generalizability and replicability, it is doubt-ful that it will have much impact on the knowledge-base of L2 classroom research. However, if it is judged by alternative criteria – for example, 'meaningfulness' and 'trustworthiness' (Mishler, 1990), then, it can be seen as affording insights that can inform the knowledge base. It would seem foolish to ignore studies such as those of Penner and Bloom, as both address key issues (i.e. the use of the learner's L1 and the implementation of learner-centred instruction) that are central to the study of the L2 classroom. Ultimately, however, the significance of such research lies not in whether it can or cannot contribute to our theoretical understanding of the L2 classroom but to its relevance to language pedagogy. As Allwright (2003: 131) noted 'who stands to gain most . . . will surely be the teacher and the learners (rather than "academic researchers")'.

Main Research Traditions

I now turn to examine the two major research traditions that figure in language teaching research – and in research in the social sciences in general. These traditions are labelled somewhat differently. Often they are referred to in terms of 'quantitative' and 'qualitative' research (see, for example, Brown and Rodgers, 2002; Mackey and Gass, 2005) but I prefer to reserve these terms to distinguish the different kinds of data that can be collected. Nunan and Bailey (2009) refer to the 'psychometric' and 'naturalistic research traditions', McDonough and McDonough (1997) to 'nor-mative' and 'interpretive' research, Grotjahn (1987) to 'analytical-nomological' and 'exploratory-interpretive'. I have chosen the terms 'confirmatory' and 'descriptive'. My aim is not to provide a 'how-to' account of these two research traditions but rather to familiarize readers with their theoretical underpinnings, the kinds of re-search designs they employ, their methods of data collection, and the ways the data has been analyzed. Throughout I will focus on research that has been conducted inside L2 classrooms.

Confirmatory Research

Theoretical underpinnings

There are a number of assumptions that underlie confirmatory research:

1. The phenomenon under study (the language classroom) exists as an objective reality that can be studied scientifically (i.e. by excluding the subjective viewpoint of the researcher as far as this is possible).
2. Confirmatory research is theory driven. That is, the research questions are derived from an explicit theory that predicts that certain types of relationships in the phenomenon being investigated will be found. The purpose of confirmatory research is to 'test' these predictions (called 'hypotheses') by providing evidence that either confirms or disconfirms them.
3. In order to form hypotheses it is necessary to divide the phenomenon being investigated into clearly-defined elements or constructs. The validity of the research depends on whether these constructs can be shown to be theoretically sound.
4. Once identified, the constructs under study can then be separately and quantitatively measured. This is commonly referred to as an etic perspective. The measurement of variables must be demonstrably reliable. That is, the researcher needs to show that no bias or inconsistency has crept into their measurement.
5. By ensuring the research is valid and reliable it is possible to arrive at conclusions about the phenomenon under study that can be applied to the wider population from which the sample being investigated was drawn. That is, the findings of confirmatory research are not limited to the specific classroom/teachers/learners under investigation.

Confirmatory studies of L2 teaching draw on theories of language teaching and learning to identify the 'variables' that can be studied. A 'variable' is a general theoretical construct. Examples of variables derived from a theory of teaching are 'production-based instruction' and 'comprehension-based instruction'. Examples derived from a theory of L2 learning are 'implicit learning' and 'explicit learning'. Some variables straddle the boundaries of teaching/learning theory. 'Focus on form' for example is a variable that was derived from a theory of L2 acquisition that claimed that attention to form in the context of meaning-focused communication constitutes the ideal condition for learning to take place, but it is also an instructional variable in that it is realized through specific instructional techniques such as corrective feedback (see Doughty and Williams, 1998). Many of the variables investigated in language teaching research are of this kind.

For research purposes, theoretical variables need to be made operational (i.e. concrete ways of investigating them have to be worked out). This often means narrowing them down to quite specific behaviours. Comprehension-based instruction, for example, might be realised in the form of listen-and-do tasks (i.e. tasks that require learners to listen to directions or descriptions and then show their understanding by some action). The key point, though, is that in confirmatory research the variables chosen for study are determined a priori by some general theory.

The relationship between variables can be of two kinds, leading to two different types of confirmatory research – experimental and correlational. Experimental research assumes a causal relationship between variables – that is variable A (called the independent variable) causes some change in variable B (called the dependent variable). In the case of language teaching research, this typically involves investigating whether some aspect of instruction (e.g. corrective feedback) results in some change in the students (e.g. a gain in grammatical accuracy). A clear example of experimental research in the field of language teaching can be found in the comparative method studies, where the effects of two different methods for teaching a language are compared in terms of measures of L2 achievement.

Correlational research assumes a link between two variables but without claiming that the link is causal. For example, the relationship between learner participation in the classroom and L2 proficiency is best seen as correlational as it is just as possible that the learners' proficiency may influence their level of participation as vice versa. Correlational relations always need to be interpreted cautiously because we cannot be sure about the direction of the relationship we have found.

In the context of the L2 classroom, the relationship between two variables is very likely to be influenced by other variables, known as moderating variables. For example, if we wanted to investigate the effect of comprehension-based versus production-based instruction on learning we would do well to take account of individual learner factors such as language anxiety. Learners with a propensity to anxiety in the classroom may learn better from comprehension-based instruction as production is inherently anxiety-creating for some learners while more self-confident learners who are prepared to take risks in using the L2 may benefit more from production-based instruction. L2 classroom researchers in the confirmatory paradigm are increasingly examining the interplay of large numbers of variables (see Chapter 10).

Design

The design of experimental and correlational studies differs and so will be considered separately.

Experimental research   A true experimental study requires the following:

1. The independent and dependent variables are identified and clearly defined.
2. Some form of intervention in the domain under study is devised with the purpose of investigating what effect the independent variable(s) has on the dependent variable(s). This is referred to as the 'treatment'.

3. A number of groups are formed, some constituting the experimental group(s) and one the control group (i.e. a group that does not receive the treatment).
4. Participants are assigned to the different groups randomly.

Most classroom-based studies, however, are not true experiments. In particular, logistical considerations generally require the use of intact classes, so random assignment of participants to groups is not possible. Classroom experimental studies are best described as quasi-experimental.

Ellis and He's (1999) study (see Table 2.1) is a quasi-experimental study. We used intact classes and also we could not include a control group as we only had access to three classes and wanted to investigate three experimental treatments (premodified input, interactionally modified input, and interactionally modified output). This constitutes a serious limitation of the study. However, we felt justified in omitting a control group because previous studies (e.g. Ellis, Tanaka and Yamazaki, 1994) had shown that both premodified and interactionally modified input resulted in greater learning of new vocabulary items than unmodified input (i.e. the control condition).

Some experimental studies investigate a single group, employing a time-series design (see Mellow, Reeder and Forster, 1996). This involves taking measures of the dependent variable at a number of different times. The idea here is to compare performance over a number of times to see whether there is evidence for a consistent pattern of change as a result of the treatment.

Complex experimental designs involving moderating variables are possible. Y. Sheen's (2008) study of corrective feedback, for example, investigated the effects of language anxiety on learner's ability to benefit from recasts of their errors (i.e. reformulations of learner utterances containing non-target forms). She obtained a measure of the learners' language anxiety and then divided the group that received recasts into two subgroups (a high-anxiety and a low-anxiety group) in order to see whether these responded differently to the recasts and whether there was any difference in the learning that resulted. She found a difference in both their response and in their learning. In other words, she showed that learners' language anxiety mediated the effect of the recasts. Such designs are important because they acknowledge that any single treatment (such as recasts) may have a differential effect depending on individual learner factors.

Experimental studies vary greatly in what constitutes the independent and dependent variables, leading to design differences. In Ellis and He's and also in Sheen's studies, the independent variable was some kind of instruction and the dependent variable was L2 learning (vocabulary in the case of Ellis and He and a grammatical feature in the case of Sheen). In such studies it is often necessary to include a pre-test to demonstrate what learners know prior to the instruction. Performance on the pre-test can then be compared to performance on a post-test (i.e. a similar test administered after the treatment). These studies also included a delayed post-test (i.e. a test administered some time after the treatment had finished). Delayed post-tests are needed to investigate whether any learning evident in the immediate post-test is durable. Other experimental studies, however, do not need to include a testing regime. In Foster and Skehan's (1996) often-cited study of tasks, for example, the independent variables were 'type of task' and 'pre-task planning' and the dependent variables were dimensions of the learners' production (i.e. fluency, complexity and accuracy) that resulted from the performance of the tasks. A testing regime only becomes essential when the research addresses whether the treatment resulted in some change in the participants (e.g. in L2 learning).

Finally, it should be noted that not all classroom experimental studies are entirely product-oriented. A product-oriented study is one that focuses on the effects of the treatment on the dependent variable (e.g. L2 learning or task performance). But L2 classroom researchers have been increasingly aware of the need to also investigate the 'processes' that arise during the treatment. Investigating the 'processes' is very important for explaining how the treatment had the effect it did (or didn't). For example, in Ellis and He (1999) we audio-recorded the actual lessons that took place during the various treatments, prepared transcripts of these and then analyzed the interactions that occurred. We showed that in the pre-modified and interactionally modified conditions where the teacher worked with the whole class the interactions resembled those that might be found in a testing context whereas those that arose in the modified production group, where the learners worked in pairs, the interactions were much more conversational with the learners working to scaffold each other's performance of the task. Process-product studies of this kind, which combine experimental research and descriptive research, are discussed further later in this chapter.

Correlational research   A correlational study aims to investigate the relationship between two or more variables. In such studies there is no 'treatment' and no a priori division of the participants into groups. Instead, the researcher obtains numerical measures of the variables under study and then investigates statistically the extent to which these variables are related.

Many correlational studies are not classroom-based. They examine learner or teacher variables by collecting data from learners outside the classroom. For example, there are a large number of studies that have examined the relationship between learners' motivation and their L2 proficiency. Often these studies involve classroom learners but they do not qualify for inclusion in this book, which, as previously explained, is concerned with teaching and its relationship to learning. However, there are also a number of classroom-based correlational studies that do examine instructional variables. Table 2.5 provides an example of such a study. Guilloteaux and Dörnyei (2008) investigated the relationship between three variables: teachers' motivating behaviour, students' motivated behaviour, and students' motivation to learn English in their courses. The first two variables were measured by observing teachers and students' behaviour in actual classrooms. The third variable was measured by means of a questionnaire. The strength of the relationships between the three variables was then investigated.

Table 2.5 Summary of Guilloteaux and Dörnyei's (2008) correlational study

Participants	Research questions	Design	Instruments	Results
Teachers and students in 20 junior high school classrooms in South Korea	The research questions addressed: 1. the relationship between teachers' motivational practice and students' motivation to learn English 2. the relationship between the students' self-reported motivation, their actual classroom behaviour, and the teachers' classroom practice	Correlational – measures of the following variables were obtained: 1. the teachers' motivational practice 2. the students' classroom behaviours 3. students' state of motivation	1. A classroom observation scheme designed to record instances of students' motivated behaviour and teachers' motivating behaviour 2. A questionnaire to measure students' motivation to learn English in their current courses 3. A post-lesson teacher evaluation scale	1. The teachers' motivational behaviour was strongly related to the students' motivated behaviour 2. It was also related (but less strongly) to students' self-reported motivation 3. Students' self-reported motivation was also related to their observed motivated behaviour

As noted above finding a relationship between two variables does not demonstrate causality. Guilloteaux and Dörnyei were very careful to acknowledge this:

> We cannot simply claim that the teachers' motivational practice increased student motivation. An alternative explanation would be the results reflect some sort of school effect. For example, the general lethargy of a demotivated student body … can demotivate a teacher, causing him or her to teach in an uninspired and uninspiring way (pp. 70–71).

However, sometimes there are grounds for claiming that that the relationship is causal. Guilloteaux and Dörnyei sought such grounds. They argued that it was unlikely there was a 'school effect' because the schools that they investigated were ecologically very similar. Thus, they argue their study suggests that 'teachers can make a real difference in their students' motivational disposition' (p. 72). Nevertheless, it would require an experimental study to confirm that this is the case.

Data collection

The data collected in confirmatory research will vary depending on the research question. In a study such as Ellis and He it was necessary to collect data that could show whether the learners had learned the target vocabulary items. In Foster and Skehan, the data collected consisted of measures derived from transcriptions of the learners' performance of the different tasks. Gulloteaux and Dörnyei collected data from within the classrooom using an observational scheme and also self-report data. In all three cases, as in all confirmatory research, the data were numerical.

There are a number of excellent accounts of the different kinds of numerical data that can be collected (e.g. Dörnyei, 2007; Ellis and Barkhuizen, 2005; Mackey and Gass, 2005). I will not attempt a thorough review here. Rather, I will give examples for some of the common variables that figure in confirmatory research (see Table 2.6). I have identified three of the most common variables in language teaching research: L2 learning, task performance, and learner factors.

The different types of data for investigating language learning are taken from Norris and Ortega's (2000) meta-analysis of experimental studies of form-focused instruction. There is a growing recognition of the need to collect 'free constructed responses' (e.g. by using communicative oral tasks) as these provide the best data for investigating whether instruction has had any effect on learners' interlanguage development. Examples of studies that have collected such data are VanPatten and Sanz's (1995) study of the effect of a particular type of instruction called Processing Instruction (see Chapter 9) and Lyster and Mori's (2006) study of the effect of different types of corrective feedback (see Chapter 8). Studies that have investigated task performance have collected a whole range of different types of data. These studies collect samples of learners' performance of different tasks, which are then analyzed to provide different kinds of measures of L2 use, including purely linguistic measures (such as fluency, complexity and accuracy) and discourse measures (such as

Table 2.6 Examples of data collection methods used in experimental research

Variable	Type of data	Examples
L2 learning	1. Metalinguistic judgements 2. Selected response 3. Constrained constructed response 4. Free constructed response	Grammaticality judgement test Multiple-choice test Sentence completion test Communicative task
Task performance	Measures of: 1. Fluency 2. Complexity 3. Accuracy 4. Negotiation sequences 5. Language-related episodes (LREs)	Mean number of syllables per minute Number of different verb forms used Percentage of error free clauses Number of successfully resolved sequences Number of LREs and successfully resolved LREs
Learner factors	1. Questionnaires 2. Tests 3. Observation	Language Anxiety Questionnaire (Horwitz, Horwitz and Cope, 1986). Modern Language Aptitude Test (Carrol and Sapon, 1959) The MOLT scheme (Guilloteaux and Dörnyei, 2008)

negotiation sequences and language-related episodes). Learner factors can figure as moderating variables (as previously explained), as dependent variables (as for example in studies that investigate the effect of some instructional treatment on learners' level of anxiety), and in correlational research (as in Guilloteaux and Dörnyei's study). Numerical data can be obtained from classroom observation schemes, from learners' responses to questionnaires or from tests of specific learner factors.

Data analysis

Given that the data in confirmatory research are numerical, the methods used to analyze them are statistical. Again, this is not the place for a detailed account of these methods. Instead I will briefly describe the main methods, leaving the reader to obtain a more detailed understanding from the numerous books that deal with statistical procedures (see, in particular, Brown, 1988 and Dörnyei, 2007).

There are two basic kinds of statistics; descriptive statistics and inferential statistics. Both are important as the results obtained from inferential statistics cannot be properly understood without reference to descriptive statistics.

Descriptive statistics provide information about the measures obtained for whole groups, although in some studies the scores obtained by individual participants are also included. Group statistics include means (i.e. the scores obtained by the individual participants divided by the number of participants) and various measures of dispersion (e.g. standard deviation and range), which provide information about the extent to which the scores of the individual participants cluster around the mean.

Inferential statistics are of two major kinds. One kind provides a measure of the extent to which the group scores are different. This kind is used in experimental studies. In part, group differences can be seen by inspecting the descriptive statistics, but these cannot tell us whether the differences could have been achieved by chance or are 'statistically significant' (i.e. are unlikely to have arisen purely by chance). There are various statistical tests that can be used for this purpose. Two of the most common are t-tests and measures of analysis of variance (ANOVAs). The former are typically used when comparing just two groups and the latter when the study involves more than two groups. Both statistics provide a statistical score (t in the case of t-tests and F in the case of ANOVAs) and also a p value, which indicates whether the score can be considered statistically significant and at what level. In general, a p value of $< .05$ is required to claim statistical significance. This means that there is only a chance of five in a hundred that the score could have been obtained by chance.

The second kind of inferential statistics provides a measure of the degree of relatedness between two variables and thus is used in correlational studies. A popular statistic of this kind is the Pearson Product Moment Correlation. This provides a score (r). A perfect correlation (never achieved in the kinds of research we will be considering) occurs when $r = 1.0$. The closer to 1.0 the r score is, the stronger the relationship. So an r score of .80 might be considered to show a strong relationship between the two variables, whereas one .10 is indicative of a weak relationship. It is also possible to calculate the p value of a correlation. Again, a value of $> .05$ is generally held to demonstrate that the relationship is statistically significant. The calculation of the p value depends on both the size of r and also the n size (i.e. the number of individual scores). With a small n size a large r score is needed to achieve significance; with a large n size a much smaller r score may be significant. Thus, if the n is very large (say several hundreds) even a weak r may become significant. With correlations, therefore, it is necessary to consider both the size of r and the p value. There are also other correlational statistics, including Multiple Regression Analysis, which seeks to show not just the strength of the relationship between two variables but also the extent to which the scores on one variable are predictive of scores on another. In this case, it becomes more possible to talk about cause and effect in a correlational study.

Descriptive Research

Theoretical underpinnings

Classroom descriptive research aims to produce qualitative and quantitative accounts of classroom processes, the factors that shape these and their implications for language learning. In many accounts of research methods the preferred term is 'naturalistic research' or 'interpretive research'. However, I have elected to use the label 'descriptive research' as this seems to me to more accurately reflect the kind of research that has taken place in L2 classrooms. In using the term 'descriptive', however, I do not wish to suggest that the research has failed to provide explanations for the phenomena investigated.

'Descriptive research' serves as a cover term for a number of different approaches. However, it is possible to identify a number of general characteristics that these have in common. These are:

1. Descriptive research adopts an emic perspective by providing a rich account of specific instructional contexts.
2. For this reason, it typically involves only a few 'cases' (e.g. teachers, learners or classrooms) and does not seek to generalize beyond these cases.
3. Researchers investigate these cases as they find them (i.e. there is no attempt to intervene through some form of instruction).
4. Descriptive research emphasizes the need to understand phenomena in their cultural and social contexts.
5. It often involves a research-then-theory approach. That is, the variables are not usually decided a priori on the basis of some theory but rather emerge as the research progresses. The findings of the research, however, may be used to build a theory.
6. It assumes that knowledge and understanding of phenomena is subjective and seeks to counter the subjectivity of the researcher by demonstrating that the research findings are consistent with the data (i.e. are trustworthy) and reflect the viewpoints of different participants.

Types of descriptive research

Descriptive research relies on observation of the phenomena under study and, in some types, on self-reports obtained from the participants involved. It is possible to group the different approaches under two broad headings: (1) interactional research and (2) ethnography.

Interactional research   Interactional research documents the interactional features of classroom discourse. A variety of tools are available for achieving this – discourse analysis, conversation analysis, and microgenetic analysis. Each of these has their own theoretical underpinnings as reflected in their different aims. Discourse analysis assumes that classroom interaction is hierarchical in structure and aims to provide a systematic description of this. Lyster and Ranta's (1997) study, for example, used discourse analysis to describe the structure of corrective feedback episodes in the classrooms they observed. Conversation analysis seeks to 'characterize the organization of interaction by abstracting from exemplars of specimens of interaction and to uncover the emic logic underlying the organization' (Seedhouse, 2004: 13). The assumption here is that there are norms that enable speakers to produce and interpret actions as, for example, in the norms that underlie turn-taking in a classroom. Microgenetic analysis aims to document change by showing how interaction assists participants to perform specific tasks collaboratively when they are unable to perform these independently. As Duff (2007) notes, a key characteristic of classroom interactional research is that it relies on the evidence available from the interactions themselves (i.e. it rarely takes into account the participants' explicit reflections on their practices).

Ethnographic research   Ethnographic research has a broader goal. It is 'the study of people's behavior in naturally occurring, ongoing settings, with a focus on the cultural interpretation of behavior' (Watson-Gegeo, 1988: 576). It emphasizes the importance of obtaining multiple perspectives by collecting a variety of data (e.g. through participant observation, interviews, assembling relevant documents, and member-checking) and using these to describe and understand common patterns of behaviour. Nunan and Bailey (2009) identify three main characteristics of ethnography: it involves longitudinal enquiry, it is comprehensive, and it views people's behaviour in cultural terms. A particular type of ethnography has figured strongly in L2 classroom research – the ethnography of communication. This focuses on the 'ways of speaking' that occur in different classroom speech communities. It differs from interactional research in that it 'looks for strategies and conventions governing larger units of communication and involves more holistic interpretation' (Saville-Troike, 1996: 354). Ethnography of communication has often been used to investigate bilingual classrooms and mainstream classrooms containing L2 learners (for example, Duff, 2002; Harklau, 1994).

Design

The design of confirmatory research is usually cross-sectional (i.e. it involves collecting data within a single or short period of time). In contrast, descriptive research can be either cross-sectional or longitudinal (i.e. data are collected over a period of time). However, there are still very few longitudinal studies of the L2 classroom.

Most (but certainly not all) interactional research is cross-sectional. It involves identifying the specific phenomenon to be studied (e.g. corrective feedback; teachers' questions; turn-taking) and formulating research questions, choosing the specific classroom(s) to investigate, observing the interactions that take place there (and, these days, audio- or video-recording them), extracting episodes relevant from the data and describing them in accordance with the procedures of the preferred research tool (discourse analysis, conversation analysis, microgenetic analysis).

Ethnographic research is emergent and therefore longitudinal in design. The scope of the research gradually narrows as it progresses. Watson-Gegeo (1988) distinguished three stages. The 'comprehensive stage' involves obtaining a general

Table 2.7 Summary of Harklau's (1994) ethnographic study

Research questions	Context	Data collection	Findings
The research questions addressed: 1. how ESL and mainstream classrooms differ as L2 learning environments 2. what students lose or gain when making the transition from ESL to mainstream classrooms	ESL and mainstream classes in a San Francisco high school with a very ethnically mixed student population. Four Chinese students were followed for four to seven semesters during which they made the transition from ESL to mainstream classes. In the final year of study a broader number of Chinese students were observed and interviewed	1. Observation of each student through full schools days 2. Samples of school work and home work 3. School records 4. Informal lunch time conversations 5. Between two and seven formal interviews of one hour's duration 6. Interviews with mainstream teachers 7. Discussions with the ESL teacher	1. Spoken language: – input not tailored to the needs of the ESL students in the mainstream classes: students often did not attend to teachers: students spoke little and generally just one or two word turns – ESL classes provided better tailored input and greater participation 2. Written language: – more and greater variety of written input and more opportunities for extended written output in ESL classes – students resorted to memorizing and repeating back language in mainstream classes but not in ESL classes 3. Structure and goals of instruction: – mainstream curriculum fixed by school internal and external factors whereas ESL curriculum looser and more adaptable to students' needs 4. Explicit language instruction: – ESL classes provided students with explicit language instruction (e.g. through feedback on written work) but mainstream teachers ignored errors 5. Socializing functions of schooling: – ESL programme helped students adjust to US life and society and helped them develop a supportive peer group in school – students unable to develop effective social relationships with students outside their own group in the mainstream classes.

picture of the situation being investigated. Its aim is to study 'all theoretically salient aspects of a setting' (p. 584). This is essential in order to enter the next stage – the 'topic-oriented stage' – where the specific topic to be investigated is identified. It is only at this stage that research questions are formulated. The final stage is the 'hypothesis-oriented stage'. This requires further data collection in order to test specific hypotheses. However, many reports of ethnographic research do not document these stages but instead describe the findings of the final stage only.

A good example of an ethnographic study is Harklau's (1994) longitudinal study of L2 learners in mainstream classrooms in California. This is summarized in Table 2.7. Harklau's study has all the hallmarks of an ethnographic study. Her research is informed by general research questions of significance to her area of study. She provides a very detailed description of the context of the research. She employed a variety of data collection methods that included both observation and the participants' self-reports. She sifted through the data to extrapolate a number of key themes, which she then discussed in holistic terms, documenting her findings with quotations from the data. Duff (2007) describes the study as 'a very complete, well-situated and synthesized account of the focal students, classes and school' (p. 979).

Data collection

Interactional research calls for data relating to the interactions that take place in the classroom. Such data can be collected in two principal ways: using an interactional analysis scheme to record the different interactional behaviours that occur or recording the interactions that take place and then preparing transcripts of these for analysis. Long (1980) distinguished three different types of interaction analysis systems: in a category system each event is coded each time it occurs, in a sign system each event is recorded only once within a fixed time span, while in a rating scale an estimate of how frequently a specific type of event occurred is made after the period of observation. One of the best-known interactional analysis systems is the Communicative Orientation of Language Teaching (COLT). Allen, Fröhlich, and Spada (1984) noted:

> The observational categories are designed (a) to capture significant features of verbal interaction in L2 classrooms and (b) to provide a means of comparing some aspects of classroom discourse with *natural* language as it is used outside the classroom (1984: 232).

Interaction analysis systems have gradually lost popularity as audio- and video-recording of classrooms has become easier. These afford richer data and an opportunity for the researcher to deliberate more carefully when coding categories. Interactional analysis systems provide quantitative data (i.e. the frequency of different behaviours). Audio- and video-recording afford both qualitative data (in the form of transcribed extracts) and quantitative data (when the data have been coded in accordance with a coding system).

Ethnographic research also employs classroom observation using interactional analysis systems or recordings but is likely to supplement these with field notes which can provide detailed contextual information not otherwise available. As illustrated in Harklau's study, ethnographic research also collects other kinds of data; participant self-reports (e.g. by means of informal and formal interviews or diaries) and documentary information.

One type of self-report that is becoming increasingly popular is 'stimulated recall'. This is often used in conjunction with an audio- or video-recording. The researcher plays back an extract from the recording and then asks the participant in the extract (the teacher or a learner) to recall the thoughts they had at the time. This method of data collection is very useful for investigating what the participants were attending to during the interaction, their affective states, and their individual perspectives on what was happening. Gass and Mackey (2000) provide an excellent account of this method.

Analysis

Quantitative data in descriptive research is analyzed using descriptive and inferential statistics. As the data typically take the form of frequency counts, a very useful statistical tool is chi-square. This allows the researcher to establish whether the distribution of frequencies across a number of different categories is statistically significant – for example, if the researcher wanted to know whether the difference in learners' repair of their errors following different kinds of corrective feedback was statistically significant. As with other inferential statistics, chi-square produces a score ($\chi2$) and an assessment of the probability of this score occurring by chance (i.e. a p value).

Qualitative data can be analyzed in a number of different ways (see Ellis and Barkhuizen, 2005: Chapter 11). In a deductive analysis, a set of predefined or expected themes or categories are used to 'code' the data. In an inductive analysis the data itself is allowed to determine the themes/categories by using what is called a 'grounded theory' approach. This involves 'examining the data first to see into what kind of chunks they fall into naturally and then choosing a set of concepts that helps to explain why the data fell that way' (Le Compte and Schensul, 1999: 46). Harklau's study employed this method. As Ellis and Barkhuizen note, the choice between deductive and inductive analysis should not be seen as mutually exclusive as many analyses involve moving to-and-fro between the two.

Hybrid research: process-product studies

Formal research in the field of language teaching is very often not 'pure' (i.e. either confirmatory or descriptive). More often than not it employs mixed forms. Grotjahn

(1987) proposed that research paradigms be considered in terms of three dimensions: (1) design, (2) type of data collected and (3) method of data analysis. Using these he describes two 'pure' research paradigms (corresponding to the distinction between 'confirmatory' and 'descriptive' research) and six 'mixed' forms. Of these mixed types, one that is very common in language teaching research is 'experimental-qualitative-statistical'. That is, the basic design is experimental, but qualitative data are collected, which are then quantified by counting the frequency of occurrence of specific categories established qualitatively. These frequencies can then be analyzed using statistical methods. This type of research is often referred to as 'process-product research'.

The importance of conducting process-product research became clear as a result of the indeterminate results produced by the method-comparison studies (see Chapter 3). Researchers began to recognize the need to investigate what happened inside classrooms when different methods were implemented. Long (1984) published an influential article entitled 'Process and Product in ESL Program Evaluation' in which he advocated the study of classroom processes as a 'supplement' to product-based enquiry. He defined 'processes' as 'a host of verbal and non-verbal teacher and student behaviors'. He gave as examples, teachers' error correction strategies and the types of questions they ask (i.e. display versus referential).

One of the best known process-product studies in L2 classroom research is Spada's (1987) study of communicative language classrooms. Spada sought to investigate the relationships between instructional differences and learning outcomes. She investigated three classes of adult-intermediate learners. To investigate instructional differences, sixty hours of classroom observation data was collected from three classes of adult intermediate-level learners using an observation scheme. She found differences in the ways in which communicative teaching was implemented. Spada also obtained pre- and post-test scores on seven proficiency measures for the learners in these classrooms. These were the product measures. She showed that there was a relationship between the classroom process variables and the learners' improvement on the product measures.

Process-product studies constitute one of the most powerful ways of investigating language teaching. They enable the researcher to investigate what happens when a particular experimental treatment is implemented. Thus they provide essential evidence for explaining the results of product-based analyses. It does not follow that externally defined treatments will result in actual differences at the process level. This can explain why no differences in learning outcomes occur. Where product differences are evident, it is possible for the researcher to explore which of the specific process features account for these differences.

Conclusion

In this chapter I have sought to provide readers with a broad brush picture of the kinds of language teaching research that will be examined in the rest of the book.

An understanding of the theoretical assumptions and methods of different research traditions – both formal and practitioner – will help readers to understand and evaluate the findings of the research.

My aim has been to *describe* the different research paradigms, not to *evaluate* them. Researchers vary in their preferred approach, some preferring practitioner to formal research and vice versa. Also, researchers have preferences for particular paradigms within each research tradition. Allwright for example promotes exploratory research as preferable to action research. Duff demonstrates a preference for ethnographic over interactional research.

My own work as a researcher has straddled the different traditions. An early study (Nobuyoshi and Ellis, 1993) was really an action research study undertaken by one of my students at that time (Nobuyoshi). Later in the 1980s (together with Maria Rathbone) I undertook a longitudinal study of the classroom acquisition of L2 German. This had elements of confirmatory research (e.g. I examined the correlations between various measures of learner differences, such as language aptitude and cognitive style, and the learners' acquisition of German as measured by both tests and progress through acquisitional sequences). But it also had aspects of descriptive research (e.g. I asked the learners to keep diaries during the six month period of the study and analyzed these in a variety of ways to investigate how they responded to the instruction they received). In the 1990s I turned to experimental research, conducting a number of studies to investigate the effects of different kinds of input on classroom learners' acquisition of vocabulary. At the end of this decade I also participated (along with Helen Basturkmen and Shawn Loewen in 1992) in a descriptive study of the 'form-focused episodes' that occurred in adult communicative ESL classrooms. This involved what I have called interactional research. Since then, my classroom research output has been largely experimental in nature but this was not motivated by any conviction of the superiority of this form of research than by the nature of the research questions I chose to investigate.

Readers will come across debates about the advantages and disadvantages of different research approaches. Descriptive researchers in the ethnographic tradition have often felt the need to justify their choice of research methodology. Duff (2007), for example, began her chapter on qualitative approaches in classroom research with this statement:

> Whereas quantitative studies of a psychometric nature or involving (quasi-) experimental designs might previously have been viewed as more legitimate forms of research within education and the social sciences, rigorous qualitative studies in classrooms and other learning environments are now increasingly accepted as an important way of generating new knowledge and moving disciplines in innovative directions (p. 973).

Duff then went on to offer eight reasons for conducting descriptive research of both the interactional and ethnographic kind. She makes a strong case. But she is also careful to acknowledge the need for confirmatory research. My own position has been that in many ways the differences in the research traditions have been overstated when it comes to considering how research can inform the practice of language teaching. I do not see language teaching research of any kind as affording 'answers' about the best way to teach but rather 'insights' that teachers need to assess to determine their relevance and applicability to their own classroom contexts. Action research, exploratory research, confirmatory research and descriptive research are in this key respect the same. In this book I intend to call eclectically on a range of research types.

3

Comparative Method Studies

Introduction

Comparative method studies are the obvious starting point for a book that seeks to provide an overview of language teaching research for, as we have seen in Chapter 1, these dominated the early years of classroom-based enquiry. The aim of a comparative method study is to investigate which of two or more types of language instruction is the more/most effective. Such studies are motivated by the understandable desire to make teaching as effective as possible. They are premised on the assumption that it is possible to identify a specific type of instruction that will 'work' more effectively than other types.

Two kinds of comparative method studies can be distinguished. First, there are 'global studies'. These are studies that have examined methods/approaches for the teaching of L2 over a long period of time and that assess learning outcomes in terms of general language proficiency or achievement. Second, there are 'local studies'. These are studies that have investigated method/approaches over a relatively short period of time and that assess learning outcomes in terms of specific linguistic features. I will consider both kinds in this chapter but the main focus will be on global studies. Local studies are considered in greater depth in subsequent chapters (see Chapter 9).

Richards, Platt and Platt (1992) define 'method' as follows:

A way of teaching language which is based on systematic principles and procedures, i.e. which is an application of views of how a language is best taught and learned (p. 228).

They go on to point out how methods differ in terms of the nature of language and of the language learning they embody (which may or may not be made explicit),

Language Teaching Research & Language Pedagogy, First Edition. Rod Ellis.
© 2012 John Wiley & Sons, Ltd. Published 2012 by John Wiley & Sons, Ltd.

their goals and objectives, the type of syllabus, the role of teachers, learners and instructional materials, and the techniques and procedures they employ. Richards and Rogers (1986) describe a number of mainstream methods (or 'approaches')[1], including the Audiolingual Method, Total Physical Response, various humanistic methods (e.g. community language learning and Suggestopedia) and communicative language teaching. In a second edition of their book (published in 2001) they extended the list of methods/approaches to include, among others, the Lexical Approach and Competency-Based Language Teaching. Methods have proliferated over the years and Richards and Rogers' list is by no means complete. In fact, the comparative method studies have examined relatively few of the different methods.

'Method', then, is a pedagogic construct enshrined in a set of principles and techniques that specify how specific acts of teaching are to be performed. As such, the method construct is problematic in two major ways (see Kumaravadivelu, 1994: 2001). The first is that the prescriptions (and proscriptions) embodied in a method view teaching as something that is *external* to the actual act of teaching itself. They position teachers as people who are simply expected to implement the method. This disempowers teachers by requiring them to function as 'actors' rather than as 'authors'. They are expected to perform the 'script' dictated by the method rather than write their own script. In other words, conformity to a method discourages teachers from theorizing their own practice and from experimenting with new possibilities. In effect, then, the method construct reinforces the gap between theory and practice and between theorists (those who devise the method) and practitioners (those who implement it). However, teachers can never just 'perform' a method; they must necessarily interpret any externally defined specifications when taking the myriad online decisions that are part and parcel of the process of teaching.

The second problem with the method construct, which is related to the first, is that it defines teaching in general terms ignoring the fact that 'language pedagogy to be relevant, must be sensitive to a particular group of teachers, teaching a particular group of learners, pursuing a particular set of goals, within a particular institutional context, embedded in a particular sociocultural milieu' (Kumaravadivelu, 2001: 538). In other words, the assumption that there is a 'best' way to teach language is mistaken. What is 'best' for one group of learners in one context may not be 'best' for a different group in a different context.

By and large the comparative method studies have ignored these problems. They have been premised on a view of teaching that sees teachers as implementers of an externally defined set of specifications about how to teach and that assumes that these specifications are broadly relevant to all (or at least a wide range) of classroom contexts. These fundamental problems need to be borne in mind when considering the research that has investigated the efficacy of different methods.

In this chapter, I will review a number of early and later global method studies, presenting the methodology employed and the results obtained by each study and then submitting each to a critical evaluation. In the concluding section I will consider whether there is still any value in conducting such studies and prepare for the alternative 'post-method' view of language pedagogy that informs how language teaching has been investigated in the following chapters in this book.

Early Comparative Method Studies

A feature of many of the early method studies was that they were carried out by teachers in their own classrooms. Another feature, as Chaudron (2001) pointed out, was that the studies these teachers conducted were methodologically flawed. However, this should not be seen as criticism, as methodological rigour in experimental research at the time of these studies was not entrenched in classroom research. Two examples will suffice to give a flavour of the early studies.

In a very early study, Bennett (1917) conducted a comparison of the German vocabulary learned by groups of junior and senior high school students in the USA. Students in each group were taught by means of 'translation study' or 'immediate study'. The former involved translating from German to English while the latter involved memorizing a passage in German with a view to being able to subsequently translate it into English. Bennett's rationale for investigating these two types of instruction was that the 'immediate study' involved greater attention to the German words 'as carriers of meaning' (p. 114). The learners were tested at various times on the words they had learned but Bennett does not provide any description of the actual format of the tests. Descriptive results are presented for the two treatments but there is no test of statistical significance. Overall, the 'immediate study' resulted in more words being learned. Bennett suggests that this was because of the greater cognitive effort demanded by the immediate study.

Where both of Bennett's treatments involved translation (the dominant method at that time), Beck's (1951) study focused on a comparison of students taught by means of a traditional approach (i.e. grammar translation) and what he called an 'oral-cultural approach'. This reflected the growing recognition in the 1950s that grammar translation was ineffective in developing learners' oral skills. In order to investigate the effects of these two methods on learning, Beck compared a group of university students enrolled in three elementary-level French courses with a group of high school students. He describes the oral-cultural treatment as follows:

> The system introduced was that of hearing the spoken language, then repeating it time and time again. Later the same phrases were read aloud and connected conversation and discourse were practiced from phrase types (p. 595).

In effect, this was a version of the Audiolingual Method. No description of the method used for the high school students is provided. It is simply assumed to have involved grammar translation. Testing is also problematic. Beck was unable to obtain any measure of the learners' oral development and so settled for testing reading, vocabulary and grammar – the only 'standard' testing instruments available. Overall the results favoured the university students. After the first course (lasting three months) they achieved the same level as the high school students achieved in one school year except in reading. After the second and third courses they demonstrated an 'amazing superiority' over high school students who had been studying French for four years. Beck offers no discussion of his results.

Clearly, neither of these studies satisfies the criterion of replicability. Descriptions of the method treatments remain sketchy, group equivalence is not clearly established, there is only limited information about the tests used to measure learning and there is no attempt to submit group scores to a test of statistical significance. However, these studies are not without interest. Bennett's study was motivated by the belief that a method that evoked greater cognitive effort would prove superior. Beck's study was based on the perceived need to develop learners' oral proficiency and the recognition that grammar translation was unlikely to achieve this. These continue to be issues of significance today and it is interesting to note that such issues figured so early in thinking about language teaching (see, for example, Laufer and Hulstijn's 2001 study of the processing depth involved in different kinds of vocabulary-learning activities).

Large-Scale Comparative Method Studies in the 1960s

A characteristic of the early studies is that they were all small-scale. In the 1960s, however, there were a number of large-scale global method studies, which are often cited by language teaching researchers, usually in order to illustrate the problems of such method comparisons (e.g. Allwright, 1988).

The 1960s were characterized by what Diller (1978) called 'the language teaching controversy'. This pitted the claims of rationalist approaches to language teaching against those of empiricists. Traditional methods such as grammar translation and the Cognitive-Code Method emphasized the provision of explicit knowledge through rule explanation, while so-called 'functional' methods such as the Audiolingual Method and the Oral Approach emphasized inductive rule learning through listening and extensive oral practice (as in Bennett's study reported in the previous section). At the time, it seemed logical to investigate which method produced the better results. It should be noted, however, that both of these methods viewed language pedagogy as necessarily and essentially requiring a primary focus on linguistic form (predominantly grammatical form) and thus were concerned with how learners achieved accuracy in an L2.

I will consider three large-scale studies; Scherer and Wertheimer (1964), Smith (1970) and Levin (1972)[2]. The projects have become known by their names – the Colorado Project, the Pennsylvania Project and GUME. After a brief account of each project I will review the various issues that these projects brought to the fore.

The Colorado Project

Scherer and Wertheimer (1964) was the first large comparative method study. It compared the Grammar-Translation Method and the Audiolingual Method by following the progress of different beginner-level, college-level students of L2 German taught by each method and tested at the end of the their first and second years of study.

The results at the end of the first year indicated the superiority of the Audiolingual Method in all tests with the exception of the translation test. However, at the end of the second year no overall significant difference between the two methods was found. While the Audiolingual Method group did better at speaking, the Grammar-Translation Method group did better in reading, writing and translation. In other words, each method resulted in learning products that reflected its instructional emphasis. Even the finding that the Audiolingual Method group did better at speaking is of doubtful value to language pedagogy in general given that special coercion was required to induce the students to study speaking (i.e. they had to punch time clocks whenever they used the language laboratory). However, the Colorado study did have a useful outcome – it led to a critical examination of the claims of the Audiolingual Method (see, e.g. Hayn, 1967).

The Pennsylvania Project

The Pennsylvania Project (Smith 1970) compared the effects of three methods on beginning and intermediate French and German classes at the high school level. The three methods were (1) 'traditional' (i.e. grammar translation), (2) 'functional skills' (essentially the Audiolingual Method), and (3) 'functional skills plus grammar'. Student achievement in the four skills of listening comprehension, speaking, reading, and writing was evaluated at mid-year and at the end of the year using a battery of standardized tests. The results in general showed no significant differences between the three methods, except that the 'traditional' group was superior to the other two groups on two of the reading tests. After two years, the 'traditional' group again surpassed the 'functional skills' group in reading ability but did significantly worse on a test of oral mimicry. No differences were found in the students' performance on the other tests. This project was subjected to substantial criticism by Clark (1969), who pointed out that the project did not ensure that the teachers of the two programmes were equivalent in experience. He also noted that although the project included a classroom observation component to ascertain whether the methods were implemented in accordance with their external specifications, different rating scales were used making it difficult to determine if the two methods were in fact distinct.

GUME (Gothenburg/Teaching/Methods/English)

Altogether six studies, all similar in design, were carried out in the GUME Project. Five involved comprehensive school students and one adult learners. Two different methods were compared: (1) the Implicit Method and (2) the Explicit Method with grammatical explanations provided in L2 English in some studies and in L2 Swedish in others. The Implicit Method is described as corresponding to 'an inductive-oriented audiolingual method' and the Explicit Method as corresponding to 'a deductive-oriented audiolingual method with generalizations in the target language'

(Levin, 1972: 84). In most of the experiments, the instruction focused on the teaching of specific grammatical structures but in one experiment the students were exposed to a range of grammatical features. A variety of different tests were used in the six studies but in every case they were either of the selected response or constrained constructed response type (see Table 2.6, Chapter 2). The results for the comprehensive school students and the adult learners differed. By and large, no significant differences between the implicit and explicit school groups were found. In some groups very little learning was evident but even in those where learning did take place the type of instruction made no difference. However, Levin interpreted the overall pattern of the results as indicating the following rank ordering of treatments; Explicit (L1 used) > Implicit > Explicit (L2 used). In the case of an older group of high school students, a clearer advantage was found for the Explicit Method. Also, the adult learner group benefitted most from the Explicit Method. In both of these groups the explicit explanation of grammar points was provided in Swedish (the learners' L1) whereas for the other explicit groups the L2 (English) was used. Levin noted that the explicit instruction also included practice exercises (i.e. it bore little resemblance to the traditional Grammar-Translation Method). He concluded that the main results 'tend to support the cognitive-code learning theory' (p. 193) but only at the upper secondary school and adult learner levels.

These studies point to the inherent difficulties of global method comparisons. They were all carefully designed studies (for their time) and yet they failed to provide a clear demonstration that one method was superior to another in terms of overall language proficiency. While short-term differences were sometimes evident, these disappeared over the long term. There are a number for reasons for the indeterminate findings. One is the age of the learners. The Pennsylvania Project investigated school-level learners and failed to find that the choice of method had any effect on such learners. GUME, however, also investigated adult learners. It found that the choice of method was a factor with these learners – the Explicit Method proving superior to the Implicit Method. Thus age (or perhaps the instructional context) appears to function as a mediating variable, influencing which type of instruction is the more effective. It is likely that there are other mediating factors (e.g. language aptitude and motivation) but GUME, which investigated these, reported no obvious interaction effects. Overall, these studies point to the inherent problem of controlling the variables involved in the implementation of a particular method – that is, variables relating to the teachers, the learners and the instructional processes. In fact, a notable lacuna in all three projects was any detailed information about the instructional processes. Thus, we do not know whether the 'external' differences between the methods were reflected in the way the instruction was conducted.

Perhaps the most serious limitation of these global method studies, however, was the nature of the testing instruments used to measure learning. These were invariably of the discrete-item constrained-response type. Such instruments are likely to favour methods that emphasize explicit knowledge of the L2. It is possible that if a test of free oral production had been included clearer differences – perhaps in favour of the Audiolingual Method – would have been evident.

Comparative Studies Investigating Superlearning

The 1970s were characterized by a growing interest in humanistic methods of language teaching (see Moskowitz, 1978). One of these – Suggestopedia and its North American adaptation known as the System for Accelerative Learning and Teaching (SALT) has been the object of a number of comparative method studies. Originating in the work of George Lozanov, a Bulgarian educator and psychiatrist, this method aimed to enhance learning (especially vocabulary learning) by inducing a relaxed state in learners so that they were open to suggestive techniques that promote subliminal learning. These techniques included the use of relaxation training, synchronised breathing, music, suggestion (e.g. that learning an L2 is easy), visualisation, vivid presentation of the target items, passive review and dramatic enactment. Lozanov claimed that such techniques result in a 100 per cent increase in learning.

Wagner and Tilney (1983) utilized many of these techniques in a study that compared the superlearning method and a traditional rote-learning method on the acquisition of 300 German words by 21 adult English-speaking learners divided into three groups. Two groups were taught by means of superlearning techniques, one receiving relaxation training and listening to Baroque classical music and the other just the relaxation training. The third group took part in traditional, rote classroom vocabulary sessions. Learning was assessed by means of an aural translation test (L1 to L2) and also alpha brain waves were measured. No differences were found between the superlearning groups and the traditional group in alpha brain waves. However, in the translation test, the traditional method proved superior. Wagner and Tilney concluded 'the combination of relaxation, special breathing, intonation, and music were not enough to produce "super" results' (p. 16).

A number of other studies investigating superlearning techniques have been published. These are surveyed by Dipamo and Job (1991). They point out that many of the studies suffered from major methodological weaknesses and that there is no clear evidence to show that superlearning techniques are superior to more traditional methods. They suggest that those studies that did show an advantage for superlearning did so because they included visualisation techniques, which other vocabulary learning research (e.g. Brown and Perry, 1991) has also consistently shown to be effective.

Comparative Studies Investigating Comprehension-Based Language Teaching

Around the same time as the Colorado, Pennsylvania and GUME projects, a number of language educators were investigating an approach to language teaching that differed quite markedly from both the inductive and deductive methods that were the focus of these three projects. This entailed teaching grammar through comprehension-based instruction rather than through production. Gary (1978) spelt out the theoretical rationale for such an approach. She argued that comprehension was prior to production in language acquisition, that forcing learners to produce in the L2 overloaded short-term memory and could have deleterious effect on acquisition, that teaching through comprehension reduced learner anxiety, and that it also exposed learners to more target language.

The key figure in researching comprehension-based language teaching is James Asher. Asher and associates (see Asher, 1977 for a review) conducted a number of studies designed to compare the effects on learning of Total Physical Response (TPR) and other methods, in particular the Audiolingual Method. The main features of TPR are (1) to delay production until learners are ready to speak, (2) to maximize exposure to the language by introducing grammatical structures through commands and (3) to postpone abstract language until learners have reached an advanced level when they are able to infer meaning from context.

A good example of the kind of study Asher undertook is reported in Asher (1977). This compared the effects of TPR and the Audiolingual Method on the level of English achieved by immigrants enrolled in English as a second language (ESL) classes. Learning was measured by the Fleming Test, a 40-item test designed to measure reading ability. Learners taught by the Audiolingual Method who were enrolled in Level 1 of the ESL programme scored 24 per cent in this test after 96 hours of instruction. Those at the same level taught by TPR scored 52 per cent after 120 hours of training. The TPR group scored almost the same as students enrolled in one of the more advanced audiolingual classes even though they had had far fewer hours of instruction. Asher (1981) summarized the results of his research into TPR in this way:

> For children and adults learning such languages as English, German, French, Japanese, Russian, or Spanish, the results were accelerated stress-free acquisition that had long-term retention. These gains also seemed to hold for people acquiring the sign language of the deaf.

Krashen (1982: 156) concluded his survey of Asher's studies by claiming that 'the TPR results are clear and consistent, and the magnitude of superiority of TPR is quite striking'. However, as Beretta (1986) pointed out, care must be taken when interpreting Asher's studies as in some of them (e.g. Asher, 1972; Asher, Kusudo and de la Torre, 1974) the tests used to measure proficiency that most clearly demonstrated an advantage for TPR were biased in favour of this method.

A number of other caveats are in order. The period of instruction in Asher's studies was relatively short. Thus we cannot be certain that production-based methods will not be equally effective in the long term. Second, the studies focused on beginner learners. Comprehension-based instruction may be less effective when learners have developed some proficiency in the L2. Indeed, advocates of comprehension-based instruction do not propose the abandonment of methods based on production but rather that 'practice in oral production should be delayed and that early language instruction should emphasize developing substantial competence in comprehension before requiring learners to talk in the new language (Gary and Gary, 1981). There were also methodological problems with Asher's studies – for example, the study referred to above did not include a pre-test. Nevertheless, the TPR studies stand out in comparative method studies as providing evidence that support the superiority of a particular method – at least in the early stages of L2 learning.

Interest in comprehension-based language instruction has continued over the years, most notably in a longitudinal study by Lightbown (1992). She reported on a project in New Brunswick, in which Canadian French children in Grades 3–6 were taught English by listening to tapes and following the written text. This was compared with an ESL programme involving oral production practice and grammar explanation. One strength of this study was that it measured learning using tests that were matched to each method, thus avoiding the bias problem discussed by Beretta (1986). Results at the end of the third year of the project showed that 'students in this program have succeeded in learning at least as much English as those whose learning had been guided by the teacher in a more traditional program' (1992: 362). They were as good even at speaking English. Lightbown et al. (2002) reported a follow-up study to the New Brunswick comprehension-based programme, looking at the same students when they had reached Grade 8 after six years of study. These students performed as well as the comparison groups on measures of comprehension and some measures of oral production but were inferior on measures of written production. The students in the regular ESL programme, for example, were more likely to mark verbs for past and were less likely to make errors like substituting 'his' for 'is'.

Another study comparing comprehension-based and production-based instruction is Shintani and Ellis (2010). This experimental study differed from Lightbown's studies in two ways. First, it was relatively short term (i.e. the instruction consisted of only three lessons) and second it focused on a specific grammatical structure – English plural –s. It investigated incidental acquisition (i.e. there was no explicit focus on the target structure; rather the learners – young Japanese children – were exposed to multiple exemplars of singular and plural nouns in instruction designed to teach them vocabulary). The comprehension-based instruction took the form of listening tasks that required a primary focus on meaning. The production-based instruction was of the present–practice–produce (PPP) kind. Acquisition of plural –s was measured by means of both comprehension and production tests. Both the comprehension-based and production-based groups outperformed a control group, which just completed the tests but there were no statistically significant differences between the two experimental groups. However, a comparison of those learners in the two groups who were complete beginners indicated an advantage for the comprehension-based instruction. Shintani and Ellis suggested that this advantage could be explained by qualitative differences in the kind of feedback the two groups experienced. In the comprehension-based instruction the feedback enabled the learners to distinguish the meanings of plural and singular nouns but in the production-based instruction the feedback was corrective (i.e. it focused on whether the learners had produced the correct noun form). Shintani (2011c) followed up with a detailed analysis of the process features of the two types of instruction, demonstrating that they differed markedly with regard to the opportunities the learners had to search for meaning and who controlled the discourse (the teacher or the learners).

The comparative method studies that have investigated comprehension-based and production-based language instruction have produced clearer results than the earlier studies that examined inductive versus deductive instruction, all of which were primarily production-based. There is fairly convincing evidence that comprehension-based instruction is as effective as production-based instruction and, in some cases, it was found to be superior for beginner learners. Asher's studies, Lightbown's report of the New Brunswick project and Shintani and Ellis' study all point in this direction. However, there is no evidence to show that comprehension-based instruction is more effective with more advanced learners and some evidence that it may be less effective than production-based instruction in the long term.

Comparative Studies Investigating Communicative Approaches

The 1970s saw the emergence of communicative language teaching at a theoretical level (Brumfit and Johnson, 1979; Widdowson, 1978; Wilkins, 1976) and a little later in published materials for learners (Abbs and Freebairn, 1982). Richards and Rogers (1986) rightly refer to the 'communicative approach' rather than the 'communicative method' as the proposals emanating from different sources differed markedly. Underlying all of them however was the belief that language was best taught not as a set of formal rules but as a tool for making meaning – as 'use' rather than 'usage' in Widdowson's (1978) terms. Thus whereas the Audiolingual Method drew on the descriptions of language provided by structural linguistics (e.g. Fries, 1952) and on behaviourist theories of learning (e.g. Lado, 1964), the communicative approach was based on functional accounts of language (e.g. Halliday, 1973), theories of communicative competence (Canale and Swain, 1980; Hymes, 1970) and nativist theories of language learning (Corder, 1967).

A weak and strong version of the communicative approach can be distinguished (Howatt, 1984). In the weak version teaching content was defined in terms of the linguistic realizations of notions and functions but the methodology remained essentially the same as in the Audiolingual Method (i.e. it involved controlled production practice and was accuracy-oriented). In the strong version, the content was no longer specified linguistically but in terms of the 'tasks' that learners were to undertake while the methodological focus was on fluency (i.e. on encouraging learners to communicate using whatever resources, linguistic and non-linguistic were available to them). Krashen and Terrell's (1983) Natural Approach can be seen as one type of strong communicative language teaching although this placed greater emphasis on the provision of comprehensible input as opposed to production and in this respect differed from mainstream communicative language teaching. Over time, the strong version morphed into 'task-based language teaching' or TBLT (Ellis, 2003;

Nunan, 1989; Willis, 1996). Also as time passed, courses that adopted PPP came to be called 'communicative' even though they were based on a traditional structural syllabus. In other words, the term 'communicative' has become a desirable label for very different conceptualizations of language teaching. This needs to be borne in mind when examining the various comparative method studies that have claimed to investigate this type of teaching.

In one of the earliest studies comparing communicative language teaching with traditional teaching, Savignon (1972) investigated the learning in three university classes of French as a foreign language. All three classes received the same number of hours of traditional instruction but one group had an additional 'communicative hour' where they performed tasks, another group an extra 'cultural hour' and the third group spent an hour each week in a language laboratory. There were no differences among the three groups on measures of grammatical proficiency but the communicative group outperformed the other two groups on measures of communicative ability. This study suggests that a mixture of traditional and communicative instruction is more effective than purely traditional instruction.

Palmer (1979) compared the effects of 'traditional' instruction and 'communicative' instruction on randomly formed groups of Thai university students. The traditional group was taught by a method involving mechanical and meaningful drills, which focused on specific linguistic features. The communicative group also followed a structural syllabus but in activities that involved an exchange of information where the students had to produce the target structures but also to process them in conversation for their communicative purposes. This can be considered a weak form of the communicative approach. Learning was measured by means of both achievement and communicative tests. The achievement tests assessed listening, grammatical accuracy, and punctuation and were of the discrete-point and integrative types. The communicative tests required students to elicit information from an interlocutor in order to identify the correct picture and to react quickly and appropriately to communication problems that arose in an oral interview. Palmer reports significant positive correlations between the communicative and achievement measures for the communicative group but none for the traditional group. Krashen (1981) noted, however, that there were no significant differences between the groups on the communicative measures. He explained this finding in terms of access to comprehensible input. While the teacher-talk in the traditional group was in the target language, it was in the students' L1 in the communicative group.

Hammond (1988) compared intact groups of students in a Spanish programme at two universities. Eight experimental groups were taught by means of the Natural Approach and 52 comparison groups were taught by means of the Grammar-Translation Method, which emphasized the deductive learning of grammar. Although in general the experimental groups outperformed the comparison groups in both a mid-term and a final examination, many of the differences were not significant. This study did show, however, that students in a communicative classroom did no worse in learning grammar than those in a traditional programme.

Another method comparison study evaluated the Communicational Teaching Project (Prabhu 1987) conducted in India with beginner-level secondary school students. Prabhu employed a task-based approach, i.e. a strong form of the communicative approach. The learners performed a series of communicative tasks first with the teacher and then individually and there was no attempt to present and practise specific linguistic items. Beretta and Davies (1985) compared the learning outcomes of the learners involved in the Project (the experimental group) and those taught by means of a 'traditional' approach involving the Structural-Oral-Situational Method (SOS) based on a structural syllabus and involving pattern practice exercises. To avoid bias in testing, Beretta and Davies devised a battery of tests that included a test that 'favoured' the experimental group (i.e. a task-based test) and one that favoured the control group (i.e. a structure test). There were also three 'neutral' tests (i.e. contextualized grammar, dictation, and listening/reading comprehension tests). The results lent general support to the effectiveness of task-based teaching. In the neutral tests, the experimental group clearly outperformed the control group. However, on the group-biased tests, while the experimental group did better on the task-based test, the control group scored higher on the structural test. Beretta and Davies concluded that the results of the evaluation supported the claim that task-based instruction produces significantly different learning from traditional form-focused instruction. They also noted that the task-based learners demonstrated superior acquisition of structures that they had not been explicitly taught and were also able to deploy what they had learned more readily.

A somewhat different approach to conducting a comparative method study was adopted by Allen et al. (1990). In all the method studies we have considered so far 'method' was defined externally (i.e. in terms of a set of prescriptions about how to teach). The study by Allen et al. was based on Stern's (1990: 106) distinction between 'experiential' and 'analytic' teaching strategies (see Table 3.1). These correspond broadly to communicative and traditional teaching. However, they conducted observations of actual lessons using an interaction analysis schedule (the Communicative Orientation of Language Teaching, or COLT) to rank the lessons in eight Grade 11 French classes in Toronto according to how experiential/analytic they were. Thus, the comparison entailed examining classrooms that varied in terms of the actual processes that had been observed to take place in them. It was hypothesized that the analytic classes would perform better on written and grammatical accuracy measures and that the experiential classes would do better on measures of sociolinguistic and discourse competence. However, when pre- and post-test measures were compared, this was found not to be the case. There were few statistically significant differences between the two most experiential and the two most analytic classes. Allen et al. admitted that the results were 'somewhat disappointing'.

Interest in comparing communicative and non-communicative approaches has continued in recent years but with a shift in theoretical orientation. Long (1991) drew a distinction between 'focus on forms' and 'focus on form'. The former involves traditional language teaching involving the presentation and practice of items drawn from a structural syllabus. The latter entails the use of various teaching strategies –

Table 3.1 Experiential and analytic features in language pedagogy (based on Stern, 1990)

Experiential features		*Analytic features*	
1.	Substantive or motivated topic or theme (topics are not arbitrary or trivial).	1.	Focus on aspects of L2, including phonology, grammar functions, discourse, and sociolinguistics.
2.	Students engage in purposeful activity (tasks or projects), not exercises.	2.	Cognitive study of language items (rules and regularities are noted; items are made salient, and related to other items and systems).
3.	Language use has characteristics of real talk (conversation) or uses any of the four skills as part of purposeful action.	3.	Practice or rehearsal of language items or skill aspects.
4.	Priority of meaning transfer and fluency over linguistic error avoidance and accuracy.	4.	Attention to accuracy and error avoidance.
5.	Diversity of social interaction.	5.	Diversity of social interaction desirable.

Source: Based on Stern, H. 1990. "Analysis and Experience as Variables in Second Language Pedagogy." In *The Development of Second Language Proficiency*, edited by B. Harley et al. Cambridge: Cambridge University Press.

such as corrective feedback – designed to draw learners' attention to linguistic form as they perform communicative tasks. Thus in both focus on forms and focus on form there is an attempt to teach linguistic forms, the difference lying in whether this takes place in a communicative or non-communicative context. This important distinction is discussed further in Chapter 8 and Chapter 9. Here we will focus on two studies that sought to compare the effects of focus on forms and focus on form on L2 acquisition.

The first study (R. Sheen, 2006) compared the effects of focus on form and focus-on-forms instruction on the acquisition of two grammatical structures – WH interrogatives and adverb placement. The study lasted seven months. The learners were Grade 6 elementary students aged between 11 and 12. The focus-on-forms instruction consisted of explicit descriptions of the target structures, controlled practice exercises and opportunities for free production (i.e. PPP). The focus-on-form instruction involved various communicative activities with the teacher instructed to provide feedback whenever errors in the production of the target structures occurred. Three types of tests were used to measure progress – an aural written comprehension test, an oral interview (scored for correct use of the target structures) and a grammaticality judgement test. None of these tests examined the learners' ability to produce the target structures in spontaneous communicative speech. Sheen provides results for only two of the tests. In the oral production test the focus-on-forms group demonstrated increased accuracy over time (but with a decline in the delayed post-test) whereas the focus-on-form group manifested no improvement. There was no statistically significant difference in the two groups' scores in the pre-test but there was in all the post-tests, in favour of the focus-on-forms group. In the grammaticality judgement test, which was administered only at the end of the study, the focus-on-forms group was also superior. On the face of it this study provides clear evidence that the focus-on-forms instruction was more effective. However, as Sheen himself noted, there were few opportunities for corrective feedback on either target structure in the focus-on-form group. Arguably, then, this type of instruction had not in fact been successfully implemented. Also, the testing regime was clearly biased in favour of the focus-on-forms group. In short, it is difficult to reach any clear conclusion based on this study except that direct teaching of the target structures resulted in the learners' ability to use them in tests that explicitly elicited them.

The second study (Laufer, 2006) that compared focus on form and focus on forms investigated vocabulary. Focus on form was operationalized as the incidental acquisition of English L2 target words. The learners (158 high school students in Israel) were exposed to the words in a reading task. They read the text and answered five comprehension questions and were allowed to use a bilingual dictionary whenever they felt the need. Focus on forms was operationalized as intentional learning of the words. The learners received a list of the words with their Hebrew translations and explanations in English and then completed two word-focused exercises. Both groups were tested by asking them to give translations or explanations of the target words. The focus-on-forms group outperformed the focus-on-form group – a result that was statistically significant. In a follow-up study both groups engaged in intentional learning of the words. They received a list of the target words with definitions, examples and translations and spent 15 minutes memorizing them. They were tested by asking them to translate the words from L1 to L2 and then in a delayed post-test from L2 to L1. No significant group differences were found for either test. Laufer concluded that where vocabulary learning is concerned focus on forms is superior. Again, however, it should be noted that the manner of testing was biased in favour of the focus-on-forms group as it closely matched the kinds of activities this group engaged in during the instruction.

It is not easy to reach clear conclusions from such a mixed bag of studies. Out of the seven studies I have considered, three (Allen et al., 1990; Hammond, 1988; Palmer, 1979) failed to find any clear differences in the learning outcomes of communicative language teaching and 'traditional' language teaching (which usually involved some form of present-practice-produce). Two studies (Beretta and Davies, 1985; Savignon, 1972) produced results that generally favoured a task-based approach. Two studies (Laufer, 2006; Sheen, 2006), both of which compared focus on form and focus on forms, found in favour of traditional language teaching. All of these evaluation studies had methodological problems of one kind or another. In particular, the manner in which the learning outcomes were assessed was often problematic. To achieve validity, it is essential to ensure that learning outcomes are not assessed in ways that are biased towards one of the approaches.

Summary

Table 3.2 summarises the 16 comparative method studies that I have reviewed in the previous sections of this chapter. It is apparent that they are a very mixed bunch. They have investigated a variety of different methods (translation, grammar translation, the Audiolingual Method, superlearning methods, Total Physical Response and other forms of comprehension-based instruction, explicit grammar teaching, and weak and strong versions of the communicative approach). They differ markedly in the learners they investigated – elementary students, high school students, university students, and adult immigrants. The instructional contexts included both 'foreign' and 'second' language classrooms. The length of the period of instruction varied enormously – from one lesson to six years. In general, the methods of testing involved selected response or controlled-response type items. Of the 16 studies only three – Savignon (1972), Beretta and Davies (1985) and Shintani and Ellis (2010) – included tests of spontaneous oral production.

As noted in the commentaries of the studies, there are methodological problems with many of them. These include:

1. In some studies the groups of learners being compared were not equivalent. Comparing school students and university students, when each received instruction with a different method, does not constitute a valid comparison. Even when the learners come from the same population of learners it is necessary to ensure equivalence by administering a pre-test. This was lacking in many of the studies.
2. The groups being compared were not taught by the same teacher in many of the studies. Thus, any differences in the effects of the instruction that were found may have resulted from differences in the instructors' teaching skills. In general, very little information is given about the teaching experience of the instructors.
3. In many of the studies no attempt was made to establish that the instructional treatments were carried out in accordance with the external descriptions of the methods. Thus, it is not clear that the methods differed in terms of actual classroom processes.
4. No account was taken of the very real possibility that different learners will benefit from different kinds of instruction. Only the GUME project investigated the interactions between individual learner differences and instructional outcomes.
5. Most of the studies lacked control groups (i.e. groups that received neither type of instruction and just completed the tests). Thus, it is impossible to determine whether any improvement in test scores was simply the result of experience in taking the tests multiple times.
6. Only four of the studies (Allen et al., 1990; Beretta and Davies, 1985; Savignon, 1972; and Shintani and Ellis, 2010) attempted to guard against test bias by ensuring that the testing battery included tests that matched the methods being compared or by administering 'neutral' tests.

Table 3.2 Summary of the comparative method studies presented

Study	Learners	Comparison	Period of instruction	Testing	Results
Bennett (1917)	Junior and senior high school students	L1 → L2 translation vs. L2 → L1 translation	Relatively short term	Vocabulary translation test	L2 → L1 translation superior – but no test of statistical difference.
Beck (1951)	One group of high school students compared with a group of university students	Grammar translation vs. oral-cultural approach	Over about one year	Reading, writing and vocabulary tests	Oral-cultural approach superior.
Scherer and Wertheimer (1964)	College level students of L2 German	Grammar translation vs. audiolingual	Two years	Speaking, reading, writing and translation tests	After one year audiolingual approach superior in all tests except translation; after two years audiolingual group superior in speaking but grammar-translation group superior in other tests.
Smith (1970)	High school learners of French and German	Grammar translation vs. 'functional' (audiolingual) vs. functional + grammar	Two years	A battery of standardized tests	After one year no differences except grammar-translation group better at reading; after two yrs grammar-translation group still better at reading but functional better at oral mimicry.

Study	Participants	Treatment	Duration	Measures	Results
Levin (1972)	Young and older groups of high school students; one group of adult learners. All L2 English	Implicit (audiolingual) vs. Explicit Method (grammar explanation plus practice)	Varying lengths in the different studies	A variety of tests but all of the selected respond or constrained response types	No differences in the groups of younger learners; Explicit Method superior for older learners when grammar explanation in L1.
Savignon (1972)	University-level learners of L2 French.	Traditional instruction vs. traditional instruction plus communicative tasks	Over a university semester	Tests of both linguistic and communicative proficiency	The traditional plus communicative tasks class outperformed the purely traditional class in a test of communicative proficiency but no difference was found in a test of grammatical proficiency.
Wagner and Tilney (1983)	Adult English-speaking learners of L2 German	Superlearning vs. traditional rote vocabulary learning	Four weeks	Aural L1 → L2 vocabulary test; measure of alpha brain waves	Traditional group superior on vocabulary test; no differences evident in alpha brain wave patterns.
Asher (1977)	Groups of beginner immigrant learners learning English	Total Physical Response vs. Audiolingual Method	90 hours of instruction	A test of reading ability	The TPR group demonstrated higher levels of achievement than the audiolingual groups.
Lightbown (1992): Lightbown et al. (2002)	Beginner learners of English in elementary school	Comprehension-based (CB) instruction vs. Explicit instruction plus oral production practice	Study lasted six years	Tests of comprehension, speaking, reading and writing	No difference after three years, including in speaking; no difference after six years except for written production (Explicit group better).

(Continued)

Table 3.2 (*Continued*)

Study	Learners	Comparison	Period of instruction	Testing	Results
Shintani and Ellis (2010)	Young Japanese children learning L2 English	Comprehension-based instruction (CB) vs. production-based instruction (PPP)	Three one-hour lessons	Discrete-point test of comprehension; Wug test; task-based production test	In general, CB superior to PPP, including on task-based production test.
Palmer (1979)	Thai university students	Communicative approach vs. Traditional Method	One semester (?)	Discrete-point and holistic achievement tests; a communicative task-based test	No significant group differences. Scores on achievement and communicative tests correlated for the communicative group but not for the audiolingual group.
Hammond (1988)	University students of L2 Spanish	Natural Approach vs. grammar translation	One semester (?)	Variety of tests	Few statistically significant differences but Natural Approach group no worse at grammar learning.
Beretta and Davies (1985)	Indian secondary school students	Task-Based Language Teaching (TBLT) vs. Oral-Situational Approach (OSA)	Two years	Three 'neutral' tests: a task-based test and a structure test	TBLT generally superior to neutral tests and one task-based test; OSA superior in structure test.

Study	Context	Comparison	Duration	Tests	Results
Allen et al. (1990)	Grade 11 French classes in Canada	'Experiential' vs. 'analytic' teaching		Battery of tests of grammatical, sociolinguistic and discourse competence	Very few statistically significant differences.
R. Sheen (2006)	Sixth grade elementary ESL classes in Canada	Focus on forms vs. focus on form	Seven months	Aural comprehension test; structured oral interview; grammaticality judgement test. All tests designed to measure accuracy of two grammatical structures	Focus on forms was superior in both structured oral interview and grammaticality judgement test.
Laufer (2006)	High school students of L2 English in Israel	Focus on forms vs. focus on form	One lesson	Translation test (L2 → L1)	Focus on forms superior; but difference disappeared after focus-on-form group also received opportunity for intentional learning of vocabulary items.

Given the heterogeneity of the studies and the methodological problems, any general conclusions must be tentative. The very early studies suffered from such major methodological problems that no conclusions can be safely drawn from them. The large-scale studies in the 1970s failed to demonstrate the superiority of any of the methods they investigated. It was this failure that led to disenchantment with global method studies and to the subsequent focus on the direct observation of classroom processes (Allwright, 1988).

Of the later studies only those that investigated comprehension-based instruction have produced results suggesting that this approach may be more effective than other approaches. Asher's studies lacked methodological sophistication but they did consistently demonstrate the superiority of TPR over the Audiolingual or Grammar-Translation Methods – at least for beginners. Shintani and Ellis' study also suggests that comprehension-based instruction produces better results than PPP – again for beginners. However, this study was short-term and investigated the acquisition of a specific grammatical feature rather than learners' general L2 proficiency. Beretta and Davies' evaluation of Prabhu's task-based approach can also be interpreted as demonstrating the effectiveness of comprehension-based instruction as much of the teaching involved students processing input (see Prabhu's 1988 account of the methodology involved). But, again, Prabhu's learners were at an elementary level of L2 proficiency. Lightbown (1992) and Lightbown et al. (2002), however, did not find the comprehension-based approach they investigated was superior to a traditional audiolingual-type approach. Also, over time, as the learners' progressed in proficiency, the traditional approach proved more effective for written production. However, there is a major difference between the way comprehension-based teaching was carried out in the Lightbown study and in the other studies. In all the other studies of comprehension-based instruction the teacher was in charge of the input that the learners' received. In the Lightbown study the learners worked independently with graded listening and reading materials. There was little teacher input. Nevertheless, in the first of her studies (which covered the first three years of instruction) the learners in the comprehension-based programme did as well as the traditional learners. A tentative conclusion might be that when comprehension-based instruction is teacher-centred and directed at beginner learners it is more effective than methods that seek to elicit production from such learners. However, there is no evidence that this advantage holds for learners at more advanced stages of proficiency.

There is little evidence to show any differences in the learning outcomes of communicative approaches and more explicit types of instruction. Savignon's (1972) study showed only that a combination of form- and meaning-based instruction was superior to purely form-focused instruction in developing communicative abilities.

The studies by Sheen (2006) and Laufer (2006) claimed to show the superiority of focus-on-forms instruction. However, both authors set out with the intention of demonstrating the superiority of this type of instruction (i.e. they sought to challenge Long's claims about focus-on-form instruction). Also, crucially, they failed to include a test that measured learners' ability to use the target features in spontaneous oral communication (i.e. the testing was biased in favour of explicit instruction).

Conclusion

As this chapter has shown, comparative method studies have not dried up despite the rejection of 'method' as a useful construct for investigating language teaching. The question that arises, then, is 'Is there anything to be gained by continuing to carry out comparative method studies'?

The case for continuing with such studies was made by R. Sheen (2006). He argued that it is dangerous to advocate new methods such as task-based language teaching on purely theoretical grounds. He is critical of the current advocacy of TBLT and focus on form because of the failure to subject the claims made on behalf of this approach to 'long-term trialling in normal classrooms' (p. 273). He proposed that comparative method studies should be carried out that are: (1) long term, (2) ensure that the groups of learners being compared are equal in terms of such variables as motivation, and (3) include learners with no previous experience of the L2. Sheen has a point. There is empirical evidence to support the hypotheses on which TBLT is based but much of this has come from laboratory-based studies and there has been no long-term study comparing the efficacy of this approach and other more traditional (e.g. focus-on-forms) approaches.

The problem is whether it is possible to devise the kind of comparative method study that Sheen desires. Sheen's own study met his first two criteria (i.e. it was long-term and the groups came from the same student population of learners). But it did not meet his third criterion. Nor did it satisfy a criterion he did not mention, namely the need for the tests used to measure learning outcomes to guard against content-bias.

Beretta (1986) provides a careful discussion of the difficulty of conducting programme-fair evaluations. He pointed out that many (perhaps most) of the comparative method studies are guilty of test-content-bias and then suggests a number of strategies for programme-fair evaluation; (1) use standardized tests, (2) design specific tests for each programme, (3) design specific tests plus programme-neutral measures (as attempted in Beretta and Davies, 1985), (4) base assessment on a specification of the behavioural objectives of each programme, and (5) base assessment on an agreed model of language proficiency such as Canale and Swain's (1980) model of communicative competence (as in Allen et al., 1990). However, he found each of these strategies problematic in different ways and concluded that, as there is no clear solution to the problem of content-fair testing, 'there are grounds for pessimism' (p. 441).

There is a further problem with comparative method studies – one mentioned several times in this chapter. It cannot be assumed that externally derived descriptions of methods will result in actual differences in classroom processes. Of the studies we have considered only Allen et al. based their comparative study on observations of actual classrooms. This is perhaps the ideal way to set about addressing this problem – use observation to identify classrooms where the instructional processes are clearly different and that match the method descriptions. However, not all researchers will be able to select classrooms pre-emptively in this way. The alternative is to conduct a process evaluation as part of a method comparison, as proposed by Long (1984). Long specified what was needed in such a process evaluation:

> ... choose categories of classroom behaviors (preferably behaviors which occur frequently and are easily recognized) which will distinguish the two programs at the classroom level (p. 416).

Of the studies examined in this chapter only Shintani and Ellis (2010) conducted such an evaluation.

We are still left with the question as to whether method comparisons are worthwhile given that 'method' as a construct is no longer viewed as a useful way of conceptualizing teaching. We began this chapter with Kumaridevelu's critique of the method construct and it is probably true that in most teaching situations, teachers no longer attempt to implement a particular method but opt instead for a varied, eclectic approach that is adapted to the needs of the particular students they are teaching. However, I believe there is still a case for method comparisons of a kind. The evidence has shown that there is little to be gained from long-term studies that seek to evaluate methods in terms of general language proficiency. But, arguably, there is still a need for more fine-grained comparative studies that examine differences in instruction in terms of learners' acquisition of specific L2 features. This is what the later studies (i.e. Sheen, 2006; Shintani and Ellis, 2010) attempted to do. Such studies, of course, are only of value if they avoid the methodological pitfalls of the earlier method studies.

In later chapters, we will be examining a number of other studies that could qualify as comparative method studies (e.g. studies that have compared processing instruction and traditional instruction based on explicit explanation and production exercises)[3]. First, though, in acknowledgement of the problems with method comparisons and the advent of a 'post-method pedagogy' (Kumaravadivelu, 2001), where teachers are given the freedom and flexibility to make their own pedagogic decisions, we will turn to a very different way of investigating language teaching – namely, the examination of the classroom processes of which actual teaching is comprised.

Notes

1. A distinction is sometimes drawn between a 'method' and an 'approach'. The former applies when there is a well-defined set of techniques based on a theory of language and language learning (e.g. the Audiolingual Method). The latter term applies when there is some variation in the specific techniques to be employed even though they are all are

informed by the same general view of language and language learning (e.g. communicative language teaching). Frequently, however, these terms are used interchangeably in the literature (see, for example, Richards and Rogers, 1986).

2. I have cited Levin (1972) as he provides a comprehensive account of all the studies undertaken in the GUME project. Another publication reporting the GUME is Von Elek and Oscarsson (1973).

3. These studies are all 'local' in nature and designed to test hypotheses based on second language acquisition research (SLA) theories rather than pedagogical proposals. In this respect they differ from the studies examined in this chapter all of which were based on theories of language teaching.

4

Second Language Classroom Discourse

Introduction

This chapter explores the classroom processes that arise when language instruction takes place. To this end it examines the nature of the oral 'discourse' found in second language (L2) classrooms. Discourse can be defined in different ways depending on the theoretical perspective but central to all definitions is the notion that it involves 'language which has been produced as a result of communication' (Richards, Platt and Platt, 1992). In examining discourse, then, it is necessary to focus on how utterances realize functional meanings and how they combine to form larger units.

At one level, 'teaching' *is* discourse. Teachers and students interact in the classroom and instruction is enacted through their interactions. It follows that observation of the discourse that arises in actual classrooms is fundamental to developing an understanding of language teaching and its relationship to learning. This chapter focuses on descriptive research of the discourse processes that arise when teachers and learners accomplish lessons.

The study of classroom discourse proceeds in one of two ways:

1. By examining the functions performed by the specific communicative acts that arise in classroom interaction.
2. By examining the structure of language lessons or parts of lessons (i.e. how the specific communicative acts interconnect to create larger units of discourse).

Observation can be conducted either by means of interaction analysis systems, by keeping field notes, or by recording lessons and preparing and analyzing transcripts. Data analysis can be quantitative (where the frequency of specific interactional

Language Teaching Research & Language Pedagogy, First Edition. Rod Ellis.
© 2012 John Wiley & Sons, Ltd. Published 2012 by John Wiley & Sons, Ltd.

features is recorded) or qualitative, as in conversational analysis and ethnographic research, which seek to understand the ways that teachers and learners interact in the way they do. See Chapter 2 for a more detailed account of the methods of data collection and analysis used in studies of L2 classroom discourse.

Observational studies of the L2 classroom flourished from the late 1960s, in part as a reaction to the disillusionment with the global method studies of that decade (see Chapter 3). They were also influenced by developments in general education research where there was a shift of interest from investigating 'methods' to 'teaching style', in linguistics where there was growing interest in the functional properties of language, and in sociology where researchers began to explore how ordinary conversation was accomplished.

Observational research of classroom discourse was motivated by two concerns. One was to obtain a record of teacher and student behaviours that could be used to provide feedback in teacher training and to encourage self-evaluation on the part of the trainee teacher. As my concern is with the use of observation for research purposes in this book, I will not examine the work that addressed this concern in detail and, instead, will focus on the second concern. This involved the attempt to document the processes that arise when instruction unfolds through the interactions that take place in the 'black box'[1] of the classroom. As Allwright (1988) noted, this was initially undertaken with a view to establishing whether the behaviours observed conformed to the prescriptions of a particular method or to identifying which techniques were 'good' and 'bad'. Subsequently, however, researchers adopted a more descriptive approach, focusing on identifying the kinds of behaviours that teachers and students engaged in, the overall structure of language classroom discourse and the way in which specific instructional activities (such as teacher questioning and corrective feedback) were enacted. This led increasingly to an attempt to go beyond simply describing classroom processes to trying to understand what motivated them and to speculating which processes were most likely to foster language learning by drawing on theories of L2 acquisition.

In this chapter, I will examine classroom discourse as a whole, in particular the kind of discourse found in teacher-centred classrooms. Specific teacher and learner behaviours will be considered in Chapters 5 and 6 respectively. I will begin with interaction analysis systems as these constituted the first means used to investigate L2 classroom discourse. I will then consider research based on discourse frameworks that aimed to provide a systematic account of the interactional structures to be found in the language classroom. This will lead into an examination of the typical types of general language use that occur. Next, I will examine research that has employed the techniques of conversational analysis. In the two sections that follow I will consider classroom discourse from the perspective of sociocultual theory and language socialization, both of which afford more theorized accounts of L2 classroom discourse. The order of these sections broadly reflects the chronological development of classroom research over the last forty plus years. It also reflects a more general movement from description to interpretation of classroom discourse. The research I will address in this chapter is 'process' research; it does not directly address to what extent and in what ways classroom discourse leads to L2 learning (the 'product'). Process-product research will be examined later in Chapter 8.

Interaction Analysis

As McKay (2006) pointed out, interaction analysis systems can be 'generic' (i.e. they are designed to capture the behaviours arising throughout a lesson) or 'limited' (i.e. they focus on some specific aspect of language teaching). I will only consider the generic type here.

An interaction analysis system consists of a set of categories describing classroom behaviours that are directly observable. As noted in Chapter 2, Long (1980) distinguished three different types of systems: (1) in a category system each event is coded each time it occurs during a lesson, (2) in a sign system each event is recorded only once within a fixed time span, while (3) in a rating scale an estimate of how frequently a specific type of event occurred is made after the period of observation. Long noted that while there are plentiful examples of category systems and sign systems for observing language lessons there are none of rating scales. All three types of systems require the direct observation of a lesson. Later systems, however, made use of transcripts of lessons (i.e. a lesson was audio- or video-recorded, a transcript prepared, and the categories coded based on a close reading of the transcript). Clearly, there are limits to the number of categories that can be reliably coded while watching a lesson while coding from a transcript allows for more complex systems and greater reliability in coding.

Early systems

Early interactional analysis systems were based on Flanders's (1970) Interaction Analysis Categories (FIAC), which was designed for use in content classrooms and was intended for use with trainee teachers rather than as a research instrument. It consisted of ten categories, the majority of which focused on teacher behaviours, which were divided into those that reflected a 'direct influence' (e.g. 'lecturing' and 'giving directions') and an 'indirect influence' ('accepts feeling' and 'asks questions'). Student behaviours were classified as 'response' or 'initiation'. Moskowitz (1968) reported a study that examined the value of Flanders' system as a means of promoting behaviour change in teacher trainees. Like Flanders, Moskowitz assumed that 'indirect' patterns of teacher behaviour were more conducive to learning than 'direct'. Moskowitz also adapted Flander's system to the foreign language classroom. The resulting instrument – the Foreign Language Interaction (FLINT) system – included a total of 20 categories reflecting the techniques viewed as desirable in the Audiolingual Method (e.g. 'use of first language (L1) and L2', 'teacher directs pattern drills', 'teacher corrects without rejection'; 'individual versus choral student response'). Like the FIAC, the FLINT system included far more teacher than student categories but subsequent systems (e.g. Krumm, 1973) became more learner-oriented.

Other early interaction analysis systems were designed for research purposes rather than for teacher training. However, like Moskowitz's FLINT system, they were based on external descriptions of a specific method on the grounds that 'inherent in any system of behaviour classification is the a priori postulating of a teaching model' (Jarvis, 1968). Jarvis' system, for example, was based on a view of teaching that involved the sequential stages of 'encountering elements of the language, imitating them, manipulating them, and finally using them in innovative real communication language'. His system consisted of two major categories – 'real language categories' and 'drill language categories' – each of which was broken down into a number of smaller categories. He also distinguished whether these categories were realized in the target language or the students' L1. Jarvis claimed that his instrument was successful in recording the teaching behaviours that distinguished more and less effective teachers in terms of the model of teaching on which the system was based. However, he insisted that it was only a 'descriptive tool', not an 'evaluative' tool. In other words, Jarvis was proposing that his system was capable of providing a measure of the extent to which a particular method was implemented. Another early interaction system was Politzer's (1970). Politzer was concerned with validating specific instructional techniques associated with the Audiolingual Method. He administered achievement tests to a group of learners in order to identify those categories in the system that showed no positive or negative correlations with the achievement measures. Allwright (1988) summed up his own account of these early systems with the comment that classroom observation had 'arrived as a basic tool for research into language teaching' (p. 42). He noted, however, that they were 'ultimately prescriptive' as they were used to try to establish to what extent teachers conformed to the audiolingual ideal.

Discourse-based interaction systems

All of these early interaction analysis systems consisted of discrete categories representing isolated behavioural acts. As a result they provided little information about how the categories interlinked to form instructional sequences. The next system we will consider drew on work by Bellack et al. (1966). This examined classroom interaction in terms of interlocking moves that constituted larger units of classroom discourse. In a later section of this chapter we will see how this framework was also drawn on by Sinclair and Coulthard (1975) to develop a complete discourse framework for describing classroom talk.

Fanselow's (1977) Foci for Observing Communications Used in Settings (FOCUS) resembled the earlier systems in that it consisted of discrete categories but differed from them in that it also showed how these categories combined to form larger units of discourse. Fanselow's aim was to provide researchers and teachers with a technical language for talking about language teaching. The system distinguished five characteristics of classroom communication: (1) the source, (2) the pedagogical focus, (3) the medium, (4) the use, and (5) the content. Each of these was broken down into a set of multiple sub-categories. To give a flavour of how the system worked Table 4.1 provides a coding for one of the classroom extracts that Fanselow analyzed in the appendix to his article. It is clear that the FOCUS system provides a much more complete description of language teaching than the earlier systems. It is doubtful, however, that such a complex system can be used for the direct observation of classes. To get round this, Fanselow suggested that it was not necessary to use the entire system as different parts of it could be used at different times. If a complete analysis was required a lesson could be recorded and transcribed. The system has two major advantages. The first, already mentioned, is that to some degree at least it captures the sequential nature of classroom discourse. The second is that the system is not tied to describing the behaviours of a particular method; it can be applied to any classroom setting.

Where Fanselow drew on the early work of Bellack et al. on classroom discourse, Allwright (1980) drew on an emerging strand of research that examined how everyday conversations were carried out. In 1974 Sacks, Schegloff and Jefferson published a paper that examined turn-taking. Allwright drew on this and on Mehan's (1974) account of how the analytical techniques used by conversational analysts (see later section in this chapter) could be applied to classroom data. Allwright's system involved both a 'macro-analysis of language teaching and learning' and a 'micro-analysis of turn-taking' in the language classroom. In his macro-analysis, Allwright distinguished three elements: (1) Samples (i.e. 'instances of the target language, in isolation or use'), (2) Guidance (i.e. 'instances of communication concerning the nature of the target language') and (3) Management activities ('aimed at ensuring the profitable occurrence of (1) and (2)'. These elements could vary in terms of their relative occurrence in a lesson, their distribution between teacher and learners, their sequencing and whether they were conducted in the target language or not. The turn-taking system consisted of two general categories: 'Turn-getting' and 'Turn-giving'. Each was broken down into a number of minor categories. For example, 'Turn-giving' could be performed by means of an 'accept' (i.e. where a classroom participant responds to a personal solicit') or 'steal' (i.e. where the classroom participant responds to a personal solicit made to another). Examples of 'turn-giving' are 'fade out' and 'make a personal solicit'. Allwright also provided 'topic' categories, distinguishing four types depending on whether the primary focus was on providing models of the target language, communicating information, communicating about pedagogical/procedural matters, or involved 'any other use of language or non-verbal communication'. Allwright then applied his system to the detailed quantitative and qualitative analysis of a university-level English as a second language (ESL) class. He emphasizes that his aim was to 'account' for the classroom data (rather than simply 'represent' it or 'explain' it. That is, he sought 'to understand why it was as it was' (Allwright, 1988: 181), in line with the general aims of conversational analysis. His analysis was highly informative and had the advantage of allocating as much attention to the learners' contributions as the teacher's. However, it is clearly very time-consuming to carry out such an analysis and, to the best of my knowledge, his system has not been utilized in further studies.

Table 4.1 Coded extract illustrating Fanselow's FOCUS system

Extract	Source	Pedagogical focus	Medium	Use	Content
Can you say something about this. (Holds up an old dirty shirt).	Teacher	Solicit	Language Non-linguistic	Present	Language: meaning
It's old.	Student 1	Response	Language	Characterize	Language: meaning
It's dirty.	Student 2	Response	Language	Characterize	Language: meaning
I don't like it.	Student 3	Response	Language	Characterize	Language: meaning
Throw it away.	Student 4	Response	Language	Characterize	Life
Touch this (Gives students a ball). (Student feels ball)	Teacher	Solicit	Language Non-linguistic Non-linguistic	Present	Language: meaning
Is it round or square?	Student	Response	Language	Attend	Language: meaning
Round (Shakes head up and down).	Teacher Student Teacher	Solicit Response Reaction	Language Para- linguistic	Present Characterize Characterize	Language: meaning Language: meaning Language: meaning

Strengths and limitations of interaction systems

At this point, I would like to take stock of what interaction analysis systems offer. To this end, I provide a summary of the key dimensions of how the different systems vary in Table 4.2, based on Long's (1980) excellent review.

Long also offered an account of the strengths and limitations of the interaction analysis system approach. He noted that many systems are easy to use and that they provide a common terminology for talking about teaching and therefore are helpful for disseminating the results of research on classrooms to teachers and other interested parties. Among the limitations he noted are the fact that the instruments focus heavily on the teacher, that the behaviours sampled are often superficial and the systems reductionist, that the systems pay no attention to the linguistic organization of classroom talk because they code isolated pedagogical acts, that they assume a teacher-centred pedagogy and that there has been no attempt at 'triangulation'

Table 4.2 Summary of different dimensions of interaction analysis systems
(based on Long, 1980)

Dimensions of systems	Commentary
Recording procedure	Sign systems do not record individual acts; category systems record each act.
Item type	Systems differ in terms of whether they contain 'low-inference' items (e.g. 'student responds to teacher's question') or 'high-inference' items (e.g. 'student hypothesizes').
Number of categories	Systems vary in how complex they are, most obviously in terms of the number of categories employed.
Multiple-coding option	Some systems allow for multiple-coding (i.e. the same event is coded in more than one category). This affects the amount of training needed to master use of a system.
Usability for real-time coding	In general it is difficult for a coder to manage more than 10 categories of the low-inference kind. More complex systems require analysis of recordings.
Focus	Many systems record verbal behaviour only and focus on the pedagogical functions of the teacher's language.
Source of variables	The systems borrow heavily from Flanders' Interaction Analysis Categories. This is 'surprising' given that second language classrooms differ markedly from content classrooms. The categories have not been validated by process-product research.
Unit of analysis	The unit of analysis can be 'arbitrary' (i.e. coding occurs within a specified short-time period) or 'analytic' (i.e. coding is in terms of moves, episodes or speech acts). The former is more 'practical' but the latter has greater potential for research.
Purpose	Some systems are intended purely for teacher training and therefore employ few categories of the low-inference type. Other systems are designed for research. Some (e.g. Fanselow's FOCUS) are intended for both.

(i.e. obtaining different perspectives on what the coded events mean to different participants). His main criticism, however, was that 'the value of analytical systems must ultimately depend on the significance for teaching and learning of the categories they contain' (p. 11) and that no attempt has been made to validate the categories they sample in terms of theory and research in second language acquisition research (SLA). This latter point was heeded by Allen, Fröhlich and Spada (1984) in the development of a new interaction analysis system. I will conclude my account of interaction analysis with a close look at this system.

The Communicative Orientation of Language Teaching
Observation Scheme

As we noted in Chapter 3, in the late 1970s the communicative approach emerged as an alternative to more traditional methods such as the Audiolingual Method and the Oral Situational Method. The Communicative Orientation of Language Teaching Observation Scheme (known as COLT) was developed to provide a system that was better suited to researching the communicative approach than existing systems. Allen, Fröhlich and Spada (1984) also took on board Long's major criticism of the earlier systems by endeavouring to identify a list of communicative behaviours based on theory and research:

> Our concept of communicative feature has been derived from current theories of communicative competence, from the literature on communicative teaching, and from a review of recent research into first and second language acquisition (Allen, Fröhlich and Spada, 1984: 233).

The scheme consisted of two parts. Part A involved real-time coding of classroom behaviours at the level of 'classroom activity'. This was chosen as the focal category on the grounds that teachers easily identify with the concept of 'activity' as this is the focus around which teaching is organized. Part B required detailed coding of the communicative features found in classroom interaction based on an analysis of a transcript of a lesson. As the COLT has been used in a number of classroom studies and arguably constitutes the best of the available interaction analysis systems, I will describe each part in more detail.

The categories comprising Part A of the COLT are shown in Table 4.3. The observer uses a coding form to conduct an observation of a lesson, first providing a written description of the activity that is taking place and noting the time at which it started and then indicating which of the categories in the other four parameters apply to the activity as it takes place. Two points are worth making about this scheme. First, many of the categories are high-inference, calling for considerable judgement on the part of the observer. This is especially true of 'Activity Type'. For example, if students are given time to plan a task before performing it, should this be coded as one activity or two separate activities? Later Spada and Fröhlich (1995) published a detailed manual that provided a classification of the different types of activities to assist observation but determining exactly what constitutes an 'activity' is still problematic. Other categories (e.g. those relating to 'other topics' in the content parameter) also involve a high level of judgement. The second point is that all the categories are pedagogic in nature (i.e. they describe aspects of teaching that most teachers would readily recognize). In this respect COLT Part A resembles the earlier interaction systems except that the categories are not based on any specific method. Rather they are generic in nature. Thus the COLT as can be used to observe any lesson irrespective of the instructional approach. Of course, to determine the instructional

Table 4.3 COLT Part A (based on Allen, Frohlich and Spada, 1984)

Parameter	*Main categories*	*Sub-categories*
Activity Type (an open-ended parameter; the observer describes the activities that occur in the lesson).		
Participant Organization (i.e. the way in which the classroom is organized for classroom interactions).	1. Whole class	a. Teacher to student or class, and vice versa b. Student to student, or student to class, and vice versa c. choral work by students
	2. Group work	a. Groups all work on the same task b. Groups work on different tasks
	3. Group and individual work	a. Individual seat work b. Mixed group/individual work
Content (i.e. the subject-matter of the activities).	1. Management	a. Classroom procedures b. Disciplinary procedures
	2. Explicit focus on language	a. Form b. Function c. Discourse d. Sociolinguistics
	3. Other topics	a. Narrow range of reference b. Limited range of reference c. Broad range of reference
	4. Topic control	a. Control by teacher b. Control shared by teacher and student c. Control by student
Student modality	a. listening b. speaking c. reading d. other (e.g. drawing)	
Materials	1. Type of materials	a. Text b. Audio c. Visual
	2. Length of text	a. Minimal b. Extended
	3. Source/purpose of the materials	a. Pedagogic b. Semi-pedagogic c. Non-pedagogic
	4. Use of the materials	a. Highly controlled b. Semi-controlled c. Minimally controlled

orientation of a lesson it will be necessary to interpret what the completed coding form shows.

Part B of the COLT consists of a set of categories designed to describe the 'communicative features' that occur within each activity. There are seven major features, each broken down into a number of sub-categories:

1. Use of target language (i.e. L1 or L2)
2. Information gap (giving information and requesting information)
3. Sustained speech (ultraminimal; minimal; sustained)
4. Reaction to code or message (form; message)
5. Incorporation of preceding utterances (correction; repetition; paraphrase; comment; expansion; clarification request; elaboration request)
6. Discourse initiation (i.e. the frequency of self-initiated turns by students)
7. Restriction of linguistic form (choral work; restricted; unrestricted).

The choice of these features is clearly based on what was, then, current thinking about language acquisition and, in particular, the role that interaction plays in it. For example, the feature 'Incorporation of preceding utterances' was motivated by research that has shown that the best environment for L1 acquisition was one where the input was closely tied to what a child has said (e.g. Ellis and Wells, 1980).

The procedures for using Part B of this system require audio-recording of a lesson. Coding begins at the beginning of each activity and continues for one minute. There is then a two minute interval before coding resumes. The frequency of each category is recorded during each one-minute period of coding.

The extract from Allen, Fröhlich and Spada (1984: 244) here illustrates the system in COLT Part B. This extract is clearly taken from a distinctly non-communicative lesson. The system is, of course, also capable of characterizing more communicative exchanges – for example, an exchange where the teacher's language involves genuine requests and the student's language unpredictable information in sustained speech.

T: What's the date today?	L2/pseudo-request/minimal speech
S: April 15th.	L2/predictable information/ultraminimal speech/limited form
T: Good.	L2/comment/minimal speech
T: What's the date today?	L2/predictable information/ultraminimal speech/ limited form
S: April 15th.	L2/predictable information/ultraminimal speech/limited form
T: Good.	L2/comment/minimal speech

Spada and Fröhlich (1995) provide a detailed explanation of how to analyze the data obtained from the COLT and also report a number of studies that used the system. Vandergrift used it to investigate the use of listening comprehension strategies by high school students in a core French programme. He found that no authentic texts were used, and there was little emphasis on global listening and listening for meaning.

Yohay and Suwa studied English classes in Japanese elementary schools. These classes were characterized by whole-class interaction and a lesson content that focused on a mixture of form, discourse and the sociolinguistic aspects of listening and speaking activities. Zotou and Mitchell's study examined the extent to which the teaching of foreign languages in Greece was 'communicative' using a modified form of the COLT. Overall they noted a persistence of traditional teacher-centred and form-centred instruction. However, some aspects of communicative language teaching were also found, e.g. the topics were generally 'broad' rather than 'narrow' and there was a strong bias towards listening and speaking. These studies suggest that the COLT can be successfully used to describe the instructional orientation of language classes but also that it may need modifying for use in specific instructional contexts.

More interesting is the use of the COLT in process-product research. Allen et al. (1990) report a study that investigated a core French programme in Canadian Grade 11 classrooms. This study was reported in Chapter 3, as, in effect, it involved a type of method comparison. It included the observation of classes using the COLT and the collection of language proficiency data using a battery of tests designed to provide measures of different aspects of communicative competence. Classes were distinguished in terms of whether they were 'experiential' or 'analytic' in orientation on the basis of the COLT observations and their proficiency scores compared. However, no significant differences were found between the experiential and analytic classes. A correlational analysis was also disappointing, with few correlations between communicative features and proficiency measures reaching statistical significance. Spada and Fröhlich (1995) report a number of other process-product studies. McKay concluded from her study of French classes in junior secondary school classrooms in Australia that communicative classrooms were not necessarily more successful that more traditional classes. Sanaoui also found no differences between experiential and analytic classes in measures of vocabulary learning. Overall, then, the attempt to demonstrate that different instructional approaches, as revealed through the use of the COLT, are associated with differences in learning outcomes has not been successful.

Final comment

Interaction analysis systems have served a valuable function in L2 classroom research. They have provided researchers with the tools they need to *describe* teaching and, in this respect, have assisted teacher trainers. The key question from a researcher's perspective, however, is whether interaction analysis schemes, including carefully designed ones such as the COLT, are capable of identifying those classroom processes that are important for L2 acquisition. In general, they have not been successful in doing so. Allen et al. (1990), for example, concluded from their own process-product study:

> A statistical analysis based on schemes such as COLT cannot be depended on to distinguish between pedagogically effective communicative activities and pedagogically ineffective ones (p. 73).

They went on to note that such schemes 'do not pay sufficiently close attention to the exchange structure of discourse'. It might be possible to remedy this problem by developing a more comprehensive interaction analysis system. But such a system runs the risk of becoming unwieldy and also there is no guarantee that observation based on a set of discrete categories will ever succeed in distinguishing more and less effective teaching. Allen et al. proposed a different approach. They suggested supplementing the COLT with a 'more detailed discourse analysis' (p. 74).

Discourse Frameworks

We noted that some of the later interaction analysis systems (e.g. Fanselow's FOCUS and Allwright's (1980) *Turns, Topics and Tasks* incorporated insights from the studies of classroom talk based on the discourse systems that originated in the 1970s. However, as category systems, they paid scant attention to how utterances combine to create larger units of discourse. We will now examine some key discourse frameworks and the insights they provided about the structure of classroom discourse.

Sinclair and Coulthard's framework

In 1975 Sinclair and Coulthard published their highly influential *Towards an Analysis of Discourse*. This drew on and extended the discourse framework of Bellack et al. (1966) by drawing on the principle of rank-scale from Halliday's (1961) systemic grammar which posited that language systems are organized hierarchically with smaller units combining to form larger ones. The advantage of such an approach is that it allowed the structure of each discourse unit to be expressed in terms of combinations of units from the rank below. Sinclair and Coulthard's framework identified the following ranks in the structure of a lesson:

1. lesson,
2. transaction,
3. exchange,
4. move, and
5. act.

They were unable to identify any structural statement for 'lesson' (the highest unit), suggesting that in this respect it has the same status as 'paragraph' in descriptions of grammar. They characterized it simply as an unordered series of transactions.

The structure of the next rank, 'transaction' could also not be clearly delineated except in terms of 'frames', which identified its boundaries. Frames were realized through a very limited of set of words – 'OK', 'well', 'right', 'now' and 'good' – and were frequently followed by a 'focus' (i.e. a metastatement about the transaction, as in this example from Coulthard (1977):

Frame: well
Focus: today I thought we'd do three quizzes (p. 123).

This combination of frame and focus constituted a 'boundary exchange'. Coulthard noted that such exchanges rarely occurred in naturally-occurring conversation. A transaction also consisted of other types of exchange – informing, directing or eliciting exchanges – but these were not tightly structured to form a transaction.

Exchanges were comprised of different combinations of 'moves' – the minimal contribution a speaker can make to an exchange. The structure of an exchange could be much more clearly defined. It typically consisted of three types of moves – 'initiating', 'responding', and 'follow-up', as in Extract 1:

Extract 1

T: Ask Anan what his name is. (initiating)
S: What's your name? (responding)
T: Good. (follow-up)

Sinclair and Coulthard found that this type of exchange, which has become known as IRF[2], was the norm in classroom discourse. They gave two reasons for this. First, it enabled the teacher to repeat a student's responding move and so make sure that the whole class was attending to it. Second, it provided a means for the teacher to 'test' whether students could give the 'correct' response to a question and to indicate whether they had done so.

The smallest unit in the framework was 'act'. Acts combine in various ways to form 'moves'. Twenty-two acts were distinguished but Coulthard (1977) reduced this to seventeen on the grounds that some of the original acts involved the same discourse function. Coulthard grouped these into three major categories – (1) 'metainteractive' (e.g. 'marker' and 'metastatement'), (2) 'interactive', which consisted of initiation options such as 'informative' and 'elicitation', response options such as 'acknowledge' and 'react', and follow-up options, such as 'accept' and 'evaluate', and (3) turn-taking options (e.g. 'bid' and 'nomination'). Sinclair and Coulthard distinguished closed-class and open-class acts depending on whether it was possible to identify the linguistic realisations of the different acts.

McTear (1975) adapted the framework for language classrooms. For example, students in the L2 classroom often produce an additional response after the follow-up move in IRF exchanges, which has since become known as 'uptake' (Lyster and Ranta, 1997):

Extract 2

T: What do you do every morning?
S: I clean my teeth.
T: You clean your teeth every morning.
S: I clean my teeth every morning.

The exchange structure is, therefore, IRF(R).

A number of other discourse systems have subsequently been developed to describe teacher-centred classroom talk. I will briefly consider one here. Nassaji and Wells (2000) developed an elaborate discourse system to describe the IRF exchanges that took place in teacher-centred subject lessons in Canadian schools. The largest unit in this framework was 'episode' defined as 'all the talk produced in carrying out a single activity or one of its constituent tasks' (p. 383). Episodes consisted of 'sequences', which in turn were made up of nuclear or bound 'exchanges'. Exchanges were composed of obligatory initiating and responding moves and could also contain a follow-up move, as in IRF exchanges. Follow-up moves, other than simple 'acknowledge' were described in terms of six functional categories ('evaluation', 'justification', 'comment', 'clarification', 'action' and 'metatalk'). This framework holds a number of advantages where the purpose is not just to describe classroom discourse but also to explore how it creates opportunities for potential student learning. The macro-category of 'episode' is better suited to that of 'transaction' for exploring classroom talk as it corresponds more closely to the way in which teaching is conceptualized and organized. The elaborated follow-up move also allows for a close examination of how IRF exchanges might afford students access to the interactional resources that foster learning. However, this framework has not been applied to language classrooms.

The initiate–respond–follow-up exchange

The IRF exchange is ubiquitous in all classrooms, including language classrooms, when the teacher controls the discourse. Lemke (1990) referred to the three-move exchange as 'triadic dialogue' and showed how dominant it was in subject classrooms. He noted that even when students initiate an exchange, the teacher is likely to respond in a manner that resembles the follow-up move in the IRF exchange. Torr (1993) based her analysis of the discourse occurring in two elementary school classrooms, one containing mainly native speakers (NSs) and other mainly non-native speaking children (NNSs), on Hasan's (1988) message semantics framework[3]. She reported that teachers dominated the interactions in both classrooms, although much more so in the NNS classroom. The basic pattern of interaction was IRF but there were differences in the quality of the questions that the two teachers asked in their initiating moves. Consolo (2000) reported that the speech of both native speaker and non-native speaker teachers of Brazilian learners of L2 English followed the typical IRF pattern. He observed 'most of the time, teachers and students rigidly observe their part in the socially defined classroom roles' (p. 105). Thus, irrespective of whether the instructional setting is a 'foreign' or a 'second' language one, IRF is the dominant pattern.

Some examples of classroom interaction will illustrate the ubiquity of the IRF exchange. As might be expected, it is clearly evident in the drill-like sequences that occur in audiolingual classrooms, as illustrated in Extract 3 from Ellis (1984a). The instructional target of the lesson was plural utterances of the kind 'These are pencils'. The 'transaction' shown in the extract begins with a frame ('now'). There follows a series of exchanges, all initiated by the teacher by means of an 'elicitation'. Where the student produces a correct response (in turns (2) and (8), both of which involve the use of singular forms), the teacher offers no feedback. Where the student fails to respond with the correct target utterance (turns (5), (12) and (15)), the teacher either repeats the original elicitation or executes a 'follow-up' move, consisting of either a 'comment' or an 'evaluate'. It is clear that the student is entirely familiar with the role she is expected to play in such exchanges. Interestingly, in this transaction the learner never succeeds in producing a complete target sentence and the teacher ultimately conspires in this, allowing the learner to respond by producing just the plural noun form (see turns 17, 18, 19 and 20).

Extract 3:
1. T: Now, Tasleem.
2. T: What is this? (Teacher holds up pen)
3. S: This is a pen.
4. T: What are these? (Teacher holds up two pens)
5. S: This are a pen.
6. T: These are ____?
7. S: Are pens.
8. T: What is this? (Teacher holds up a ruler)
9. S: This is a ruler. . . .
10. T: What are these? (Teacher holds up two rulers)
11. S: This is a . . . art . . .
12.   This are a rulers.
13. T: These are rulers.
14. T: What are these?
15. S: This are a rulers.
16. T: Not 'a'.
17.   These are ____?
18. S: Rulers.
19. T: Rulers.
20. S: Rulers.

IRF exchanges are less prevalent in task-based lessons although even here the IRF exchange can easily take over, especially when the teacher elects to focus the students' attention on linguistic form, as in Extract 4 from a task-based lesson.

Extract 4:
T: Write down one thing about last week or last weekend.
S: I had been? I had been?
T: Past simple. I saw. I went.
S: I had b____, I had?
T: Past simple.
S: (Student writes down verb) That's right.
S: I ran.
T: Not I had been because you need two things in the past. So last weekend I went to the movies.

Here the teacher opens an IRF exchange with a 'directive', the student responds (incorrectly), and the teacher follows-up with a 'comment', which also re-establishes the original directive. The student again responds incorrectly and the teacher again comments on this. Finally the student produces the correct form which leads to an 'acknowledge' from the teacher. The student then says the correct form (i.e. the additional 'response' move noted by McTear) and the teacher again follows up, this time with a more elaborate metacomment.

There are obvious reasons why the IRF exchange is so prevalent. The power differential between teachers and students confers on the former the right to control the discourse. Teachers exercise this right as a means of ensuring that the discourse proceeds in an orderly manner. The IRF exchange (with the teacher taking the initiating role) prevents turn-taking becoming unruly and helps to focus students' attention on what is being said. Berry (1981) pointed out that when the primary knower is also the initiator of an IRF exchange, it is necessary to complete the exchange of information by confirming or disconfirming the response move (i.e. through a follow-up move). She noted that the situation is very different when the initiator is the secondary knower and the responder is the primary knower. Such exchanges involve an open request for information and do not require a follow-up move. Thus, it is the teacher taking on the role of both 'initiator' and 'primary knower' that leads to the typical IRF exchange found in classrooms. Berry's account suggests that if the IRF exchange is to be displaced as the dominant feature of classrooms, the teacher has to either abandon the role of 'primary knower' or to allocate the initiating role to the students.

The key question, however, is to what extent the IRF exchange affords or deprives learners of the interactional resources that promote learning. In general, educators and SLA researchers have viewed IRF exchanges as limiting opportunities for learning. IRF is associated with the pedagogy of transmission (Barnes 1976), affording learners few opportunities for extended utterances, limiting the range of language functions to be performed and providing few occasions for negotiating meaning as communication breakdown is infrequent. As Van Lier (1996) put it, 'in the IRF exchange, the student's response is hemmed in, squeezed between a demand to display knowledge and a judgement on its competence' (p. 151). Lerner (1995) argued that the follow-up move was especially limiting in that it restricts learner participation by removing the opportunity for the learner to respond further to the teacher's question. Kasper (2001) noted that L2 pragmatics research has unequivocally demonstrated that 'the IRF routine is an unproductive interactional format for the learning of pragmatics and discourse' (p. 518).

However, an alternative view is possible. Van Lier went on to acknowledge that IRF exchanges can also facilitate students' contribution by scaffolding their attempts to use the L2. Much depends on how the exchange is enacted. Thus, if the initiation move involves teacher questions that 'introduce issues as for negotiation' (Nassaji and Wells, 2000: 400) richer contributions from students can arise. Also, where the follow-up move serves to extend the student's response and to make connections with what has gone before and what will follow, rather than just evaluate the student's response, the discourse can become less pedagogic and more conversational. Ohta (2001) found that the Japanese learners she investigated appropriated the language they were exposed to in IRF exchanges for use in subsequent group work. Gourlay (2005) showed how teachers in business English lessons with L2 learners exploited the IRF exchange by means of 'embedded extensions', which introduced new input and allowed students to engage in covert activities where they enacted their own agendas. Van Lier (2000b) argued that the contribution that IRF makes to learning depends on the depth of processing involved and proposed an 'IRF continuum' (p. 94), with 'recitation' at the bottom end, 'precision' at the top and 'display' and 'cognition' at intermediate levels.

From these studies it is clear that IRF is not a monolithic structure but, in fact, highly varied. Van Lier (1996) identified the following dimensions in which it can vary: (1) conduct of initiation (i.e. a general, unspecific elicitation directed at the whole class or a specific, personal elicitation directed at a single student), (2) response function (i.e. whether the teacher's follow-up move requires students to repeat something, to recall material from their memory, or to express themselves more precisely), and (3) pedagogical purpose (i.e. display or assessment orientation). Clearly, the IRF exchange is capable of affording a greater range of learning opportunities than was once thought. This will be clearly evident in a later section of this chapter when we revisit the IRF exchange from the perspective of conversational analysis and sociocultural theory.

However, there has been no study that has attempted to establish an empirical link between the IRF exchange and L2 acquisition. To date, the research has focused on simply describing this aspect of classroom discourse and identifying the factors responsible for it. The various claims concerning its contribution to language learning are based entirely on theoretical positions or on extrapolations from L1 acquisition research – for example, the importance that some SLA theorists (e.g. Long, 1983a) have attached to the negotiation of meaning or, from a sociocultural perspective, to scaffolding. While there are studies that demonstrate the facilitative effect of negotiation, there are no studies that demonstrate that a classroom rich in such features leads to faster learning than a classroom where the IRF prevails.

Other classroom discourse patterns

Although IRF exchanges tend to dominate, other kinds of exchange can also be found. Van Lier (1988) pointed out that it is easy to overstate the lack of flexibility evident in L2 classroom discourse. He found that although the discourse is often strictly controlled by the teacher through IRF exchanges, learners do sometimes initiate exchanges, and 'schismic talk' (talk that deviates from some predetermined plan) also occurs, at least in some classrooms. Other studies (for example, Ernst, 1994; Johnson, 1995) have also pointed to the variety of discourse that is possible in teacher-led exchanges.

Task-based teaching affords opportunities for student-initiated discourse, as illustrated in Extract 5, where the teacher and the students are clarifying the name that one group of students has chosen to give to itself:

Extract 5:
1. S1:   My group has a name.
2. T: What name?
3. S1:   Best.
4. T: Bess' group.
5. S1:   Best.
6. T: Oh, best. Okay.
7. S2:   Best.
8. T: Best. Not group three. The best. That's a lovely name.

This extract is much more conversational in nature with the student taking the initiating role and the teacher first seeking clarification and then confirming and accepting the group's chosen name.

Johnson (1995) provides a number of examples of student-initiated talk in an ESL classroom with low-proficiency learners. In Extract 6[4], one of the students (Wang), opens the sequence by naming a film he wants to talk about. The teacher then encourages Wang to elaborate on the topic using expansions to help him say what he wants to say. The resulting discourse is very different from the standard IRF structure. This seems to help Wang as his utterances become progressively well-formed as the interaction continues. There is no follow-up move. But at the end of the sequence the teacher takes over control of the discourse with a mock warning to the rest of the students, thereby opening up an opportunity for another student to take a turn. As Johnson (1995: 25) herself points out there are features of this interaction that are very similar to those found in adult-child conversation, and which have been shown to assist L1 acquisition (see, for example, Ellis and Wells, 1980).

Extract 6:
1. Wang: Kung Fu.
2. T: Kung Fu? You like the movie *Kung Fu*?
3. Wang: Yeah . . . fight.
4. T: That was about a great fighter? . . .
             A man who knows how to fight with his hands.
5. Wang: I fight . . . my hand.
6. T: You know how to fight with your hands?
7. Wang: I fight with my hand.
8. T: Watch out guys, Wang knows karate.

Gibbons (2007), drawing on Wells (1999) identifies four conditions that need to be met for what she calls 'progressive discourse' to take place in the classroom:

1. A need for ideas not just to be shared but to be questioned.
2. A classroom ethos that encourages students to share their own ideas.
3. Control of the discourse does not rest entirely with the teacher.
4. Learner control of the interpersonal language needed to participate in classroom talk.

All of these conditions are met in the extract above. The crucial issue for the language classroom is who controls the discourse, in particular, i.e. who establishes the topic of the talk and its development (Ellis, 1999). A skillful teacher can then find ways of building on the student's contributions.

Negotiation of meaning sequences

One particular type of discourse structure that has attracted considerable interest from SLA researchers is that which arises when negotiation of meaning occurs. This occurs when the listener fails to fully understand what the speaker has said and attempts to remedy the problem. Varonis and Gass (1985) developed a framework to describe the structure of such 'non-understanding routines' where negotiation takes place. It consists of a 'trigger', i.e. the utterance or part of an utterance that creates a problem of understanding, an 'indicator' which indicates that something in a previous utterance was not understood, a 'response' to the indicator, and finally a 'reaction to the response', which is optional. The 'indicator–response–reaction to the response' portion of a non-understanding sequence is called a 'pushdown', because it has the effect of pushing the conversation down rather than allowing it to proceed in a forward manner. The model is recursive in that it allows for the 'response' element itself to act as a 'trigger' for a further non-understanding routine.

Non-understanding routines occur frequently in everyday talk involving L2 learners but much less frequently in teacher-centred classrooms, mainly because the prominent IRF exchange is designed to minimize the possibility of communication breakdown. Pica and Long (1986) found that there was very little negotiation of meaning in elementary ESL classrooms in comparison to NS–NNS conversations outside the classroom. Negotiation of meaning is much more likely to occur in task-based lessons where the primary focus is on meaning and where the teacher does not act as the 'primary knower' and 'initiator' of exchanges. A good example of a negotiation of meaning sequence can be seen in Extract 5. The trigger here occurs in (3) as presumably the teacher expected the student to give the name of a person. The teacher responds with an indicator (4), which also tries to resolve the problem. This produces a response from the learner in turn (5) and a reaction to the response from the teacher in turn (6). Turns (7) and (8) confirm that the communication problem has been resolved.

Negotiation sequences such as this are more likely to occur when a learner initiates the exchange and the teacher is positioned as the person with the responsibility of resolving the communication problem. They are less likely to occur when the teacher initiates an exchange as learners are often reluctant to signal that that they have not understood. However, negotiation of meaning does occur sometimes in teacher-initiated exchanges, as illustrated in Extract 7. The teacher begins the exchange with an open question, which leads to the student clarifying what he does in the mountains (i.e. 'walking'). The teacher confirms his understanding and then the rest of the sequence focuses on the choice of the best word to describe the student's activity.

Extract 7:
1. T: Are you a mountain climber?
2. S: No, walking.
3. T: Walking in the mountains.
4. S: Trekking.
5. T: Ah.
6. S: Tracking, tramping.
7. T: Trekking, trekking. Or in New Zealand?
8. S: Tramping.
9. T: Tramping.

It is easy to see how such sequences can assist acquisition. In Extract 7, the learner is provided with a number of synonyms for 'walking in the mountains' and also guided to the word favoured in New Zealand. Strong claims have been made for the role that negotiation of meaning sequences can play in language learning (see, for example, Long, 1983; 1996). We will examine these later in Chapter 8.

Final comment

Discourse analytic frameworks such as that of Sinclair and Coulthard have provided researchers with the tools needed to describe L2 classroom talk rigorously and in detail. They have shifted the focus of attention away from discrete categories of talk to an examination of contingency (i.e. how one utterance interlocks with the preceding and following utterances to create structured patterns of discourse). Arguably, this affords a much more illuminating account of classroom discourse. However, there has been no study that has attempted to establish an empirical link between different patterns and L2 acquisition. To date, the research has focused mainly on simply describing aspects of classroom discourse and identifying the factors responsible for them. The various claims concerning their contribution to language learning are based entirely on theoretical positions or on extrapolations from L1 acquisition research. While there are studies that demonstrate the facilitative effect of negotiation, there are no studies that demonstrate that a classroom rich in such features leads to faster learning than a classroom where the IRF prevails.

Types of Language Use

Other researchers have adopted a more holistic approach to describing the communicative behaviours that arise in the L2 classroom by distinguishing different types of language use. As with the discourse analytic frameworks this approach was often motivated by theoretical accounts of how interaction provides learning opportunities. In Ellis (2008) I described a number of attempts to characterize types of language use[5].

McTear (1975) identified four types of language use based on the extent to which the language focused on the code or on meaning:

1. mechanical: no exchange of meaning is involved;
2. meaningful: meaning is contextualized but there is still no information conveyed;
3. pseudo-communicative: i.e. new information is conveyed but in a manner that is unlikely in naturalistic discourse;
4. real communication: i.e. spontaneous speech resulting from the exchange of opinions, jokes, classroom management, etc.

Mechanical and meaningful language use involves a focus on the code, while real communication by definition entails genuine information exchange with pseudo-communicative language use lying somewhere in between. Readers might like to look at the various extracts from classroom discourse in the previous sections of this chapter and decide which of McTear's four types each one represents. It is not always easy to decide!

In Ellis (1984a), I distinguished 'address' (who talks to whom) and 'goal' (the overall purpose of an interaction). The description of address types was based on the participatory structures that can occur in a language classroom (i.e. whether the interactions involve the teacher (or an individual student) interacting with the whole class, the teacher addressing an individual student, or a student interacting with other students in small group work. Three goals were specified: (1) core goals, where the focus is on the language itself (medium), on some other content (message), or embedded in some ongoing activity such as model-making (activity); (2) framework goals associated with the organization and management of classroom events; and (3) social goals. I discussed interactional sequences taken from an ESL classroom in Britain to illustrate how the type of goal influences the discourse, and then speculated about the learning opportunities each type affords. I pointed out that interactional events with core goals are likely to restrict learners to a responding role, whereas framework and social goals provide opportunities for them to initiate discourse and to perform a wider range of language functions.

In Van Lier's (1988) framework, there are four basic types of classroom interaction, according to whether the teacher controls the topic (i.e. what is talked about) and the activity (i.e. the way the topic is talked about). Type 1 occurs when the teacher controls neither topic nor activity, as in the small talk sometimes found at the beginning of a lesson or in private talk between students. In Type 2 the teacher controls the topic but not the activity; it occurs when the teacher makes an announcement, gives instructions, or delivers a lecture. Type 3 involves teacher control of both topic and activity, as when the teacher elicits responses in a language drill. In Type 4 the teacher controls the activity but not the topic, as in small group work where the procedural rules are specified but the students are free to choose what to talk about. In a further development of this framework, Van Lier (1991) added a third dimension – the function that the language serves. He followed Halliday (1973) in distinguishing three types of function: (1) ideational (telling people facts or experiences), (2) interpersonal (working on relationships with people), and (3) textual (signalling connections and boundaries, clarifying, summarizing, etc.).

Johnson (1995) adopted a similar holistic approach based on a distinction between 'academic task structures' (i.e. how the subject matter is sequenced in a lesson and the sequential steps involved) and 'social participation structures' (i.e. how the allocation of interactional rights and obligations shapes the discourse). These two structures are interrelated. Where the academic task structure is rigid, the social participation structures are also tightly controlled. In such cases, classroom communication becomes ritualized. In contrast, when the academic task structure and social participation structure are more fluid, classroom communication can become highly spontaneous and adaptive. Johnson considered that topic control plays a crucial role in determining how fluid the communication is. Drawing on Ellis (1990) and Van Lier (1988), she suggested the 'optimal conditions' for L2 acquisition. These include, creating opportunities for students to have a reason for attending to language, providing ample opportunity for students to use language, helping students to participate in language-related activities that are beyond their current level of proficiency, and offering a full range of contexts that cater for a 'full performance' of the language. Johnson argued that these optimal conditions are more likely to occur in discourse where the academic task structure and social participation structure are more relaxed.

These broad frameworks have been developed through descriptive studies of language classrooms, utilizing detailed analysis of transcripts of actual interactions. They are macro-analytic rather than micro-analytic in nature and thus cannot serve as schemes for describing the way discourse unfolds in L2 classrooms. However, as Ellis, Van Lier and Johnson demonstrate, they enable researchers to characterize the general nature of the discourse found in different classrooms and in different types of instructional activities and to speculate how different types of language use might affect L2 learning.

Conversation Analysis and the L2 Classroom

Conversation analysis (CA) (see Chapter 2), like discourse analysis (of which it is sometimes treated as sub-type), seeks to describe the organization of conversational discourse by investigating 'how participants understand and respond to one another in their turns at talk' (Hutchby and Wooffitt, 1998: 14). Analysis is entirely bottom-up and data-driven (i.e. there is no reference to a priori norms or structures) and assumes that no detail can be dismissed. For this reason, conversational analysts base their work on very narrowly transcribed conversations. Markee (2005) set out what he considered the minimal requirements for a CA transcript. They need to document:

> ... how members hesitate, pause, or become silent during talk, how they speed up or slow down their delivery, how they modulate the volume of their speech, how they emphasize certain words or sounds through stress, and how they overlap each other's talk (p. 358).

He then added that if video-recording were used to collect data it would also be possible – and desirable – to include information about gestures, embodied actions and eye-gaze behaviours. Clearly, CA involves the painstaking transcription and analysis of data. Here is a transcript of an extract from a teacher-fronted L2 classroom (from Markee, 2005: 357) that illustrates the kind of detail that conversation analysts seek to include. A key of the transcript conventions can be found in Markee (2005: 360–361).

Extract 8:
01. T: [X _____
02. T: → U:: HM (0.6) ART<u>U</u>RO ((*L1 turn to look at T*)
03. L6:   [X
04. L6:   → [yes
05. T: [. . . X _____
06. T: → [OR GONZALO ((*As T relocates next turn to L1. L6 turns his gaze away
07.   from T and turns back to face front*))
08. T: _____
09. T: ?H <u>WHY</u>: D'YOU THINK GERMAN . . . .

As its name suggests, CA focuses on naturally-occurring conversations, which, as we have already seen do not regularly occur in classrooms. Markee and Kasper (2004) noted that conversational analysts treat classroom talk as 'a type of institutional talk that is empirically distinct from the default speech exchange system of ordinary conversation' because 'teacher-fronted classroom talk is an unequal power speech exchange system' (p. 492). However, Seedhouse (2004) took a different approach, arguing that a range of interactions occur in classrooms and showing how these both differ from and, in some ways, resemble conversations.

Classroom CA has focused on the same types of interactional organization as those found in conversation – turn-taking and repair. I will briefly report the key findings for both types and then consider 'off-task talk'. Finally, I will examine how participants' identities can influence the organization of classroom discourse.

Turn-taking

Ethnomethodological studies of naturally occurring conversations (for example, Sacks, Schegloff, and Jefferson, 1974) have identified a number of rules that underlie speaker selection and change: only one speaker speaks at a time; a speaker can select the next speaker by nominating or by performing the first part of an adjacency pair (for example, asking a question that requires an answer); a speaker can alternatively allow the next speaker to self-select; and there is usually competition to take the next turn. Turn-taking in institutional settings, however, is often different because, as Seedhouse (2004) pointed out 'the organisation of turn-taking is constrained and related to the institutional goal, and this is the case in the language classroom' (p. 168).

Classroom researchers frequently highlight the differences between turn-taking in natural and classroom settings. McHoul (1978), for instance, showed that in the latter there is generally a strict allocation of turns in order to cope with potential transition and distribution problems and that who speaks to whom, at what time, is firmly controlled. As a result there is less turn-by-turn negotiation and competition while individual student initiatives are discouraged. Lörscher (1986) examined turn-taking in English lessons in different types of German secondary schools and found that turns were almost invariably allocated by the teacher, the right to speak returned to the teacher when a student turn was completed, and the teacher had the right to interrupt or stop a student turn. Lörscher argued that these rules are determined by the nature of the school as a public institution and by the teaching-learning process. Van Lier (1988) set out to identify how turn-taking in the L2 classroom differs from that found in ordinary conversation. He identified the following 'basic rule' governing classroom turn-taking:

1. In L2 classrooms, whenever centralized attention is required:
    a.   one speaker speaks at any one time;
    b.   many can speak at once if they say (roughly) the same thing, or at least if (a proportion of) the simultaneous talk remains intelligible.
2. If not (a) or (b), repair work will be undertaken (p. 139).

Interest in the turn-taking mechanisms found in classroom discourse has continued over the years. Markee (2000) identified the following general characteristics of turn-taking in classroom talk:

- the pre-allocation of different kinds of turns to teachers and learners,
- the frequent production by learners of turns in chorus,
- the frequent production of long-turns by the teacher and short-turns by the student,
- the requirement that learners produce elaborated sentence-length turns in order to display knowledge,
- a predetermined topic.

Table 4.4 Aspects of turn-taking mechanisms in four different instructional contexts (based on Seedhouse, 2004)

Contexts	*Aspects of turn-taking*
Form and accuracy contexts	Tight control of turn-taking Adjacency pair consisting of teacher prompt and learner production Optional evaluation and follow-up
Meaning-and-fluency contexts	Turn-taking sequences more varied than in form and accuracy contexts Turn-taking managed by students Also, when turn-taking is managed by the teacher the crucial factor is whether interactional space is available to students to nominate and develop a topic
Task-oriented contexts	The types of turns are constrained by the nature of the task Learners have to actively construct a turn-taking system There is a tendency towards linguistically simplified language as a result of a focus on 'getting the task finished' (p. 131)
Procedural contexts	Typically no turn-taking (teacher conducts an unbroken monologue) Three possible variants: – a student seeks clarification – teacher asks a display question – teacher may ask a learner to verify the procedure

As previously noted, Markee saw turn-taking of this kind as a reflection of 'unequal power speech exchange systems'.

The most detailed account of turn-taking in the L2 classroom can be found in Seedhouse (2004). Drawing on an extensive and varied database of language lessons from around the world, Seedhouse argued that it was not possible to view classroom discourse in terms of a single-exchange system. He showed that the way in which the organization of interaction takes place varies according to context. He distinguished four different classroom contexts: (1) form-and-accuracy contexts, (2) meaning-and-fluency contexts, (3) task-oriented contexts, and (4) procedural contexts (i.e. where the teacher explains how to carry out an activity). Table 4.4 summarizes the main features of the turn-taking mechanisms that occurred in each of these contexts.

Seedhouse emphasizes 'the reflexive relationship between the pedagogical focus of the interaction and the organization of turn-taking and sequence' (p. 138). However, he also admitted that despite its flexibility, the classroom speech exchange systems he examined 'remain identifiably L2 classroom interaction' (p. 139) and that conversational exchanges are difficult if not impossible in the L2 classroom. In an earlier publication he wrote:

> As soon as the teacher instructs the learners to 'have a conversation in English', the institutional purpose will be invoked, and the interaction could not be a conversation

... To replicate conversation, the lesson would have to cease to be a lesson in any understood sense of the term and become a conversation which did not have any underlying pedagogical purpose ... (Seedhouse, 1996: 18).

In other words, truly conversational exchanges are only possible in 'off-the-record' interactions.

We can see two related issues running through these accounts of classroom turn-taking. The first is the tension between the felt need to identify a set of general characteristics of classroom speech exchange systems and the recognition that there is considerable variety as well. This variety derives in part from the fact that the participants are able to transgress from the 'basic rule' that guides turn-taking and in part from the fact that turn-taking mechanisms differ according to the pedagogic purpose. The second issue concerns the differences between L2 classroom turn-taking mechanisms and those found in ordinary conversation. Studies of classroom turn-taking often take as their point of comparison the speech exchange system of ordinary conversation.

Repair

Conversational analysts view repair, like other types of conversational activity, as a joint production. Early studies focused on repair in naturally occurring conversations. They defined repair as the treatment of 'trouble' (i.e. anything that the participants consider is impeding communication). In this respect, then 'repair' includes a wider range of discourse phenomena than both negotiation of meaning and 'corrective feedback', which concerns the repair work undertaken to address trouble of a purely linguistic nature (i.e. learner errors). Corrective feedback is examined in the following chapter.

Sacks, Schegloff and Jefferson (1974) distinguished different types of repair in conversations in terms of who initiates the repair (the speaker or the hearer) and who carries it out. The four basic types they found were (1) self-initiated self-repair, (2) self-initiated other repair, (3) other-initiated self-repair, and (4) other initiated-other repair. In conversations, (1) is clearly the preferred type of repair. (4) is the least preferred.

Later research (for example, Kasper, 1985; Markee and Kasper, 2004; Seedhouse, 2004; Van Lier, 1988) has examined repair in classroom contexts. The general finding is that 'the organization of repair varies with the pedagogical focus' (Seedhouse, 2004: 142). This is not surprising given that patterns of turn-taking have been found to be similarly variable (see section on turn-taking). In line with this position, Seedhouse distinguished what he calls 'didactic repair' in form-and-accuracy contexts and 'conversational repair' in meaning-and-fluency contexts.

Didactic repair arises when the teacher is trying to elicit a linguistically correct utterance from a student and the student fails to provide it. Typically, the teacher initiates the repair allowing the student the opportunity to self-repair. If the student still fails, the teacher carries out the repair. Seedhouse noted that teachers often require students to produce the *identical* utterance they are targeting and that repair-work can ensue even if the learner produces a linguistically correct utterance, which is viewed as unsatisfactory in some way (e.g. it is an incomplete sentence). However, sometimes teachers adopt a different repair strategy in form-and-accuracy contexts, as in this extract from Ellis (1988):

Extract 9:
1. T: Nun, erm, auf der nächsten Seite.
         Und warum sind sie im Schirmgeschaft? Mary.
         (Now, on the next side. And why are they in the umbrella shop? Mary.)
2. S1: Erm, sie sind im Schirmgeschaft, weil, erm.
         (They are in the umbrella shop because . . .)
         (.2.) sie (.) möchten eine Schirm kaufen.
         (They would like an umbrella to buy.)
3. T: Was meinen die anderen? Ist das richtig, was Mary sagt? (.3.) Roger, Sie schutteln den Kopf. Verstehen Sie? Sie schutteln den Kopf. Shaking your head. Wie sagen Sie es? Warum sind sie im Schirmgeschaft?
         (What think the others? Is that right what Mary says? Roger, you shake the head. Understand you? You shake the head . . . . How say you it? Why are they in the umbrella shop?
4. S2: Erm, weil sie einen Schirm kaufen möchten.
         (Because they an umbrella to buy would like.)
5. T: Weil Frau Meyer einen Schirm kaufen möchte. Und Mary sagte, weil Frau Meyer möchte einen Schirm kaufen.
         (Because Frau Meyer an umbrella to buy would Like. And Matt said, because Frau Meyer would like an umbrella to buy.)

Here, the teacher elects to invite another student to repair S1's grammatical error. This is a strategy that is often recommended by language-teaching methodologists (e.g. Edge, 1989) but, in fact, occurs relatively rarely.

Seedhouse found that in meaning-and-fluency contexts conversational repair is much more likely to occur. Purely linguistic problems are often ignored and the teacher is often prepared to accept highly simplified learner language. Instead, repair-work occurs when there is a breakdown in communication, and, in particular when it is necessary to establish factual accuracy, as in this example:

Extract 10:
1. T: what about in China? Well, Hong Kong. China, do you have a milk van?
2. L: er, China (.) no, no milk.
3. T: no milk?
4. L: yeah, shop, er, city, city.
5. T: ah, at the shop, at the shop.
         (Nunan, 1989: 142; cited in Seedhouse, 2004).

Such sequences involve the negotiation of meaning discussed earlier. Seedhouse claimed that 'overt correction is undertaken only when there is an error which impedes communication' (p. 153). However, as we will see in Chapter 5, this is not always the case. Ellis, Basturkmen, and Loewen (2001), for example, have shown that didactic repair is in fact quite common in communicative activities.

Repair sequences afford potential learning opportunities in that they make problems explicit and provide solutions. In contrast, what Waring (2008) termed 'explicit positive assessment' may deprive learners of learning opportunities. Waring examines a number of teacher-student sequences where the teacher provides a positive assessment of a student contribution by mans of expressions such as 'good', 'excellent' and 'perfect' and showed how this serves to close a sequence and thereby 'preempt any further talk on the issue by implicating the latter as unnecessary and unwarranted' (p. 589). He suggested that, as a result, opportunities for further exploration of a linguistic point – 'the "stuff" of learning' – are suppressed.

Off-task talk

As previously noted, Van Lier (1988) found that classroom discourse is not as tightly regulated as is sometimes made out and that opportunities for 'schismic talk' occur. Markee (2005) coined the term 'off-task talk' to refer to 'talk as interaction that diverges from whatever topic(s) teachers designate as the current class agenda' (p. 197). He then examined in detail an example of such talk, where one learner invited another learner to a party during a class where the official topic was the reunification of East and West Germany. Markee showed that this off-task talk occurred when an 'interactional gap' opened up as a result of the teacher failing to frame a new topic when attempting a topic change. It arose as a result of the two learners taking on identities other than that of students (i.e. as 'inviter' and 'invited') while at the same time maintaining a 'skillful schizophrenia' by concurrently orienting to the norms of their 'conversation' and the ongoing institutional talk of the classroom. Markee argues that such 'hybrid contexts of talk' afford special opportunities for language learning.

Identity in classroom talk

As Markee's study shows, another interesting angle that can be explored through conversational analysis is how the identity of classroom participants affects the interactions that take place between teacher and students. Richards (2006) drew on Zimmerman's (1998) three aspects of identity. (1) 'Discourse identity' refers to the identities that participants adopt in the moment-by-moment organization of an interaction – for example, as current speaker, listener, questioner, challenger or repair initiator. (2) 'Situated identity' is the identity that arises from the typical roles the participants perform in a specific situation. In the case of the classroom, the key situated identities are those of 'teacher' and 'student'. (3) 'Transportable identity' refers to the personal identity (or identities) that an individual can draw on and be made relevant to the talk. By way of example, Richards described his personal identity as 'a white, middle-aged English male' or 'father of two teenage daughters'. He proposed that the L2 classroom is characterized by a 'default identity' (i.e. 'teacher' and 'student') but noted that this is 'not binding'. He then provided extracts from L2 classrooms that illustrate the default position (where teacher-dominated IRF exchanges figure), a change in discourse identity (where a student becomes the 'primary knower'), a change in both discourse and situated identities (where the teacher temporarily takes on the role of 'learner'), and an orientation to an aspect of transportable identity (where the teacher and student act as members of their respective cultures). Richards' point is that the interactional patterning of lessons varies enormously depending on the type of identity brought into play. His extracts show that involvement is highest when the interactants depart from their default identities, in particular when transportable identities come into play. He suggested that teachers may be able to enrich the interactional resources made available to students by introducing transportable identities into the classroom, for example through personal revelation[6].

The following brief extracts illustrate the differences that Richards detected in the discourse originating from the default identity position and that arising from the introduction of a transportable identity. In the first extract (from Bye, 1991 cited in Richards, 2006: 61–2) the teacher functions very much as 'teacher', insisting on the rights this identity confers on him to regulate the content of student turns, thus demanding the students perform as 'student'.

Extract 11:
1. T: Who could make a sentence about Perry – or about – yeah make a sentence about Perry please.
2. S1:   Perry who?
3. T: No we won't ask any questions yet. Just Make a sentence.
4. S2:   Which one?
5. T: No – no questions.
6. S2:   Ah – it's Barry.
7. T: tell me something about Perry.
8. S2:   He wash . . .

In the second extract, S1 transports his identity as a maker of war models into the talk in order to explain why he likes the 'swastika' insignia and to refute the teacher's assumption that he does not understand the significance of this.

Extract 12:
1. S1:   But in fact, in Taiwan, many, many boys like the swasi-, swastika.
2. T: But I feel they don't really understand.
3. S1:   No, we understand. You know why. After, after . . . .

4. S2:   Really? (Sceptically to S1.)
5. S1:   Yeah, like me, you know, I played, no I made, the, the, the model. You
          know? The war models 'muo shin'.
6. S3:   Game.
7. S1:   Yeah.
8. S3:   Game. World War II game.
9. S1:   No, no, no not game, muo shin. You know?
10. T: A model.
11. S1:   Yeah, to make a tank . . . .

The discourse in these two extracts is markedly different. The first shows the
teacher insisting on the IRF format – working to achieve the response he requires
in order to evaluate it. In the second, as Richards pointed out, 'there is no evidence
of situated identity and nothing "institutional" about the talk'. Implicit in Richards'
discussion of these two episodes is the assumption that 'institutional' talk is less
likely to afford opportunities for L2 development than the 'conversational' talk that
can arise when the teacher and students activate a transportable identity.

Final comment

Like, the discourse analysis systems we considered in the previous section and unlike
interactional analysis systems, conversational analysis has illuminated some of the
key characteristics of sequential talk in the classroom. Its contribution is essentially
twofold. First, it has given us highly detailed descriptions of how classroom discourse
unfolds, uncovering the 'hidden' social norms that shape it. Second, it has shown
that classroom discourse is not as monolithic as earlier work based on discourse
analytic systems suggested. There is considerable variety, reflecting the pedagogic
purposes and the discourse identities that inform how participants interact.

CA studies of L2 classrooms are deliberatively atheoretical. They emphasize the
need to simply observe and describe classroom talk without any preconceived notions
of what might take place or what might be important (e.g. for learning). This is both
a strength and a weakness. It ensures a more or less unbiased account of classroom
processes. However, it tells us nothing about how these processes affect L2 learning
nor does it allow us to speculate about which processes might be important for
learning. Aware of this limitation, CA classroom researchers (such as Waring 2008)
have increasingly aligned themselves with a theory that does address the relationship
between interaction and learning. In the next section we examine the descriptive
work on L2 classroom discourse that has originated from this theory.

Sociocultural Theory: Scaffolding

The primary claim of Sociocultural Theory or SCT (and one shared by many conversation analysts) is that language learning is dialogically based. That is, acquisition
is seen as occurring *in* rather than *as a result of* interaction. Interaction mediates

learning not by providing learners with 'data' which they then process internally but by affording opportunities to collaboratively produce new linguistic forms. In other words, when learners produce a new linguistic form for the first time in discourse, 'development' takes place. Subsequently 'learning' occurs when the form has become internalized. Evidence that this has occurred is obtained by showing that a linguistic feature that learners could initially only produce with the help of scaffolding can subsequently be produced independently – that is, when it can be shown that the learner has moved from 'other regulation' to 'self-regulation'.

In this chapter, we will not examine how learning takes place. Instead we will focus on 'scaffolding' – that is, the process by which one speaker (an expert or a novice) assists another speaker (a novice) to perform a skill that they are unable to perform independently[7]. This is achieved by the joint construction of a Zone of Proximal Development or ZPD (i.e. a site of potential development where learners are helped to perform a skill collaboratively). Scaffolding is thus both a discourse and cognitive construct, as Wood, Bruner and Ross's (1976) early definition makes clear. They identified the following features of scaffolding:

1. Recruiting interest in the task.
2. Simplifying the task.
3. Maintaining pursuit of the goal.
4. Marking critical features and discrepancies between what has been produced and the ideal solution.
5. Controlling frustration during problem solving.
6. Demonstrating an idealized version of the act to be performed.

For scaffolding to be effective in assisting learning it needs to be tuned to the learner's developmental level (i.e. it should be neither too much or too little).

What then does scaffolding look like at the discourse level? Ohta (2001) proposed that classroom discourse consists to a large extent of 'interactional routines', suggesting that learners 'acquire facility in L2 interaction through progressively expanded involvement' in such routines, moving from 'peripheral participation to more and more active involvement' (p. 187). She explored the potential of a routine we have already examined in detail – IRF – focusing on how this helps learners of L2 Japanese to develop the interactional competence involved in producing appropriate listener responses (e.g. the use of *ne* as an aligning expression), which occur frequently in ordinary Japanese conversation. Ohta showed how the follow-up move of the IRF exchange allows the teacher to model listener responses. She noted that in all the classrooms she investigated 'teachers used a variety of listener responses, including using *ne* for assessments, expressions of alignment, and confirmation questions' (p. 190). She suggested that these demonstrate the teachers' interest in student talk and thus increase the salience of her responses. In addition, listener responses in IRF exchanges can also serve a structural function in the discourse, signalling a topic shift is about to occur. In another interactional routine – a greeting sequence that conventionally includes reference to the weather – a teacher scaffolded the students' use of '*soo desu ne*' as shown in Extract 13.

Extract 13:

1. T: hai ja hajimema:su (.) ohayoo gozaima:::su
        (Okay let's begin. Good morning).
2. Ss: Ohayoo gozaimasu.
        (Good morning).
3. T: Kyoo wa iya na tenki desu ne:
        (the weather is unpleasant today ne:
4. Ss: So desu ne:
        (It is ne:)
5. T: Iya:: soo desu ne::
        (Unpleasant it is ne ::)

                              (Ohta, 2001: 195).

The teachers did more than simply model the use of *ne*; they also gave explicit guidance in its use (e.g. by requesting students to produce '*soo desu ne*' chorally). Ohta's discussion of listener responses is of interest because it shows how the kinds of sequences that discourse analysts have identified can provide scaffolding opportunities. However, Ohta admitted that teacher-centred discourse while beneficial in exposing learners to exemplars of *ne* also constrains students' actual use of it. She pointed to the importance of a peer learning setting as a site for the development of interactional competence.

Another example from the growing body of research that has examined classroom discourse from an SCT perspective can be found in Guk and Kellogg's (2007) interesting comparison of the kinds of scaffolding used by a teacher when interacting with students and by students interacting amongst themselves in a Korean primary school. The teacher orientates strongly towards language as a system, breaking down sentences into small pieces. Scaffolding is achieved by means of demonstration, requests for repetition, leading questions and initiating solutions – techniques that Vygotsky (1978), the founding father of SCT, himself identified. The following extract illustrates these techniques:

Extract 14:

1. T: Repeat after me. Dahye is stronger than Yeseul.
2. Ss: Dahye is stronger than Yeseul.
3. T: Than Yeseul.
4. Ss: Than Yeseul.
5. T: Keokkuro hamyeon mueorahuyo?
        (How would you say it the other way?) Yeseul is . . .
6. Ss: Yeseul is weaker . . .
7. T: . . . . Weaker than Dahye.
8. Ss: Yeseul is weaker than Dahye.

In contrast, in group work the students work with larger chunks and focus more on co-constructing discourse. Guk and Kellogg suggested that the two forms of discourse complement each other, with the teacher-class discourse supplying the intermental mediation that learners need to create a ZPD and the student-student discourse the opportunity to internalize what has been learned. We will examine the role of group work in L2 classes in greater detail in Chapter 6.

Scaffolding, then, is the interactive work that helps construct a zone of proximal development. Ultimately, then, scaffolding is defined in terms of what it is claimed to bring about (i.e. a ZPD). There are two problems here. The first is that there is no rigorous description of the discourse features involved in scaffolding. We do not know precisely what the discourse characteristics of the collaborative work called 'scaffolding' actually consists of, and, importantly, we do not know what does not constitute scaffolding. The second problem concerns the operationalization of ZPD. In order to know whether a ZPD has in fact been constructed we need to be sure that the learner is not capable of performing the skill without assistance (i.e. that development has not in fact already taken place). In fact, this is rarely demonstrated, and certainly not in the above extracts. It is all too easy to claim that a sequence of talk is illustrative of a scaffolded ZPD but much more difficult to convincingly demonstrate that it is.

I will conclude this section with a discussion of one study that has gone some way to overcoming these problems of definition. Anton (1999) drew on Stone's (1993) definition of 'prolepsis' as 'a special type of conversational implicature in which the necessary context is specified *after* the utterance rather than before it' (p. 174). Stone went on to suggest that this challenges the listener to reconstruct the speaker's view, which may have a transforming effect. Anton examined interactions involving two foreign language teachers, who differed markedly in their interactional styles. One adopts a distinctive proleptic style, as in Extract 15, where the teacher is encouraging the learners to think about the form of the language:

Extract 15:
1. T :   So, alors, qu'est-ce qui passé ici? Quelle est la difference ici? Quelle est la difference ici? Quelle difference est-ce que vous pouvez remarquer ici dans les trois exemples?
         (So, what's happening here? What's the difference? What difference can you see in these examples?)
2. SI: Être
         (to be).
3. T: Être, oui, on utilize le verbe être, n'est-ce-pas? Pur former le passé compose, n'est-ce-pas? Est-ce-qu'il y a d'autres differences que vous pouvez remarquer?
         (To be, yes, we use the verb to be right? In order to form the past right? Any other difference that you can see?)
4. S2:   New verbs.

This exchange follows the familiar IRF pattern but the questions are open-ended, designed to help the learners to reflect on form and to lead them to verbalize a rule. Anton argued that this kind of proleptic teaching constitutes 'effective assistance (i.e. a scaffold)' (p. 308). It contrasts with the style of the second teacher, who adopts a more traditional transmission model of instruction by providing his own grammatical explanation and, as a result, dominates the interaction. Anton, there-fore, examined scaffolding in terms of a clearly defined discourse category (prolep-sis). Again, though, she provided no evidence that this helps to construct a ZPD for the learners. There is nothing in the microgenetic analyses of the extracts she discussed that clearly demonstrates that the learners are developing new knowledge or transforming old knowledge. One way in which this might be achieved is through the examination of discourse over time (i.e. longitudinally). This allows us to see how the learner progresses in the performance of a skill (i.e. from a stage of assisted performance to a stage of independent use). There are studies that have under-taken this (e.g. Aljaafreh and Lantolf, 1994; Ohta, 2001), which we will examine in Chapter 8.

Ethnographic Accounts of the L2 Classroom

Classroom ethnographers aim to provide an emic and holistic account of classrooms as 'cultural scenes'. To this end the employ multiple data collection methods (e.g. video- and audio-recordings, field notes, interviews, diaries) which are then sub-jected to qualitative analysis in order to describe and understand the way in which the participants behaved (see also Chapter 2 and, in particular, the description of Harklau's (1994) study). My concern here, however, will not be with ethnography in its broadest sense but microethnographic accounts of the way in which class-room participants interact. Erickson and Mohatt (1982) distinguish ethnography and microethnography in this way:

> While general ethnography reports overall narrative descriptions of events, mi-croethnography attempts to specify the processes of face-to-face interaction in the events by which the 'outcomes' of those events are produced.

Microethnography constitutes one way of conducting an ethnography of com-munication, with the focus on the discourse features and structures of classroom events.

In an early and influential study, Philips (1972) investigated the differences be-tween Indian and non-Indian children's participation in classroom interaction in an Indian reservation school in Oregon (USA). She noted that the basic frame-work was teacher-controlled interaction and, within this, distinguished a number of 'participant structures'. In the first type, the teacher interacts with all the students, addressing either the whole class or an individual student in a whole-class context with the students responding chorally or individually. The teacher may solicit vol-untary student responses or nominate a specific student to respond. In the second type, the teacher interacts with a smaller group of students. Student participation is mandatory and individual rather than choral. The third structure involves the stu-dents working independently at their desks. Individual students can choose to make contact with the teacher and engage in private talk with her. The fourth structure involves small group work where the students communicate amongst themselves.

Often there is a student 'chair', who functions as a proxy teacher. Philips reported that the way in which the non-Indian children participated in classroom discourse varied according to the participant structure. They rarely participated in Types 1 and 2, even when called on to do so. However, after a while, they initiated contact with the teacher as frequently as the non-Indian children in Type 3 and they became fully involved in Type 4 interactions and functioned more collaboratively than the non-Indian children. Philips' study highlights two crucial points about classroom discourse. It demonstrates the significance of cultural differences in understanding how and why students from different ethnic backgrounds interact in classrooms. It shows that the type of participant structure has a marked influence on when and how students take part in interaction.

Philip's study suggests that the Indian children she investigated failed to socialize effectively into the discursive practices of the classroom. More recent ethnographic and microethnnographic studies have drawn explicitly on socialization as a construct to investigate how learners develop the interactional competence they need to participate in L2 classrooms. Schieffelin and Ochs (1986) defined language socialization as the practice by which novices in a community are socialized both to the language forms and, through language, to the values, behaviours, and practices of the community in which they live. Thus, it entails 'socialization through the use of language and socialization to use language' (p. 163). As such, it affords a promising way of examining the complex relationship between classroom social behaviour and language learning.

Zuengler and Cole (2005) reviewed a number of studies of socialization in educational settings, seeing these as sites of 'secondary socialization' (i.e. 'primary socialization' takes place in the home and family). A focus of several of the studies reviewed by Zuengler and Cole is the 'interactional routines' that occur in L2 classrooms – such as 'greeting', 'attendance' and 'personal introduction' (Kanagy, 1999). Because these are highly predictable in structure and repetitive, learners are able to discover what constitutes appropriately socialized behaviour. Other ethnolinguistic studies conducted within the language socialization paradigm have examined the participatory patterns of L2 students in mainstream classrooms. Duff (2003) found that in such classrooms the L2 learners were often silent and that even when they did participate actively their turns were shorter, more cautious and less audible than students who had been living in Canada longer. Zuengler and Cole concluded their review by emphasizing that the socialization of L2 learners is a complex and fluid phenomenon that is 'potentially problematic, tension producing, and unsuccessful' (p. 306) as a result of differences between home and classroom socialization practices or in some cases differences between the classroom socialization practices that learners have internalized from their previous experience of language classrooms and the socialization practices of their current classroom.

In order to document how classrooms socialize L2 students into the interactional management of classroom talk, longitudinal studies are needed and these are relatively rare. An excellent example of a longitudinal study is Cekaite's (2007) account of one learner's interactional competence developed over one year in a Swedish reception immersion classroom. Cekaite examined in great detail the teacher-fronted classroom talk that this learner (Fusi) participated in. She identified three phases in Fusi's development. In the first phase Fusi was mostly silent. In the second phase, she attempted to participate inappropriately through 'aggravated direct disagreements' with the teacher. In the third phase, she demonstrated mastery of 'timely self-selections', thereby 'displaying her knowledge of the sequential organization of classroom activities' (p. 58) and had become 'a socially competent actor' (p. 59). This study is of special interest because it illustrates the interrelatedness of Fusi's developing interactional and linguistic competence. Cekaite also makes the important point that how learners position themselves within an L2 classroom community is not static but changes over time; Fusi moved from being a peripheral participant to a fully active participant.

The focus of ethnolinguistic accounts of L2 classrooms, such as Cekaite's study, is not the structure of teacher-led classroom talk or even specific interactional phenomena such as turn-taking or repair work. Rather they examine interactional repertoires in general, documenting these in great detail through reference to minutely-analyzed extracts of classroom talk. A pervasive finding of such accounts is the important role that interactional routines play in assisting learners to both master the rules of engagement and also develop their linguistic repertoires.

The studies to date have investigated 'second' rather than 'foreign' language classrooms. In the former, the L2 serves as not just the target language but also the medium of instruction. In the latter, however, this may or may not be the case. There is a need for microethnographic accounts of foreign language classrooms to examine how the interactional management of classroom talk is handled when two languages are available.

Conclusion

In this chapter, I have taken a broad brush approach to investigating second language classroom discourse, starting with the early interactional analysis systems which examine classroom talk in terms of discrete categories, moving on to different approaches to describing the structure of classroom communication and concluding with approaches based on theoretical views of language learning. This work covers several decades. It has evolved from a primary concern for description – to satisfy the need for a technical language for talking about teaching-as-interaction – to an increasing concern for understanding why teacher-led discourse takes the form it does and how it relates to language learning. It has grown in complexity as researchers moved from the direct observation of language classrooms to analyzing in great detail transcriptions of audio- and video-recorded lessons. There has also been a gradual shift in the direction of qualitative ways of looking at classroom discourse. Where the early interactional analysis and discourse systems were devised to quantify aspects of whole lessons, conversational analysis, microgenetic and ethnolinguistic methods focused on the detailed analysis of specific interactional sequences.

What have we learned from these varied accounts? One way of answering this question is by highlighting the key characteristics of L2 classroom discourse that emerge out of the research. These are:

1. Teachers control the discourse

In teacher-centred classrooms, teachers often dominate the discourse, both quantitatively (they typically occupy two-thirds or more of the total talk) and qualitatively through their control of the topics talked about and the turn-taking mechanisms.

2. IRF exchanges

The teacher's dominance is achieved through a particular type of exchange – initiate–respond–follow-up. This enables the teacher to determine who talks, when and about what. It serves as a mechanism for ensuring orderly discourse in the classroom. It also provides the teacher with a means for evaluating individual student responses for the public good. The IRF exchange is by far the most common discourse pattern found in L2 classrooms where the teacher is teaching the whole class.

3. Other discourse patterns

Despite the prevalence of the IRF exchange, other patterns do occur. What I have called framework language (Ellis, 1984a) provides opportunities for students to initiate interactional sequences. Talk that centres round 'transportable identities' also leads to a much more conversational type of discourse, where teachers and learners adopt symmetrical roles and sometimes even swop roles. Certain types of instruction – for example, what Allen et al. (1990) called 'experiential' teaching (in contrast to 'analytical teaching') or what Seedhouse (2004) called 'meaning-and-fluency contexts' (as opposed to 'form-and-accuracy contexts') result in a range of discourse features more akin to those in ordinary conversations. Task-based teaching, in particular, offers an escape from the dominance of the IRF exchange.

4. Participant structure

Another useful way of characterizing the variety that can occur in classroom communication systems is in terms of participant structure (i.e. the ways in which verbal interaction is organized in the classroom). Students work by themselves or in pairs or in small groups. Even in teacher-centred classrooms not all the interaction is between the teacher and the whole class. Teachers talk to individual students, sometimes with the whole class as an audience but sometimes privately. The kind of talk that arises in these participant structures differs. In this chapter I have focused on those participant structures that occur in whole class interaction. In Chapter 6, however, I will examine the participant structures associated with small group work.

5. Repair

A common feature of classroom discourse is the need to engage in repair work when some kind of problem arises. The problem may be 'communicative' (i.e. the participants fail to understand each other) or 'linguistic' (i.e. when the learner makes an error). In the former, repair is conducted through the 'negotiation of meaning'. In the latter it is more didactic in nature and typically managed by the teacher. The structure of repair sequences differs accordingly.

6. Scaffolding

Scaffolding remains a somewhat illusive construct but nevertheless a useful one in that it has both a discourse and cognitive side to it. It refers to the attempts made by one speaker (typically the teacher) to assist another speaker to perform a skill or a linguistic feature that they cannot manage by themselves. Many of the examples of scaffolding we have examined in this chapter involve IRF exchanges. 'Prolepsis', for example, is typically conducted through IRF but involves the use of open-ended questions that guide learners to an understanding of some linguistic phenomenon. Clearly, though more conversational types of scaffolding, when they occur, can help construct contexts for learning.

7. Interactional sequences

A number of studies have noted the existence of 'interactional sequences' – the discourse episodes that arise in the execution of common classroom routines. These may have social origins (as in greeting sequences) or instructional origins (as in the management of typical learning activities). Ernst (1994) provides an excellent example of how teachers can exploit classroom routines. She described how an elementary school teacher conducted a 'talking circle'. This had a regular five-part structure consisting of (1) getting ready, (2) entry into the circle, (3) a core phase, when students had the chance to talk about topics of interest to them, (4) the teacher's exposition of her agenda for the week, and (5) moving on. Each part involved identifiable interactional sequences. Such sequences serve a dual purpose. They help learners unfamiliar with the norms of classroom behaviour to socialize into them (as Cekaite showed in her study) and they assist linguistic development through the frequent and highly contextualized use of vocabulary and grammar.

In much of the research there has been an implicit and sometimes explicit comparison between classroom discourse and conversational discourse. This comparison has been motivated by an assumption that classrooms would foster language learning more effectively if the talk that took place in them was more 'natural'. After all, the aim of most language instruction is to develop learners' communicative abilities. How, then, can this be achieved if the kind of classroom discourse that learners are asked to participate in differs markedly from the natural discourse they aspire to participate in? Edmondson (1985) captured this problem neatly with his 'teacher's paradox', which states: 'We seek in the classroom to teach people how to talk when they are not being taught. (1985: 162)'.

Pedagogic discourse does differ from naturally occurring discourse and, as we have seen, in some respects is quite restricted. In the opinion of some, pedagogic discourse constitutes a 'falsification of behaviour' and a 'distortion' (Riley, 1977).

However, other researchers see it as inevitable and even desirable (for example, Edmondson, 1985 and Cullen, 1998). Also, as I noted above, classroom discourse is not invariably pedagogic. A better way of viewing the classroom might be as 'co-existing discourse worlds' (Kramsch, 1985). Kramsch argued that the nature of classroom discourse will depend on the roles the participants adopt, the nature of the learning tasks, and the kind of knowledge that is targetted. Instructional discourse arises when the teacher and the students act out institutional roles, the tasks are concerned with the transmission and reception of information and are controlled by the teacher, and there is a focus on knowledge as a product and on accuracy. Natural discourse is characterized by more fluid roles established through interaction, tasks that encourage equal participation in the negotiation of meaning, and a focus on the interactional process itself and on fluency.

The key issue of course, is the relationship between interaction and language learning. Does pedagogic discourse foster learning? Will language learning take place more efficiently if the discourse is more natural (i.e. more conversational)? What are the characteristics of an 'acquisition-rich' classroom? These are better questions than the questions we examined in Chapter 3. They take us inside the classroom, where learning takes place. They view instruction not in terms of externally-defined methods but as discourse processes. There are two ways of addressing these questions. One is to speculate how different classroom processes afford learning opportunities by drawing on theories of language learning. This is the approach we have seen in this chapter. The problem is that theories differ in what they see as the processes important for learning. For example, there is no consensus about the value of IRF exchanges nor of the relative contributions of the discourse that typifies form-and-accuracy and meaning-fluency contexts. The other way is to conduct process-product studies (i.e. studies that investigate the relationship between the behaviours that characterize different types of classroom discourse and learning outcomes). We will examine such studies in Chapter 8.

Notes

1. The term 'black box' was used by Long (1980) to reflect the fact that at the time of writing little was known about what actually transpired in the classroom (i.e. the 'black box') when teaching took place.
2. Following Mehan (1979), the IRF exchange is also sometimes referred to as IRE (i.e. Initiate-Respond-Evaluate). Hall and Walsh (2002) suggested that the two labels are not synonymous, with IRE implying a transmission model of teaching and IRF a more inquiry-based approach.
3. Hasan's (1988) framework involves analyzing the 'messages' (corresponding loosely to clauses) in terms of both their semantic features and their contribution to the discourse as a whole. The basis of the framework is Halliday's distinction between the three macro-functions of language: experiential, interpersonal and textual.
4. Readers might also like to read Seedhouse's (2004) account of this extract from a conversation analytic perspective.

R. Ellis

5. All of the macro-analytic frameworks were developed to describe the types of language use that occur in face-to-face instruction. The extent to which they are applicable to computer-mediated communication (CMC) is uncertain. There have been attempts to characterize the types of language use found in CMC, often in terms of the different functions performed by the participants' utterances. Collentine (2009) reviews this literature and also develops her own framework. This contains categories like 'assertive discourse', 'humour' and 'interpersonal discourse'.

6. Richards also acknowledges that there are practical, pedagogic and moral reasons why it might not be possible to engage in personal revelation.

7. Other terms have also been used to refer to the kind of discourse that scaffolds learning – 'collaborative dialogue' (Swain, 2000), 'instructional conversation' (Donato, 2000) and 'assisted performance' (Tharp and Gallimore, 1988).

5

Focus on the Teacher

Introduction

In the last chapter I examined the kinds of talk that arise in teacher-directed classroom discourse. 'Discourse' by definition involves a consideration of how utterances combine sequentially through the contributions of both teacher and learners. In this chapter I intend to focus more narrowly on the teacher's language.

Extracting the teacher's contribution from the total discourse runs the risk of distorting the true nature of the communication that takes place in the second language (L2) classroom. In part, at least, the way the teacher chooses to communicate must necessarily be influenced by the learners' contributions. Nevertheless, I believe a focus on the teacher's use of language is justified for a number of reasons. First, as we noted in Chapter 4, it is the teacher who makes the major contribution to L2 discourse. Walsh (2002) listed 10 general features of English as a foreign language (EFL) classroom discourse, which I have reproduced in Table 5.1. Of these 10 features, seven refer solely to teachers. The same features and the same degree of teacher dominance apply to other types of language classrooms (e.g. second and immersion classrooms).

Second, theoretical views of L2 acquisition emphasize the role of input in the language learning process. N. Ellis (2002: 175), for example, argued that language learning is essentially 'frequency learning'. Noting that 'the real stuff of language acquisition is the slow acquisition of form-function mappings and the regularities therein' (he showed that type frequency[1] is the primary determinant of how learners construct such mappings implicitly. It follows that the input that learners are exposed to in the classroom will influence the course of language learning. While teachers are not the sole source of input (other sources are the instructional materials and the

Language Teaching Research & Language Pedagogy, First Edition. Rod Ellis.
© 2012 John Wiley & Sons, Ltd. Published 2012 by John Wiley & Sons, Ltd.

R. Ellis

Table 5.1 Ten features of discourse in the EFL classroom (Walsh, 2002)

1. Teachers largely control the topic of discussion.
2. Teachers often control both content and procedure.
3. Teachers usually control who may participate and when.
4. Students take their cues from teachers.
5. Role relationships between teachers and learners are unequal.
6. Teachers are responsible for managing the interaction which occurs.
7. Teachers talk most of the time.
8. Teachers modify their talk to learners.
9. Learners rarely modify their talk to teachers.
10. Teachers ask questions (to which they know the answers) most of the time.

learners themselves) they constitute the major source in many classrooms. Thus an understanding of the nature of the 'input' that teachers provide – and how this differs from the kind of input learners experience in naturalistic settings – is potentially of great importance for understanding how classrooms create contexts for language learning.

The third reason for electing to focus narrowly on the teacher is that it allows for the detailed examination of a number of key aspects of language use in the L2 classroom and reflects what has been a common approach to researching the L2 classroom. These aspects are:

1. teacher-talk;
2. teacher questions;
3. teacher's use of the learners' first language (L1) (including the use of code-switching);
4. the teacher's use of metalanguage;
5. corrective feedback.

In addition, focusing on the teacher allows for an examination of the growing body of research that has investigated teachers' beliefs and how these influence their teaching behaviours. I will now proceed by systematically examining these different aspects.

Teacher-Talk

Studies of how native speakers address L2 learners has shown that they frequently use a special register known as 'foreigner-talk'. This is characterized by a number of 'modifications' (i.e. there are distinctive differences in how native speakers (NSs) talk to non-native speakers (NNSs) as opposed to other native speakers). The modifications affect all levels of language – pronunciation, lexis, grammar and discourse. They can be 'grammatical' (e.g. the use of full rather than contracted forms) or 'ungrammatical' (e.g. the omission of functors such as copula – *be*, articles, subject pronouns and verb/noun inflections). Foreigner-talk can serve a number of different functions in NS–NNS talk: (1) it assists effective communication by making it easier for the interlocutors to understand), (2) it signals, implicitly or explicitly, the NS's attitudes towards the NNSs (i.e. by establishing an affective bond or, in some cases, by signalling NS status through 'talking down'), and (3) it teaches the target language (TL) implicitly. 'Teacher-talk' can be thought of as a sub-variety of 'foreigner-talk'. However, it differs from it in some interesting ways.

Key characteristics of teacher-talk

Chaudron (1988: Chapter 3) provided a comprehensive survey of early teacher-talk studies. His research indicates that teachers modify their speech when addressing L2 learners in the classroom in a number of ways and also that they are sensitive to their learners' general proficiency level. His main findings can be summarized as follows:

- In general, the research confirms the finding for L1 classrooms – namely, that the teacher takes up about two-thirds of the total talking time.
- While there is considerable evidence of variability among teachers and programmes, the general picture is one of teacher dominance in that teachers are likely to explain, question, and command and learners to respond.
- Teachers, like native speakers tend to slow down their rate of speech when talking to classroom learners as opposed to other native speakers and also do so to a greater extent with less proficient learners. However, there is considerable variability among teachers.
- Teachers are likely to make use of longer pauses when talking to learners than to other native speakers.
- Teachers tend to speak more loudly and to make their speech more distinct when addressing L2 learners.
- Teachers tend to use high-frequency words resulting in a lower type–token ratio. They vary their use of vocabulary in accordance with the learners' proficiency level. However, one study (Wesche and Ready, 1985) found no significant vocabulary modifications in university lectures to L2 learners.
- There is a trend towards shorter utterances with less proficient learners, but some studies which use words per utterance as a measure report no modifications. The degree of subordination tends to be lower, but again results have been mixed. Teachers use fewer marked structures such as past tense.
- Ungrammatical teacher-talk is rare. However, it has been observed to occur in teaching contexts where the teacher is endeavouring to establish an affective bond with students of low-L2 proficiency.
- Teachers have been found to use more self-repetitions with L2 learners, in particular when they are of low-level proficiency.

Many of these modifications are the same as those found in foreigner-talk but some seem to reflect the special characteristics of classroom settings – in particular the need to maintain orderly communication and to conform to target language norms.

Teacher-talk and L2 acquisition

Interest in teacher-talk was motivated in part by research which demonstrated that 'caretaker-talk' (i.e. the formal and interactional modifications that arise in talk to young children) facilitates L1 acquisition because it helps children to 'map native-language input' (Kuhl, 2000: 1185). Some L2 researchers hypothesized that teacher-talk might help L2 acquisition in a similar way. Krashen (1981), for example, suggested that teacher-talk, like other simple codes, is 'roughly tuned' to the learner's developmental level and in this way constitutes 'optimal' input. He based this claim on his Input Hypothesis, which states that to acquire an L2, learners need access to 'comprehensible input'. Teacher-talk is one way of providing such input.

The key issue, however, is whether teacher-talk does in fact promote acquisition. In fact, there are no studies that have investigated this empirically by attempting to demonstrate which features of teacher-talk correlate with measures of learning or to establish causal links between teacher-talk and acquisition. Rather the approach has been that of identifying those features of teacher-talk that are optimal for language learning on theoretical grounds. Wong Fillmore (1985), for example, identified a number of features of teacher-talk that she claimed were facilitative of acquisition in kindergarten classrooms with both L1 and L2 speaking children: avoidance of translation, an emphasis on communication and comprehension by ensuring message redundancy, the avoidance of ungrammatical teacher-talk, the frequent use of patterns and routines, repetitiveness, tailoring questions to suit the learners' level of proficiency, and general richness of language. In a similar vein, Walsh (2002) identified a number of characteristics of teacher-talk that, in his view, either inhibited or increased learner participation. Learning potential was increased if the corrective feedback was direct (as opposed to indirect), if teachers provided 'content feedback' (i.e. personal reactions made to learners), frequently 'pushed' learners by requesting confirmation or clarification, allowed extended wait-time, and scaffolded learners' production. Learning opportunities were inhibited if the teacher attempted to ensure the smooth progression of the discourse by means of 'latching' (i.e. completing student turns for them), echoing students' contributions, and interrupting students' in mid-flow. Such studies, however, do not show whether those features of teacher-talk viewed as optimal do assist learners to acquire the L2.

It should also be noted that not all researchers are convinced that simplified teacher-talk is beneficial. White (1987), for example, disputed the claims of the Input Hypothesis, arguing that 'the driving force for grammar change is that input is incomprehensible, rather than comprehensible' (1987: 95). White's idea was that failure to understand a sentence may force the learner to pay closer attention to its

Table 5.2 A teacher-educator's perspective on teacher-talk (based on O'Neill, 1994)

Teacher-talk is useful when the following conditions are met:
1. It is broken into sense groups.
2. It is simplified but not unnatural.
3. It is more redundant than 'ordinary speech' and words and structures are naturally repeated or 'recycled' at regular intervals.
4. It is broken into 'short paragraph' segments to encourage or invite students to interrupt, comment, and ask questions.
5. When new vocabulary or structure is taught, typical examples are given.
6. The teacher gets regular feedback through questions – especially 'open questions'.
7. The teacher uses other devices to get feedback such as student physical responses.
8. A variety of elicitation and explanation techniques are used (e.g. use of context, enactment, illustration).
9. A variety of correction techniques are employed, including both covert and overt types.
10. It is between 95 per cent and 85 per cent comprehensible.

syntactical properties in order to obtain clues about its meaning. White went on to argue that simple codes, such as teacher-talk, may actually deprive learners of the input they need to achieve high levels of proficiency and may encourage fossilization.

Teacher-talk and teacher education

Teacher-talk is the defining feature of many classrooms. It is not surprising, therefore, to find that teacher educators have paid considerable attention to it. Drawing partly on research and more generally on their own experience as language teachers, they have drawn up lists of what they view as the conditions that need to be met for teacher-talk to work for acquisition. In Table 5.2, I list the ten conditions that O'Neill (1994) proposed. Interestingly, O'Neill also challenged the common view expressed by teacher educators that teachers should aim to talk 'less' so the students can talk 'more', seeing merit in the teacher providing and adjusting input. While it might be possible to challenge some of O'Neill's conditions (for example, it is by no means clear that a 'variety of correction techniques' is the most effective way to conduct corrective feedback), they broadly reflect the conditions that classroom researchers might also identify.

Other teacher educators have adopted a different approach. They have encouraged teachers to reflect on their own practice of teacher-talk by preparing transcriptions of lessons and then examining them in terms of predetermined features of teacher-talk (such as amount of teacher-talk, rate of speech, types of questions, metalanguage, use of the L1 and feedback). Thornbury (1996) and Walsh (2006) report studies that investigated the use of such training practices with teachers. Warren-Price (2003) reports an interesting action-research study in which he investigated his own use of teacher-talk and reported how becoming more aware of his classroom actions enabled him to reduce the amount of teacher-talk-time.

Final comment

There have been few studies of teacher-talk since Chaudron's review. One reason for their demise is that register-like descriptions are viewed as being of limited value because they fail to take account of the individual, contextual, and sociocultural factors that shape teachers' choice of language on a moment-by-moment basis. It was for this reason that more recent L2 classroom research has adopted a discourse perspective on the classroom (see Chapter 4). However, researchers have continued to show interest in the specific aspects of teacher-talk (rather than in its general properties). In the following sections of this chapter we will explore what they have discovered about these aspects.

Teacher Questions

Teachers, whether in content classrooms or language classrooms, typically ask a lot of questions. Hargie (1978), for example, surveyed a number of early studies of content classrooms, noting it was not surprising that researchers had paid a great deal of attention to teachers' questions given their sheer volume. Long and Sato (1984) observed a total of 938 questions in six elementary-level English as a second language (ESL) lessons. One reason for the prevalence of questioning is undoubtedly the control it gives the teacher over the discourse. Thus, a teacher question is likely to occupy the first part of the ubiquitous three-phase initiate–respond–follow-up (IRF) exchange. However, as Dillon (1997) noted, the classroom is 'a complex of multiple contexts and processes, involving various kinds of questioning' (p. 105) with their frequency and type varying depending on whether the context involves 'recitation' or 'discussion'. Not surprisingly, then, there are very different views about the contribution that teacher questions can make to language learning.

Taxonomies of teacher questions

Much of the work on questions has centred on developing taxonomies to describe the different types. In one of the earliest taxonomies, Barnes (1969; 1976) distinguished four types of questions he observed in secondary school classrooms in Britain: (1) factual questions ('What?'), (2) reasoning questions ('How?' and 'Why?'), (3) open questions that do not require any reasoning, and (4) social questions (questions that influence student behaviour by means of control or appeal). Barnes made much of the distinction between closed questions (i.e. questions that are framed with only one acceptable answer in mind) and open questions (i.e. questions that permit a number of different acceptable answers). Barnes also pointed out that many questions have the appearance of being open, but, in fact, when the teacher's response to a student's answer is examined, turn out to be closed; he called these pseudo-questions.

Long and Sato (1984) modified Kearsley's (1976) taxonomy of questions to account for the different types of teachers' questions they observed in ESL lessons in the USA (see Table 5.3). The key distinction in Long and Sato's taxonomy lies in the two types of epistemic questions – referential questions and evaluative questions (more generally referred to as 'display questions'). This distinction is similar but not identical to the open/closed distinction of Barnes. Referential questions are likely to be open, while display questions are likely to be closed, but it is possible to conceive of closed referential questions and of open display questions[2].

Other taxonomies have focused on different aspects of teachers' questions. Koivukari (1987), for example, was concerned with depth of cognitive processing. Rote questions (those calling for the reproduction of content) are considered to operate at the surface level, while two kinds of 'comprehension' questions (those calling for the reproduction of content and those calling for the generation of new content) operate at progressively deeper levels. Håkansson and Lindberg (1988) distinguished questions in terms of their form (i.e. 'yes/no' questions, alternative questions, or WH questions), cognitive level (i.e. questions that require reproduction of information or convergent thinking), communicative value (i.e. whether they were referential or display), and orientation (i.e. whether the question is focused on language or real-life content). Håkansson and Lindberg's taxonomy is one of the most comprehensive available.

Whereas there are few problems in assigning teachers' questions to formal categories, difficulties arise with functional, communicative, and cognitive categories. These are 'high inference' and often call for substantial interpretative work on the part of the analyst. For example, the teacher's questions in the following example from White (1992) might be considered display in that they were clearly designed to elicit a specific grammatical structure but also referential in that they concerned an area of the student's private life that the teacher had no knowledge of.

T: How long have you worn glasses? How long have you had your glasses?
S: I have worn glasses for about six years.
T: Very good. Same glasses?

Such 'pseudo-communication' (McTear, 1975) makes the coding of questions problematic. Also, a question can serve more than one purpose and thus can belong simultaneously to more than one type. Questions of the kind 'What is the capital city of Japan?' are clearly (in most contexts) display questions but when asked by a teacher they also serve to maintain control over the discourse. Teachers' questions are frequently multi-functional.

Table 5.3 Long and Sato's (1984) taxonomy of teacher questions (based on Kearsley, 1976)

Type of question	Definition	Example
1. Echoic	Questions that ask for a repetition of an utterance or confirmation that an utterance has been interpreted as intended.	Pardon? What? Huh?
2. Epistemic	Questions that serve the purpose of acquiring information.	
a. Referential	Questions intended to provide contextual information about situations, events, actions, purposes, relationships or properties.	Where did you go for your holiday this year?
b. Evaluative	Questions that aim to establish the addressee's knowledge of the answer.	What city is the capital of Japan?
3. Expressive	Questions that convey attitudinal information to the addressee.	'Are you coming or aren't you?
4. Social control	Questions used to exert authority by maintaining control of the discourse.	'Are you listening to me?'
a. Attentional	Questions that allow the questioner to take over the direction of the discourse.	'Can I say something now?'
b. Verbosity	Questions asked only for the sake of politeness or to sustain conversations.	'How's your daughter getting on these days?'

Studies of teacher questions

Studies of teachers' questions in the L2 classroom have focused on the frequency of the different types of questions, wait-time (the length of time the teacher is prepared to wait for an answer), the nature of the learners' output when answering questions, the effect of the learners' level of proficiency on questioning, the possibility of training teachers to ask more 'communicative' questions, and the variation evident in teachers' questioning strategies. Much of the research has been informed by the assumption that L2 learning will be enhanced if the questions result in active learner participation and meaning negotiation.

In general, language teachers prefer closed, display questions. Long and Sato (1984) found that the ESL teachers in their study asked far more display than referential questions (476 as opposed to 128). This contrasted with native-speaker behaviour outside the classroom where referential questions predominate (999 as opposed to two display questions in the sample they studied). They concluded that 'ESL teachers continue to emphasize form over meaning, accuracy over communication' (1983: 283–4). Other studies (for example, White and Lightbown, 1984; Early, 1985; White, 1992) also showed that display/closed questions are more common than referential/open questions in the L2 classroom.

Teachers also seem to prefer instant responses from their students. White and Lightbown (1984) found that the teachers in their study rarely gave enough time for students to formulate answers before repeating, rephrasing, or redirecting the question at another student. The shorter the wait-time is, however, the fewer and the shorter the student responses are.

One way in which teachers' questions might affect L2 acquisition is in terms of the opportunities they provide for learner output. Brock (1986) found that responses to referential questions (mean length = 10 words) were significantly longer than responses to display questions (mean length = 4.23 words) in four advanced ESL classes at the University of Hawaii. Similar results have been obtained by Long and Crookes (1992), Nunan (1990a), and White (1992), suggesting that the findings are fairly robust. However, as White illustrated, it does not follow that all display questions produce short responses. There is little opportunity for an extended learner response in exchanges such as the following:

T: What's this?
S: It's a cup.
T: Good.

(Long and Crookes, 1992).

However, this is not the case in the following exchange based on a reading comprehension lesson, even though it also begins with a display question:

T: Did anyone manage to find some reasons for this?
S: With the decline of religion there is no pressure on woman to get married.

(White, 1992: 26).

Banbrook (1987) also showed that referential questions can elicit responses of varying lengths and complexity. Wu (1993) found that Hong Kong secondary students produced longer and more complex utterances in response to display questions. It should be noted, however, that the length of the student's response to a question is only one of several possible measures of learner output. Of equal interest, perhaps, is the length of the sequence initiated by a question. In this respect, Long and Crookes (1992) report that display questions elicited more student turns than referential questions. Lee (2006) also found that display questions sometimes underwent continuous interactional revisions as the teacher and students jointly negotiated their meaning over several turns. Clearly, more work is needed to tease out the relationship between question type and learner output.

Very few studies have examined the relationship between teachers' choice of questions and the learners' proficiency level. In Ellis (1985), I found no difference in the use a teacher made of open and closed questions with two learners over a nine month period, but I did find evidence to suggest that the cognitive complexity of the questions changed, with more questions requiring some form of comment as opposed to object identification evident at the end of the period. Kosiarz (1985; cited in Nizegorodcew, 2007) found no overall differences in the proportions of display and referential questions directed at learners of different proficiency levels by Polish teachers of English. However, she did report differences in the questioning strategies used. The teachers were more likely to repeat a question for low-proficiency learners and use a probing strategy involving open questions with higher-level students.

Most of the research has focused narrowly on the individual questions that teachers ask and the learners' responses to them. A better approach might be to examine questioning strategies, as in Kosiarz's study. Wu (1993) identified five such strategies used by Chinese teachers of English in Hong Kong secondary schools: (1) rephrasing by expressing a question in a new way, (2) simplifying an initial question, (3) repeating the question, (4) decomposing an initial question into two or more parts and (5) probing by following up a question with one or more other questions. Wu found that the most effective strategy was (4) as this encouraged students to elaborate on their initial response. Hall (1998) also found that one teacher of Spanish as a foreign language made effective use of additional questions that prompted students to elaborate by expanding their responses, justifying or clarifying opinions and making connections to their own experiences. Such use of questions serves as one way in which teachers can extend the follow-up move of the IRF exchange (see Chapter 4).

Given the indeterminate nature of the findings of many of the studies, it might seem premature to prescribe questioning strategies in teacher education. A number of studies, however, have investigated the effect of training teachers to ask specific types of questions. Brock (1986) and Long and Crookes (1992) found that instructors given training in the use of referential questions did respond by increasing the frequency of this type of question in their teaching. Koivukari (1987) found that training led to teachers using more 'deep' comprehension questions and fewer superficial rote questions, and was also able to demonstrate that an experimental group showed improved comprehension scores from this treatment.

Variation in teachers' questioning strategies

It is almost certainly a mistake to assume that the questioning strategies evident in one teaching context will be the same as those in another. Wu (1993), in the study referred to above, showed that teachers in two secondary schools in Hong Kong did not conform entirely to the general pattern reported in other studies. Thus, while they did ask more closed than open questions they also asked more referential than display questions. Wu also noted that in this teaching context many of the questions failed to elicit any response whatsoever from the students unless the teacher nominated a specific student to respond due to a cultural inclination to avoid participating publicly in the classroom. Wu's study suggests that great care is needed in making generalizations about both teachers' questions and students' responses.

Several studies have pointed to the necessity of acknowledging individual variation in teachers' questioning strategies within the same teaching context. Studies by Long and Sato (1984), Long and Crookes (1992), and Koivukari (1987) all reported extensive differences although these researchers did not always draw the reader's attention to them explicitly. Banbrook and Skehan (1990) provided illustrative evidence to argue that there is both intra- and inter-teacher variation. They identified three sources of intra-teacher variation: '(a) general teacher variation, (b) variation that takes place over the phases of the lesson and (c) variation in question-asking . . . that is the consequence of the teaching tasks or activities engaged in' (1990: 150). They argued that although variation in teachers' questions is well attested, its parameters are not yet well understood. Perhaps the clearest evidence of how teachers vary can be found in Spada and Lightbown's (1993) classroom study. They reported that one of the teachers in their study asked more than five times as many spontaneous questions (defined as questions unrelated to the teaching materials or genuinely open questions) than two other teachers in an intensive ESL class in Canada. They also suggested that this had a beneficial impact on the learners' acquisition of question forms.

Socially-oriented studies of teacher questions

In the main, the studies of teachers' questions in the L2 classroom have been 'etic' in orientation. That is, they have attempted to code questions in terms of a predetermined classification system and then quantify the different types. In Van Lier's (1988) view, however, a more 'emic' approach might be more rewarding. Van Lier commented:

> the practice of questioning in L2 classrooms, pervasive though it is, has so far received only superficial treatment . . . An analysis must go beyond simple distinctions such as display and referential to carefully examine the purposes and the effects of questions, not only in terms of linguistic production, but also in terms of cognitive demands and interactive purpose (1988: 224).

More recent qualitative, socially-oriented accounts of teachers' questions have sought to challenge the received view that certain types of questions (for example, display questions) impact negatively on acquisition because they fail to engage learners in the kinds of language use believed to be facilitative.

The sociocultural context may influence teachers' choice of questioning strategies. Poole (1992), suggested that the use of display or closed questions in most of the classrooms that have been studied may reflect the caretaker practices evident in white, middle-class Western society. Teachers from such a background ask questions because they provide a means by which an expert (the teacher) and a novice (the learner) can jointly construct a proposition across utterances and speakers. Poole suggested that this may be why such questions are so ubiquitous and why they are difficult to get rid of – teachers are being asked to reject a strategy that they feel to be culturally warranted.

McCormick and Donato's (2000) semester-long study of ESL teachers' questions was premised on a view of instruction as goal-directed actions. From this perspective, the role of teachers' questions can only be understood in relation to the goals they are trying to achieve. McCormick and Donato sought to show that simply assigning questions to some predetermined functional category is misleading. They argued that questions need to be viewed as 'dynamic discursive tools' that serve 'to build collaboration and to scaffold comprehension and comprehensibility'. They sought to demonstrate this by examining questions in relation to Wood, Bruner, and Ross's (1976) scaffolding framework (see Chapter 4) Finally, Ho (2005) examined the questions asked by three non-native speaking ESL teachers in Brunei to demonstrate the dangers of assigning teachers' questions to fixed categories and to argue, like McCormick and Donato, that display-type questions can be purposeful and effective in terms of institutional goals.

Final comment

One clear finding from all the studies mentioned in this section is that teachers ask a lot of questions. In many classrooms, these are closed/display questions. But clearly the type of questioning varies considerably from one teaching context to another, from one teacher to another and in a single teacher depending on the nature of the instructional activity. There has been a gradual shift in the way in which teachers' questions have been researched, with more recent studies adopting an emic perspective. The later studies are less inclined to see teacher questions as inhibiting learning opportunities in the classroom and instead emphasize the role that teacher questions can play in assisting teachers to achieve their varied instructional purposes and, in particular, in helping to scaffold learning.

Use of the Learner's L1

In this section we will consider only the teacher's use of the students' L1 in the L2 classroom. We will reserve consideration of the students' use of their L1 to the next chapter. There is virtue in such a division as the pros and cons of L1 use by teachers and students need to be examined separately. Unfortunately, this has not always been recognized in discussions of L1 use.

Differing opinions about the use of the L1 in L2 classrooms

Clearly classrooms vary in the feasibility of the teacher speaking in the learners' L1. In multilingual classrooms of the kind found in many second-language contexts, the teacher cannot be expected to make use of the variety of L1s spoken by the students. However, in foreign language contexts, where the students all speak the same L1 and the teacher is likely to be a native speaker of their language, use of the L1 is both feasible and, in many ways, natural.

The importance of taking into account differences in the teaching context has been eloquently made by Edstrom (2009). Her comment points to the need to not just consider macro-contexts (second versus foreign language settings) but also the micro-contexts that are dynamically constructed as a lesson takes place. It follows that L1 use cannot be determined a priori:

> Decisions about appropriate L1 use are in large part inextricably tied to classroom circumstances and cannot be predetermined nor easily generalized from one context to another (p. 14).

In fact, though, commentators have attempted to establish general guidelines. They have expressed markedly different positions regarding the value of the teacher using the students' L1. In Ellis (1984a) I argued that the teacher should use the students' L1 as little as possible in order to maximize students' exposure to L2 input. Harbord (1992) similarly argued that L1 use should be minimized and certainly not employed to save time in setting up pedagogic activities. This is a view that is often promoted by official policy. In Korea, for example, elementary teachers are instructed to use English in English lessons at all times. Cummins (2005) described the general assumptions that underlie two-way bilingual immersion programmes – instruction should be exclusively in the target language, translation should be avoided, and the two languages be kept rigidly separate. In other words, avoidance of the L1 is recommended in foreign language, second language and immersion contexts.

In contrast, Cook (2001) recommended that teachers use the L1 to explain grammar, organize tasks, discipline students, and implement tests. He noted that code-switching is a natural phenomenon in settings where speakers have a shared language. Other commentators, such as Atkinson (1987), have adopted an intermediate position by attempting to distinguish pedagogically valid and invalid uses of the L1. Nizegorodcew (2007) is a good example of this approach:

> The L2 teacher should communicate with her students in the target language unless the affective or instructional circumstances make her momentarily code-switch to the L1 (p. 167).

Cummins (2005) argued the need for two-way cross-language transfer in mainstream bilingual classrooms. Creese and Blackledge (2010) similarly argued for what they call 'translanguaging' as a bilingual strategy, reporting a study that showed how this can be effectively implemented in Gujarati and Chinese community schools in the United Kingdom.

These different positions draw on different theoretical frameworks. From an interactionist perspective, emphasis needs to be given to ensuring learners receive maximum exposure to L2 input. In contrast, in sociocultural theory the L1 is seen as a useful cognitive tool for scaffolding L2 learner production and facilitating private speech (see, for example, Anton and DiCamilla, 1999; and Swain and Lapkin, 2000). Theories of L2 motivation also lend support to the use of the L1 as a means of reducing learner anxiety and creating rapport in the classroom. My concern here, however, is not to review the varying and often conflicting views about the teacher's use of the L1 but to focus on what research has shown about its actual use in L2 classrooms. The following review will focus on three aspects of L1 use – the extent to which teachers resort to the L1, the specific purposes they use it for and the relationship between teachers' beliefs and their actual use of the L1.

The use of the L1 in language classrooms

As I have already noted, learners in second language classrooms typically come from a variety of language backgrounds and so there is no common L1 for the teacher to use. L1 use in second language contexts is more generally discussed in terms of the learners' use rather than the teacher's. Auerbach (1993), for example, made a compelling case for the use of the learners' L1 in ESL classroom in majority-language contexts such as the USA (see Chapter 6). All the studies considered in this section investigated foreign language classrooms where the teacher was a speaker of the students' mother tongue.

Not surprisingly, there is considerable variation in the extent to which teachers make use of the L1 in foreign language contexts. Duff and Polio (1990) investigated 13 foreign language classrooms in a US university. They recorded three sessions in each classroom. They distinguished utterances that were entirely in the target language from those that were in English (the L1) or were 'mixed' (i.e. contained both L1 and L2 words). All the teachers were native speakers of the target language. Polio and Duff reported that some teachers used the target language exclusively, others used it most of the time, and still others hardly at all (one teacher used the target language exclusively for less than 10 per cent of the time). Another interesting finding from this study was that the teachers varied very little in their use of the L1 across the three sessions (i.e. the proportion of utterances in the target language varied very little). It would seem, then, that these teachers were consistent in the extent to which they relied on the L1 possibly because the lessons they taught were textbook-based and followed a similar format. Turnbull (2000) investigated four secondary-level teachers of French and also found considerable variation in the amount of L1 use (i.e. from 28 per cent to 76 per cent). Macaro (2001) investigated six student teachers of foreign languages in the United Kingdom. Overall, the trainee teachers made relatively little use of the L1 (the mean for the six teachers was 4.8 per cent) but, as in other studies, there was considerable variation among them, and in contrast to the teachers in Duff and Polio (1990), a considerable range of L1 use from one lesson to another. Kim and Elder

(2005) also reported considerable variation in the use of the target language and the L1 by seven secondary school foreign language teachers in New Zealand. A number of factors are likely to influence teachers' overall choice of language – institutional policy, the students' proficiency level, the instructional approach (clearly the L1 is likely to be used more in grammar translation than in communicative language teaching), and teachers' own beliefs about the utility of the L1.

More interesting than the amount of L1 use, are the particular functions that the L1 serves. In a follow-up study, Polio and Duff (1994) identified a number of different uses of the L1, each of which they explored qualitatively through illustrative extracts from the lessons. Table 5.4 summarizes their main findings. Kim and Elder (2005) analyzed L1 use in terms of Ellis' (1984a) distinction between 'core' and 'framework' goals (see Chapter 4). They found that the teachers varied considerably in whether they manifested greater use of the L1 in interactions with framework or core goals. They also noted that the type of lesson influenced the teachers' choice of language: lessons involving task-based activities resulted in less use of the L1.

Teachers' beliefs about the use of the L1

A number of studies have explored the relationship between teachers' beliefs about the use of the L1 and their actual use. Macaro (2001), in the study referred to above, reported that conflicts existed between teachers' personal beliefs and their actual practice. For example, one teacher professed a commitment to conducting the whole lesson in the target language, but Macaro found that she used the L1 to explain the meaning of words, to reprimand students and for procedural instructions. Interestingly, this teacher shifted from a 'virtual position' (i.e. total exclusion of the L1) to a 'maximal position' (i.e. ideally teachers should use the target language but sometimes teachers need to resort to the L1). For this teacher, then, the exigencies of accomplishing a language lesson led her to acknowledge that some uses of the L1 were legitimate. Edstrom (2006) compared her own beliefs about the use of the L1 and her actual practice in a beginning-level university Spanish class. Edstrom was broadly committed to maximizing the use of the target language but found that she resorted to the L1 for grammar instruction, classroom management and to address comprehension problems. She identified three reasons for her use of the L1; the need to establish rapport and solidarity with the students, the impossibility of achieving certain goals (such as cultural awareness) through the target language, and the sheer effort of maintaining communication throughout a lesson in the L2. Song and Andrews (2008) examined the beliefs of four university level Chinese teachers of English and their L1 use. The teachers varied in terms of whether they were pro- or anti-L1 use. Again, there was not always a close relationship between these teachers' beliefs and their classroom practice. In part, this could be explained by the content of the syllabuses they were working from, with language- or culture-oriented syllabuses more likely to lend themselves to L1 use. All of these studies demonstrate the gap between an 'ideal' and the reality of the classroom.

Table 5.4 Functions of teachers' L1 use (based on Polio and Duff, 1994)

Categories of L1 use	Description	Findings
Classroom administrative vocabulary	Use of L1 words to refer to aspects of the culture of the university classroom (e.g. 'review section', 'mid-term', 'homework'.	The L1 words were typically inserted into TL utterances.
Grammar instruction	Use of the L1 to explain grammatical concepts.	This was very common and involved whole utterances in the L1.
Classroom management	Use of the L1 to set up learning activities.	Some teachers used the L1 exclusively; others code-switched (i.e. used a mixture of English and the TL).
Empathy/solidarity	The use of the L1 for interpersonal and rapport-building purposes.	Some teachers used the L1 to digress from instructional sequences in order to background their role as teachers (e.g. joking in the L1).
Practising English	The use of the L1 by students to help their teacher's non-native English.	Students provided English equivalents for TL items.
Unknown vocabulary/ translation	The use of the L1 to show the meaning of TL items.	Teachers used the TL item first and then gave the LI translation.
Lack of comprehension	The use of the L1 to resolve students' comprehension problems.	This was 'surprisingly uncommon'.
Interactive effect	The teacher responded to a student using the L1 by using the L1 him/herself.	There appeared to a reciprocal effect – the use of the L1 by one participant led to its use by another.

Final comment

Theoreticians and many teachers share the view that it is important for the teacher to maximize exposure to the L2 in the classroom. Turnbull and Arnett (2002), in a review of the research on teacher's use of the target language and L1, claim that there is a 'near consensus' on this issue. However, it is also clear that teachers often do make use of the learners' L1 even when they adhere to a 'maximal position' about the use of the target language. Also, in the opinion of some commentators, using the L1 is desirable not just because it helps teachers to meet the practical needs of managing life in a classroom but also because it can help language learning. What is missing from the research on this issue are studies that have attempted to investigate to what extent the teacher's variable use of the target language and the L1 affect learning. Claims and counter-claims about the relationship between L1 use and learning have run far ahead of the evidence.

One thing is clear, as Song and Andrews (2008) pointed out, teachers' attitudes and practices regarding the use of the L1 'cannot be changed by coercion' (p. 201). In other words official policy is unlikely to have much impact on how much or for what purposes teachers use the L1. Kang (2008), for example, reports a study of one Korean elementary teachers' response to the 'teaching English through English' policy in Korea, showing that the teacher neither fully believed in this policy nor practiced it. If change is needed it is more likely to be brought about by encouraging teachers to reflect on their own practices (Edstrom, 2009).

Use of Metalanguage

We have already noted that teachers often use the learners' L1 when providing metalinguistic explanations of grammatical points. However, they also use the target language, especially with more advanced learners. In this section we will examine the case for using metalanguage and the research that has investigated both teachers' beliefs about its use and their actual practice.

Defining 'metalanguage'

The term 'metalanguage' can have both a broad and a narrow definition. Berry (2005) argues for the broad definition – 'any language about language (that is, comments on the code' (p. 17) – but acknowledges that the narrow definition has prevailed in applied linguistics (i.e. the technical terminology used to talk about language). Indeed this is the meaning I attributed to the term when I defined metalingual knowledge as 'the technical terminology needed to describe language' (Ellis 1994: 714). However, I have also acknowledged (see Ellis, 2004) that metalanguage includes both highly technical terms (e.g. 'dative alternation') and also semi-technical terms (e.g. 'word' or 'sentence'). Defined in this way the distinction between the broad and narrow definition that Berry makes is not so clear. For me, metalanguage is the language used to talk about language. It implies 'metalinguistic awareness' on the part of the user, but as Berry rightly points out, this can exist independently of metalanguage (i.e. a person can perform a conscious and reflective judgement about the grammaticality of a sentence without recourse to any metalanguage).

Do teachers need metalingual knowledge?

The need for teachers to have access to a rich metalanguage is debatable. The debate centres on the utility of teachers using metalanguage in their teaching. Alderson

(1997) questioned whether university teachers of foreign languages in the United Kingdom were right to assume that metalanguage was an essential element of teaching even at this level:

> Many university modern language teachers bemoan the 'fact' that their students do not have any metalanguage ... If students simply need metalinguistic knowledge in order to understand language classes because such metalanguage is in common use, one possible option is to change the way one teaches, and avoid using any metalanguage (p. 2).

Alderson's doubt about the use of metalanguage was informed by his finding that there was no relationship between learners' own knowledge of metalanguage and their language proficiency (see, Alderson, Clapham and Steel, 1997). However, as Berry (2005) points out other studies (e.g. Renout, 2001) have reported a correlation between learners' metalingual knowledge and language proficiency. In any case, it does not follow that because there is no relationship between the *learners'* metalingual knowledge and proficiency that such knowledge is of no value to *teachers*. It is quite feasible that the teachers' adroit use of metalanguage assists language acquisition (i.e. the development of proficiency). Indeed there is some evidence that this is the case.

The debate about the value of teachers using metalanguage reflects a larger issue – namely, whether language teaching should treat the target language as a 'tool' for communication or an 'object' to be dissected and studied as 'accumulated entities' (Rutherford, 1988). Clearly when teachers use metalanguage they are treating the language as an 'object'. However, as we will see, teachers can make effective use of metalanguage in communicative-type lessons as well as more traditional, form-focused lessons.

Hu (2010) gave four reasons why teachers should be able to use metalanguage: (1) many learners possess a rich metalinguistic knowledge and teachers need to be able to tap into this, (2) explicit discussion of language is advantageous at times, even in communicative lessons, (3) the use of metalanguage allows for 'explanatory precision', and (4) metalanguage can help learners make the link between what they already know and new knowledge. Hu, like many commentators, concludes by suggesting that metalingual comments need to be integrated into meaning-focused pedagogy.

Studies of teachers' use of metalanguage

Relatively few studies have examined teachers' use of metalanguage and those that have done so have focused more or less exclusively on grammatical terminology. Brumfit, Mitchell and Hooper (1996) looked at teachers' use of metalanguage in foreign language classrooms in Britain and reported that this dealt more or less exclusively with 'language as a system' to the neglect of sociolinguistic and pragmatic aspects of language. Borg (2003) reviewed a number of studies of teachers' declarative knowledge about grammar, which showed that teachers often lack an adequate level of grammatical knowledge. Interestingly, non-native speaking teachers were found to demonstrate higher levels of grammatical knowledge than native speaking teachers (Andrews, 1999).

Borg (1998) conducted a qualitative study of one teacher's pedagogical beliefs and their relationship to his actual practice. He reported that this teacher used grammatical terminology quite freely but also manifested doubts about its value (e.g. on one occasion when a student asked about the name of a tense the teacher replied 'The name doesn't matter'). When asked about his use of metalanguage, the teacher replied that it was helpful because students enjoy an 'intellectual spot' in a lesson but that care had to be taken to ensure that 'nobody feels alienated in any way' (p. 20). This teacher also indicated in what ways metalanguage assisted his teaching: (1) it provided an effective means for communicating about language, (2) it facilitated diagnostic work, and (3) it helped learners to become autonomous investigators of language. These views about the value of metalanguage were in stark contrast to those promulgated in this teacher's initial training, which emphasized the need to avoid the use of grammatical labels.

Borg (1999) investigated how four teachers' cognitions about the use of metalanguage were reflected in their actual use of it in the classroom. He found that 'with respect to the use of terminology, all four teachers had developed stances which did overlap in certain aspects, but which were clearly individualized' (p. 118). For example, Hanna thought that grammatical jargon was unnecessary, could alienate students and did not promote the use of the language. She avoided terminology but did respond to students' requests about grammatical concepts. Eric (the same teacher as in Borg, 1998) saw greater merit in the use of grammatical terminology and promoted talk about language. Borg concluded by noting that the teachers' beliefs about metalanguage were not related directly to their practices both because these sometimes conflicted with other beliefs and because the decisions they took about when to use terminology were interactive (i.e. were undertaken in real time in accordance with the micro-contexts that arose in a lesson). In a later study, Phipps and Borg (2009) also noted a number of tensions between teachers' beliefs and practices. One teacher, for example, stated he preferred not to present rules to students but did so because he felt it would motivate and engage them. To explain this discrepancy, Phipps and Borg distinguished teachers' 'core beliefs' (e.g. 'it is important to respond to students' expectations') and their 'peripheral beliefs' (e.g. 'teachers should minimize the use of metalanguage when presenting grammatical structures') and argued that when there is a conflict teachers act in accordance with their core beliefs as these are more firmly grounded in experience.

Basturkmen, Loewen, and Ellis (2002) investigated the extent to which teachers used metalanguage in lessons based on communicative tasks. A clear finding was that the teachers did use metalanguage in such lessons. Interestingly, it occurred more frequently in teacher-initiated form-focused episodes (i.e. where the teachers elected to draw attention to language even though no linguistic or communicative problem had arisen) than in reactive episodes where the teachers corrected students' errors. Altogether metalanguage occurred in 32 per cent of the total form-focused episodes in these lessons but most of the terms used were of a semi-technical nature (for example, 'mean', 'question' and 'verb'), reflecting the teachers' assessment of their students' general lack of metalanguage.

The role of metalanguage in L2 learning

A number of studies (e.g. Alderson, Clapham and Steel, 1997; Berry, 2009; Renout, 2001) have examined the relationship between learners' metalingual knowledge and language proficiency with mixed results. However, only a few studies have examined the effect of teachers' use of metalanguage on learning. Basturkmen, Loewen and Ellis (2002) examined whether metalanguage was related to student repair of their errors, an aspect of learner language that has been hypothesized to be important for learning. They found no evidence of any relationship, although this may simply have reflected the low incidence of metalanguage in the communicatively oriented discourse they investigated. Other studies of corrective feedback have investigated the effect of metalinguistic comments on learning. These are considered in the next section.

Final comment

Researchers' views about the value of teachers' use of metalanguage in the classroom differ markedly and this appears to be reflected in teachers' own beliefs and practice. It is clear, however, that teachers' use of metalanguage is widespread with adult L2 learners. It is also clear that metalingual comments are not restricted to form-and-accuracy contexts; they also occur in meaning-and-fluency contexts. The research to date has focused on grammatical terminology. Teachers appear to make few metalingual references to sociolinguistic or discourse aspects of L2 use. The extent to which the teacher's use of metalanguage assists language acquisition remains largely unstudied to date. There is some evidence that it can help learners to participate more effectively in interactions focused on the production of specific target language features.

There is widespread acceptance in teacher education circles that teachers need to 'know' the grammar of the target language (i.e. they should be able to provide explicit explanations of grammatical points). 'Grammar' is a content strand in just about all pre- and post-experience training courses. In some contexts (e.g. Hong Kong), knowledge of metalanguage is seen as an essential component of teachers' technical knowledge (see, for example, Coniam and Falvey, 2002) and they are tested on it (e.g. by assessing to what extent teachers are able to identify and explain learner errors).

Corrective Feedback

Of all the different aspects of the teacher's language, corrective feedback (CF) has received the most attention. In this chapter we will be concerned only with descriptive studies of corrective feedback (i.e. studies that document teachers' beliefs about CF and how they handle learner errors in classroom contexts). We will not consider the substantial number of laboratory studies of CF nor the classroom-based experimental studies of CF (see Chapter 8 and Chapter 9). Also, the focus will be entirely on errors that occur in oral interaction – there will be no consideration of written CF.

Corrective feedback in SLA and language pedagogy

Corrective feedback has attracted the attention of both SLA researchers and teacher educators. The term 'corrective feedback' is used by researchers who draw on interactionist-cognitive theories of L2 acquisition. It refers to the specific move that corrects a learner error. The term 'repair' (see Chapter 4) is the preferred term of conversational analysts. It refers to complete episodes where some kind of problem arises and is addressed. Here we will be concerned with the corrective feedback moves performed by teachers.

Second language acquisition (SLA) researchers are concerned with whether corrective feedback has any effect on learners' interlanguage development and, for those who argue it does, what type of CF is most effective. There is currently no agreement about whether CF is desirable and even less agreement about how is should be undertaken. Teacher educators also vary in the advice they give to teachers about how to conduct CF. A brief inspection of some popular teacher handbooks (e.g. Harmer, 1983; Hedge, 2000; Ur, 1996) reveals both the importance that teacher educators attach to CF and also the differences that exist regarding whether teachers should correct, what errors should be corrected, when and how correction should be undertaken and who should provide the correction (i.e. the teacher or the students).

Corrective feedback figures in both cognitive and sociocultural theories of L2 acquisition[3]. Cognitive theories emphasize that CF is most likely to assist acquisition when the participants are focused primarily on meaning in the context of producing and understanding messages in communication, commit errors and then receive feedback that they recognize as corrective. In this way, learners are helped to see how a particular linguistic form realizes a particular meaning in context. Cognitive theories emphasize the importance of learners noticing the errors they have made and then comparing their own erroneous production with the teacher's corrective feedback move. Some theorists (e.g. Lyster, 1998a) have argued that 'uptake' (i.e. the learner's self-repair of an error following CF) promotes acquisition but other researchers (e.g. Long, 2007) have disputed this, arguing that CF works for acquisition because of the input it provides rather than through opportunities for learner self-repair. As we will see, this dispute underlies the type of CF that different researchers claim is most beneficial.

In sociocultural theory (SCT), learning is 'participation' rather than 'acquisition'; that is, it is mediated through and evident in social interaction rather than in the mind of the learner (see Chapter 4). According to SCT, there is no single set of characteristics of social interaction that constitute affordances for all learners. Rather, affordances arise out of the successful tailoring of the interaction to the developmental level of individual learners. They occur when the interaction enables the participants to construct a 'zone of proximal development' for the learner – that is the learners come to be able to perform a language feature through the scaffolding provided by an interlocutor when they are not able to do so independently. The aim of corrective feedback, therefore, is to assist the learner to move from other-regulation in the zone of proximal development to self-regulation, where the learner is finally able to use a linguistic feature correctly without assistance. It follows from this view of CF that what constitutes a facilitative form of correction for one learner might not be so for another, either because it is pitched at a level too far in advance of the learner or because it fails to 'stretch' the learner by posing a sufficient challenge.

In language pedagogy the key questions regarding the practice of CF are:

1. Should learner errors be corrected?
2. If so, when should learner errors be corrected?
3. Which learner errors should be corrected?
4. How should learner errors be corrected?
5. Who should correct learner errors?

(Hendrickson, 1978).

Various answers to all five questions have been proffered. Ur (1996) noted that different language teaching methods have adopted very different positions to (1). For example, correction is seen as essential in the Audiolingual Method, but undesirable in Humanistic Methods such as Suggestopedia. A common position regarding (2) is that CF has a place in 'accuracy' work but not in 'fluency' work. Harmer (1983), for example, argued that when students are engaged in communicative activity, the teacher should not intervene by 'telling students that they are making mistakes, insisting on accuracy and asking for repetition etc.' (p. 44). However, there are also arguments for responding to learner errors immediately even in fluency work (i.e. it can help students to realize their own meanings in correct language). Various proposals have been advanced for deciding which errors to correct. For example, some methodologists have drawn on Corder's (1967) distinction between 'errors' resulting from gaps in learners' L2 knowledge and 'mistakes' due to lapses of concentration. They suggest that teachers should focus on the former rather than the latter. But again, alternative positions are possible. It could be argued for example, that learners need to have their attention drawn to their mistakes as this will help them avoid them in the future (Johnson 1988). There are also different opinions about how to answer question (4). Some commentators favour indirect forms of correction on the grounds they are less threatening to learners while others recommend more direct forms as these are more likely to be attended to. Ur's (1996) approach was to raise a number of questions for teachers' to consider and then to offer answers based on her own practical teaching experience. There is greater consensus regarding (5). Handbook writers frequently recommend that teachers first allow students to self-correct and if this fails try peer-correction. Such a view, however, contradicts the expressed wish of students, who have been shown to favour teacher correction.

These differences in theoretical and pedagogical viewpoints are not really so surprising. CF is a complex phenomenon. There are no theoretical certainties and no easy rules-of-thumb for teachers to follow. As Hyland and Hyland (2006) pointed out, CF is a form of 'social action' and as such will automatically vary in accordance with how a specific context is constructed by the participants – as we have already seen in the discussion of 'repair' in the language classroom in Chapter 4. Similarly, Breen (2001) argued that language classes are social events and that, as such, CF needs to take account of the socio-affective factors that influence how participants in a classroom interact.

Teachers' beliefs about corrective feedback

Differences are evident in what individual teachers think about feedback and how they handle it (see, for example, Schulz, 2001). While teachers generally feel the need to correct learner errors, they differ with regard to what errors they think need correcting, who ideally should do the correcting (the teacher, the student who committed an error or another student as in peer feedback), when they should correct (e.g. some teachers express the belief that it is wrong to correct errors that arise when learners are performing communicative tasks or engaged in expressive writing) and how they should correct.

Teachers' and students beliefs about CF do not always coincide. Lasagabaster and Sierra (2005) reported a study where they asked teachers and university-level learners to watch a commercial video and judge the effectiveness of the CF. Both teachers and learners concurred that 'more time, longer explanation, and the use of different correction strategies' (p. 112) were needed. However, Yoshida (2008) reported a gap between Japanese as a foreign language teachers in Australia and their students, with the teachers demonstrating a preference for recasts (see definition in Table 5.5) and the students a preference for the chance to self-correct.

Early studies of corrective feedback

Much of the earlier research on CF was descriptive in nature. A number of studies (e.g., Allwright, 1975; Chaudron, 1977; Long, 1977) set out to develop typologies of CF strategies with a view to identifying which strategies teachers' typically use and how consistent they are in their use of them. These typologies testify to the point already made – corrective feedback is highly complex. Chaudron's system, for

Table 5.5 Taxonomy of teachers' corrective strategies (Lyster and Ranta, 1997: 46–49)

Corrective strategy	Definition	Example
Explicit correction	'the explicit provision of the correct form . . . the teacher clearly indicates that what the student said was incorrect'	S: La note pour le shot. T: Oh, pur la, oh, pur ça. Tu veux dire pour la piqure. Piqure. Oui?
Recasts	'reformulation of all or part of student's utterance, minus the error'	S: L'eau erable? T: L'eau d'erable.
Clarification requests	'indicate to students either that their utterance has been misunderstood by the teacher or that the utterance is ill-formed in some way'	S: Est-ce que, est-ce que je peux fait une carte sur le . . . pur mon petit frère sur le computer? T: Pardon?
Metalinguistic feedback	'contains comments, information, or questions related to the well-formedness of the student's utterance, without explicitly providing the correct form'	S: Euhm, le, le elephant. Le elephant gronde. T: Est-ce qu'on dit le elephant?
Elicitation	This is of three kinds: the teacher (1) elicits completion of his/her own utterance, (2) uses a question to elicit the correct form, (3) asks a student to reformulate his/her utterance.	S: Le chien peut court. T: Le chien peut court? Le chien peut . . . .
Repetition	'the teacher's repetition, in isolation, of the student's erroneous utterance'	S: Le . . . Le girafe? T: Le girafe?

example, consists of a total of 31 'features' (corrective acts that are dependent on context) and 'types' (acts capable of standing independently).

The research showed that some errors are more likely to be treated than others (e.g. lexical errors receive more attention than grammatical errors), although, of course, this is likely to vary considerably from teacher to teacher. It also showed that there is considerable variation among teachers regarding the frequency with which errors are corrected and the preferred manner in which they are corrected. Teachers often simultaneously provide more than one kind of feedback on the same error. However, they do not correct all errors and are less likely to correct an error if it occurs frequently. Also, on occasions, teachers have been observed to correct 'errors' that have not in fact been made (Edmundson, 1985).

Two general characteristics of teachers' error correction practices emerge from these early studies - their imprecision and inconsistency. Imprecision is evident in the fact that teachers use the same overt behaviour (e.g. 'repetition') to both indicate that an error has been made and to reinforce a correct response. Nystrom (1983) commented: 'teachers typically are unable to sort though the feedback options available to them and arrive at an appropriate response'. Inconsistency arises when teachers respond variably to the same error made by different students in the same class, correcting some students and ignoring others. Such inconsistency is not necessarily detrimental, for, as Allwright (1975) pointed out, it may reflect teachers' attempts to cater for individual differences among the students and to balance their cognitive and affective needs.

Types of corrective feedback

Later descriptive studies have continued to examine the different strategies that teachers use to correct learner errors. In an often-cited study, Lyster and Ranta (1997) identified the strategies used by teachers in French immersion classrooms in Canada. See Table 2.2 in Chapter 2 for a summary of this study. The strategies are defined and illustrated here in Table 5.5. Lyster and Ranta noted that some teacher corrective moves involve multiple strategies (e.g. repetition occurred together with all the other feedback types). Other studies have shown that the same strategies are found in other types of language classrooms. An important point about this taxonomy is that it can be applied to both correction that is didactic (i.e. directed purely at linguistic correctness) and communicative (i.e. directed at resolving a communication problem). In other words, CF can involve both a 'negotiation of form' and a 'negotiation of meaning'.

The strategies shown in Table 5.5 differ along two dimensions, Strategies can be input-providing (i.e. the correct form is given to the student) or output-prompting (i.e. the student is prompted to self-correct). They can also be implicit (i.e. the corrective force of the feedback move is hidden) or explicit (i.e. the corrective force is overt).

Table 5.6 classifies Lyster and Ranta's strategies in terms of these two dimensions.

However, while the distinction between input-providing and output-prompting strategies is relatively clear-cut, the difference between implicit and explicit strategies

Table 5.6 Two dimensions of CF strategies

	Implicit	*Explicit*
Input-providing	• Recasts	• Explicit correction only
Output-prompting	• Repetition	• Metalinguistic clue
	• Clarification requests	• Elicitation

Table 5.7 Regulatory scale – implicit to explicit (Aljaafreh and Lantolf, 1994: 471)

 0 Tutor asks the learner to read, find the errors, and correct them independently, prior to the tutorial.

 1. Construction of a 'collaborative frame' prompted by the presence of the tutor as a potential dialogic partner.

 2. Prompted or focused reading of the sentence that contains the error by the learner or the tutor.

 3. Tutor indicates that something may be wrong in a segment (for example, sentence, clause, line) – 'Is there anything wrong in this sentence?'

 4. Tutor rejects unsuccessful attempts at recognizing the error.

 5. Tutor narrows down the location of the error (for example, tutor repeats or points to the specific segment which contains the error).

 6. Tutor indicates the nature of the error, but does not identify the error (for example, 'There is something wrong with the tense marking here').

 7. Tutor identifies the error ('You can't use an auxiliary here').

 8. Tutor rejects learner's unsuccessful attempts at correcting error.

 9. Tutor provides clues to help the learner arrive at the correct form (for example, 'It is not really past but some thing that is still going on').

10. Tutor provides the correct form.

11. Tutor provides some explanation for use of the correct form.

12. Tutor provides examples of the correct pattern when other forms of help fail to produce an appropriate responsive action.

Source: Based on Aljaafreh, A., and J. Lantolf. 1994. "Negative Feedback as Regulation and Second Language Learning in the Zone of Proximal Development." *The Modern Language Journal*, 78: 465–83.

is not. Implicit and explicit CF constitute poles on a continuum rather than a dichotomy. Aljaafreh and Lantolf (1994) developed a 'regulatory scale' to reflect the extent to which the oral feedback provided by a writing tutor was implicit or explicit. For example, asking learners to find and correct their own errors constitutes an implicit strategy, while providing examples of the correct pattern is a highly explicit strategy. An intermediate level occurs when the tutor indicates the nature of an error without identifying it for the learner. The complete scale is shown in Table 5.7. This scale was developed within the framework of sociocultural theory to investigate the role that corrective feedback can play in scaffolding learners' zones of proximal development. The underlying assumption was that corrective feedback would be effective if it was fine-tuned to the learner's development (i.e. provided the minimal assistance needed to induce a self-correction).

Given the prevalence of recasts in classroom CF, it is not surprising that this strategy has received special attention from researchers. Long (2007) sees recasts as an implicit strategy but other researchers (e.g. Nicholas, Lightbown, and Spada, 2001) have shown that the corrective force of some recasts is in fact quite explicit. Loewen and Philip (2006), for example, investigated the different characteristics of recasts in terms of linguistic focus, length, number of changes and segmentation. Such descriptions are useful because they enable researchers to examine the relationship between different types/characteristics of recasts and learner repair (i.e., whether the learner's response successfully incorporates the correction) and acquisition (i.e., whether as a result of exposure to a recast the learner is subsequently able to use the corrected form more accurately). Studies that have attempted this will be considered in subsequent chapters.

Choice of corrective strategy

Descriptive studies have examined the frequency with which teachers use the different CF strategies. One of the clearest findings is that teachers have a strong preference for correcting students using recasts. Lyster and Ranta (1997) reported that 55 per cent of the teacher turns containing feedback in immersion classrooms were recasts. The next most common type was elicitation, followed, in order, by clarification requests, metalinguistic feedback, explicit correction and repetition. However, there is variation both in individual teachers' choice of corrective strategy and also according to the instructional context. Lyster and Ranta noted that one teacher who taught more advanced-level students used a smaller percentage of recasts than the other teachers.

Yoshida's (2008) study helps to explain why teachers vary in the practice of CF. This study used a stimulus recall interview to examine teachers' choice of, and learners' preferences for, different CF types. The findings shed light on when and why teachers use recasts, elicitation and metalinguistic feedback. For example, the teachers claimed they used recasts because of the time limitation of classes and in response to learners' differing cognitive styles. On the other hand, the teachers stated they used prompts (e.g. elicitation or metalinguistic clue) when they felt sure that the learner was able to self-correct the error.

Studies conducted within the ambit of sociocultural theory have been less concerned with the frequency of use of different types of CF and more concerned with qualitative aspects of CF. In sociocultural theory, corrective feedback is seen as a key element in how teachers can assist a learner to achieve self-regulation through self-correction and thereby ultimately learn how to use a feature correctly without assistance. Aljaafreh and Lantolf, in the study referred to above, provided a detailed analysis of selected CF protocols to show how the degree of scaffolding provided by the tutor for a particular learner diminished (i.e., the help provided became more implicit over time). This was possible because the learners assumed increased control over the L2 and therefore needed less assistance. In more recent research, Poehner and Lantolf (2005) and Poehner (2008) have developed this line of research through what they call 'dynamic assessment'. Poehner asked the learners to construct a past-tense oral narrative in French after watching a short video-clip. They were given no feedback or mediation in this first task. Then they repeated the task after watching a second clip. This time 'they interacted with a mediator who offered suggestions, posed questions, made corrections, and helped them think through decisions concerning selection of lexical items, verb tense, and other language difficulties' (Poehner and Lantolf, 2005: 246). This interactive assistance, which was provided in the learner's L1, was 'highly flexible, emerging from the interaction between the student and the mediator'. Poehner and Lantolf showed how the native-speaker interlocutor (the 'tester') varied the specific mediating strategies he used at different times with the same learner and also with different learners. For example, in the case of one learner, he initially used quite direct clues (for example, 'in the past') and subsequently, when addressing the same linguistic problem, more indirect means (for example, 'there's something there with the verb').

Timing of corrective feedback

A final issue of interest is the timing of CF – whether it should be provided at the time an error is committed or whether it can be delayed. We have already noted that teachers vary in their belief about this, some preferring to correct online and others to delay correction, especially when students are engaged in a communicative activity. All of the research reported in the previous sections addressed immediate CF. There has been little attention paid to how teachers conduct delayed CF. An interesting exception is Rolin-Ianzati (2010). She identified two different approaches that teachers of L2 French used when providing delayed feedback following a role-play activity. In both cases the teachers initiated correction but in the first approach they provided the correction themselves while in the second they attempted to elicit correction from the students. The teachers she investigated were systematic in the approach they chose in a university introductory French course. For example one teacher invariably opted for the first approach, while another teacher used the second for most corrections. Overall she found a slight preference for the first approach. However, the teachers varied considerably in how they actually implemented their chosen approach. For example a teacher might elect to initiate student self-repair but then go on to review a particular error if students failed to self-correct.

Final comments

The focus of this section has been on the descriptive research that has examined teachers' beliefs about CF and their actual practice of it. The research shows that teachers often do have definite beliefs about both the need for CF and how best to implement it. However, there is not always a close match between their beliefs and their practice, in part because CF is essentially a social event that requires teachers to respond variably to errors depending on the specific instructional context they are working in and the individual learners receiving correction. As a result, teachers are often imprecise and inconsistent in how they deal with errors.

The research has demonstrated a number of core corrective strategies. These can be classified along two dimensions – implicit versus explicit and input-providing versus output-prompting. Typologies of strategies have allowed researchers to investigate the frequency with which different strategies are used by teachers. A clear finding is a preference for recasts (an input-providing strategy). Recasts cause minimum interruption to the flow of an interaction and are also non-face threatening to students. Qualitative studies of CF have been undertaken within the framework of sociocultural theory. They seek to show how teachers can 'scaffold' learner self-correction by selecting a strategy at the right level of implicitness/explicitness. With the exception of one study, the research has only examined immediate CF. There is a clear need for more research on delayed CF.

Teachers' Cognitions About Language Teaching

A distinction is sometimes drawn between three kinds of teacher cognitions: (1) knowledge (i.e. things we know and view as conventionally accepted facts), (2) assumptions (i.e. the temporary acceptance of facts which have not been demonstrated and (3) beliefs (i.e. the acceptance of propositions about which there is actual or potential disagreement). However, as Woods (1996) noted, the boundaries between these three constructs are unclear. He saw beliefs, assumptions and knowledge as interwoven into a system he called 'BAK'. My focus in this section, however, will be on 'beliefs', which following Abelson (1979), can be characterized as non-consensual, often abstract, evaluative, held with different degrees of commitment and potentially conflictual.

Types of 'beliefs'

Different types of beliefs can be distinguished. Ajzen (1991) proposed that human behaviour is guided by three kinds of beliefs. Behavioural beliefs link a specific behaviour to a particular outcome. In the case of language teachers an example might be:

> Maximizing the use of the target language in the classroom will result in faster language learning.

Normative beliefs are those beliefs sanctioned by a specific community that a person belongs to. For Korean teachers of English, such a belief might be:

> It is necessary to use the target language at all times in an English lesson.

Control beliefs reflect a person's estimation of whether it is feasible or practical to attempt a particular behavioural goal (e.g. the use of the target language). For example,

> It is sometimes alright to use the L1 to ensure that students understand how to carry out a learning activity.

Beliefs constitute complex and dynamic systems (Feryok, 2010). They are shaped by a variety of factors including the teacher's previous classroom experiences as a student, their own experiences of learning an L2, their previous teaching experiences and their teacher training/ education.

Another distinction is important for understanding why teachers behave in the way they do. Argyris and Schön (1974) drew a distinction between 'espoused theory' and 'theories of action'. The former is comprised of explicit beliefs that are used to explain what people believe they should do or what they would like others to think are guiding their actions. The latter is comprised of the beliefs that actually motivate a person's actions. The beliefs that comprise a person's theory-of-action may be implicit in part and only become explicit through reflection. Making beliefs explicit can effect change in a person's espoused theory.

This theoretical background helps us to understand why teachers' stated beliefs are not always reflected in their observed behaviours in the classroom. Dissonance can exist between behavioural and normative beliefs and, even more so, between behavioural/normative beliefs and control beliefs. Various personal and situational factors will influence which particular type of belief underlies teachers' actions. As a result, what teachers espouse as their theory of language teaching may correspond only loosely to their theory-of-action.

Research on teacher beliefs and practices

Borg (2009b) provides a succinct historical overview of teacher cognition research. It began in the 1970s when researchers started to question the value of method studies and of investigating generic teaching behaviours predictive of learning. Educational researchers now recognized that 'teachers were not robots who simply implemented, in an unthinking manner, curricula designed by others' but rather, 'exerted agency in the classroom – they made decisions before and while teaching' (Borg, 2009b: 1). Educational researchers switched from viewing teaching as 'behaviours' to seeing it as 'thoughtful behaviours'. However, this interest in teacher cognitions took time to impact on the study of language teaching and it was not until the mid-1990s that researchers began to examine L2 teacher cognitions. From this time there has been a steady interest in this line of research. Borg (2003), for example, reviewed a total of 64 studies and there have been many more since. As Borg noted, many of these studies focused on grammar teaching, including teachers' views about metalanguage (see earlier section).

This chapter has already examined a number of teacher belief studies. From these a number of general points emerge:

1. Inconsistencies between teachers' stated beliefs and their actual practices are common. We have seen evidence of this in teachers' beliefs about the use of the L1, metalanguage and corrective feedback.
2. Teachers' declarative beliefs may not closely match their procedural beliefs. As Andrews (1999) noted, it is important to examine both the declarative and the procedural dimensions of teachers' belief systems.

3. Teachers' belief systems can be inherently conflictual, creating what Golembek (1998) called 'hot spots', which have to be resolved through the immediate context of action.

4. Not all espoused beliefs are equal. Phipps and Borg (2009) distinguished 'core beliefs' and 'peripheral beliefs'. Thus, teachers may act in accordance with their peripheral beliefs only if they feel that these do not conflict with their core beliefs.

5. For many teachers, a core belief concerns the need to attend to their students' own wants and their affective needs. Thus, for example, even if teachers believe it wrong to use the L1, they may still use it to establish rapport with their students. Similarly, they may believe it best to avoid the use of grammatical terminology but still do so if asked a question about grammar by a student.

6. Teachers' beliefs sometimes conflict with institutionally mandated practices (e.g. regarding the use of the L1 in the classroom or the type of syllabus they are expected to follow), in which case they may sometimes act in accordance with their own beliefs and at other times conform to the mandated practices.

7. Purely personal factors may cause a teacher to suspend action based on a firmly held belief. Edstrom (2009), for example, noted that even though she was committed to maximal use of the target language, she sometimes resorted to the use of the L1 when she was tired at the end of a lesson.

8. There may be a lack of congruence between teachers' beliefs and their students' beliefs. The need to resolve this may also result in variable teaching behaviours.

9. Finally, teachers' belief systems are not fixed; they are dynamic, evolving as a result of new teaching experiences and teachers' reflections on their teaching practices.

10. Teachers' beliefs tend to be influenced much more by their own experiences of teaching and learning in classrooms than by their knowledge and understanding of research.

I will conclude this section with a brief look at a study that illustrates many of these general points about teachers' beliefs as well as the kind of methodology used to research them. Basturkmen, Loewen and Ellis (2004) investigated three ESL teachers' beliefs about 'focus on form' and their actual practice of this in task-based lessons. Focus on form refers to the attention to form that arises incidentally when learners are primarily focused on meaning. This attention can be initiated by the teacher or by the students. Basturkmen et al. (2004) elicited the teachers' beliefs by means of in-depth interviews and cued-response scenarios (i.e. the teachers were presented with a set of scenarios of typical classroom situations and asked to comment on what they would do in these situations). The teachers' task-based lessons were audio-recorded and episodes where a focus on form occurred were identified. Finally, each teacher was presented with transcripts of four of their focus-on-form episodes and invited to verbalize their thoughts about their interactive decision making in these specific contexts.

The teachers all expressed very definite views about how and when to focus on form. For example, they all considered student-initiated focus-on-form episodes undesirable on the grounds that they interrupted the communicative flow of a task-based lesson. They also expressed the belief that form should not be attended to unless there was a communicative need and were strongly in favour of student self-correction. However, there were also differences among the three teachers regarding which forms required attention (i.e. vocabulary, pronunciation or grammar) and how they should be corrected. Also, all the teachers manifested inconsistencies in their beliefs. For example, one teacher indicated that recasting a student's erroneous utterance was an effective way of focusing on form but also believed that error correction was best delayed until the task was completed. There were also clear examples of mismatches between the teachers' stated beliefs and their actual practice of focus on form. For example, they were seen to attend to form even though no communication problem had occurred. When confronted with these discrepancies between beliefs and practice they simply acknowledged the discrepancy and attempted to justify their actions. In other words, they did not consider the discrepancies problematic.

This study illustrates several of the general points above. There was a lack of congruence between stated beliefs (espoused theory) and actual practice (theory-in-action). There was evidence of conflictual beliefs but, in this case, no evidence that these created 'hot spots' that the teachers felt a need to resolve. The fact that they corrected linguistic errors even though they believed they should only attend to errors that created communicative difficulty can be explained in terms of the distinction between 'core' and 'peripheral' beliefs. Fundamental to these teachers practice was their felt need to assist their students to learn the language and this overrode the more peripheral belief that the communicative flow of the lesson should be maintained.

It is clear that any understanding of how teachers teach requires an examination of their beliefs about teaching. But it is equally clear that simply investigating their stated beliefs is inadequate as these do not always closely correspond to their actual practices. The practices themselves need to be investigated to provide evidence of teachers' procedural beliefs. The relationship between teachers' declarative and procedural beliefs remains a fertile site for study. A key issue for teacher educators is how technical knowledge about language teaching impacts on both teachers' espoused beliefs and their personal practical knowledge, a point addressed in Chapter 11.

Conclusion

The aim of this chapter has been to examine research that has focused narrowly on the teacher. It has attempted to answers two key questions: (1) What do teachers say and do when they teach an L2? (2) Why do they do it? To answer the first question I have focused on a number of general and more specific aspects of teacher-talk. To answer the second question I have examined the beliefs that teachers hold about these different aspects and the extent to which these beliefs inform their practice of teaching. There is, of course, a more compelling question that needs answering – namely (3) How can what teachers say and do facilitate language learning? A fair conclusion is that we now have a substantial amount of information regarding the answer to (1) and that we have an increasing understanding of how to answer (2).

By and large, though, we still know very little about (3) although some researchers have not been shy in drawing on theories of language learning to propose how teachers can best promote language learning. These theories differ in how they conceptualize the teacher's contributions to classroom discourse and how they view their role in language learning. I will conclude by considering two broad theoretical perspectives – the cognitive perspective that informs mainstream second language acquisition research and the socio-interactional perspective that is becoming increasingly influential (see Ellis, 2010b). These two perspectives have been reflected throughout this chapter and are summarized in Table 5.8.

Table 5.8 Focus on the teacher – cognitive and social perspectives

Focus	*Cognitive perspective*	*Socio-interactional perspective*
Teacher-talk	Teacher-talk that is well-adjusted to the level of the students will guarantee the 'comprehensible input' needed for L2 acquisition. Adjustments need to take place at the phonological, lexical, grammatical and discourse levels.	How teachers talk to students needs to take account of the goals of specific activities and the micro-contexts they give rise to. Thus, no general teacher-talk characteristics can be identified as universally facilitative of L2 learning. Register-like studies of teacher-talk cannot adequately account for the way teachers talk to students.
Teacher questions	Open, referential and cognitively demanding questions where teachers allow ample wait-time for students to respond will create the interactional conditions most likely to foster L2 acquisition.	Teachers need to vary the types of questions they ask in accordance with the goals they are trying to achieve and the specific classroom context/activity. More important than the specific type of question is the questioning strategies that can be employed to scaffold student responses.
Use of the L1	Teachers need to maximize their use of the target language – especially in foreign language contexts – in order to ensure that learners have sufficient L2 input for acquisition to take place. Thus, they should avoid the use of the L1 even in interactions centred on framework or social goals.	Code-switching is a natural phenomenon and thus should be permitted in the L2 classroom. Teaching is not just about 'providing input' but also about establishing rapport and the use of the L1 may be essential for achieving this. Also, the teacher can make effective use of the L1 to scaffold learners' use of the L2.

(Continued)

Table 5.8 (*Continued*)

Focus	Cognitive perspective	Socio-interactional perspective
Use of metalanguage	Metalanguage may assist the development of learners' explicit knowledge which may indirectly facilitate the processes responsible for the development of implicit knowledge. Metalingual explanations may also serve to prompt learners to experiment with new L2 forms in their production.	The use of metalanguage is socially motivated. Teachers need to be responsive when their students indicate a need for metalingual explanations. Given that the central purpose of the L2 classroom is to learn the L2 it is natural that teachers and students will orientate to the target language as an object and this can be facilitated by use of metalanguage.
Corrective feedback	Distinct corrective feedback strategies can be identified and investigated in terms of the extent to which they promote noticing of target features, learner repair of their errors and L2 acquisition. Teachers have demonstrated a clear preference for recasts but these may not always be noticed by students in a classroom context and may not be the most effective for assisting L2 acquisition.	The choice of corrective feedback strategy is contextually determined, with different types figuring more or less prominently in different macro- and micro-contexts. Effective corrective strategies are those that are adjusted to the individual learner.
Teacher beliefs	Teachers hold general beliefs that influence the decisions they make with regard to the different aspects of language use. These beliefs are amenable to change through both external inputs (e.g. a teacher training course) and through reflection on personal experience.	There is no simple correlation between a teacher's declarative beliefs and their actual practices. In order to cope with specific classroom situations, a teacher may disregard one belief in order to act on another. Practice is governed by procedural beliefs which are grounded in the teacher's social experiences rather than by declarative beliefs founded on a technical understanding of language and language teaching.

The cognitive perspective views teachers as providers of 'data' for language learning. It informs the search for those universal features of teacher-talk that will enhance learning. In contrast, the socio-interactional perspective views teachers as possessing a variety of beliefs and resources which will be drawn on variably to cope with the heterogeneous situations that arise in accordance with their previous social encounters in classrooms. There is perhaps no need to choose between these perspectives. We do need to know what the typical characteristics of teacher-talk are and whether these are likely to facilitate learning. Equally we need to develop an understanding of the social (and personal) factors that cause teachers to modify how they communicate with learners in different contexts and what the outcomes of such modification are.

Notes

1. Learners are more receptive to features in the input that have high type frequency (for example, the *–ed* inflection on regular past tense verbs in English) than to items with low type frequency (for example, the vowel change in 'swim/swam').
2. An example of a closed referential question might be 'How many children do you have?' If the speaker does not know the answer to the question it is 'referential' but clearly there is only one possible answer. An example of an open display question is when a teacher asks 'Can you give me an example of a polite request?' Here there are a number of possible answers but the purpose of the question is to test whether the student knows what a polite request is.
3. I have excluded any mention of accounts of corrective feedback based on Universal Grammar (UG). While there is some variation in the different UG-positions, in general CF is viewed as playing no or only a very limited role in L2 acquisition on the grounds that it constitutes a form of negative evidence. UG is seen as only responsive to positive evidence (i.e. to the data available from meaning-focused input).

6

Focus on the Learner

Introduction

There has been much less research on the learner's contribution to classroom discourse, probably for the obvious reason that learners typically contribute a lot less to the discourse than teachers and do so in quite limited ways. In classrooms dominated by initiate–respond–follow-up (IRF) exchanges, for example, the learner is frequently limited to the 'response' move. However, a number of studies have explored different aspects of the learner's contribution especially in the context of small group work, where there is more opportunity for learners to talk. Much of the more recent research has been informed by sociocultural or socialization theory; that is, it has attempted to identify ways in which classroom learners construct learning opportunities in interactions with the teacher or among themselves and how they develop the interactional competence needed to become a member of a classroom community.

I will begin by examining a number of longitudinal studies that have described the path that learners follow in developing linguistic, sociolinguistic and interactional competence in the classroom. I will then look at a number of key aspects of classroom learner language followed by a review of the research that has investigated small group work.

Longitudinal Studies of L2 Classroom Learners

Ortega and Iberri-Shea (2005) pointed out that 'many questions concerning second language learning are fundamentally questions of time and timing' (p. 27) and these are best answered through longitudinal studies. Their survey of longitudinal studies

Language Teaching Research & Language Pedagogy, First Edition. Rod Ellis.
© 2012 John Wiley & Sons, Ltd. Published 2012 by John Wiley & Sons, Ltd.

in the years 2002–4 revealed a total of 38 but interestingly none of these investigated learners within a classroom setting (as opposed to a naturalistic or mixed setting). In fact, there have been surprisingly few longitudinal studies of learners that have been based on observations of language use within a classroom setting[1]. One reason for this is the problem of obtaining enough data through observation, as individual learners often talk very little in the classroom.

Early studies focused on learners' grammatical development in order to investigate whether this followed a similar pattern to that reported for naturalistic learners. A little later the focus switched to how classroom learners developed pragmatic competence. More recent studies have adopted an ecological perspective; that is, they have tried to show how learners integrate or fail to integrate into their classroom communities over time and how this affords or deprives them of learning opportunities. In this section I will review longitudinal studies of classrooms learners' grammatical development, pragmatic development and socialization.

Classroom learners' grammatical development

One of the key findings of early research into naturalistic acquisition was that second language (L2) learners seemed to follow a relatively fixed and universal order of acquisition and also progressed through a series of stages involving 'transitional constructions' when acquiring structures such as English negatives and interrogatives (see, for example, the collection of papers in Hatch, 1978b).

This led researchers to ask whether classroom learners (i.e. learners who were entirely or primarily dependent on the classroom for learning) manifested the same pattern of development as naturalistic learners. This was an important question because the answer entails some significant implications for the role of instruction in the learning process. Three early studies investigated the order and sequence of acquisition.

1.   Felix (1981)

This was an eight-month study of 34 L2 learners of English in a first year class of a German high school. The students received one 45-minute period of English teaching five days a week with practically no opportunity for exposure outside the classroom. The type of instruction was traditional. Felix noted that 'there was hardly any room for spontaneous utterances; in their verbal products students were expected to strictly conform to the type of pattern presented by the teacher' (p. 90). Felix examined the learners' acquisition of negatives by inspecting the language they produced in language drills to see if there were any utterances that resembled those produced by naturalistic learners. The learners had no difficulty in using 'no' as an external negator but were unable to produce negative elliptic sentences (e.g. 'No, it isn't') until the third month, even though this pattern was the first to be taught. They were often unable to produce well-formed main verb negation sentences even though they received lengthy explanations of the grammatical rules for tense and number marking. For example, they used 'don't' and 'doesn't' randomly at the beginning of a negative sentence (e.g. 'Don't I like cake?'), in much the same way as has been reported for naturalistic learners. However, there were also differences between these classroom learners and naturalistic learners. They reached a high level of accuracy in elliptic negative sentences by the third month whereas this is one of the last features to be acquired naturalistically. Also a majority of the students' negative utterances were well-formed. What stands out from Felix's study is that even though the learners only had the opportunity to produce English in drills, their negative utterances nevertheless manifested many of the characteristics of naturalistic acquisition. Felix also investigated interrogatives with similar findings (e.g. many of the learners' utterances reflected those belonging to the early stages of the naturalistic acquisition of interrogatives).

2.   Ellis (1984a)

Unlike Felix, I examined the communicative speech produced inside an English as a second language (ESL) classroom. The learners were a Portuguese-speaking boy aged 10 years and two Punjabi-speaking ESL children aged 11 and 13 years. On arrival in London, they were placed in a language unit for recently arrived immigrants. All three learners were complete beginners at the start of the study, which lasted for two school years. Initially the two learners were entirely reliant on the classroom for their L2 input but over time they also had some limited contact with English outside. My analysis was based entirely on the communicative utterances these learners produced in their classrooms.

The developmental profile for negatives was more or less the same for all three learners and was very similar to that reported for naturalistic learners. Their first negatives were verbless, consisting of 'no' plus some other word (e.g. 'no very good'). A little later 'no + verb' utterances began to appear (e.g. 'No coming'). Other negator forms (i.e. 'not' and 'don't') also appeared. Later still, utterances where the negator was attached to a modal verb emerged (e.g. 'This man can't read). However, it was not until the end of the first school year in the case of the Portuguese boy and well into the second school year for the two Punjabi-speaking learners that negatives with auxiliary verbs 'do', 'is' and 'have' appeared.

Interrogatives also followed a well-defined pattern of development. Initially, the learners simply repeated the teacher's question. Then they began producing verbless intonation questions and some formulaic-type questions (e.g. 'What's this?'). Creative WH and yes/no questions occurred more-or-less simultaneously, initially as single words (e.g. 'Where?') and then more fully-formed as they analyzed the components of the earlier formulaic questions. However, it was some time before they regularly used subject-verb inversion in questions. Overall, the development of interrogatives was slower than that of negatives. I suggested that this slowness could be explained by the fact that in a classroom environment intonation questions (an early acquired form) serve as the natural way of asking questions.

This sequence of acquisition for negatives and interrogatives resembles that reported by Cancino, Rosanksy and Schumann (1978) for naturalistic learners of English. The same utterance types were evident and the stages of development essentially identical.

Table 6.1 Summary of Lightbown's (1983) study

Purpose	To examine the relationship between the use of *–ing* and *-s* morphemes in the teachers' language and in textbooks and the learners' use of the same morphemes in their speech.
Participants	Francophone students enrolled in Grade 6 ESL classes in Canada.
Classroom data	Audio-recordings of 15 class sessions for three Grade 6 groups at two weekly intervals over the course of a school year.
Textbook data	Copies of the textbooks used in the ESL classes – *Look, Listen and Learn* and *Lado English Series.*[a]
Learner data	Audio recordings of learners performing an oral communication game in pairs once in Grade 6 and twice in Grade 7.
Analysis	Obligatory occasion analysis used to calculate accuracy levels for V*ing* and *–s* morphemes in learners' speech. Frequency count of the verb forms appearing in the students' text books; frequency count of the verb forms appearing in six selected examples of Grade 6 teachers' speech.
Results	No direct relationship evident between the frequency of verb forms appearing in textbooks/teachers' speech and the frequency of use of the same forms in the learners' speech. A delayed effect was evident; extensive practice of V*ing* in Grade 5 resulted in overuse of this morpheme in Grade 6. The subsequent decline in frequency of V*ing* in the input and increase in frequency of uninflected verb forms led to learners showing a later preference for uninflected forms.
Conclusion	'By forcing learners to repeat and overlearn forms which have no associated meaning to contrast them with other form(s), we may be setting up barriers which have to be broken down before the learners can begin to build up their own interlanguage systems' (p. 239).

[a]Lado, R. and R. Tremblay. 1971. Lado English Series, 4 Vols (Canadian edition). Montreal: Centre Educatif et Culturel.

3.   Lightbown (1983)

This study reported on the acquisition of English by French-speaking students in Quebec (see Table 6.1 for a summary of the whole study). It followed 36 Grade 6 students through to Grade 7. The students had approximately 120 minutes of English in Grade 6 and 200 minutes in Grade 7. Lightbown noted that the students had few contacts with English outside the classroom. Data were collected from outside the classroom by means of a communication game played by individual students with a researcher. As in my study, therefore, the data reflected the learners' communicative use of the L2.

Lightbown investigated four grammatical morphemes – copula *be*, auxiliary *be*, Verb+*ing* and third person *–s*. She found that the overall accuracy order of these morphemes was different from that reported in morpheme studies of naturalistic learners. The main difference involved Verb+*ing*, which was performed much less accurately by the classroom learners. Lightbown found that there was a sharp decrease in accuracy of this feature from Grade 6 to Grade 7. Thus, whereas the Grade 6 learners preferred the V*ing* form ('He's taking a cake') the Grade 7 learners were more likely to opt for an uninflected verb form (e.g. 'He's take a cake'). This contrasts with the order reported for naturalistic learners, where the uninflected verb form typically precedes the use of an inflected verb form. Lightbown suggested that the students might have been over-exposed to Verb+*ing* in Grade 5 and as a consequence 'overlearned' it. However, when the frequency of exposure to Verb+*ing* subsequently declined, the natural tendency to use uninflected forms reasserted itself.

Overall, these studies demonstrate that the process of L2 acquisition in classroom and naturalistic contexts is very similar. Interestingly, this appears to be true for both foreign and second language classrooms. Even in classrooms where there is little opportunity for spontaneous, communicative speech, learners seem to resort to the same strategies as those observed in untutored learners. However, there is also evidence that the linguistic environment of the classroom has some influence on the course of L2 development. First, Felix's study showed that learners were sometimes able to produce target-like utterances from the start when performing drills. Second, Lightbown's study suggested that the acquisition order can – at least, temporarily – be disturbed as a result of input that exposes learners to one particular feature (Verb+*ing*). In a classroom context, learners produce both controlled and spontaneous speech. The effects of instruction are more likely to be evident in the former. When classroom learners are communicating spontaneously they are likely to draw on the same natural processing mechanisms that figure in untutored acquisition.

There is one other important point to make about these studies. Instruction can be viewed in two very different ways – as a 'syllabus' that determines the order in which grammatical features are taught and as 'input' that learners are exposed to through the interactions that take place. The effect of direct instruction on L2 acquisition will be considered in a later chapter (Chapter 9). Here we are more concerned with how classroom 'input' shapes incidental acquisition (i.e. the learning that takes place when the students are not focused on learning specific features of the L2). What seems to be the case is that a lot of the learning that goes on inside a classroom is incidental in nature and that it results in a similar pattern of development to the incidental learning that goes on in naturalistic settings.

Classroom learners' pragmatic development

Most studies of interlanguage pragmatics – whether of naturalistic or instructed language learners – have been cross-sectional. Here I will consider two longitudinal classroom-based studies.

1. Ellis (1992)

I investigated two children's acquisition of requests over a 21-month period. The classroom context – the same as that in Ellis (1984a) (see previous section) – provided ample opportunities for these ESL learners to produce requests in English, with both learners producing substantial numbers mainly in interactions involving framework goals. There was clear evidence of developmental progression. Initially, the learners' requests were verbless (e.g. 'big circle') and when requests with verbs first appeared they were formulaic in nature (e.g. 'leave it'; 'give me'). However, within six months the learners were able to produce imperative requests using a variety of lexical verbs and also conventionally indirect requests using the formula 'Can I have a ___?' From this time a greater a variety of requesting strategies began to appear (e.g. want statements and strong hints) and also variations on the 'Can I have ___?' formula (e.g. the use of 'Could ___?' and 'Can you ___?). By the end of the period of study, both learners were able to use a variety of devices to perform requests. However, the classroom environment also seemed to restrict the types of requests produced. For example, verbless requests continued to occur quite frequently right up to the end of the period of study. Also, the learners' requests were directed at a fairly small set of classroom goods (e.g. pencils, books, colours) and to the performance of a predictable set of actions (e.g. sitting, standing, moving, starting, stopping); thus there was little opportunity to perform requests with a heavy imposition on the addressee. Also there was no opportunity to address a non-intimate or socially distant addressee and this limited the need for these learners to elaborate their requests or to vary their request strategy according to addressee (i.e. the teacher or another student). I concluded 'the sheer routineness of classroom business may have provided a context for the acquisition of basic request forms but may not have encouraged the acquisition of more elaborate forms' (p. 18).

In this respect, the results of my classroom study were very different from those of Achiba (2003), who investigated the naturalistic acquisition of requests by a seven-year-old Japanese girl living in Australia. Achiba showed that this girl learned to vary her choice of request strategy depending on the goal of her requests and also that the choice of strategy according to goal changed over time. Although Achiba acknowledged that the girl's development of requests was not complete by the end of the study, it is clear that she made much greater progress than my two classroom learners. While it would be wrong to generalize on these two studies, it seems that the classroom does not afford the same opportunities for the development of sociolinguistic competence as naturalistic settings.

2. Belz and Kinginger (2003)

This study examined US university students' use of German informal second-person pronoun (T) forms in a tele-collaborative course where the students communicated via email and in synchronous chat rooms with native-speaking German students who were training to become teachers of English. Belz and Kinginger examined the 14 US students' development in the use of T forms over a two-month period. They noted that in the very first email contact, the German students invariably used T forms when addressing their US partners. In contrast, all of the US students used either the formal address (V) forms exclusively or a mixture of T and V forms in their initial communication with their German partners. In so doing the US students ignored both their German partner's use of T forms and also the explicit advice they had received from their instructor to use T forms. Nine of the 11 students who used V forms inappropriately subsequently received peer assistance from their German partners (i.e. they were explicitly instructed about the need to use T forms to display solidarity). Belz and Kinginger distinguished three different patterns of development in the US students that followed this peer assistance. Abrupt development occurred when a learner abandoned the use of V forms entirely once they had received peer assistance about the correct use of address forms. Gradual development occurred when, following peer assistance, a learner switched from primarily using V forms to primarily using T forms but still manifested some use of V forms. The third pattern of development – persistent variation – was considered to have occurred when the relative percentage of V used after peer assistance was greater than it was before.

Belz and Kinginger positioned their study within a sociocultural and socialization theoretical framework. That is, they sought to show how the learning experiences of particular individuals could account for the varied microgenetic development that they observed in this group of learners. They argued that the precise nature of the social practices that the learners engaged in mediated their idiosyncratic developmental pathways. In emphasizing the historically constituted nature of individual learners' acquisition of T forms, this study differs from the longitudinal studies considered above, which were more concerned with documenting universal aspects of L2 development.

Classroom learners' socialization

Whereas Belz and Kinginger's study adopted a socialization perspective, it was primarily focused on how learners acquired the linguistic means for performing a specific pragmatic function. The final two longitudinal studies are drawn from a rapidly expanding branch of classroom research – ethnographic discourse accounts of classroom learners that were directed at the 'understanding of roles, interrelationships, and intentionalities in ecologies of second language learning' (Ortega and Iberri-Shea, 2005: 37). In other words, this research is less concerned with learners' linguistic development and more concerned with how they are socialized into the practices of the classrooms in which they were learning. Acquisition is defined in terms of the interactional competence needed to function as a member of a community of practice (Lave and Wenger, 1991) in a local classroom context. It is documented through case studies of individual learners.

1. Lantolf and Genung (2002)

The learner that was the focus of this study – PG (a doctoral student and an experienced language learner) – enrolled in an intensive summer programme in Chinese in order to fulfill a degree requirement. Lantolf and Genung describe how she adapted to the requirements of the instructional methods employed by the Chinese instructor. The course was taught quite traditionally. Each lesson focused on a specific grammatical structure which was drilled mechanically and then practised through scripted dialogues, which the students were expected to memorize. In addition, there were English to Chinese translation exercises with the teacher calling on the students in a fixed sequential order. Lantolf and Geunung focused on how the type of instruction influenced the learner's use of private speech and her motives for learning Chinese.

In a previous German language class, PG reported having used private speech outside the classroom to figure out how to communicate in the language. However, this did not occur in the case of the Chinese language class. Instead, PG mentally rehearsed the dialogues she would have to perform in class and just practised the translations she would be called on to produce in class the next day. In the penultimate week of the course, however, the instructor introduced more communicative, open-ended questions. This led to PG using the same type of private speech she had engaged on during her German class. That is, she began to try to work out how to say things communicatively in Chinese.

PG began her Chinese course with an expectation that it would provide her with communicative opportunities to learn the language. When she discovered that it did not she was faced with a dilemma. She could either accept the instructor's traditional approach or resist it. Her initial response was one of resistance. She found that the subservient role she was expected to adopt as a student was an 'affront to her integrity as a person'. She tackled both the course instructors and the programme director, pointing out the inappropriateness of an audiolingual pedagogy for a course that purported to teach colloquial Chinese and complaining about the instructor's negative attitudes to the students. However, her comments fell on deaf ears. PG responded by readjusting her motive for taking the course. Whereas she had started off with a real desire to learn Chinese, she now determined to just aim at obtaining a passing grade and adapted herself to 'comfortable routine of drill'. As a result, when the instructor introduced a free-form question and answer activity in the penultimate lesson, she reacted negatively as this now conflicted with her motive of simply completing her degree requirement.

The point that Lantolf and Genung seek to make through this case study is that 'it is the quality of the social framework and the activity carried out within that framework that determine learning outcomes' (p. 176). That is, classroom learners are required to function within a community of practice and this determines how they react mentally and physically. PG shifted traumatically from a 'higher cognitive motive' involving an intrinsic interest in learning Chinese to a 'lower cognitive motive' involving rote learning and when suddenly required to act in a manner compatible with her initial motive but incompatible with her secondary motive she expressed resentment.

2. Morita (2004)

This study examined the academic socialization of a group of Japanese women enrolled in a variety of master-level courses in a Canadian university. The focus of the study was on the problems that these students had in participating actively in their classes. Morita collected data by means of classroom observations, weekly self-reports from the students, and interviews. She identified three principal themes in the struggle to participate in their classroom communities.

First, all the students faced a major challenge in establishing themselves as competent members in their classroom communities. The students developed an identity as less competent class members than other students as a result of the difficulties they experienced in fully understanding reading materials and lectures and in contributing to discussions. However, although this was a general problem for all the students, some of them were able to develop an identity as competent classroom members in some of their courses. Also, their identity varied from course to course:

> The same students could participate differently and negotiate different identities in different classroom contexts or in similar contexts over time (p. 584).

For example, Lisa, who was studying for an MEd in a Teaching English as a Second Language TESL programme, found herself unable to participate effectively due to concerns about her linguistic competence and her anxiety and insecurity, but she experienced 'significant personal transformations' (p. 585) over time. For example, she came to reject her identity as a 'non-native speaker' and to see herself as an 'English speaker' and, as a result, was able to participate more freely in class discussions.

Second, Morita explored in detail the 'voices behind the silence in the classroom'. The students acknowledged the linguistic and cultural reasons that are often given for Japanese women's reluctance to assume the right to speak in a classroom context, but also pointed to a number of other reasons – their limited content knowledge, their personal tendencies and preferences, their marginal status, their role as relative newcomers and the instructor's pedagogical style. Morita observed that even if they appeared to be passive, they were actively negotiating their multiple roles and identities in the classroom. Nanako, for example, changed her attitude towards her own silence after she had asked the instructor for advice and found that he did not consider her silence a problem. As a result she now felt able to remain 'legitimately silent' and began to see her outsider status as a strength. However, in other courses her silence continued to constitute a problem for her. In other words, Nanako's silences in her different courses 'had different meanings, causes, and outcomes as she positioned herself or was positioned variously in them' (p. 589).

The third theme Morita identified concerned the role played by the students' agency and how they positioned themselves or allowed themselves to be positioned. The students responded to being positioned as marginal members of their classes in a variety of ways. Some employed a variety of strategies to gain fuller membership (e.g. speaking up in earlier stages of a discussion). Some sought support from their instructors. Some elected to remain on the periphery of discussions. Still others attempted to resist their marginalization. Rie, for example, who as a third generation Korean in Japan had experience of what it meant to struggle as minority student, sought to negotiate her power and identity in the two multicultural education courses she was taking. In one she succeeded in constructing herself as a valued member but in the other was unable to escape from her marginal status even though she actively resisted it by challenging the instructor to make adjustments to the way she taught. In this case 'although Rie projected herself as a legitimate but marginalized participant, the instructor constructed Rie essentially as someone with a deficit' (p. 593).

Mori's study illuminates how students' identities and membership of classroom communities both shapes and is shaped by their participation. These Japanese learners all experienced 'silence' as a problem but for different reasons and they addressed it in different ways. Some were able to successfully struggle against their 'ascribed identities' but others were less successful. The study also highlights the 'local' nature of classroom communities and warns against trying to find universal explanations for students' apparent non-participation.

Both of these studies illustrate a number of important points about student participation in classrooms. The first is that classrooms constitute social contexts that require learners to participate in certain ways. Learners' socialization is the process of conforming to or modifying these requirements. The second point is that, for a variety of reasons, learners may find the process of socialization a struggle and may succeed or fail to socialize to their own satisfaction. The third point is that learners can elect to resist the requirement to socialize by asserting their own agency, challenging the instructor and thereby seeking to change the classroom context. The fourth point is that learners have multiple identities and which identity they draw on will influence their motivation to socialize or resist socialization. In this respect, then, classrooms are not so different from naturalistic settings – they are sites where learners have to decide whether they wish to assert their 'right to speak' (Norton, 1997) or to accept their assigned identities.

Final comment

The longitudinal studies considered in this section are representative of a general shift in the way in which classroom learners have been investigated over the last three decades. The early studies were informed by research in second language acquisition research (SLA), were descriptive in nature, and were focused more or less exclusively on grammatical aspects of the L2. Later studies switched attention to pragmatic aspects of learner-language. More recently, studies have been informed by socio-interactional theories of learning, focusing on how classrooms as social contexts shape the way learners behave and on how learners themselves can help to construct the local contexts in which they are learning. The earlier studies provide us with detailed information about the course of L2 learning in a classroom but have little to say about the forces that shape this learning. The socialization studies broaden our conceptualization of what it means to 'learn' in a classroom and also provide rich information about the factors involved. Arguably, these studies complement each other. We do need answers to questions like 'Does instructed L2 acquisition follow the same or different route of development to naturalistic L2 acquisition?' But we also need to acknowledge that L2 development involves much more than the acquisition of linguistic systems and we also need to deepen our understanding of why learners participate in the way they do in specific classroom contexts and the possible implications of this for language learning.

Aspects of Learner-Talk in the L2 Classroom

The longitudinal studies we examined in the previous section highlighted a number of aspects of learner-talk in L2 classrooms. In this section we will explore the research than has examined these aspects. The aspects I have chosen to consider are:

1. silent period and private speech;
2. formulaic speech;
3. structural and semantic simplification;
4. use of the first language (L1);
5. use of metalanguage;
6. discourse features;
7. uptake;
8. language play.

I will examine research that has investigated learner-talk relating to these aspects in both teacher-led lessons and in small group work.

Silent period and private speech

Some naturalistic learners have been found to undergo a quite lengthy silent period. Classroom learners, however, are often obliged to speak from the beginning and thus do not have the option of remaining silent until they are ready to start speaking. However, a number of studies of classroom learners have shown that a silent period is still common, especially in kindergarten or early elementary school classes. Itoh and Hatch (1978), for instance, described how their subject, Takahiro – a two-and-a-half-year-old Japanese boy – refused to speak English at an American nursery school for the first three months. Cekaite (2007) reported that Fusi, a seven-year-old Kurdish girl who was more or less a complete beginner was 'generally silent' during the first few months in a Swedish immersion classroom. Iddings and Jang (2008) similarly reported that Juan, a newly immigrated Mexican student, underwent a lengthy silent period in a mainstream kindergarten classroom. However, not all learners – even young children – elect to remain silent initially. Gibbons' (1985) survey of 47 children learning L2 English in Sydney primary schools revealed considerable individual variation, with a mean length of just two weeks' silence. It is also interesting to note that in studies that report a silent period, the learners were not completely silent but often produced some formulaic expressions right from the beginning. Fusi for example, made use of a 'handful of conventionalized phrases' such as summoning the teacher by name or simple requests.

The question arises as to why some learners opt for a silent period while others do not. Saville-Troike (1988) suggested that the reason may lie in differences in the learners' social and cognitive orientation. She distinguished other-directed and inner-directed learners. The former 'approach language as an interpersonal, social task, with a predominant focus on the message they wish to convey', while the latter 'approach language learning as an intrapersonal task, with a predominant focus on the language code' (p. 568). She suggests that while other-directed learners do not typically go through a silent period, inner-directed learners do.

Another key question is whether any language learning is taking place during the silent period. Krashen (1981) argued that it provides an opportunity for the learner to build up competence via listening. Evidence in support of such a position comes from Iddings and Jang's study. They documented Juan's involvement in the Quiet Mouse activity, where a student was chosen to walk around the classroom with a puppet to pick the quietest student. Iddings and Jang describe how Juan first contributed to this routine activity non-verbally but was clearly attending to the language used by other students (e.g. He, be quiet!'; 'I'm quiet, pick me!') and eventually began to produce such utterances himself. In effect, the process by which Juan was socialized as a participant in this activity served also as a process of language acquisition. Another possibility is that although learners may be silent in a social sense, they still engage in private speech, which mediates acquisition. Saville-Troike used a radio-microphone hung round the neck of the children she studied to record their 'silent speech'. She found that five of the children who went through a silent period manifested private speech (i.e. they repeated other speakers' utterances, recalled and practised English words and phrases, created new linguistic forms, substituted items in utterances, expanded them and rehearsed utterances for overt social performance). All five learners eventually began to speak, using at first single words, memorized chunks, and repetitions of other children's L2 utterances. However, a sixth child who manifested a silent period, failed to engage in silent speech and, unlike the others, remained silent throughout the study (approximately 18 weeks), apparently not learning any English. It is possible, then, that the silent period is an opportunity for learners to experiment with 'speaking' through private speech and that this assists the emergence of social speech.

Probably the most extensive study of private speech in interactive contexts is Ohta's (2001) study of adult classroom learners of L2 Japanese. Like Saville-Troike, Ohta found the instances of private speech varied greatly across students. Two students hardly produced any but one student produced an average of 54 instances per class. Interestingly, the teacher-fronted setting resulted in a higher incidence of private speech than pair or group work, which led Ohta to suggest that the students needed a 'certain amount of privacy' (p. 66) to engage in it. Ohta considered a number of ways in which these learners' private speech may have assisted internalization: it provided a basis for further rehearsal of linguistic forms in inner speech; it enabled the learners to test out hypotheses without the pressure that accompanies speech in social interaction; it had an assimilative function; and it helped to keep the learners actively involved in classroom work.

By and large the silent period has been investigated in classrooms involving young L2 learners in classrooms where the L2 functions as the medium of instruction. With the exception of Ohta's research, little is known about the extent to which learners in other classroom settings engage in a silent period.

Formulaic speech

Wray (2000) defined a formulaic sequence as:

> A sequence, continuous or discontinuous, of words or other meaning elements, which is, or appears to be, prefabricated: that is stored and retrieved whole from the memory at the time of use, rather than being subject to generation or analysis by the language grammar (p. 465).

Formulaic speech differs from creative speech, which is speech that has been constructed by drawing on underlying abstract patterns or rules. Krashen and Scarcella (1978) distinguished two types of formulaic sequences. Routines are whole utterances learnt as memorized chunks (for example, 'I don't know'); patterns are utterances that are only partially unanalyzed and have one or more open slots (for example, 'Can I have a ____?'). In Ellis (1984c), I also suggested that formulaic speech can consist of entire scripts, such as greeting sequences, which the learner can memorize because they are fixed and predictable.

Researchers have suggested a number of criteria for determining whether an utterance is formulaic. The following are the criteria proposed by Myles, Hooper, and Mitchell (1998: 325). A formulaic sequence:

1. is at least two morphemes in length,
2. is phonologically coherent (i.e. fluently articulated, non-hesitant),
3. is unrelated to productive patterns in the learner's speech,
4. has greater complexity in comparison with the learner's other output,
5. is used repeatedly in the same form,
6. may be inappropriate (syntactically, semantically or pragmatically or otherwise idiosyncratic),
7. is situationally dependent, and
8. is community-wide in use.

Read and Nation (2004) pointed out that no single criterion is adequate in itself and emphasized the need to consider multiple criteria. However, the key criteria applied in the studies of early-learner language referred to below appear to be (3) and (4).

Formulaic sequences have been observed to be very common in naturalistic L2 acquisition. Studies of instructed learners (e.g. Ellis, 1984b; Eskildsen, 2009; Girard and Sionis, 2004; Kanagy, 1999; Myles, Hooper and Mitchell, 1998; Myles, Mitchell and Hooper, 1999; Weinert, 1987) have also shown them to be prevalent in classrooms. Interestingly, these studies show that they occur in all kinds of instructional settings – ESL classes, foreign language classes, and immersion classes.

In Ellis (1984b), I observed that the three classroom learners I studied learnt formulas to enable them to meet their basic communicative needs in an ESL classroom, where English functioned as the medium of instruction. I was able to show how specific formulas were worked on systematically by learners. For example, the 'I don't know' formula was built on by combining it with other formulas:

> That one I don't know.
> I don't know what's this.

It was also broken down, so that 'don't' came to be used in similar but different expressions:

> I don't understand.
> I don't like.

'Know' was eventually used without 'don't':

> I know this.

and with subjects other than 'I':

> You don't know where it is.

I concluded from my study that formulas are important for beginner learners because they provide them with the linguistic means for performing functions that are communicatively important to them and also provide them with an entry point for the development of the rule-based knowledge they need to produce creative utterances.

Myles, Hooper and Mitchell (1998) investigated the rote-learned formulas used by 16 beginner French-as-a-foreign language learners. They tracked the unanalyzed use of 'j' + verb in the formulas *j'aime*, *j'habite* and *j'adore* in communicative language activities performed over a two-year period. The students' initial use of these formulas reflected the fact that the early activities required the exchange of personal information. However, they were then subsequently used inappropriately in tasks that called for third-person reference, for example,

La garcon j'aime le cricket (= the boy I like cricket).
Elle j'aime le shopping (= she I like shopping).

Over time many of the learners succeeded in segmenting the subject pronoun from the verb, often with a struggle:

J'ai . . . no oh . . . elle habite le town
(= I have .. no oh . . . she lives in town).
Mon soeur . . . . j'ai adore umm . . . elle adore la euh . . . elle fait les magasins
(= my sister . . . I have love . . . she loves the . . . she goes shopping).

Myles et al. suggested that 'the need to establish explicit reference (third person, in particular) triggered the breakdown of the chunks' (p. 351–2). In other words, the analysis of the formulas was linked to the creative use of subject pronouns in non-formulaic utterances. Drawing on the same data, Myles (2004) characterized the overall pattern of development as:

Formulaic sequences → verb extraction → morphosyntactic elaboration.

Not all learners progressed along this developmental path, however. For example, while some had freed the subject pronoun for use by the end of the second year of the study and had more or less dropped the inappropriate use of the formulas for third-person reference, others were only beginning to do so and still others had not yet begun to break down the formulas. The learners also varied considerably in the extent to which they acquired formulaic sequences. Myles suggested that their rate of L2 development depended on the extent to which they acquired formulaic sequences.

Eskildsen (2009) investigated one adult ESL learner (Carlos), collecting data of his classroom speech over a four-year period. He showed how this learners' use of 'can' evolved from low-scope patterns to utterance schemas. For example, early use of 'can' was restricted to four basic patterns: (1) I can + verb, (2) Can you + verb, (3) Can I + verb and (4) You can + verb. He noted that these utterances were 'multi-word expressions' (i.e. they consisted of 'a recurring sequence of words used together for a relatively coherent communicative purpose', p. 338) and that they were 'interactionally and locally contextualized' (p. 353). Over time Carlos developed a range of interrelated utterance schemas that allowed him to use 'can' with different subject pronouns and in declarative, negative and interrogative sentence types. Carlos displayed 'a constant development toward a richer and more varied linguistic inventory in response to richer and more varied interactional needs' (p. 349). However, Eskilden concluded that Carlos did not appear to reach a final level of constructional knowledge. Thus, Eskilden's study provides evidence of a 'item-based path of learning' but also suggests that even after a considerable period of time, classroom learners such as Carlos may not reach a full abstract representation of grammatical forms that first appeared formulaically. This conclusion mirrors Ellis' (1992) conclusion that there may be limits to classroom learners' L2 development.

Kanagy's (1999) study examined the interactional routines that occurred in a Japanese immersion classroom. She noted that the routines varied in the degree of formulaicity, with a greeting routine being the most fixed in form, content and response required, and a personal introduction routine offering greater variety. Kanagy reported that her study supported my own claim (Ellis, 1984a) that learners are able to store predictable discourse stretches as scripts and to activate them in appropriate contexts. She showed how initially the learners were directed by the teacher to play their part in the scripts but over time they were able to do so more independently. She also found that some students were eventually able to apply the L2 scripts from familiar routines to new situations. However, when expressing their own meanings, the children's creative speech remained at the one-word level throughout the year.

Formulaic sequences have been hypothesized to serve a number of different functions in the L2 classrooms (see Girard and Sionis, 2004). They appear to be strongly linked to the communicative needs of the classroom situation. In classrooms where the L2 functions as the medium of instruction, formulas are frequently linked to framework goals (e.g. they enable learners to obtain the materials they need, signal when they need help, defend their rights vis-a-vis other students). They also assist learners to carry out learning activities by, for example, claiming the right not to answer a teacher's question (by means of the 'I don't know' formula), or by fulfilling the demands of communicative tasks (as in the study by Myles, Hooper and Mitchell, 1998). They also serve a psycholinguistic function by helping to increase fluency and by providing 'islands of reliability' (Raupach, 1983) during which they can engage in online planning about what to say next. Finally, they may assist the acquisition of a creative rule system.

There is, however, disagreement about whether formulas are broken down and the parts fed into the learners' abstract rule systems. Krashen and Scarcella (1978) claimed that formulaic speech and rule-created speech are unrelated. According to this view, learners do not unpack the linguistic information contained in formulaic sequences, but rather internalize L2 rules independently through attending to input. In contrast, N. Ellis (1996) suggested that the analysis of chunks serves as a primary means by which learners bootstrap their way to grammar, a view supported for classroom learners in the studies by both Myles, Hooper and Mitchell and Girard and Sionis in two very different classroom settings. Eskilden (2009), however, questioned whether learners achieve full abstract representations. What is clear, however, is that formulaic sequences constitute a stage in the process of acquisition for classroom learners in much the same way as they do for naturalistic learners. Irrespective of whether formulaic sequences play a role in acquisition it is clear that they are a major feature of L2 learner-talk in many classrooms.

Structural and semantic simplification

A characteristic of formulaic sequences is that they are typically well-formed whereas early creative speech is characterized by structural and semantic simplification. For example, a learner may produce a grammatically correct negative utterance (e.g. 'I don't know') as a formula while at the same stage of learning produce markedly non-target-like creative negative utterances (e.g. 'No coming'; 'No looking my card'). In such creative utterances, structural simplification is evident in the omission of grammatical functors such as auxiliary verbs, articles and bound morphemes like plural –*s* and past tense –*ed*. Semantic simplification involves the omission of content words – nouns, verbs, adjectives and adverbs – which would normally occur in native-speaker speech. Simplification is a feature of early interlanguage but also occurs later on when a learner is under pressure to communicate.

Given that the goal of language instruction is to assist learners to produce well-formed speech, a question of some interest is whether the kind of structural and semantic simplification observed in the speech of naturalistic learners is also evident in the speech of classroom learners. This is likely to depend on whether the learners have the opportunity to produce creative speech. In classrooms, where learner production is tightly controlled by means of drills or rote-learned dialogues, simplified speech may be quite rare. As Corder (1976) noted:

> . . . learners do not use their interlanguage very often in the classroom for what we call 'normal' or authentic communicative purposes. The greater part of interlanguage data in the classroom is produced as a result of formal exercises and bears the same relations to spontaneous communicative use of language as the practising of tennis strokes to playing tennis (p. 68).

However, even in formal language activities, interlanguage talk is not entirely absent (see, for example, Extract 3 in Chapter 4 and the account of Felix's (1981) study above). Also, in classrooms, where the L2 is both the medium and object of instruction and where there are plentiful opportunities to participate in communicative tasks, simplified speech is likely to occur quite frequently.

There is, in fact, plenty of evidence to show that classroom learners do simplify their speech both structurally and semantically. In Ellis (1984a) I provided a number of examples, comparing the learners' creative speech with their 'modelled' speech, as shown in Table 6.2.

Girard and Sionis (2004) provide similar examples in the speech of French-speaking children in a partial English immersion classroom. Their learners drop subjects (e.g. 'Is sleeping'), omit the copula ('Axel bigger Theo smaller') and morphological inflections ('He run'), and overextend formulaic patterns (e.g. 'Can I have a chips?'). Cekaite (2007) gives examples of Fusi's L2 Swedish creative speech. When the teacher refers to her as 'lilla Fusi' ('little Fusi') she responds in a determined manner 'nej lilla' (= 'I am not little'). When the teacher points out that that there is only one dog in the picture ('jag ser bara en hund har' = 'I am only seeing one dog here') she insists 'har tva' (= 'here two'). Myles et al. (1999) provide examples from the French-as-a-foreign language classroom they studied. The English-speaking students misused pronouns (e.g. 'tu aime' = 'she likes'), misformed questions (e.g. 'aimes?' = 'do you like?'), omitted the main verb (e.g. 'il j'ai' = 'he likes'), and misused intonation questions (e.g. 'Richard tu adores?' = 'does he love?').

Table 6.2 Examples of creative and modelled speech in the speech of ESL learners

Creative speech	Modelled speech
Lakbir blue (= Lakbir's dress is blue)	My name is John
Eating at school (= You eat meat at school)	It is raining
Sir, kick (= He has just kicked me)	It is snowing
You here (to teacher) (= Record the girl sitting here)	Show me 'ruler' on the board (repeating teacher's instruction)
Finish, Baljit? (= Have you finished, Baljit?)	I am writing
Me breaktime (= I'm going now it is breaktime)	I am not sleeping
Miss, my book finish (= My exercise book is full)	My name is Tasleem
	I spy with my little eye (repeating after teacher)

These studies show that structurally and propositionally simplified speech is prevalent in L2 beginner-level classrooms. In this respect, classroom L2 acquisition resembles naturalistic acquisition. Klein and Perdue (1997) and Perdue (2000) identified similar types of simplified speech in the L2 production of migrant workers in various European countries. They suggested that early-untutored L2 acquisition is characterized by what they called the 'pre-basic variety' (involving purely nominal utterance organization) and the 'basic variety' (involving utterances with verbs but only in non-finite form). It would seem that instructed L2 acquisition can involve very similar varieties.

Use of the L1

We considered the teacher's use of the L1 in Chapter 5, noting that there are marked differences in opinions about such use and also that teachers are likely to use the L1for management purposes and for empathy/solidarity (among other functions) even if they are strongly committed to maximal use of the L2. Here we consider the learner's use of the L1.

Early immersion programmes permit students to use their L1 in the beginning stages. While the teacher is expected to use the target language at all times, students are allowed to respond to questions or seek assistance in their L1. The assumption is that over time students will make the switch to use of the L2. However, although this does happen, immersion learners continue to speak in the L1 at times. Tarone and Swain (1995) showed that older learners (i.e. fifth and sixth graders) in French immersion programmes in Canada increased use of their L1 over time when interacting with each other. Tarone and Swain suggested that this was because of the increasing pressure on the students to perform important interpersonal functions such as play, competition, and positioning within their peer group. Lacking access to vernacular-style French, they resorted to use of L1 English. If this is true of immersion classrooms, it is likely to be even more so in foreign language classrooms, where the learners' limited L2 proficiency makes social interaction with other students in the L2 even more problematic.

Another study that investigated early immersion was Broner (2001). This study set out to systematically examine learners' relative use of their L1 and the target language, using VARBRUL – a statistical tool that enabled the researcher to identify the contributions of a number of different variables to the choice of language. Broner investigated three L2 learners over five months in a fifth grade Spanish immersion classroom. The analysis showed that the children sometimes used their L1 with another learner but never with the teacher. With peers, the use of the L1 was affected by the content of the activity, social relationships and whether the children were on-task or off-task. The L1 also played an important role in language play (see later section in this chapter).

The L1 can also be seen as a cognitive resource for L2 students. For example, learners, especially those of low-L2 proficiency, may be better able to develop ideas for L2 writing assignments if they conduct pre-writing activities in their L1. Stapa and Majid (2009) found that Malaysian students who generated ideas for a written essay in Bahasa Melayu produced essays that were awarded significantly higher marks than those of a comparison group that generated ideas in L2 English. Scott and De la Fuente (2008) also found an advantage for the use of the L1 when intermediate college learners of French and German performed a consciousness-raising task in groups. They reported that a group that were allowed to use their L1 performed the task 'collaboratively in a balanced and coherent manner' whereas a comparison group that performed the same task in the target language exhibited 'fragmented interaction and little evidence of collaboration' (p. 100).

One of the most potentially valuable uses of the L1 is in metatalk. Metatalk is of two kinds; there is the metatalk that learners employ to establish what kind of 'activity' to make of a task and also what operations to employ in performing it and there is the metalinguistic talk that arises when learners focus explicitly on language in the course of accomplishing a task. I will consider the first use here, reserving the second to the next section when I consider learners' use of metalanguage. Platt and Brooks (1994) described how university-level learners of L2 Spanish used their L1 (English) to talk about a jigsaw task, its goals, and their own language production. Brooks and Donato (1994) described how third-year high school learners of L2 Spanish used the L1 to establish their goals in a two-way information-gap task that required them to describe where to draw shapes on a matrix sheet consisting of unnumbered small squares. They found that even though the teacher carefully explained the task goals, the learners often felt the need to discuss these between themselves in their L1.

Much of the current work on learners' use of the L1 in the classroom has drawn on sociocultural theory. According to this, the L1 can serve the function of 'mediating' learning of the L2. Mediation can occur collaboratively through social talk but also through private speech (i.e. 'audible speech not adapted to an addressee' Ohta

(2001: 16). Both social mediation and private speech can take place in the L2 but learners often elect to use their L1.

L2 learners use the L1 in collaborative tasks to scaffold each other. Anton and DiCamilla (1999) examined the collaborative interaction of adult learners of Spanish. These learners used the L1 not just for metatalk but also to assist each other's production in the L2, as in Extract 1, where the students are composing a text about the eating habits of Americans:

Extract 1:
1. G: I don't know the word for snack.
2. D: Um . . .
3. G: Ohm so you just say 'in the afternoon'.
4. D: We we could . . . in the afternoon.
5. G: So what time in the afternoon?
6. D: Um . . .
7. G: Or do we want to just say in the afternoon?
8. D: Let's say . . .
9. G: Por la tarde?
10. D: Por la tarde . . . comen . . . what did they eat?

In this extract, the L1 is used to 'overtly address the problem of accessing the linguistic items needed to express their idea' (p. 237). Anton and Dicamilla note that this use of the L1 often arose when the students were faced with a cognitive challenge. When there was no problem, the learners created text directly in the L2.

Anton and DiCamilla 's study examined learners in a foreign language setting where the use of the L1 is perhaps most likely to occur as the students have a shared L1. Storch and Wigglesworth (2003), however, showed that L1 use has a role to play in second language classrooms as well. Drawing on sociocultural theory, they investigated the amount of L1 use by six pairs of students (each with a shared L1) in a heterogeneous ESL class in Australia, the functions served by the L1 and the students' attitudes to its use. Three pairs of students hardly used the L1 at all. Storch and Wigglesworth then told the other three pairs that they should feel free to use their L1 if they felt it would be helpful. However, only two of these pairs subsequently did use it between 25 and 50 per cent of the time. It served four functions: (1) task management, (2) task clarification, (3) discussing vocabulary and meaning, and (4) deliberating about grammar points. Interestingly, the students' use of their L1 was clearly related to their expressed attitudes. Those students who made little use of it thought that doing so would slow down the activity and also that they should use the L2 as much as possible. However, a majority of the students also felt that using their L1 would have helped them complete the tasks more efficiently. This study suggests that second language learners may be more resistant to utillizing their L1 than foreign or immersion language learners but that when they do so they exploit it as a mediational tool in similar ways.

Sociocultural researchers have also examined L1 use in learners' private speech. Lantolf (2006) presented evidence to suggest that learners, including those of advanced proficiency, may experience difficulty in self-regulating by means of the L2. He referred to a study by Centano-Cortes and Jimenez-Jimenez (2004), which audio-recorded native speakers of both Spanish and English solving a number of cognitively challenging problems presented on a computer in Spanish. The native speakers of Spanish produced only two brief private speech utterances in the L2, while the English speakers produced much more. This led Lantolf to suggest that 'the material circumstances of a particular task (in this case, the task language) influence which language an individual is likely to access for cognitive regulation' (p. 72). The English speakers' L2 private speech was limited in a number of ways. The intermediate-level learners only used Spanish for reading aloud the problems to be solved; they switched to their L1 as they tried to reach a solution. The advanced-level learners did make fuller use of the L2 while working through a problem but interestingly were not very successful in achieving a solution when they did so. In other words, when it comes to solving linguistic problems, the learners benefitted from drawing on their L1 for private speech.

In short, the L1 is used by classroom learners profitably in both social talk and private speech. It serves three main functions. First, it serves an interpersonal function, enabling learners to socialize with each other. Second, it plays an important role in metatalk, helping learners to establish reciprocity regarding their goals and procedures for carrying out an activity. Third, it enables learners to solve problems associated with their limited L2 resources.

However, it also worth enquiring what constitutes unprofitable use of the L1. Clearly, if learners do not make the effort to use the L2, acquisition will be impeded – as Storch and Wigglesworth's students were fully aware of. It is all too easy for learners who share a common L1 to avoid any difficulty they experience in using the L2 by resorting to the L1. Sociocultural researchers, however, have preferred to focus on the effective uses of the L1 and have had little to say about its ineffective uses.

Use of metalanguage

In Chapter 5 we examined the teacher's use of metalanguage. Here we will examine the learners' use of metalanguage, beginning with a look at studies that have examined the extent to which learners' possess L2 metalingual knowledge and then considering the actual uses they make of it.

The bulk of the research has focused on learners' knowledge of metalingual terms for talking about grammar (as opposed to other tasks of language such a pronunciation and vocabulary). Some studies (e.g. Alderson et al., 1997; Berry, 2009; Clapham, 2001; Elder, 2009; Elder et al., 1999; Han and R. Ellis, 1998) have addressed learners' general knowledge of metalingual terms. Of these, all except Clapham investigated 'breadth' of knowledge (i.e. the extent of learners' knowledge). Clapham's study showed the importance of investigating 'depth' (e.g. the extent to

Table 6.3 Selected studies of L2 learners' metalingual knowledge

Study	Participants	Instrument	Results
Green and Hecht (1992)	300 German-speaking high school and university learners of L2 English	Correcting sentences containing errors and explaining errors	Overall the learners could state the correct rule only 46 per cent of the time (but university learners 86 per cent)
Alderson (1997)	599 British university students of foreign languages	Test of receptive knowledge of grammatical explanations of rules and of grammatical terms	The mean metalanguage score was 49 per cent. Scores were higher for terms than rules. Best known terms were 'verb', 'noun' and 'subject'; least known terms were 'predicate', 'finite verb' and 'auxiliary verb'
Han and Ellis (1998)	30 mixed background learners enrolled in US intensive English language programme	Oral interview that required learners to explain verb complement errors in sentences; scale of metalinguistic knowledge developed	Mean metalingual comment score was 111.40 out of 170 with a minimum of 3 and a maximum of 147
Elder et al. (1999)	334 students of foreign languages at the University of Melbourne, Australia	Same as Alderson et al.	Similar results as in Alderson (1997)
Butler (2002)	80 Japanese learners of mixed L2 English proficiency	Participants' reasons for choosing articles in a cloze task	The learners were generally able to provide some kind of explanation for the choice of articles in a cloze task
Berry (2009)	Approximately 100 students each from university English majors in Poland, Austria and Hong Kong	Productive test of knowledge of grammatical terms	Means scores out of a possible total of 50 were Poland 23.87, Austria 21.33, and Hong Kong 22.55. Most known terms were 'noun', 'verb' and 'plural' and least known terms were 'finite verb', verb phrase' and 'concord'
Elder (2009)	249 mixed background L2 learners of English drawn from different learning contexts	Receptive test of ability to choose correct explanation of errors and of grammatical terms	Mean score for whole sample was 21 (out of a total of 40); L2 learners outscored native-speaking university students in knowledge of grammatical terms

which subjects can identify metalingual terms in a variety of sentence types). A few other studies have also examined learners' ability to verbalize grammatical rules explicitly (Butler, 2002; Green and Hecht, 1992; Hu, 2002). Some of these studies also examined the relationship between learners' metalingual knowledge and their general L2 proficiency.

Two basic methods have been used to investigate learners' metalanguage. The first involves designing a test of breadth of knowledge of metalingual terms. This can involve a test of receptive knowledge as in Elder (2009) (i.e. learners are presented with a short L2 text and asked to find examples of specific grammatical features from the test) or productively as in Berry (2009) (i.e. learners are presented with a list of grammatical terms and asked to first tick the ones they know and then exemplify them in a word or phrase). The second method involves asking learners to verbalize their understanding of specific grammatical features. One way in which this has been done (as, for example, in Green and Hecht, 1992) is by presenting a number of sentences that contain a grammatical error and asking the learners to first identify the errors and then explain them.

Table 6.3 summarizes a number of studies that have investigated the extent of L2 learners' metalanguage. These studies have investigated different learner populations. A number investigated university learners of foreign languages (e.g.; Alderson, Clapham and Steel, 1997; Berry, 2009; Elder, 1998; Green and Hecht, 1992). They reported varying levels of metalingual knowledge. For example, Green and Hecht found that German university students could state the correct rule 86 per cent of the time. However, Alderson et al. and Berry both reported that the learners they investigated scored less than 50 per cent on a test that focused on knowledge of metalingual terms. However, a direct comparison of these populations is not possible as the instruments used to measure metalingual knowledge were different. What does seem to be the case is that even university learners of foreign languages often have quite limited knowledge of grammatical terminology. Thus, while they can be expected to know terms like 'noun' and 'verb' they are unlikely to know terms like 'finite verb' or 'concord'. Other studies (e.g. Elder, 2009; Han and Ellis, 1998) have investigated second language or mixed populations of learners. Both of these studies show mean levels of metalingual knowledge in excess of 50 per cent but direct comparison with university learners of foreign languages is, again, not really possible. Second language learner populations appear to demonstrate larger standard deviations indicating greater within group variation in their metalingual knowledge. This may reflect differences in the extent to which they have experienced formal instruction. Elder (2009), for example, reported a significant correlation between number of years of formal study and scores on a test of grammatical terminology. Roehr and Ganem-Guttierez (2009) reported that cumulative years of study of other L2s and formal study of the L2s they investigated jointly accounted for 45 per cent of the variance in metalingual knowledge of university-level learners of L2 German and Spanish.

An important question is whether there is any relationship between metalingual knowledge and general language proficiency. This has been investigated in a number of studies (e.g. Alderson et al., 1997; Elder, 2009; Elder et al., 1999; Han and Ellis, 1998; Roehr, 2008). The findings are quite mixed. Some studies report significant correlations between levels of metalinguistic knowledge and written L2 proficiency. However, these are often very low. For example in the study by Alderson et al., the highest correlation between metalanguage total scores and C-test scores, which largely measured grammatical knowledge, was only .47. Han and Ellis (1998) failed to find a significant relationship between metalingual comments and scores on the SLEP Test or the TOEFL. These different results may reflect differences in the way both metalingual knowledge and L2 proficiency were measured. Elder (2009), for example, found that metalinguistic knowledge correlated more strongly with TEOFL scores than IELTS and not at all with a diagnostic test of L2 ability. It should also be noted that correlations are always difficult to interpret. Finding a statistically significant correlation does not allow us to conclude that metalingual knowledge contributes to L2 proficiency, only that the two are related in some way. However, it does seem reasonable to conclude that metalingual knowledge plays a role in learners' developing L2 proficiency[2].

All of these studies examined classroom learners' metalingual knowledge by means of various kinds of tests administered separately from the conduct of actual language teaching. Of greater interest, perhaps, is the extent to which learners make use of metalanguage during language lessons. A number of studies have investigated this. In the first of these, Basturkmen, Loewen and Ellis (2002) identified 30 different metalingual terms used by the students during task-based lessons (a smaller number than their teachers – see Chapter 5). The terms employed by the students most frequently were those that other studies have shown learners are most likely to know (e.g. 'sentence' and 'noun').

Other studies have documented learners' 'languaging about language' (Swain, 2006). When performing a variety of tasks such as dictogloss and reformulation[3] she noted that such metalinglistic talk serves two purposes: 1) it articulates and transforms learners' thinking into 'an artifactual form' and (2) it provides a means for further reflection on this form. Often it is conducted in the learners' L1.

A good example of the role played by learners' 'languaging about language' is Fortune's (2005) study. This explored the use of the metalanguage by adult intermediate and advanced-level English as a foreign language (EFL) learners in two British universities when they performed dictogloss tasks in triads or pairs. Fortune distinguished four types of metalanguage as shown in Table 6.4. He also distinguished different types of metalinguistic terms: (1) technical terms of the kind found in linguistic description, (2) non-technical terms frequently used in making generalizations (e.g. the use of 'general' and 'specific' to talk about article usage, and (3) non-technical terms used in metalinguistic interactions (e.g. 'it sounds right'). The advanced learners used more metalanguage than the intermediate-level learners (i.e. 46 per cent as opposed to 29 per cent) in the episodes where language became the object of talk. The advanced learners were also more likely to use metalanguage to formulate rules (i.e. Type M + R). In general, both groups of learners used technical and non-technical terms correctly. Perhaps the most interesting finding of this study,

Table 6.4 Types of metalanguage used by learners in a dictogloss task (Fortune, 2005)

Type	Definition	Example
M	Metalanguage used but without any of the features in the other types.	A. Shall we put 'the' or 'an' before 'earthquake'? B. 'The', I think.
M + G	Metalanguage includes the use of grammatical terminology.	A. 'An earthquake'? Or is it the definite article? B. Definite.
M + R	Metalanguage includes a grammatical rule or generalization as the reason for a decision.	A. Is it 'an earthquake' or 'the earthquake'? B. We use 'the' when something's been mentioned before.
M + T	Metalanguage includes knowledge of the textual context as a reason for a decision.	A. Before 'the earthquake'? B. No, 'an earthquake'. The story isn't about a particular earthquake, but any earthquake.

Source: Based on Fortune, A. 2005. "Learners' Use of Metalanguage in Collaborative Form-Focused L2 Output Tasks." *Language Awareness*, 14: 21–38.

however, was that the use of metalanguage was associated with more prolonged attention to a specific lexical or grammatical form (i.e. the students were more likely to re-engage with the form after it had been initially attended to). This study demonstrated that, for adult learners, the use of metalanguage in small group work based on tasks that invite a focus on form (such as dictogloss) is not only quite common but also potentially facilitative of language learning.

Many learners – especially adult learners – possess substantial metalinguistic knowledge of the L2. While there is uncertainty regarding the extent to which such knowledge is important for developing L2 proficiency, there is clearer evidence that it assists learners to focus on form when performing tasks. We will return to 'languaging about language' in Chapter 8 when we will consider studies that have examined its role in language learning.

Discourse features

So far we have focused on a number of discrete aspects of learner language in L2 classrooms. We will now consider the nature of the learner's contribution to classroom discourse. We have already noted that this is often quite limited as learners are frequently restricted to the responding move in the ubiquitous IRF exchange. However, opportunities for more varied and extended use of the L2 do arise. For example, there are opportunities for learners to initiate exchanges, to ask questions and for self-repetition, all of which have the potential to facilitate learning.

One of the factors that seems to determine the quality of learner participation in classroom discourse is the degree of control the learners exercise over the discourse – a point we considered in Chapter 4. Cathcart (1986) studied the different kinds of communicative acts performed by eight Spanish-speaking children in a variety of school settings (recess, seatwork, free play, ESL instruction, playhouse, interview, and storytelling). She found that interactions where the learners initiated talk were characterized by a wide variety of communicative acts and syntactic structures, whereas the situations where the teacher had control seemed to produce single-word utterances, short phrases, and formulaic sequences. Other researchers have also found marked differences in the quality of learners' participation depending on the kind of activity they are involved in. House (1986), for instance, compared the performance of advanced German learners of L2 English in a role-play situation, where they had considerable freedom, and a teacher-led discussion. She found that the learners confined themselves to an 'interactional core' in the discussion, failing to use 'discourse lubricants' such as topic introducers (e.g. 'You know . . .') and various kinds of supportive and amplifying moves. In contrast, the role-play conversations sounded much more natural.

Van Lier (1988) identified a number of turn-taking behaviours that he considered indicative of learner initiative (for example, the turn is off-stream, introducing something new or disputing a proposition in a previous turn). He went on to challenge McHoul's claim that 'only teachers can direct speakership in any creative way' (1978: 188). He noted that in the L2 classroom data he collected the learners frequently did self-select. Van Lier argued that learners need such opportunities because they allow for experimenting with language that is at the cutting edge of their linguistic development. Boyd and Maloof (2000) also examined instances of active student talk in ESL classrooms. They focused on students' digressions from a teacher-nominated topic and how these could be exploited by the teacher to create opportunities for language learning.

Further evidence of learner-initiated discourse in L2 classrooms can be found in Ellis, Basturkmen, and Loewen's (2001) study of 'pre-emptive focus on form'. This refers to episodes that arose in the context of task-based lessons where either the students or the teacher initiated attention to linguistic form in the absence of any attested learner error. The study found that the majority of the pre-emptive focus-on-form episodes, dealt with vocabulary, were direct (i.e. they dealt with form explicitly rather than implicitly) and were generally initiated by the students rather than the teacher. Students were also more likely to incorporate the form that was the focus of an episode into an utterance of their own when they had initiated the episode than when the teacher had initiated it. This may have been because student-initiated focus on form addressed an actual gap in students' knowledge whereas teacher-initiated focus on form only dealt with forms that the teacher hypothesized might be problematic.

One way in which learners can seize the initiative is by asking questions. As Mc-Grew (2005) noted 'questions may be the most acceptable way for students to initiate topics' (p. 62). Learner questions offer opportunities for a radically different type of classroom discourse from that typically seen in teacher-controlled discourse. However, they are infrequent in many classrooms and perhaps for this reason there have been few studies of them. Ohta and Nakane (2004) investigated student questions in Japanese language classes. They found that the students asked few questions in teacher-fronted lessons (only 20 in 40 hours of instruction) but directed somewhat more (23 in total) at the teacher while working in groups. Their study then focused on how the teachers responded to the students' questions. In general, the teachers provided direct answers, which Ohta and Nakane suggested were potentially facilitative of L2 acquisition. They argued that such exchanges enabled the students to act as equal partners in the discourse and provided them with solutions to their real problems. McGrew (2005) investigated the information-seeking questions that learners asked in a third-semester Modern Hebrew class in a US university. He distinguished four main categories of questions: (1) lexical (i.e. questions about the meaning or form of words), (2) grammatical (i.e. questions about syntax), (2) meta-pedagogical (i.e. questions about classroom activities and procedures) and (3) substantival (i.e. real-world questions not directly connected with the Hebrew-learning agenda of the class). Out of a total of 77 learner questions, 28 were lexical, 22 grammatical, 19 meta-pedagogical and 10 substantival. The learner questions almost always involved a simple initiation followed by a teacher response (i.e. IR rather than IRF). Questions directed at other learners were uncommon. More than half of the questions were posed in the learners' L1.

Another aspect of the learner's contribution to classroom discourse that has attracted attention is repetition. This is of course a common feature of some types of language instruction (e.g. audiolingual drill practice) but it also occurs quite naturally when learners are performing more communicative activities. From a cognitivist perspective, such repetition assists production by providing more time for the learner to engage in micro- and macro-conversational planning and may assist acquisition by consolidating what is being learnt (Skehan, 1998). From a sociocultural perspective, too, repetition is seen as a valuable tool for achieving self-regulation.

Duff (2000) investigated instances of repetition in learners' speech involving young learners, adolescents, and young adults in high school language immersion classes in Hungary and university foreign language classrooms in the US. She showed how repetition serves a variety of social, cognitive, linguistic, and affective purposes. She also illustrated through the analysis of two extended sequences how repetition in drill-like activities can become burdensome when insisted on by the teacher. Interestingly, however, this caused the learners to diverge from the teacher's topic by introducing their own, less taxing but more meaningful topic. In this respect, then, the enforced repetition led to a favourable shift in the discourse that afforded the learners more opportunity for initiative.

Other studies have focused on learners' use of repetition in group work interactions. DiCamilla and Anton (1997), for example, showed how learners' repetition helped to establish intersubjectivity. They examined five dyads collaborating in writing a composition. They repeated phrases, words, and sometimes syllables as a means of accepting and extending each other's contributions. DiCamilla and Anton emphasized that repetition does far more than increase the frequency of input, or make the input comprehensible; it serves as a socio-cognitive tool for accomplishing the task.

Roebuck and Wagner (2004) showed that classroom learners can be taught to use repetition as an effective tool. They trained students in a fourth-semester university Spanish course to use repetition (for example, by requiring them to repeat part of the teacher's question before answering it). They found that the students subsequently used unscripted repetition in peer interviews and also in more demanding dramatizations. They noted that the training was especially beneficial for weaker students.

These studies of learners' contributions to classroom discourse demonstrate that classrooms do afford opportunity for varied used of the L2, including those that resemble conversational discourse. The features that researchers have chosen to investigate – learner initiations, questions and repetitions – have been chosen both because such features can be found with some regularity in classrooms and because there are theoretical grounds for believing that they provide 'affordances' for language learning. However, to date, no process-product study has produced evidence of a causal connection between these features and L2 acquisition.

Uptake

Uptake is also a discourse feature. However, I have elected to consider this in a separate section as it has received a lot of attention from researchers and also because there are strong, theoretical grounds for claiming that it contributes more directly to L2 learning.

'Uptake' is a term that has been used to refer to a discourse move where learners respond to information they have received about some linguistic problem they have experienced. The move typically occurs following corrective feedback (CF), as in Extract 2.

Extract 2:
1. S: I have an ali[bi].
2. T: you have what?
3. S: an ali[bi].
4. T: an alib-? An alib[ay].
5. S: ali [bay].
6. T: okay, listen, listen, alibi.
7. SS: alibi.

The linguistic problem here arises in turn (1), where a student mispronounces the word 'alibi'. The teacher responds in (2) with a request for clarification, signalling that there is a linguistic problem. (3) is an uptake move but the student fails to

Table 6.5 Types of uptake move (Lyster and Ranta, 1997)

A. Repair
  1. Repetition (i.e. the student repeats the teacher's feedback).
  2. Incorporation (i.e. the student incorporates repetition of the correct form in a longer utterance.
  3. Self-repair (i.e. the student corrects the error in response to teacher feedback that did not supply the correct form).
  4. Peer-repair (i.e. a student other than the student who produced the error corrects it in response to teacher feedback).
B. Needs repair
  1. Acknowledgement (e.g. the student says 'yes' or 'no').
  2. Same error (i.e. the student produces the same error again).
  3. Different error (i.e. the student fails to correct the original error and in addition produces a different error).
  4. Off-target (i.e. the student responds by circumventing the teacher's linguistic focus).
  5. Hesitation (i.e. the student hesitates in response to the teacher's feedback).
  6. Partial repair (i.e. the student partly corrects the initial error).

repair the pronunciation error. This results in explicit correction by the teacher in (4), a further uptake move in (5), which again fails to repair the error, more explicit correction by the teacher in (6), and a final choral uptake move in (7), where the class as a whole now pronounces 'alibi' correctly. From this example, it should be clear that uptake following corrective feedback can be of two basic kinds – 'repair' (as in turn 7) or 'needs repair' (as in turns 3 and 5). Lyster and Ranta (1997) also distinguished different categories of these two basic types, as shown in Table 6.5.

Ellis, Basturkmen and Loewen (2001) defined 'uptake' more broadly. They noted that there are occasions in communicative lessons where teachers or learners themselves pre-empt attention to a linguistic feature (e.g. by asking a question). In student-initiated exchanges, the student still has the opportunity to react, for example, by simply acknowledging the previous move or by attempting to use the feature in focus in his/her own speech. Extract 3 provides an example of this type of uptake (see turn 3). In teacher-initiated exchanges, learner uptake is also possible, for example, when the learner repeats the linguistic form that the teacher has identified as potentially problematic.

Extract 3:
1. S: You can say just January eighteen<th>?
2. T: jan- january eighteen?, January eighteen? Mmm
       It's okay, It's a little casual (.) casual. Friends (.)
       January eighteen, okay, but usually January THE
       eighteenth or THE eighteenth of January.
3. S: January THE eighteenth.
4. T: the, yeah, good.

To take account of this type of uptake Ellis et al. proposed the following definition:

1. Uptake is a student move.
2. The move is optional (i.e., a focus on form does not obligate the student to provide an uptake move).
3. The uptake move occurs in episodes where learners have demonstrated a gap in their knowledge (e.g. by making an error, by asking a question or by failing to answer a teacher's question).
4. The uptake move occurs as a reaction to some preceding move in which another participant (usually the teacher) either explicitly or implicitly provides information about a linguistic feature.

It should be noted, however, that most of the research that has examined learner uptake has been based on the narrower definition (i.e. uptake as the move following corrective feedback).

A number of studies have investigated learner uptake. Many of these have been laboratory-based and have examined one-on-one interactions between a learner and a researcher. I will not consider these here. Instead I will focus exclusively on classroom studies that have investigated to what extent learners are successful in repairing the linguistic problem that led to the uptake move.

In a series of articles, Lyster and co-researchers (for example, Lyster, 1998a; 1998b; Lyster and Ranta, 1997) examined the nature of French immersion students' uptake of corrective feedback. Lyster (1998a) examined the relationship between different types of corrective feedback (see Table 5.5 in Chapter 5) and uptake. He found that learner repair of lexical and grammatical errors was more likely after elicitations, requests for clarification, and metalinguistic clues (which he called 'negotiation of form' and later renamed 'prompts') than other types, in particular recasts. For example, 61 per cent of the repairs of grammatical errors occurred after negotiation of form and only 39 per cent after explicit correction or recasts. Lyster and Ranta concluded that uptake with repair is more likely 'when . . . the correct form is not provided to the students . . . and when signals are provided to the learner that assist the reformulation of the erroneous utterance' (p. 58). Oliver (2000), in a study of ESL classes, also reported a low level of uptake following recasts. However, she noted that there was no opportunity for uptake following approximately one-third of the teachers' recast moves because the teacher continued his or her turn without giving the student a chance to respond. If the 'no chance' exchanges were excluded, the rate of uptake was quite high – 'impressive' in Oliver's opinion.

The extent to which recasts or other types of corrective feedback elicit uptake is influenced by a number of contextual variables. Lyster and Mori (2006) reported differences in uptake and repair according to the instructional context, in this case two different immersion contexts – French immersion in Canada and Japanese immersion in the USA. Corrective feedback consisting of prompts induced higher levels of uptake and repair in the French immersion context but recasts did so in the Japanese immersion context. On the basis of these findings they advanced the 'counterbalance hypothesis', which predicts that the extent to which different CF strategies lead to uptake/repair is influenced by whether the overall instruction orients learners to attend to form, as it did in the Japanese immersion programme, or to meaning, as it did in Canada. Oliver (2000) found that learner uptake of feedback was also more likely in a teacher-fronted lesson than in a pair-work situation. She suggested that this was because many of the recasts in the pair-work situation consisted of confirmation requests where the appropriate response was simply 'yes' or 'no'. Finally, Oliver and Mackey (2003) found differences in both the frequency of feedback, uptake, and modified output in the specific contexts within child ESL classrooms. Feedback occurred most frequently in explicit language contexts. Uptake and modified output were also more likely to occur in explicit language contexts. Feedback, uptake, and modified output were least frequent in management-related exchanges. It is clear, then, that uptake varies depending on both macro-factors such as the instructional setting and micro-factors such as the participatory structure of the classroom and the purpose of specific interactions.

Ellis, Basturkmen and Loewen (2001) investigated uptake using their broader definition of this construct. In a study that examined instances of uptake in 12 hours of communicative ESL teaching in New Zealand, they found that it was generally frequent and successful – to a much greater extent than reported in studies of uptake in immersion classrooms (Lyster and Ranta, 1997). Uptake was also higher and more successful in reactive focus on form and in student-initiated pre-emptive focus on form than in teacher-initiated focus on form. Other factors that influenced the level of uptake were the source of focus (whether it involved the negotiation of meaning or of form) and the complexity of an episode (whether the solution to the problem involved one or more than one exchange). In reactive focus-on-form episodes (FFE), recasts resulted in a high level of uptake that was also generally successful. Also, there was a trend for explicit treatment of error to result in more uptake than implicit treatment. Alcon-Soler (2009) reported very similar results to those in Ellis et al. for 14–15-year-old Spanish EFL learners. The level of successful uptake was not as high as in Ellis et al. but, again, total uptake was higher in the student-initiated and reactive focus-on-form episodes than in the teacher-initiated episodes. Explicit and complex FFEs were positively related to uptake whereas implicit FFEs were negatively related.

These studies show that learner uptake is common in many classrooms and also is often successful (i.e. learners are generally able to repair their linguistic problems when provided with assistance from the teacher). They also show that the extent of the uptake and of its success varies according to both the instructional context and the type of assistance they are given. From the perspective of sociocultural theory, the very act of repairing a linguistic problem can be considered evidence of acquisition. However, from an interactionist-cognitive perspective, as Long (2007) argued, it is necessary to demonstrate that learners are capable of using the feature that has been uptaken on their own, without assistance, before any claim about acquisition can be made. Some studies have investigated whether this takes place. We will consider these in Chapter 8.

Language play

The final aspect of learner language in the L2 classroom we will consider is 'language play'[4]. Cook (1997) defines 'language play' as 'behaviour not primarily motivated by human need to manipulate the environment and to share information for this purpose and to form and maintain social relationships – though it may indirectly serve both of these functions' (p. 227). It involves creating patterns of sound (e.g. rhyme and alliteration) and of structure (i.e. through creating patterns and parallelisms). It also involves playing with units of meaning (e.g. by creating neologisms). Language play figures naturally in the language of both children and adults – in games, riddles, literature, jokes and conversational banter.

Cook's definition of 'language play' emphasizes its creative, fun aspect. Lantolf (1997), adopting a sociocultural theoretical perspective, offers a very different definition based on the idea of 'rehearsal'. For him language play is evident when learners talk aloud to themselves, repeat phrases to themselves silently, make up sentences in the L2, imitate sounds in Spanish or when random snatches of the L2 pop into their heads. Lantolf specifically denies that this can kind of play is 'fun'. Rather it is a form of private speech that is utilized to scaffold learning.

In an attempt to operationalize these two senses of language play, Broner and Tarone (2001) distinguished a number of observable characteristics of language play as 'fun' and as 'rehearsal'. I have listed these in Table 6.6. These characteristics provide a basis for examining instances of both kinds of language play in the classroom.

Broner and Tarone discussed a number of examples of language play that occurred in the speech of three children in a Spanish immersion class. They examined examples of both ludic play and play-as-rehearsal. Extract 4 serves as an example of the former. The play in this extract centres around a pun and an insult, both of which Broner and Tarone noted were common in the children's speech. Leonard begins by questioning the difference between 'cerebro' and 'celebro' and when he continues to mix up the two words, Carolina exploits his confusion to insult him (turn 6) and then giggles. This has all the qualities of language play as fun.

Table 6.6 Observable characteristics of language play as 'fun' and as 'rehearsal' (based on Broner and Tarone, 2001)

Language play as 'fun'	Language play as 'rehearsal'
Accompanied by smiles or laughter	Is not marked by laughter
Accompanied by marked shifts in pitch or voice quality or both	Is marked primarily by a shift in volume (*sotto voce*) rather than in voice quality or pitch
Uses language forms known to be mastered by the speaker	Uses language forms known to be new to the speaker
Creates a fictional world of reference	Does not create a fictional world of reference
Appears to be addressed to an audience	Appears to be addressed to the self

Extract 4:
1. Leonard: cerebro: celebro (brain: I celebrate).
2. Carolina: cerebro (brain).
3. Leonard: cerebro? (brain?)
4. Carolina: cerebro (brain). You know the thing in your heads.
5. Leonard: si yo no tengo/selebro (if I don't have I celebrate).
6. Child A: You don't have one.
7. Carolina: giggles.

Extract 5 illustrates language play as rehearsal. The teacher introduces a new word ('volumen') and defines it. She then asks a question. However, Carolina does not answer it publicly. Rather she repeats the new word sotto voce to herself. Clearly, this is a word new to her and equally clearly there is no fictional world being created.

Extract 5:
1. Teacher: volumen, volumen se llama el espacio que hay dentro del algo (volume, volume the space that's inside something is called volumen)
y como se mide el volumen? (Waits for a response) (and how is volumen measured?)
2. Carolina: volumen: (whispering to herself) (volume).

Broner and Tarone also point out that there are times when both types of language play are evident in the same episode.

Further examples of both types of language play can be found in Bushnell (2008), this time in a second semester Japanese as a foreign language classroom in an American university. This study shows that adults as well as children engage in language play. Drawing in part on Broner and Tarone's earlier article, Bushnell identifies a number of ways in which language play creates 'affordances' for language learning:

- it can lower affective barriers,
- it can increase enhance memorizability,
- it can help learners to develop the ability to speak in other 'voices',
- it may promote destabilization and restructuring,
- it allows learners to commit face-threatening acts in an acceptable manner,
- it provides an opportunity for extended multiparty interaction where there is a focus on linguistic form, and
- it serves as a resource for organizing and engaging in social interaction.

Drawing on her own examples of language play, Bushnell shows how the learners reorganized the instructional tasks they were given in the form of 'task-as-play (i.e. they used on-task language in their language play). As such, she argued that language play need not be seen as unwanted 'off-task' behaviour.

There is, however, no actual evidence in either Broner and Tarone or Bushnell's studies to show that the 'affordances' provided by language play resulted in language learning[5]. In fact, in one instance (that shown in Extract 5), the language play may have interfered with the acquisition of the correct form (i.e. the children later used the wrong term – celebro – in a presentation to the rest of the class).

Learner-Talk in Small Group Work

This chapter concludes with a look at the research that has investigated small group work. In fact, many of the studies referred to in the previous sections reported on learner behaviour in small groups. Most of the studies that have investigated learners use of the L1, metalanguage, discourse features such as repetition and questions, and language play have been based on data collected from learners working in pairs or small groups. Only uptake has been studied in relation to teacher-class interaction. The predominance of small group work as a site for investigating learner language is not surprising as researchers need data to analyze and they are more likely to obtain sufficient samples of learner-talk from group work interactions than from teacher-class interactions. The focus of this section will be on the different approaches that have been used to investigate learner-talk in small group work.

Comparisons of learner-talk in teacher-fronted classrooms and small group work

One of the earliest approaches involved comparing learner-talk in teacher-fronted and small group work interactions. Long et al. (1976) reported that students working in small groups produced a greater quantity of language and also better quality language than students in a teacher-fronted, lockstep classroom setting. Small group work provided more opportunities for language production and greater variety of language use in initiating discussion, asking for clarification, interrupting, competing for the floor, and joking. Pica and Doughty (1985a), however, found no difference in the overall quantity of interactional adjustments in a one-way task performed in a lockstep setting and in small group work, but when they replicated this study using a two-way task (Pica and Doughty, 1985b), they did find significant differences. Thus, these two studies showed that group work results in more negotiation of meaning but only if the task is of the required-information exchange type. Rulon and McCreary (1986) investigated the effect of participatory structure on the negotiation of content, defined as 'the process of spoken interaction whereby the content of a previously encountered passage (aural or written) is clarified to the satisfaction of both parties' (1986: 183). They found little difference between small group and teacher-led discussions with regard to length of utterance, syntactic complexity, or interactional features, but they did find that significantly more negotiation of content occurred in the small group discussions. Zhao and Bitchener (2007) compared the focus-on-form episodes (FFEs) – occasions when there was attention to a specific linguistic form during communicative activities – that arose when the same tasks were performed by the teacher working with the whole class and the learners working alone in groups. They found that there were more reactive FFEs in the teacher-class context but more student-initiated FFEs in the group work. They also reported that there was much less uptake in the teacher-class interactions. This was because teachers often did not provide learners with the opportunity to uptake. However the percentage of successful uptake (i.e. where learners repaired their errors) was the same in both.

From these studies it is clear that group work can provide opportunities for very different kinds of interaction from those found in lockstep lessons. This has led some researchers to claim that group work interaction is more likely to facilitate acquisition than teacher-directed interaction. Group work has been promoted on both pedagogical and psycholinguistic grounds.

Long and Porter (1985) listed five principal pedagogical arguments for recommending small group work:

1. Group work increases language production opportunities.
2. Group work improves the quality of student talk.
3. Group work helps individualize instruction.
4. Group work promotes a positive affective climate.
5. Group work motivates learners.

They then went on to consider the psycholinguistic rationale for group work. Drawing on the kinds of studies referred to in the preceding paragraph, they suggested that group work was advantageous for language learning for the following reasons:

1. Quantity of practice (i.e. there is more opportunity for language practice in group work than in lockstep lessons).
2. Variety of practice (i.e. in group work learners can perform a wide range of language functions).
3. Accuracy of student production (i.e. learners have been shown to use the L2 just as accurately in group work as in lockstep lessons).
4. Correction (i.e. students engage in self- and other-corrections to a greater extent in group work than in lockstep teaching).
5. Negotiation (i.e. students engage in more negotiation of meaning sequences when performing communicative tasks in group work than in teacher-led lessons).
6. Task (i.e. group work lends itself to the performance of two-way tasks that elicit negotiation of meaning sequences).

Long and Porter's article constitutes a convincing case for the use of group work.

However, not all researchers and educators are convinced of the advantages of group work. They have noted a number of potential limitations. One concerns the ephemeral nature of spoken discourse. Williams (1999) suggested, for example, that group work may not be conducive to students paying attention to form. She found that beginner and intermediate proficiency learners rarely focused on form while performing communicative tasks and when they did so it was only when the teacher was in attendance. Advanced-level learners addressed form more frequently. However, the actual forms attended to by learners, irrespective of their proficiency, were lexical; there were very few occasions when they addressed grammatical problems.

Other researchers have queried the acquisitional value of the 'interlanguage talk' that takes place in groups. Both Pica and Doughty (1985a) and Porter (1986) found that interlanguage talk is less grammatical than teacher-talk. Thus, it is possible that exposure to incorrect peer input may lead to fossilization. Prabhu (1987) argued that for task-based teaching to be effective learners needed to be maximally exposed to good models of the L2 and for this reason rejected the use of group work in favour of teacher-led task-based lessons.

Given that at least some of the time learner production in group work will contain errors, an important question is how learners handle these. Porter (1986) reported that ESL learners rarely corrected their partners' errors wrongly during group work – only 0.3 per cent of the time. They also rarely repeated their fellow-learners' errors. Ohta (2001) examined the extent to which beginner-level learners of L2 Japanese repeated the errors of other students either immediately or subsequently and reported that other-repetition of errors only occurred approximately 8 per cent of the time. These studies suggest that learners may not be so disadvantaged after all by the input they receive from their fellow learners.

Another limitation of group work, however, is potentially more serious. Learners appear to lack any sociolinguistic need to adjust their speech to take account of social context. Porter (1985) found that L2 speakers did not provide sociolinguistically appropriate input and suggested that learners may not be able to develop sociolinguistic competence from each other. This, however, may be a limitation not just of small group work but of classroom interaction in general, as suggested by Ellis' (1992) study of two learners' requesting strategies, which was discussed earlier in the chapter.

As Pica (1994) noted, the effectiveness of group work depends very much on the specific context. Factors such whether the group is monolingual or heterogeneous, the cultural background of the learners, and the nature of the classroom task influence outcomes. Pica concluded that while group work definitely has a role in the classroom, it does not guarantee success in L2 learning.

Studies informed by cognitive-interactionist theories of L2 learning

Cognitive-interactionist theories of L2 learning view language learning as something that takes place inside the head of the learner as a result of interacting in the L2. That is, interaction provides learners with the input, which they process internally, and opportunities for L2 production, both of which have been hypothesized to help them build and restructure their interlanguages. Research based on such theories has investigated the interactions that occur during group work in terms of the opportunities that they provide for negotiation of meaning (see Chapter 4) and for L2 production that is fluent, complex and accurate.

Researchers in this tradition have investigated what task design variables and task implementation variables promote negotiation of meaning in pairs or in small group work. Many of these studies were conducted in a laboratory setting rather than a classroom. Indeed, some researchers have queried whether the kinds of tasks that have been investigated – information-gap and opinion-gap tasks – are very effective in promoting negotiation of meaning in a classroom. Foster (1998), for example, examined these types of tasks performed by adult ESL learners in the United Kingdom and concluded that they resulted in relatively little negotiation of meaning or modified output. Foster suggested that one reason for this was that the students treated the tasks as 'fun' rather than as providing opportunities for learning.

Other studies based on interactionist- cognitive theories of learning have focused on learners' L2 production in collaborative discourse. Bygate (1988), for example, suggested that group work facilitates acquisition by affording learners opportunities to build up utterances through the use of satellite units (i.e. words, phrases, or clauses that constitute either moodless utterances that lack a finite verb or some kind of syntactically dependent unit, as in Extract 6).

Extract 6:
1. S1:   at the door.
2. S2:   yes in the same door I think.
3. S3:   besides the man who is leaving.
4. S2:   behind him.

Bygate argued that the use of satellite units allows for flexibility in communication, gives the learner time to prepare messages, and enables messages to be built up collaboratively, thus helping to extend learners' capabilities. More recent studies of learners' production in group work (e.g. Foster and Skehan, 1996) have investigated the effects of task-design and implementation variables on the fluency, complexity and accuracy of their use of the L2 when performing tasks in groups.

Given that many of the studies of small group work have involved the use of 'tasks', I will reserve a detailed discussion of them until the next chapter.

Studies informed by sociocultural theory

As we have already seen, a growing number of studies have made use of the theoretical constructs and methodology of sociocultural theory to explore the acquisitional benefits of group interaction. An underlying premise of these studies is that effective scaffolding does not require expert-novice interaction (i.e. interaction involving the teacher) but can take place in novice-novice interactions (i.e. in peer interactions).

Studies by Donato (1994) and Swain and her co-researchers (e.g. Kowal and Swain, 1994); Swain and Lapkin, 1998), among others, have documented the collaborative dialoguing that can occur in pair work or small group work when learners engage in discussions about problematic language points. For example, Kowal and Swain (1994) investigated how Grade 8 French immersion students performed a dictogloss task, showing that they were often able to decide collectively what forms to use to reconstruct a text. However, Kowal and Swain also noted that heterogeneous dyads worked less effectively together, possibly because 'neither student's needs were within the zone of proximal development of the other' (p. 86) and because they failed to respect each other's perspective. These studies are considered in greater detail in Chapter 8.

Perhaps the most complete study of group work from a sociocultural theoretical perspective is Ohta's (2001) account of beginner learners in a Japanese foreign language classroom. Ohta proposed that learners were able to assist each other because of the different roles performed by speakers and listeners. Speakers struggle to produce utterances in the L2 because of the limitations of working memory and the need to process output consciously. Listeners on the other hand are under less pressure and so are able to notice errors in their partner's production and to anticipate and formulate what will come next. This is what makes 'assisted performance' possible. Ohta documented various ways in which this assistance takes place. She showed that learners would sometimes fail to notice an error in their own production but notice it in the production of others and draw their attention to it. Thus:

> Even learners who are unable to produce a particular grammatical structure on their own were able to assist a partner with the same task when they afforded the abundant attentional resources of the listener's role (p. 85).

Through the detailed analysis of sequences of pair and group work talk she identified the various scaffolding techniques that helped learners to construct Zones of Proximal Development. When a listener observed a partner struggling to produce an utterance he/she would wait to give their partner time to complete it, or prompt him/her by repeating a syllable, or co-construct the utterance by providing a syllable, word or phrase that contributed towards its completion or, sometimes, provide an explanation in the L1 (English). These techniques were also used when a learner made an error. In addition, the listener would draw the speaker's attention to the error or correct it or ask the teacher for assistance. Ohta emphasized the reciprocal nature of assisted performance: 'this is the key to peer assistance – that both peers benefit, the one receiving assistance and the one who reaches out to provide it' (p. 125).

Ohta's examples of peer interaction demonstrate how effective it can be in creating affordances for learning. However, as we have already noted, the quality of talk in group work varies. Of considerable interest, therefore, is what specific characteristics of this talk are indicative of the collaboration needed for learning. Storch (2002) reported an analysis of the patterns of dyadic interaction found in ESL students' performance of a range of tasks. She identified four basic patterns based on two intersecting dimensions involving (1) mutuality (i.e. 'the level of engagement with each other's contribution') and (2) equality (i.e. 'the degree of control or authority over a task') (p. 127). Storch investigated the relationship between the different patterns of dyadic interaction and language development, measured in terms of the extent to which 'learning', as evidenced in the interactions, led to 'development', as evidenced in subsequent tasks. She reported that the most collaborative dyad (i.e. the dyad manifesting high mutuality and high equality) achieved more instances of transfer of knowledge than both the dominant/passive and the dominant/dominant dyads.

Studies of learner variables affecting group work

Fairly obviously the characteristics of the learners who make up groups will influence the quantity and quality of the talk that they engage in. One variable of particular interest is the learners' L2 proficiency. Do groups work more effectively if the learners are similar or differ in their L2 proficiency?

Porter (1986) found that intermediate learners got more input and better quality input from advanced learners than from other intermediate learners while advanced learners got more opportunity to practise when they were communicating with intermediate learners. Porter felt that mixed pairings offer something to both sets of learners.

In a very careful study involving a task that required the resolution of a number of 'referential conflicts' (the subjects were given maps that differed in a number of ways), Yule and McDonald (1990) examined the effects of proficiency in mixed-level dyads, where in some interactions the sender of the information was of low proficiency and the receiver high proficiency (L>H) and in others the opposite (H>L). They found that the L>H interactions were at least twice as long as the H>L interactions. Furthermore, negotiated solutions to the referential problems were much more likely to take place in the L>H condition than in the H>L (a 67.5 per cent success rate as opposed to 17.5 per cent). Where mixed-ability pairings are involved, therefore, success (and perhaps also acquisition) is more likely if the lower-level learner is in charge of the key information that has to be communicated.

Flanigan (1991) investigated pairs of non-native-speaker elementary school children. In this study, the more linguistically competent children were asked to assist the less competent in how to use a computer in a graded reading and listening 'station'. Flannigan found that little negotiation of meaning took place, as the less proficient learners lacked the ability to respond. Also, although the more proficient children made use of the same discourse strategies as those observed in studies of adult caretakers and teachers (i.e. repetitions, expansions, explanations, rephrased questions, and comprehension checks), they made no attempt to simplify their talk grammatically or lexically. This study also suggests that proficiency is a significant factor when constituting pairs or groups.

Overall, these studies support mixed-proficiency-level groups, especially when pressure to communicate is placed on the learners with less proficiency. They also point to another possible limitation of group work – L2 learners may fail to utilize the kinds of modifications found in 'teacher-talk' (Chapter 5) that have been hypothesized to facilitate acquisition.

Preparing learners for working in groups

One way of reconciling the potential advantages and limitations of group work is to ensure that the learners engage cooperatively with each other and support each other's language learning. Naughton (2006) described a study in which the effects of training university learners of L2 English in cooperative strategies (the use of follow-up questions, requesting and giving clarification, repair by means of recasts, and requesting and giving help) were examined. Naughton reported that the cooperative strategy training had a positive effect on both overall participation (measured by the number of turns taken) and the students' use of interaction strategies (in particular the use of follow-up questions and repair) in subsequent group work.

Another way of developing effective group work is to engage learners in discussing and reflecting on their own behaviour while working in groups. Ewald (2004) reports an interesting study that serves as an excellent example of 'exploratory practice' (Allwright, 2003: Chapter 2). She invited the students in her first-year undergraduate Spanish course to watch some skits that illustrated the kinds of problems she and other teachers had noted arose in small group work. The problems included students failing to find the correct activity in their workbook, looking bored and uninterested, signalling comprehension even when they hadn't understood, off-task behaviour, and attempting to hide this when a teacher approached. Ewald provided evidence to show that as a result of watching and discussing these skits, the students modified their behaviour in three main ways. They engaged in personal reflection about their own behaviour in groups. They developed a much greater sense of community and they attempted to improve the effectiveness of their participation in group work. Subsequently, these students were observed to make more effort to work collaboratively and to stay on task.

Final comment

What emerges from this brief account of what is now an enormous body of research on group work is that peer interaction is of potential benefit to language learning. A number of studies have shown that what transpires in group work assists learning, whether this is defined in terms of the social interaction that occurs during group work or in subsequent independent use of the L2. However, for group work to be effective, certain key conditions need to be met. Learners have to be on task, they have to engage collaboratively, there has to be attention to form, and the talk has to be beneficial to all the participants. It is, however, perhaps less clear whether groups are more effective when they are homogeneous or heterogeneous, with the studies considered above reporting mixed results. The studies I have examined also suggest that group work is not always the most effective way of providing opportunities for learning in a classroom and that its putative benefits are sometimes overstated. Clearly, though, group work affords learners opportunities for using and learning the L2 in ways that are unlikely to arise regularly in lockstep teaching.

Much of the research on group work has been motivated by the growing interest among both researchers and teachers in task-based teaching. In the next chapter we will return to some of the research we have considered here when we examine the research that has investigated the use of tasks in the L2 classroom.

Conclusion

This chapter has identified a number of potentially important characteristics of learner-talk in the classroom:

1. While opportunities for 'creative language use' may be somewhat limited in many classrooms, they clearly do occur, especially in the talk that centres on framework goals (i.e. in the language used to manage classrooms activities) and in small group work based on communicative tasks. Lockstep teaching can also afford learners with opportunities for creative language use.
2. There are close similarities between the order and sequence of L2 acquisition in classroom and naturalistic learners as manifest in the learners' creative language use.
3. Key features of learner language evident in naturalistic learners – a silent period, formulaic sequences, structural and semantic simplification – can also be found in the speech of classroom learners.
4. The nature of many classrooms makes it inevitable that learners will draw on their L1 as a tool for both managing instructional tasks and learning. Similarly, classroom learners are likely to develop knowledge of metalingual terms that can support their performance of instructional tasks and potentially assist learning. Both the L1 and metalanguage can be seen as tools that learners can use to support their learning.
5. The extent to which classroom learners have the opportunity for more varied use of the L2 – such as language play – will depend to a considerable extent on whether they are able to perform an initiating – and not just a responding role – in classroom discourse. Learner questions serve as one way in which they can take the initiative.
6. An aspect of learner language in the classroom that is of potential importance for learning is the successful incorporation of a linguistic form that has been the subject of attention into their own speech (i.e. uptake).
7. Group work provides a context that allows learners to maximize the use of the L2 for learning, whether through the opportunity to negotiate for meaning or to scaffold fellow learners' attempts at L2 production. IRF exchanges (see Chapter 4) occur rarely in group work. However, group work is not always effective

in promoting the kind of learner-talk that will facilitate acquisition. There are obvious dangers of being over-exposed to use of the L1 or to 'interlanguage talk'. For group work to be effective, learners may need to be made aware of the problems that often arise and to reflect on solutions to them.

These aspects of learner-talk all relate to 'participation' – they define the qualitative nature of the learner's participation in classroom discourse[6]. As in the previous chapter, I have been primarily concerned with their description rather than with demonstrating how they assist acquisition. Thus, the question remains as to the relationship between 'participation' and 'acquisition' (Sfard, 1998). From a sociocultural theoretical perspective, participation *is* learning as it constitutes a step towards self-regulation. From an interactionist-cognitive perspective, however, participation is only a source of learning – learning takes place inside the learner's head and can only be claimed to have occurred when there is evidence of some change in the learner's interlanguage system. I have endeavoured to remain neutral about how 'participation' should be conceptualized in this chapter. My position has been that no matter how learner participation is conceptualized it clearly needs to be investigated if we are to understand the L2 classroom and its potential for language learning.

One final point that emerges from this chapter is that the L2 classroom should never be treated as monolithic in nature (and there is a danger in some of the research of viewing it this way). Classrooms are complex social contexts and they vary enormously. Furthermore, they are not just fixed and static social contexts. They are dynamic, constantly changing, in part at least because of the part played by learners in helping to construct and reconstruct them, as Morita's (2004) study discussed earlier so clearly showed.

Notes

1. There have been a number of longitudinal studies of L2 classroom learners based on data collected from outside the classroom. A good example of such a study is Klapper and Rees (2003). They examined two groups of university-level learners of L2 German over the entire length of their course (four years) and collected product-only data by means of tests administered at entry, the end of Year 2, and the start and end of Year 4. My concern in this chapter, however, is primarily with studies that document learners' development in terms of oral production data collected through observing them in their classrooms.
2. Research by Roehr (2008) has shown that there is a relationship between learners' metalingual knowledge and their language aptitude. Roehr goes so far as to claim that 'learners' ability to correct, describe, and explain highlighted L2 errors and their L2 language analytic ability may constitute components of the same construct' (p. 173).
3. Dictogloss is a technique developed by Wajnryb (1990). It makes use of a short text that has been selected or devized to have a structural focus. The text is read at normal speed, sentence by sentence, while the learners note down key words and phrases (i.e. the content words). The learners then work in groups to try to reconstruct the text collaboratively.

Reformulation (Cohen 1982) requires students to revise a draft of their own piece of writing after receiving a native speaker reformulation of their draft.

4. A related notion to 'language play' is 'humour'. This is an aspect of language that many teachers explore to considerable effect. For those interested in this topic see Bell (2009).

5. Tocalli-Beller and Swain (2007) report a study that examined learners' discussions of riddles such as 'When is a door not a door? When it is ajar' and showed that such discussions did result in the learning of the words that were the key semantic triggers in such riddles (e.g. 'ajar').

6. Quantitative studies of learner participation and its relationship to language learning are considered in Chapter 8.

7

Investigating the Performance of Tasks

Introduction

This chapter examines research that has investigated how tasks are performed in second language (L2) classrooms. The focus is exclusively on the performance of tasks rather than on the learning that results from the performance. As tasks serve as the organizational unit of task-based language teaching (TBLT), I will begin with a brief discussion of this. I will then provide my definition of 'task', distinguishing it from 'exercise'. Tasks vary in terms of how they are designed and also how they are implemented in the classroom. Thus, in the next section I describe the key design and implementation variables. A key question is whether these variables impact on the way a task is performed. I discuss the case for claiming that this is not possible because learners will always impose their own interpretation on a task, (i.e. the activity that results cannot be predicted on the basis of the task workplan). I will then argue, that while tasks cannot be viewed as determining performance, it is nevertheless possible to identify likely ways in which different tasks will be performed as a result of their specific design features and the way they are implemented. I then outline the main ways in which researchers have examined 'performance' (i.e. in terms of specific discourse measures such as 'negotiation of meaning' and general aspects of production such as 'fluency' and 'accuracy'). All this paves the way for the main purpose of this chapter – a review of the research that has investigated how the design and implementation variables impact on the way tasks are performed. Finally, I will briefly look at a different approach to investigating the performance of tasks – through micro- and macro-evaluations of task-based teaching.

Language Teaching Research & Language Pedagogy, First Edition. Rod Ellis.
© 2012 John Wiley & Sons, Ltd. Published 2012 by John Wiley & Sons, Ltd.

Task-Based Language Teaching

TBLT constitutes a strong form of communicative language teaching. Howatt (1984) in his history of English language teaching distinguished 'weak' and 'strong' forms of communicative language teaching in terms of whether the aim is 'learning to use English' or 'using English to learn it'. In the case of the former, an attempt is made to teach and practise communication; in the case of the latter, an attempt is made to create opportunities for communication in the classroom on the grounds that language is best learned through communicating. The weak version of communicative language teaching is evident in notional-functional language teaching, where the aim is to teach and practise the linguistic exponents of specific notions (such as 'possibility') and functions (such as 'requesting'). The strong version is evident in a number of different approaches, including Krashen and Terrell's (1983) Natural Approach, content-based language teaching and TBLT.

TBLT emerged in the 1980s, notably in Prabhu's Communicational Language Teaching Project (Prabhu, 1987: Chapter 3). It gathered steam as a 'fluency-based' approach underpinned by the findings of second language acquisition research (see Long, 1985) and by support from teacher educators (see Nunan, 1989). The 1990s saw a number of key publications that addressed such issues as how to select tasks that would be most beneficial for language learning (Pica, Kanagy and Falodun, 1993), how to design a task-based syllabus (Long and Crookes, 1992), how to conduct a task-based lesson (Willis, 1996) and how to construct task-based language tests (Norris, Brown and Hudson, 2000). The first decade of the twentieth century witnessed a host of books devoted to TBLT (e.g. Bygate, Skehan and Swain, 2001; Ellis, 2003; Nunan, 2004; Samuda and Bygate, 2008). In this decade also books began to appear that provided accounts of actual TBLT lessons and courses (e.g. Edwards and Willis, 2005; Leaver and Willis, 2004; Van den Branden 2006). Inevitably, TBLT has attracted critics too, notably R. Sheen (1994) and Swan (2005).

TBLT does not constitute a well-defined method. Rather it is an 'approach' based on a set of general principles. Van den Branden, Bygate and Norris (2009) distinguished three basic dimensions of language education which serve to identify the core principles of TBLT:

1. Holistic versus discrete learning (i.e. 'whether language should be treated as discourse in use rather than discrete bits', p. 2).
2. Teacher-centred versus learner-driven education (i.e. whether it is the teacher who controls the discourse or whether primacy is given to student-initiated discourse).
3. Communication-based versus form-focused instruction (i.e. whether the primary focus of the instruction is on meaning and achieving mutual understanding or on form and achieving accuracy).

TBLT is an approach that emphasizes holistic learning, it is learner-driven and it entails communication-based instruction. It contrasts with traditional approaches (such as present–practice–produce – PPP), which are based on discrete learning, are teacher-centred and emphasize form and accuracy. However, as Van den Branden, Bygate and Norris (2009) pointed out, the three dimensions are not really dichotomous but rather offer 'gradations of pedagogical choice' (p. 3). Indeed, some proponents of PPP would dispute the characterization of this approach I have just given. Similarly, not all advocates of TBLT would view it as I have just described.

In fact, TBLT, does not constitute a unified approach – there are a number of different versions (Eckerth, 2008a). In Ellis (2009) I distinguished three different approaches to TBLT – Long's (1985), Skehan's (1998) and my own (Ellis, 2003). I discussed these in terms of five characteristics (1) the provision of opportunities for natural language use – what Widdowson (2003) refers to as 'authenticity'), (2) learner-centredness (as manifested in the centrality of small group work), (3) focus on form (i.e. whether the approach includes devices for focusing learners' attention on form while they are communicating), (4) the kind of task (i.e. whether unfocused or focused) and (5) the rejection of traditional approaches to language teaching (e.g. PPP). I showed that the only characteristic that all three approaches share are (1) – the emphasis on creating contexts for natural language use – and (3) focus on form. However, they differ in terms of how attention to form is to be achieved, with Long emphasizing corrective feedback, Skehan task-design and pre-task planning, and myself a variety of ways in the pre-task, main task and post-task phases of a task-based lesson. Major differences in the three approaches are evident with regard to (2) (i.e. I do not see group work as an essential characteristic), (4) (i.e. Skehan favours just unfocused tasks whereas Long and myself also see a role for focused tasks) and (5) where Long and Skehan view traditional structural teaching as theoretically indefensible I see it as complementary to TBLT. Table 7.1 summarizes my comparison of these approaches.

Table 7.1 A comparison of three approaches to TBLT (based on Ellis, 2009)

Characteristic	Long (1985)	Skehan (1998)	Ellis (2003)
Natural language use	Yes	Yes	Yes
Learner-centredness	Yes	Yes	Not necessarily
Focus on form	Yes – through corrective feedback	Yes – mainly through pre-task	Yes – in all phases of a TBLT lesson
Tasks	Yes – unfocused and focused	Yes – unfocused	Yes – unfocused and focused
Rejection of traditional approaches	Yes	Yes	No

Source: Ellis, R. 2009. "Task-Based Language Teaching: Sorting Out the Misunderstandings." *International Journal of Applied Linguistics*, 19, no. 3: 222–246.

What all three of these approaches have most clearly in common is the centrality of 'tasks' as the means for conducting language teaching. I will now return to a consideration of what a 'task' is.

Defining 'Task'

The term 'task' is sometimes used with the same generic meaning as 'activity', as for example in Breen's (1989) definition of the term:

> ... a structured plan for the provision of opportunities for the refinement of knowledge and capabilities entailed in a new language and its use during communication (p. 187).

Breen went on to state that a task could be 'a brief practise exercise' or 'a more complex workplan that requires spontaneous communication of meaning'. The term is often used in Breen's general sense. However, it has taken on a narrower meaning in TBLT research.

My own narrower definition of task is based on four key criteria:

1. The primary focus should be on 'meaning' (by which is I mean learners should be mainly concerned with processing the semantic and pragmatic meaning of utterances).
2. There should be some kind of 'gap' (i.e. a need to convey information, to express an opinion or to infer meaning).
3. Learners should largely have to rely on their own resources (linguistic and non-linguistic) in order to complete the activity.
4. There is a clearly defined outcome other than the use of language (i.e. the language serves as the means for achieving the outcome, not as an end in its own right).

In Ellis (2010a), I showed how these criteria can be used to distinguish between a 'task' and 'a situational grammar exercise'[1]. Whereas the latter may satisfy criteria (2) and (3), it does not satisfy (1) as the learners know that the main purpose of the activity is to practise correct language rather than to process messages for meaning. Nor does it satisfy (4) as the outcome is simply the use of correct language. I illustrated these differences in two instructional activities that make use of the same semantic content but, in performance, afford very different pragmatic uses of language. The two activities are reproduced here. 'Going Shopping' is a situational grammar exercise, designed to provide practice in the use of 'some' and 'any'. 'What can you buy?' is a task. The primary focus is on meaning, there is an information gap, the learners have to use their own linguistic resources, and there are outcomes that can be checked not for linguistic accuracy but for factual correctness.

Going Shopping

Look at Mary's shopping list. Then look at the list of items in Abdullah's store.

Mary's Shopping List

1.	oranges	4.	powdered milk
2.	eggs	5.	biscuits
3.	flour	6.	jam

Abdullah's Store

1.	bread	7.	mealie meal flour
2.	salt	8.	sugar
3.	apples	9.	curry powder
4.	tins of fish	10.	biscuits
5.	coca cola	11.	powdered milk
6.	flour	12.	dried beans

Work with a partner. One person is Mary and the other person is Mr. Abdullah. Make conversations like this.

Mary: Good morning. Do you have any _____?
Abdullah: Yes, I have some. / No I don't have any.

What can you buy?

Student A:

You are going shopping at Student B's store. Here is your shopping list. Find out which items on your list you can buy.

Mary's Shopping List

1.	oranges	4.	powdered milk
2.	eggs	5.	biscuits
3.	flour	6.	jam

Student B:

You own a store. Here is a list of items for sale in your store. Make a list of the items that Student A asks for that you do not stock.

1.	bread	7.	mealie meal flour
2.	salt	8.	sugar
3.	apples	9.	curry powder
4.	tins of fish	10.	biscuits
5.	coca cola	11.	powdered milk
6.	flour	12.	dried beans

The Design and Implementation of Tasks

Tasks can differ in terms of how they are designed and how they are implemented in the classroom. Both design and implementation variables can potentially influence how a task is performed. The key design and implementation variables are considered in the next section as a precursor to discussing the research that has investigated them.

Design variables

Different types of tasks can be identified depending on the design variables involved.

1.   Tasks can be 'unfocused' or 'focused'. Unfocused tasks are tasks that are designed to provide learners with opportunities for communicating using language in general. Focused tasks are tasks that have been designed to provide opportunities for communicating using some specific linguistic feature (typically a grammatical structure). However, focused tasks must still satisfy the four criteria stated above. For this reason the target linguistic feature of a focused task is 'hidden' (i.e. learners are not told explicitly what the feature is). Thus, a focused task can still be distinguished from a 'situational grammar exercise' as in the latter learners are made aware of what feature they are supposed to be using. In other words, learners are expected to orient differently to a focused task and a situational grammar exercise.

2.   Tasks can also be 'input-providing' or 'output-prompting'. Input-providing tasks engage learners in listening or reading, while output-prompting tasks engage them in speaking or writing. Thus, a task can provide opportunities for communicating in any of the four language skills. Many tasks are integrative; that is, they involve two or more skills.

3.   Tasks also differ in terms of the type of 'gap' they contain. Prabhu (1987) distinguished three types of gap: (1) an information gap (as in the 'What can you buy task?' above), (2) an opinion gap (where students all have access to the same information which they use as a basis for discussing the solution to some problem), and (3) a reasoning gap (where students are required to derive some new information from given information through processes of deduction or practical reasoning).

4.   Another significant distinction concerns whether the task is 'closed' (i.e. there is just one or a very limited number of possible outcomes) or 'open' (i.e. there are a number of different outcomes that are possible). In general, information-gap and reasoning-gap tasks are 'closed' while opinion-gap tasks are 'open'.

5.   Tasks vary in complexity. A number of different factors influence the complexity of a task, for example, whether the task language relates to the here-and-now (as when describing a picture that can be seen) or the there-and-then (as when narrating a movie after watching it). Another factor that can affect complexity is whether the task involves a single activity (e.g. listening to someone describe a route and drawing

the route in on a map) or a dual activity (e.g. listening to someone describe a route and drawing in both locations missing on the map as well as the route taken).

This list is not exhaustive. Other design variables concern whether the task is monologic or dialogic, the nature of the input provided by the task (e.g. how structured it is and how familiar the topic is to the students), and the nature of the output (i.e. whether it is oral or written and how complex it is). These – and other – design variables potentially impact on how students' perform a task (see Chapter 7 in Ellis, 2003).

Implementation variables

Implementation variables refer to the different methodological options available for exploiting tasks in the classroom. Key variables that have been investigated include:

1.   Lockstep versus pair work or small group work. A misunderstanding that has arisen about TBLT is that tasks must be performed in pairs or small groups. In fact, this is not an essential feature of TBLT. Tasks are often performed in this way but they can also be performed in lockstep lessons, with the teacher taking one role and the students another role. One potential advantage of performing a task in lockstep is that it provides opportunities for 'focus on form', for example through the kinds of corrective feedback discussed in Chapter 5. 'Focus on form' is discussed later in the chapter.

2.   Including a pre-task stage where learners are pre-taught the linguistic forms (lexical and/or grammatical) that will be needed to perform the task. A key question here is whether and to what extent the learners then try to make use of the forms they have been taught while performing the task.

3.   The extent to which the task positions the learners as 'speakers' and/or 'listeners'. For example, a describe-and-do task, that requires one participant to describe a set of objects and the other participant to identify the correct objects and then locate them in the rightful position on a board can be performed 'non-interactively' (where one participant is the 'speaker' and the other the 'listener/doer') or 'interactively' (where the listener is able to request clarification whenever needed).

4.   Allocation of roles in a task according to various individual learner factors. In the last chapter we say that Yule and McDonald (1990) found that learners were more effective in resolving the referential conflicts inherent in an information-gap task if the 'speaker' role was allocated to the learner with lower proficiency and the 'listener' role to the learner with higher proficiency. Other variables that might influence the allocation of roles are the learners' first languages (L1s) (i.e. the task can be performed by same or different language pairs), their sex (i.e. the task can be performed by same or different sex pairs), or their personality (e.g. an extrovert learner can be paired with a more introverted learner).

5.   The extent to which there is opportunity for strategic planning. In many studies, learners have been given time to prepare for the performance of the task before they are asked to perform it. Such planning can be 'unguided' (i.e. the learners are simply instructed to prepare for the task) or 'guided' (i.e. the learners are advised to focus on the specific linguistic forms they will need to perform the task).

6.   The extent to which there is opportunity for online planning. Learners can be given a time limit for performing the task, which pressurizes them to plan rapidly as they perform the task. Alternatively, no time limit is set, in which case learners can pause as much as they need in order to work out what to say next.

7.   Learners can be asked to repeat a task. This can be carried out without any changes to the task or by modifying the design of the task or by manipulating one of the other implementation variables.

8.   A post-task requirement. For example, learners can simply be asked to perform the task or they can be informed that after performing the task they will be required to report the task outcome to the rest of the class. Willis (1996) sees the 'report' stage as an essential feature of the task-cycle.

The Cognition Hypothesis

Robinson's (2007) Cognition Hypothesis provides a theoretical basis for making predictions about how design and implementation variables affect the performance of a task. He sees some variables as 'resource-directing' in the sense that they vary in the demands they make on the learner's attention and, in so doing, cause the learner to focus on specific linguistic forms and thus potentially promote interlanguage development. Task variables that are resource-directing include whether the task requires: (1) reference to events happening in the 'here-and-now' or to events that took place in the past elsewhere (in the 'there-and-then), (2) reference to a few easily distinguishable features or to many similar features, (3) reference to easily-identifiable locations or to locations where no support is available, (4) transmission of simple information or provision of reasons for intentions, beliefs or relations.

Other variables are characterized as 'resource-dispersing'. These vary in the procedural demands they make on the learners' attentional and memory resources but do not affect the extent to which they draw attention to specific linguistic forms. Resource-dispersing variables do not promote the acquisition of new L2 forms but do enhance automaticity. Examples are: (1) providing or not providing strategic planning time, (2) providing or not providing background knowledge prior to performance of the task, (3) a task with or without a clear structure, (4) a task involving a few or many steps to complete it and (5) a task that requires just one thing or many things to be done. Robinson makes specific predictions about how task complexity will affect the fluency, accuracy and complexity of learners' production. Studies that have investigated these are considered later in this chapter.

'Task' Versus 'Activity'

In the research we will consider in this chapter, the independent variable is 'task' – or rather the specific design features and implementation variables that the researcher is interested in. The dependent variable differs from study to study. In some studies it is the 'process' of performing the task, measured in a variety of ways. In other studies, it is the task 'outcome' (e.g. whether a learner has drawn in the route on a map correctly)[2]. In the next section I will examine how process features have been measured. First, though, it is necessary to point out that not all researchers are convinced that specific variables will determine how a task is performed.

The key issue is the relationship between task-as-workplan and task-as-process (Breen, 1989). If there is no correspondence between the task-as-workplan and the task-as-process it will not be possible to predict what kinds of language use will result from the performance of tasks.

Sociocultural theorists have argued that it is not possible to predict the 'activity' (i.e. the process) that results from a 'task' as learners are likely to interpret the task-as-workplan differently in accordance with their own goals and motives. There is, in fact, plenty of evidence to demonstrate that the task-as-workplan does not always result in the anticipated use of language. Coughlan and Duff (1994) showed that the 'activity' that resulted from a task varied from learner to learner and also from performance to performance by the same learner. Using the techniques of conversational analysis, Mori (2002) examined how a 'zadankai' task (i.e. a task involving a discussion between small groups of learners of Japanese and native speaker visitors to the classroom) panned out. She reported that what unfolded as the learners engaged in the discussions, was not exactly what was intended by the task. The task-as-workplan required the learners to ask the native speaker questions and to comment on the replies and allow the native speaker to ask them questions. In actuality, in one group the task-in-process took the form of a structured interview, with the students functioning as the interviewer and only minimally acknowledging the native speaker's responses before moving on to the next question. Seedhouse (2005a) argued that the discrepancy between the predicted and actual language use resulting from a task was so great that a task could only be defined in terms of the language processes that arose in its performance.

These studies investigated unfocused tasks. The problem becomes even more acute with focused tasks. It is very difficult to design production tasks that make the use of the target feature obligatory. Learners are adroit at using their strategic competence to get round having to use a linguistic feature they do not know or cannot access easily.

However, the distinction between task-as-workplan and task-as-process has been overstated. While 'task' and 'activity' are not isomorphic there clearly is a relationship between them as will become apparent when we consider the research that has investigated tasks. It is possible to design and implement tasks in ways that will lead learners to prioritize specific aspects of language. Also, as we will see, studies of focused tasks have shown that in at least some cases it is possible to design tasks that result in the required use of the target structure. Thus, while it is obviously important to recognize that learners will vary in how they perform a particular task – and to explore the nature of this variation – it is also necessary to acknowledge that the design of a task and the way that it is implemented will influence the kind of language that learners produce.

Measuring Task-Based Language Production

Learners' production has been measured in two primary ways – either in terms of the kind of discourse deemed to be theoretically significant for learning or in terms of the general qualities of the learners' spoken output.

Discourse-based measures

Researchers have been interested in the extent to which dialogic tasks elicit attention to form. That is, although a task requires a primary focus on meaning it does not prohibit secondary attention to linguistic form. Indeed, interactionist-cognitive theories of L2 acquisition (e.g. Doughty, 2001) argue that for acquisition to take place learners need to attend to form *while* they are struggling to understand and produce meaningful messages. Sociocultural theories claim that the process of 'languaging' – talking about language (Swain, 2006) – enables participants to scaffold zones of proximal development and thus to construct utterances that are beyond their independent abilities. These theories have given rise to three principal discourse measures.

1.   Negotiation of meaning

A negotiation of meaning sequence occurs when there is a breakdown in communication that leads to the interlocutors attempting to remedy this through talk. It consists of a 'trigger' followed by an 'indicator' (where a speaker indicates a problem has arisen) and a 'response' (where an attempt is made by the first speaker to resolve the problem). Such sequences were discussed in Chapter 4 (see Extract 7 for an example). A number of studies have examined how task design and implementation variables affect the frequency of negotiation sequences or of the conversational strategies involved in negotiation (e.g. requests for clarification, recasts, or repetitions). An underlying assumption is that tasks that induce higher frequencies of negotiation sequences or of particular conversational strategies (such as recasts) will be more effective in promoting learning.

2.   Language-related episodes

Swain (1998: 70) defined a language-related episode (LRE) as 'any part of a dialogue in which students talk about the language they are producing, question their language use, or other- or self-correct'. LREs include negotiation sequences but they also include sequences where there is no communication breakdown (i.e. where the talk about language is focused explicitly on linguistic form), as in this example from Kim (2009: 258).

Extract 1:

Learner A:　She find the money.

Learner B:　No . . . It should be . . . she found the money . . . past.

Learner A:　Ah . . . sorry . . . she found the money.

Such episodes can result in (A) a correct resolution to the linguistic problem (as in extract 1), (B) an incorrect resolution, or (C) they can remain unresolved. Researchers have investigated the frequency with which LREs address pronunciation, vocabulary, grammar or some pragmatic aspect of language. They have investigated what impact they have on learning by administering tailor-made tests to assess whether individual learners' participation in an LRE results in acquisition of the specific form addressed in the LRE.

3.　Focus-on-form episodes

This term was coined by Ellis, Basturkmen and Loewen (2001). Whereas LREs have been investigated in the talk that results from pair or group work, focus-on-form episodes (FFEs) have been investigated in lockstep lessons. An FFE is an occasion where the participants attend to some aspect of linguistic form while engaged in performing a communicative task. Three types can be distinguished:

a.　Responding FFEs where one of the participants – usually the teacher – responds to an utterance produced by another participant – usually the student – that is problematic either because its meaning is not clear or because it contains a linguistic error.

b.　Student-initiated FFEs where a student initiates a focus on a specific linguistic feature because of a gap in his/her knowledge. Such FFEs typically begin with a student question.

c.　Teacher-initiated FFEs where the teacher initiates a focus on a specific linguistic feature because he/she thinks it may be problematic for the students.

Extracts 2–4 illustrate these three types.

Extract 2: Responding FFE

S:　they looking the Glockenspiel today morning.

T:　today morning? (quizzical look) (.) this morning.

S:　this morning.

T:　this morning, good, yeah.

Extract 3: Student initiated FFE

L1:   what's mean positive.
L2:   that means mmm.
T: they are optimistic mm okay she she feels good about the future.
L1:   mhm.
L2:   oh.
T: she feels like the future will be good for her.

Extract 4: Teacher initiated FFE

T: so if he's committed theft, what is he.
L1:   um he was in prison for two years,
T: yeah that's where he was, what do we call the person who commits theft.
L2:   thief.
T: thief.
L3:   thief.
T: yeah okay.

Research has examined the frequency of different types of FFE, the extent to which each type promotes uptake and, in one study (Loewen, 2005), the relationship between FFEs and learning.

In addition to these discourse measures, conversational analysis has been widely employed to examine the orderliness, structure and sequential patterns of the interactions that arise in the performance of different tasks. Conversational analysis has also been employed to demonstrate the nature of the 'activity' that learners construct out of a 'task' and the microgenetic development of some specific linguistic or interactional feature over time (e.g. Belz and Kinginger 2003: Chapter 6).

General aspects of L2 production

Skehan (1996) proposed three general aspects of language use that could be investigated in research on tasks:

1. *Accuracy* refers to 'how well the target language is produced in relation to the rule system of the target language' (Skehan, 1996: 23). Learners who prioritize accuracy are seeking control over the elements they have already fully internalized and thus adopt a conservative stance towards L2 use.
2. *Complexity* is the extent to which learners produce elaborated language. There are two senses in which language can be considered elaborated. First, as Skehan (2001) suggests, learners vary in their willingness to use more challenging and difficult language. Language that is at the upper limit of their interlanguage systems, and thus is not fully automated, can be considered more complex than language that has been fully internalized. Secondly, complexity can refer to the

learner's preparedness to use a wide range of different structures. Complexity will depend on learners' willingness to take risks by experimenting linguistically.

3. *Fluency* is the production of language in real time without undue pausing or hesitation. Fluency occurs when learners prioritize meaning over form in order to get a task done. It is achieved through the use of processing strategies that enable learners to avoid or solve problems quickly.

The focus here is very much on the language produced by individual students rather than the interactions they participate in. Specific linguistic measures of each of these aspects have been developed. Some of the most common of these are shown in Table 7.2. (See Ellis and Barkhuizen (2005) for a full account of the different measures used for each aspect).

Table 7.2 Selected measures of fluency, accuracy and complexity

Aspect	*Measure*	*Method of calculation*
Fluency	1. Syllables per minute	After dysfluencies have been removed, the number of syllables is counted and divided by the total speaking time.
	2. Mean length of pauses	The length of each pause and then the total length of all pauses is calculated. This is divided by the total number of pauses.
	3. Number of repetitions	The total number of times a word, phrase or complete utterance is repeated are counted.
Accuracy	1. Percentage of error free clauses	The learners' production is divided into clauses and each clause examined to see if it contains an error or is error-free. The number of error-free clauses is divided by the total number of clauses and expressed as a percentage.
	2. Target-like use of a specific grammatical feature	A specific grammatical feature is selected for analysis (e.g. past tense). Obligatory occasions for the use of this feature are identified and the number of times the learner supplies or fails to supply the target feature identified. Accuracy is expressed as a percentage of correct suppliance.
Complexity	1. Amount of subordination used	The learner's production is divided into clauses and the number of (1) total clauses and (2) subordinate clauses is calculated. (2) is then divided by (1)[3].
	2. Lexical richness (type–token ratio)	The total number of different words used (= types) is divided by the total number of words (= tokens) used[4].

The relationship between task characteristics and these three aspects of language production has been theorized in two different ways. As we have already seen, Robinson (2001) argued from the perspective of his Cognition Hypothesis that different tasks will result in learners prioritizing either accuracy/complexity or fluency. Like Robinson, Skehan (1998) maintained that learners would need to choose between fluency or 'form' when performing tasks but also claimed that a trade-off would sometimes occur between the two aspects of form, namely accuracy and complexity (i.e. if learners elected to prioritize accuracy, complexity might suffer and vice versa). These different claims were based on different theoretical models of working memory, with Skehan arguing for a single-limited-capacity model and Robinson for a multiple-resources model. According to single-limited-capacity models, more complex and less automatized tasks consume more attentional capacity, thus obliging the learner to choose which aspect of language to prioritize. According to a multiple-resources model attention can be allocated to different aspects of a task as long as these do not belong to the same domain (e.g. form or meaning), thus making it possible for attention to be allocated to both complexity and accuracy at the same time.

Researching Tasks

We are now in a position to investigate what research has found out about how learners perform tasks. In this chapter, I want to focus on the *performance* of tasks rather than on the relationship between task performance and acquisition, which I will consider in the next chapter. Here I will examine the following:

1. The impact of task design and implementation variables on learners' comprehension in input-based tasks.
2. The impact of task types on the interactive behaviour of L2 learners (e.g. in terms of negotiation of meaning and language-related episodes).
3. The impact of manipulating task design and implementation features on L2 output in terms of fluency, accuracy and complexity.
4. The extent to which focused tasks are successful in eliciting the specific linguistic features that they are targeting.
5. The nature of the various focus-on-form techniques that occur in task performance.

There is one other important topic – the role played by individual learner factors such as working memory and language classroom anxiety in mediating how learners perform tasks and the learning that takes place. I will reserve a consideration of this for Chapter 10 where I look at research on individual learner differences in the L2 classroom.

It should be noted that much of the research on tasks has been carried out in a laboratory setting, perhaps because it is much easier to manipulate design and implementation variables in such a setting than in a classroom. A key question, therefore, is whether there is any difference in the effect that tasks have on performance depending on the setting. I will begin by considering this question.

Effects of setting on task performance

Doubts about the relevance of laboratory-based studies to our understanding of tasks have been voiced by a number of researchers and teacher educators. The principal reason for these doubts lies in the claim that 'laboratory studies omit all kinds of contextual factors that contribute very significantly to the impact of a task' (Samuda and Bygate, 2008: 261).

A number of studies have investigated the effects of setting on task performance. The first three reviewed here did so by examining how specific types of tasks that had figured in earlier laboratory-based research were performed in classroom contexts. The tasks were of the required- versus optional-information exchange types (i.e. two-way information gap tasks versus opinion-gap tasks). The final study reported a direct comparison of task performance in laboratory and classroom settings. The focus of all the studies was on negotiation of meaning.

Foster (1998) set out to investigate whether information gap and opinion-gap tasks elicited similar amounts of negotiation when performed in a classroom setting in pairs or in small groups compared to a laboratory setting (as reported in previous research). Foster found that negotiation occurred relatively rarely in the adult English as a second language (ESL) classroom she investigated. She suggested that rather than engage in the painstaking, frustrating and face-threatening nature of extensive negotiation, the learners opted for a 'pretend and hope' rather than a 'check and clarify' strategy. Also, whereas the laboratory studies had reported a higher incidence of negotiation in information gap tasks than in opinion gap tasks, Foster found no difference. In other words, the task type had no effect on the frequency of negotiation in the classroom.

Foster's study has been partially replicated in two further studies. Slimani-Rolls (2005) investigated adult learners of L2 French performing similar tasks to Foster's (i.e. information/opinion gap tasks) in their normal classroom. Slimani-Rolls commented 'the normal classroom environment was protected as far as possible' with the teacher acting as the researcher collecting data. She reported a reasonable level of negotiation similar to that reported in the laboratory-based studies, with the two-way information gap task resulting in higher levels of meaning negotiation than both the one-way information gap and opinion gap tasks. However, there was considerable individual variation in the amount of negotiation, with 25 per cent of the learners producing 60 per cent of the meaning negotiation and 20 per cent producing none at all. Also, there was little evidence of meaning modification – e.g. students responded by simply confirming that they had understood. In terms of the quality of the students' performance of the tasks, Slimani-Rolls showed that the one-way information-gap task and the opinion-gap task offered 'more scope for language manipulation and more opportunities for genuine communication' (p. 208). In conclusion, Slimani-Rolls emphasized learner idiosyncrasy resulting from their different perceptions of what was involved in performing the tasks – as sociocultural accounts of tasks have claimed is likely to happen (see section on 'task' versus 'activity').

Eckerth (2008b) also replicated Foster's study. In this case, the learners were university students of L2 German. He reported somewhat greater amounts of negotiated input moves and modified output moves than Foster. But like Foster, he found no effect for task type. Like both Foster and Slimani-Rolls, he found that students tended to simply respond 'yes' or 'no' to informed guesses made by an interlocutor when performing the information-gap tasks. He also found considerable individual variation in negotiation patterns among the students.

None of these studies carried out a direct comparison between tasks performed in a laboratory and in a classroom setting. Gass, Mackey, and Ross-Feldman (2005), however, set out to do this. They asked students enrolled in a third semester university Spanish course to perform three tasks (two information-gap tasks and one opinion-gap task) in dyads in a laboratory setting with the researcher present and in their normal classroom setting. They reported no statistically significant differences in three aspects of interaction (negotiation of meaning, language-related episodes, and recasts) in the two settings. They argued that the results of their study demonstrated that laboratory-based research findings could be cautiously generalized to classroom settings. It should be noted, however, that whereas Foster examined the amount of production involved in negotiation, Gass et al. used absolute frequency counts. Thus a direct comparison with Foster's study is not possible. Eckerth (2008b) also cast doubt on whether Gass et al.'s classroom really functioned as a classroom. He noted that the students were asked to complete the three tasks in an uninterrupted succession and that the three tasks were all completed in nearly the same time. He concluded 'while the classroom may have looked like a classroom, it may not have been perceived as such by the students'.

These studies addressed whether the setting influenced the amount and types of negotiation that occurred when learners performed tasks. Mackey and Goo (2007) reported a meta-analysis of task-based studies that examined whether the setting had any effect on the learning that resulted from interactive tasks. They found that the mean effect sizes of post-tests were significantly larger in studies conducted in laboratory settings than in studies conducted in classrooms. In other words, the interactions that resulted from performing tasks had a greater effect on learning when they occurred in laboratory settings.

Clearly, the issue of whether learners perform tasks in similar ways in a laboratory compared with their normal classroom is an important one. If the answer is 'yes', then, as Gass, Mackey and Ross-Feldman pointed out, it will be possible to extrapolate from the findings of laboratory studies to the classroom and draw implications for language pedagogy. However, if the answer is 'no' then major doubts about the relevance of laboratory-based studies to language pedagogy will arise. These studies do not provide a definitive answer to this question. It is clear that tasks can generate similar types of negotiation whether performed in a laboratory setting or a classroom but not necessarily in similar amounts. Questions also arise about the quality of the negotiated sequences, with Foster, Slimani-Rolls and Eckerth all reporting that the negotiations they observed taking place in the classroom were 'shallow' (i.e. involved little extended negotiation and little modified output). This may be one reason why task-based interaction might be less conducive to learning when carried out in a classroom. However, the finding that gives rise to the greatest concern regarding the applicability of laboratory-based findings to language pedagogy is the considerable variation in individual learners' contribution to negotiation in classroom settings. In a laboratory, learners may feel the need to 'play the game' to the best of their abilities; in a classroom, some learners may see little point in pursuing negotiation when a communication problem arises.

In accordance with the purpose of this book I intend to limit my discussion of the research in the following sections to studies that have actually been carried out in the classroom. It should be noted, however, that deciding whether a particular study was classroom-based is not always easy. For example, Mackey, Kanganas and Oliver (2007) conducted a study that investigated the effects of task familiarity. This involved dividing a normal class in half and teaching them in different rooms to ensure that each half did not become familiar with a particular task. Given that this study involves an artificial manipulation of the normal classroom setting I have not included it in this review. Also, in a number of cases, it proved quite impossible to determine whether a study had been conducted in a classroom or a laboratory setting. I have excluded such studies.

Input-based tasks and learner comprehension

Input-based tasks are tasks that do not require production on the part of the learner. They are non-reciprocal tasks (Ellis, 2001b). That is, they provide the learners with oral or written input in the form of instructions or descriptions and require them to demonstrate understanding non-verbally (e.g. by an action, selecting the right picture, finding the differences between two pictures, completing a map, or making a model). See Duran and Ramaut (2006) for examples of input-based tasks. Such tasks are well-suited to beginner learners who have not yet developed sufficient proficiency to engage in L2 production. They cater to the 'silent period' (see Chapter 6). However, more complex input-based tasks also have a role to play with advanced learners.

The rationale for such tasks draws on theories that emphasize the role of comprehensible input in L2 acquisition. Krashen (1985), for example, argued that the 'fundamental principle' of L2 acquisition is that 'acquisition' (i.e. the subconscious process of internalizing new linguistic forms and their meanings) will occur automatically if learners receive comprehensible input. He argued that input is made comprehensible through simplifying the input and providing learners with contextual support (e.g. pictures). Other researchers such as Schmidt (1994; 2001) have disputed the claim that acquisition is a subconscious process and argued that attention to input needs to be conscious for acquisition to take place (i.e. it involves 'noticing'). Two somewhat different claims arise about the relationship between comprehension and language learning from these different positions. Krashen saw comprehension as essential for learning. For Schmidt, comprehension may facilitate learning but does not guarantee it unless 'noticing' also occurs. Long (1983a; 1996) argued that input that is interactionally modified through the negotiation of meaning is especially beneficial for comprehension. In this case, an input-based task needs to involve learners in responding minimally to the input by requesting clarification when they do not understand. Such tasks, however, are still essentially input-based.

In Ellis (2003) I reviewed a number studies based on 'listen-and-do' tasks (i.e. Ellis and He, 1999; Ellis and Heimbach, 1997; Ellis, Tanaka and Yamazaki, 1994; Loshcky, 1994; Pica, Young and Doughty, 1987)[5]. A good example of such a task can be found in Ellis, Tanaka and Yamazaki (1994). Their Kitchen Task required learners to listen to directions about where to place various objects in a matrix picture of a kitchen. The objects were depicted in small numbered pictures. The product outcome of the task was the matrix picture of the kitchen with the numbers of the small pictures entered in different locations. These studies were directed at investigating the effects of three kinds of input on L2 comprehension (as manifest by learners' performance of the task) – baseline input, pre-modified input and interactionally modified input. Baseline input was derived by asking native speakers to perform the task with other native speakers. Pre-modified input was prepared by adapting the baseline input, based on the kinds of modifications native speakers make when communicating with L2 learners (see Chapter 4). Interactionally modified input was produced when learners were allowed to request clarification of baseline input. Examples of these three kinds of input are provided in Table 7.3.

Most of the studies involved adolescent or adult learners. They demonstrated that tasks involving interactionally modified input resulted in better comprehension than those providing baseline or pre-modified input. However, the studies failed to consistently show that tasks consisting of pre-modified output assisted comprehension. Heimbach and Ellis' study which investigated young children found that even when the children had the chance to request clarification many of them failed to do so with the result that their level of comprehension was very low.

Many of the adolescent and adult learners in these studies also made no effort to interact by requesting clarification. However, in the case of older learners it would seem that active negotiation is not essential for comprehension. Pica (1991) reported a study that compared the comprehension of (1) negotiators, who had opportunities to actively negotiate, (2) observers, who observed the negotiators but did not themselves negotiate, and (3) listeners, who performed the task later, listening to the teacher read directions based on the interactionally modified input but with no opportunity to interact. The comprehension scores of the three groups were not significantly different.

One possibility is that the advantage found for tasks involving interactionally modified input arises simply because the learners had more time to process the input in this condition. Ellis and He (1999) investigated whether this was the case by ensuring the amount of time allocated to the pre-modified and interactionally

Table 7.3 Three types of input in a listen-and-do task

Type of input	Example
Baseline	Can you find the scouring pad? Take the scouring pad and put it on top of the counter by the sink – the right side of the sink.
Premodified	Can you find the scouring pad? A scouring pad – 'scour' means to clean a dish. A scouring pad is a small thing you hold in your hand and you clean a dish with it. Take the scouring pad and put it on top of the counter by the sink – on the right side of the sink.
Interactionally modified	T: Can you find the scouring pad? Take the scouring pad and put it on top of the counter by the sink – the right side of the sink. S1: One more time. T: OK. Can you find the scouring pad? Take the scouring pad and put it on top of the counter by the sink – the right side of the sink. S2: What is a scouring pad? T: Scouring pad is uh . . . you hold it in your hand and you wash dishes with it. OK? S2: Once again. A: Once again? Can you find the scouring pad? Take the scouring pad and put it on top of the counter by the sink – the right side of the sink.

modified groups was the same. Interestingly, in this study there was no statistically significant difference in the comprehension scores of the two groups.

Interactionally modified input can also sometimes prove disadvantageous. Giving learners the opportunity to interact can sometimes lead to input that overloads them with input with the result that comprehension is impeded rather than facilitated (see, for example, Ehrlich, Avery and Yorio, 1989). However, when I re-examined the data from Ellis, Tanaka and Yamazaki in Ellis (1994), I found that every direction was comprehended better by the interactionally modified group than by the pre-modified group irrespective of how elaborated the input was in each direction.

These studies all involved listening tasks. There have also been a number of studies that have investigated the effects of modifying written input on reading comprehension (see, for example, Chaudron's (1988) review; Yano, Long and Ross, 1994; Oh, 2001; and Urano, 2002). Three types of input have been examined; base-line, pre-modified and elaborated (i.e. involving such rhetorical devices as examples, definitions, paraphrases and explicitly marked thematic structure). The latter cor-responded to the 'interactionally modified input' in the listening tasks. The studies indicated that, in general, the elaborated input resulted in higher levels of reading comprehension especially for beginner learners. However, it is doubtful whether these studies really involved 'tasks'. The students were asked to read the passage for no other purpose than to answer the comprehension questions (i.e. there was no communicative outcome).

Table 7.4 Task design and implementation variables investigated in interaction studies (based on Ellis, 2003)

Design variables	*Implementation variables*
1. Required vs. optional information exchange	1. Participant role (e.g. listener vs. active participant)
2. Information gap: one-way vs. two-way	2. Task repetition
3. Task outcome: open vs. closed tasks	3. Interlocutor familiarity (i.e. participants familiar with each other vs. not familiar)
4. Topic (e.g. topic familiarity)	4. Interlocutor proficiency
5. Discourse mode (e.g. narrative vs. description)	
6. Cognitive complexity (e.g. context-embedded vs. context-reduced)	

Tasks and learner–learner interaction

The tasks we will consider here differ from those considered in the previous section in that they were performed by students working in pairs or small groups rather than with the teacher in lockstep lessons. In Ellis (2003: Chapter 3) I reviewed research that had investigated the impact of various task-design and implementation variables on learner–learner interaction. The variables I considered are listed in Table 7.4. Looking back on the studies that I reviewed then, it is apparent that very few of them were conducted in a classroom. They were almost all laboratory-based studies. There was a good reason for this. The studies were designed to investigate very specific variables and this necessitated strictly controlling how they were performed, something that was much easier to achieve outside of the classroom than inside it. However, this very fact again raises questions about the relevance of laboratory task-based studies to the classroom. The studies I will now review are those that examined task-based interaction in a classroom-context only.

1.   Design variables and interaction

As noted in the section on small group work in Chapter 6, Pica and Doughty (1985a; 1985b) found that small group work in language classrooms only resulted in more negotiation work than teacher-fronted lessons when the task was of the required information type. Newton (1991) found almost double the quantity of negotiation in tasks where the information provided was split among the learners compared to tasks where the information was shared. Foster (1998) reported that required-information exchange tasks consistently elicited more negotiation and more modified output than the optional-information exchange tasks, especially when the students worked in pairs, although, as noted above neither type of task elicited much negotiation. Gass, Mackey and Ross-Feldman (2005) compared the negotiation of meaning that arose from three tasks (one was an optional-information task and the other two required-information exchange tasks) when performed in a classroom. They reported a much higher incidence of negotiation of meaning and language-related episodes in the required-information exchange tasks.

However, differences in the amount and quality of negotiation can also be seen in tasks of the same basic type. Fujii and Mackey (2009) reported a study that compared Japanese university-level English as a foreign language (EFL) students' performance of two open-ended decision-making tasks conducted in pairs. The Survival Ranking Task asked learners to rank 10 items in order of their importance if they were stranded in a desert. The Homestay Decision Task presented learners with two potentially face-threatening and problematic scenarios for students staying with a host family together with some possible strategies for dealing with these. This study found a much higher incidence of feedback in the interactions that arose from the Survival Ranking Task. There were also differences in the types of feedback elicited by each task. For example, clarification requests were the most frequent feedback strategy in the Survival Ranking Task whereas confirmation checks were the most frequent in the Homestay Decision Task. A general finding of this study, however, was that both tasks produced a relatively small amount of interactional feedback. Thus, once again, optional-information tasks were shown to be less than ideal in eliciting negotiation of meaning or language-related episodes.

Pica's (2002) study of content-based classrooms for high-intermediate ESL learners provides further evidence of the limitation of optional-information tasks. The classes revolved around open discussions of literature and films. Following a detailed analysis of recorded lessons, Pica reached the following conclusion:

> The discussions were interesting and meaningful with respect to subject-matter content. However, as open-ended communication activities, they drew attention away from students' need for input and feedback that contained negative evidence on crucial form-meaning relationships in their L2 development. The discussions involved teachers and students in using language to discuss content, but did not focus on the L2 forms used to encode content meaning, particularly when the students' own production of form was itself not target-like (p. 16).

Pica went on to suggest that although the discussion task was an obvious choice for this kind of class 'as a task for L2 learning, it falls short of meeting conditions that satisfy learners' needs for positive, and particularly, negative evidence, relevant to L2 learning'.

An interesting classroom study by Hardy and Moore (2004) investigated two different task-design features. They examined 'structural task support' and 'content familiarity' in a computer-mediated classroom. In the former, high support was defined as a high amount of linguistic information, a clear ordering of parts of the task, and a requirement to select a response, while low task support entailed little linguistic information, left open the sequence needed to achieve a solution, and imposed no need for learners to construct their own response. 'Content familiarity' was operationalized in terms of the students' familiarity with the plot, characters, and cultural setting of the video material that comprised the input for the tasks. The results showed that low support resulted in more negotiation (broadly defined to include content as well as meaning) than high support. The ordering of the tasks was also a factor. When a task with low structural support was preceded by a task with high structural support, it led to more negotiation than in the reverse order. However, content familiarity had no effect on negotiation and there was also no evidence of any interaction between the two design variables.

Task types have also been found to influence the extent to which L2 learners make use of their L1 when interacting together. De La Colina and Mayo (2009) investigated Spanish undergraduate EFL students' use of their L1 when performing three tasks in self-selected pairs – a jigsaw task, a dictogloss and a text reconstruction task. In line with other research on the use of the L1 (see Chapter 6), they found that it was employed for two main purposes – metacognition (i.e. talk about the task) or metatalk (i.e. talk about talk). English (the L2) was used more or less exclusively in the jigsaw task to describe the content of the pictures although the L1 figured in very limited ways (e.g. expressing helplessness or completing a sentence they could not manage in English). In contrast, the L1 was the main language of the other two tasks, with English used only to produce or read aloud passages from the text. The greatest difference across tasks occurred in the number of episodes devoted to meta-talk with text reconstruction generating the most and the dictogloss the smallest. Storch and Aldosari (2010) also reported that task type had a greater effect than L2 proficiency on adult EFL learners' use of their L1 (Arabic). A text-editing task elicited considerably more use of the L1 than a jigsaw or composition task.

Finally, a number of recent studies have been based on Robinson's (2007) Cognition Hypothesis. That is, they investigated how combinations of design and implementation variables influenced different aspects of interaction involving learners. However, once again most of these studies were carried out in a laboratory. Kim (2009) is an exception. She asked 34 adult learners enrolled in an intensive English programme in the US to perform two picture narration tasks and two Spot-the-Difference tasks during regular class periods. These tasks differed in complexity as shown in Table 7.5. Kim investigated the effect of task complexity on the learners' production of language-related episodes. The predictions of the Cognition Hypothesis were only partially supported. For example the group of high proficiency learners produced more LREs in the Picture Narration task and more correctly resolved LREs when performing the complex version (in line with the Cognition Hypothesis) but the low-proficiency learners produced more when performing the simple narration task. In the case of the Spot-the-Difference task the low-proficiency group produced more LREs and more correctly resolved LREs when performing the simple version – again in line with the Complexity Hypothesis. However, different results were obtained for the high proficiency group, which produced a more or less identical number of LREs and correctly resolved LREs in the simple and complex version of the tasks[6].

Table 7.5 Simple and complex tasks in Kim (2009)

	Task 1 *Picture narration*	*Task 2* *Picture narration*	*Task 3* *Spot-the-Difference*	*Task 4* *Spot-the-Difference*
Simple	No reasoning required		Few elements in the picture	
Complex		Reasoning required		Many elements in the picture

Source: Kim, Y. 2009. "The Effects of Task Complexity on Learner–Learner Interactions." *System*, 37: 254–268.

2. Implementation variables and interaction

Of the implementation variables listed in Table 7.4, only task repetition, and interlocutor proficiency have been investigated in classroom-based studies.

Ko, Schallert and Walters (2003) investigated the effects of interaction on task repetition. In this study, each student told a story to two classmates and the teacher, engaged in negotiation-of-meaning exchanges with them about the story, and then retold the story to a group of other students. The effect of retelling the story was measured using a seven-point rating scale that evaluated different aspects of the students' stories. Out of the 21 students, 11 scored higher for the retold story than the original one, while 10 scored the same or lower. In other words, not all the students told better stories at the second attempt. The critical factor turned out to be the quality of scaffolding that occurred during the first telling. Ko, Schallert, and Walters showed that effective scaffolding was very much a co-construction, with the learners playing as important a role as the teacher. Pinter (2007) also showed that repeating a task (in this case a Spot-the-Difference task) could lead to improved task performance. The young beginner-level children in this study 'turned the task into a fast-moving game that they tackled with confidence' (p. 201) when they were given the opportunity to repeat it.

A number of studies have investigated the effects of the interlocutors' level of proficiency on interaction. These studies built on Yule and McDonald's (1990) laboratory study of mixed proficiency dyads performing tasks. Kim and McDonough (2008) compared the occurrence and resolution of LREs when an intermediate-level learner of Korean as a second language performed a dictogloss task with a learner of the same level and with a more advanced learner. The results showed that the interlocutor's proficiency had a significant effect, with the learners producing and successfully resolving more lexical LREs when they interacted with a more advanced learner. The proficiency pairings also influenced how the intermediate-level learners interacted (i.e. whether in a passive, dominant or collaborative role). Correctly resolved LREs were most likely to occur in collaborative interaction with an advanced interlocutor, a finding also reported by Watanabe and Swain (2007).

Of considerable interest is another implementation variable not considered in Ellis (2003), namely whether there is any advantage to a task being performed interactionally as opposed to individually. Storch (2007) compared ESL students completing a text-editing task in pairs and individually. There was no difference in the accuracy of their edited texts. However, Storch argued that performing the task in pairs was advantageous because it afforded opportunities for using the L2 for a range of functions, which would promote language learning. Clearly, though there is a need for more studies that examine this implementation variable.

Final comment

There is clear evidence from these studies that task type influences how learners interact. A general finding is that in a classroom context required-information exchange tasks such as Spot-the-Difference result in more negotiation of meaning and more language-related episodes than optional information tasks of the opinion-gap kind. There is also some evidence to suggest that L1 use occurs less frequently in required-information exchange tasks. However, as yet, there is insufficient evidence to suggest that a complex task results in more language-related episodes than a simple version of the same task when both are performed in a classroom. Regarding implementation variables, task repetition and interlocutor pairings according to proficiency have been found to affect the quality of task performance.

There is clearly a need for more classroom-based studies that investigate the effect that task types and implementation variables have on learner–learner interaction. There is also a need for more studies like Hardy and Moore's (2004) that investigate combinations of task characteristics and like Kim's (2009) that investigate whether theoretical claims regarding the effect of task complexity are supported when tasks are performed in the classroom. There is also a need to investigate how contextual variables impact on interaction when tasks are performed in different classrooms.

Tasks and L2 production

Another line of research on tasks involves examining learner production (i.e. the language that individual learners produce when performing dialogic or monologic tasks). In these studies, researchers have investigated the effects of various design and implementation variables on the fluency, complexity and accuracy of learners' production. Table 7.6 summarizes the design and implementation variables that I examined in my 2003 book. Again, many of the studies I considered were conducted in a laboratory setting[7] but I will only review classroom-based studies here. Of the design variables listed in Table 7.6, 'contextual support', 'topic', 'shared versus split information', 'closed versus open outcome', the 'inherent structure of the outcome' and 'discourse mode' have been investigated in classroom-based studies.

Arslanyilmaz and Pedersen (2010) provided contextual support by asking learners to watch a subtitled video of a performance of a task prior to performing tasks in an online chat classroom. The learners produced more fluent and more accurate

Table 7.6 Task design and implementation variables investigated in L2 production studies (based on Ellis, 2003)

Design variables	Implementation variables
1. Contextual support	1. Strategic (pre-task) planning
2. Number of elements to be manipulated	2. Online (within-task) planning
3. Topic	3. Rehearsal (task repetition)
4. Shared vs. split information	4. Post-task requirement
5. Dual vs. single task	
6. Closed vs. open outcome	
7. Inherent structure of the outcome	
8. Discourse mode (e.g. argument vs. description)	

language when provided with the subtitled similar task videos than when they were not so provided.

Lange (2000) asked adult ESL students to perform two opinion-gap tasks that were identical in design but differed in topic. She found that her Prison Task resulted in significantly more talk than her Heart Transplant Task. However, there was no difference in the accuracy of verb forms. Newton and Kennedy (1996) reported a number of differences in the language produced by adult ESL learners at the upper-intermediate level when performing shared- and split-information tasks (e.g. the shared information tasks led to greater use of conjunctions – a measure or complexity). However, as these tasks also differed in terms of discourse mode (i.e. argument versus description) it is not possible to decide which variable was responsible for the differences.

Tong-Fredericks (1984) compared a problem-solving task with a closed outcome and role-play tasks with open outcomes. She reported that the closed task elicited more spontaneous speech and a wider range of language functions. The role-play tasks resulted in a rigid question-and-answer structure but also greater attention to accuracy and more complex language. Brown (1991) also found that an open task elicited more complex language use (i.e. 'hypothesizing') than a closed decision-making task.

Brown (1991) also investigated the inherent structure of the outcome of a task by comparing 'tight' and 'loose' tasks. The former structured the learners' performance by means of questions and a rigid set of sub-tasks. However, Brown found no difference in any of his measures of production, possibly because the tasks did not differ in terms of the inherent structure of their content. Foster and Skehan (1996) reported a study that investigated the effects of task structure in relation to opportunities learners had for strategic planning. They found that planning had a greater effect on accuracy in tasks with a clear inherent structure. They suggested that learners were able to devote attention to accuracy during planning because the clear structure of the tasks removed the need for planning content.

Turning to the implementation variables, a number of classroom-based studies have investigated strategic planning (see Table 7.7). Strategic planning (typically

Table 7.7 Classroom-based studies of the effects of strategic planning

Study	Learners	Research questions	Method	Dependent variables	Results
Foster (1996)	32 intermediate ESL learners in the UK	What effect does planning time have on students' fluency, complexity and accuracy? Planning time = 10 minutes.	Three tasks: 1. personal information 2. narrative 3. decision-making. First five minutes analyzed. 3 groups: (1) guided planning, (2) unguided planning and, (3) control.	Fluency: – number of pauses – total silence – repetitions. Complexity: – variety of past tense forms – clauses per c-unit.	Planners paused less, were silent less and produced fewer repetitions than non-planners. Planners used a greater variety of past tense forms and produced more clauses per c-unit especially with guided planning in more cognitive demanding tasks (i.e. task (3). Unguided planning benefitted accuracy but only in tasks (1) and (3) (i.e. not in the narrative task).
Foster and Skehan (1996)	As in Foster (1996)	General hypothesis – planning will have an effect on fluency, complexity and accuracy. The effects of planning will depend on both type and task complexity.	As in Foster (1996)	Fluency: – reformulations – replacements – false starts – repetitions – hesitations – pauses (1 second or longer) – silence total. Complexity: – clauses/c-units – variety of verb forms Accuracy: – error-free clauses – lexical errors.	Fluency: For tasks (1) and (3) planning (but not type of planning) led to fewer pauses and less silence but for task (2) guided planning had a greater effect than unguided. In (3) planning led to more repetition, hesitation and replacements. Complexity: Clear planning effects for subordination (detailed planning > undetailed planning > no planning). Greater variety of past tense forms found on tasks (1) and (2) but not (3). Accuracy: More error-free clauses in planning conditions for tasks (1) and (3) but not for (2). No difference between guided and unguided planning.

Study	Participants	Research question	Task / design	Measures	Findings
Skehan and Foster (1997)	40 pre-intermediate ESL learners in UK	What effect does planning have on oral task performance?	As in Foster (1996). Two variables examined: – planning time (10 minutes) – post-task (public performance).	Fluency: – number of pauses greater than 1 second. Complexity: – clauses per c-unit Accuracy: – error-free clauses.	Planners paused less than no-planners in the (1) personal and (2) narrative tasks but not in the (3) decision-making task. Planners produced more complex language in tasks (1) and (3) but not (2). Planners were more accurate than non-planners but only in the narrative task. Some evidence that post-task led to greater fluency in task (2) and greater accuracy in task (3).
Skehan and Foster (2005)	61 intermediate-level ESL students	The study investigated the effects of guided vs. unguided planning and also the effects of planning at two different times (first five mins and second five minutes) during a task performance	Decision-making task (assigning sentence for crimes committed). Three groups: – no planning – 10 minutes guided planning – 10 minutes unguided planning.	Fluency: – end of clauses pauses – mid-clause pauses – filled pauses – length or run – reformulations – false starts. Complexity: – subordinate clauses per AS unit Accuracy: – error free clauses and clause length.	Fluency: Both planning conditions produced fewer end of clause pauses than the no planning group at both times. Detailed planners produced more filled pauses than undetailed and no planners but only at Time 2. Complexity: Detailed planners produced more subordinate clauses than other two groups but only at Time 1. Accuracy: Detailed planners produced more accurate speech than no planning but only at Time 1.

(Continued)

Table 7.7 (*Continued*)

Study	Learners	Research questions	Method	Dependent variables	Results
Mochizuki and Ortega (2008)	56 first-year high school students in Japan (beginner level)	What effect does guiding learners to attend to a specific grammatical feature have on performance of this feature in a task?	Picture story retelling task with audio-narrative stimulus. One-way task. Three groups: 1. No planning – students retold story immediately after listening to it and while looking at the pictures. 2. Unguided planning – five minutes. 3. Guided planning – five minutes – students received handout about how to make relative clauses.	Fluency: – mean number of words per minute Complexity: – mean length of T-unit – mean number of clauses per T-unit – number of relative clauses per T-unit Accuracy: – frequency of use of relative clauses – degree of accurate use of relative clauses.	Fluency: – trend for non-guided planners to be more fluent than no planning and guided planning group Complexity: – no group differences in general complexity Accuracy: – guided planners produced more and more accurate relative clauses than the unguided planners.

operationalized as allowing learners 10 minutes to plan what to say before they performed the task) has been found to have a clear effect on learner production. This effect is evident in all three aspects of language use (i.e. fluency, complexity and accuracy) but is perhaps most clearly evident in fluency (i.e. in a reduction in the number of pauses and total silence).

The nature of the planning (i.e. whether it was 'undetailed' or 'detailed') also influences production. Detailed planning involved providing guidance on how learners might use the planning time at their disposal to consider the grammar, vocabulary and the organization of what to say. Undetailed planning involved simply asking the learners to plan. Detailed planning leads to more complex language (e.g. greater subordination) and sometimes to more accurate language use.

These studies also show an interaction between task type and strategic planning. The Foster and Skehan studies included three tasks: (1) a personal information task, (2) a narrative task and (3) a decision-making task. Foster and Skehan (1996) argued that (1) is the easiest because the information is familiar to the learners and is well-structured. (3) is considered the most difficult because the information to be communicated is not familiar and is not clearly structured for the learners. The effect of the strategic planning on fluency appears to be clearer in the simpler tasks. Skehan and Foster (1997), for example, reported that planners paused less than no-planners in (1) and (2) but not in (3). Foster and Skehan (1996) found that the planners actually repaired more than the non-planners in (3) (i.e. became less fluent in this dimension). The relationship between task complexity, planning and L2 complexity is less clear. Foster and Skehan (1996) found that strategic planning led to greater grammatical richness in their personal information and narrative tasks but not in the decision-making task but in Skehan and Foster (1997) they reported that planning resulted in greater grammatical complexity in the personal and decision-making tasks but not in the narrative task. In the case of accuracy, the effects of planning appear to be more clearly evident in narrative tasks.

In Ellis (2005b), I identified two other types of planning – task repetition and online planning. However, these planning types have only been investigated in laboratory-based studies. Only one classroom study (Foster and Skehan, 1997) investigated the effect of including a post-task requirement (i.e. informing learners that they would have to perform the task a second time before the whole class). This study reported that the effect of the post-task requirement on fluency, complexity and accuracy was generally very weak.

More recent task-based studies of L2 production (e.g. Gilabert, 2007; Gilabert, Baron and Llanes, 2009; Robinson, 2007) have drawn on Robinson's Cognition Hypothesis to investigate the effects of task complexity on fluency, complexity and accuracy but they have all been laboratory-based. This is somewhat disappointing as these researchers are explicitly interested in the application of the Cognition Hypothesis to language pedagogy. Until it can shown that this has explanatory value in the classroom, doubts must exist about its relevance to language teaching.

Focused tasks

The research I have considered in the previous sections involved unfocused tasks. In this section I will examine the research that has investigated focused tasks (i.e. tasks that were designed to elicit specific linguistic features). Such tasks are important because they enable the researcher to pre-test learners' knowledge of the target features and thereby to measure in a post-test to what extent performance of the task results in learning. However, in this chapter I will only consider to what extent *focused* tasks successfully elicit the specific linguistic features that they targetted, reserving consideration of the learning that results to Chapter 8. It should be noted, however, that from a sociocultural theoretical perspective use of the target feature when performing the task is itself considered evidence of learning.

In an important paper, Loschky and Bley-Vroman (1993) noted that there were three ways in which what they called 'structure-based communication tasks' could be designed to provide a focus on specific target features:

1. 'Task-naturalness' (i.e. where the target structure may not be necessary for completion of the task but nevertheless can be expected to arise naturally and frequently in performing the task). The example Loschky and Bley-Vroman provided is of a task that involves the exchange of information about a travel itinerary. They suggested that this will lead naturally to the use of the Present Simple Tense (e.g. 'You leave Honolulu at 7:10.') but acknowledge that it could also be performed using other ways of expressing the future (e.g. 'will' or 'going to').
2. 'Task utility' (i.e. where the targetted feature is not essential for completing the task but is 'useful'). An example might be a Spot-the-Difference task that requires learners to make reference to the location of specific objects through the use of prepositions).
3. 'Task-essentialness' (i.e. where learners *must* use the feature in order to complete the task successfully – if they fail to use it they will not be able to achieve a satisfactory outcome). However, Loschky and Bley Vroman acknowledge that it may be impossible to design tasks that make the production of the target feature essential and that task-essentialness can only be achieved by receptive tasks.

   Thus, the best that might be achieved in the case of focused production tasks is task-naturalness or task utility.

Given that it is not possible to achieve task-essentialness a key question is whether the focused task does elicit use of the targetted feature. Table 7.8 summarizes the findings of a number of classroom studies that have employed focused tasks[8]. It is clear that at least some structure-based production tasks do result in the use of the target structure but that this depends on the structure (e.g. question forms are likely to be easier to elicit than passive verbs). Focused tasks are also likely to be

Table 7.8 Selected studies of structure-based production tasks

Study	Type of focused task	Feature targetted	Use of feature
Tuz (1993)	Information gap picture task	Adjectival order in English noun phrases e.g. 'a square red clock'	Learners failed to use target feature even though they had practised it previously in controlled exercises.
Sterlacci (1996)	Opinion gap	English modal verbs	18 out of 19 learners used the target structure in a written communicative task; learners were not aware that modal verbs had been targetted by the task.
Kowal and Swain (1997)	Consciousness-raising task (dictogloss)	French present tense forms	Learners did not focus specifically on present tense forms.
Samuda (2001)	Opinion-gap task	Epistemic modal verbs	Learners failed to use modal verbs; instead they relied on lexical means to express degrees of probability.
Boston (2010)	Opinion-gap narrative task	Passive Voice	Learners largely failed to use the passive voice even when they had been primed to do so.

more effective in developing control over partially acquired structures than entirely new structures[9]. Sterlacci's learners, for example, clearly already knew modal verbs whereas Samuda's learners did not. It is worth pointing out that 'a failed focused task still successfully performs as an unfocused task' (Boston, 2010: 172). In other words, even if a focused task does not succeed in eliciting the target feature it is still of potential pedagogic value.

As structure-based production tasks are not always successful in eliciting use of the target structure, the question arises as to whether it is possible to methodologically prompt learners to use the target structure when they perform the task. One way might be to pre-teach the target structure. The danger here is that the 'taskness' will be subverted as learners respond by treating the task as a situational grammar exercise that requires the display of correct language rather than as a communicative activity. A second way might be to 'prime' the use of target structure. This involves exposing learners to exemplars of the target structure in the expectancy that 'when speakers have a choice between alternative structures they produce the structure that was previously produced or heard' (McDonough, 2006: 181). Boston (2010) reported an interesting study in which he attempted to prime learners' use of the passive voice in a narrative task. However, the attempt was unsuccessful as the learners who received the prime still opted for use of the active voice. The third way is to utilize some kind of focus-on-form technique (as in Samuda, 2001). This technique has been found to be successful but relies to a considerable extent on the teacher intervening in the performance of the task. It will be considered in the following section.

An alternative type of focused task that has been shown to be somewhat more successful in eliciting use of the target feature is a consciousness-raising (CR) task. Whereas structure-based production tasks are built around content of a general nature (e.g. stories, pictures of objects, opinions about the kind of person you like), CR tasks make language itself the content and thus invite 'languaging about language'. However, CR tasks can still be considered 'tasks' in the sense that learners are required to talk meaningfully about a language point using their own linguistic resources. That is, although there is a linguistic feature that is the focus of the task, learners are not required to use this feature, only think about it and discuss it. Indeed, some studies that have employed CR tasks (such as Kowal and Swain, 1997) have found that learners do not actually produce the structure targetted by the task. Other studies, however, have found that they do. Eckerth (2008b), for example, investigated two L2 German CR tasks – a text-reconstruction task and a text-repair task where students worked in pairs to agree on a correct version of a text given to them. Eckerth found that these tasks resulted in very similar patterns of talk to unfocused tasks (e.g. similar amounts of speech production and negotiation of meaning) he also found that the tasks resulted in the learners not only attempting to use the target structures but also in struggling to achieve a metalinguistic understanding of how they worked. Moreover, the learners were not just focused on formal accuracy but rather 'attended to the way in which form, meaning, function and context interact' (p. 104). The extent to which CR tasks evoke use and discussion of the target feature depends in part on the nature of the task. Pesce (2008), for example, reported that a cloze-task stimulated more intensive discussion of Spanish imperfecto and indefinido verb tenses than a narrative task, where the learners were more focused on the propositional content of the task.

As I noted earlier, not all versions of TBLT involve the use of focused tasks and those that do differ in the kind of focused task they view as central. Skehan (1998) argued that focused tasks are unnecessary as unfocused tasks will in any case predispose learners to utilize clusters of linguistic features and, with appropriate design and methods of implementation, will ensure attention to accuracy. Long (1991) saw focused tasks as useful as they provide an opportunity for learners to engage in negotiation of meaning involving use of the target structure. In Ellis, (2003) I argued for the use of a variety of focused tasks, including CR tasks. I have also argued that both negotiation of form as well as negotiation of meaning has a role to play in helping learners focus on the target feature. I will now look at research that has investigated this type of negotiation.

Focus on form

Long (1991) defined focus on form as follows:

> Focus on form overtly draws students' attention to linguistic elements as they arise incidentally in lessons whose overriding focus is on meaning or communication (pp. 45-46).

Two kinds of focus on form can be distinguished: planned focus on form and incidental focus on form. Planned focus on form involves the use of focused tasks in which case the specific form to be focused on is predetermined. Incidental focus on form involves the use of unfocused tasks in which case the forms that will be focused on cannot be predetermined. However, students and teacher may need or elect to attend to various forms while performing the task. In this case, of course, attention to form will be extensive rather than intensive – that is, many different forms are likely to be treated briefly rather than a single form addressed many times.

The rationale for focus on form rests on the claim that L2 learning is most effectively promoted if learners have the opportunity to attend to form while engaged in meaning-focused language use. Long (1991) argued that only in this way can attention to form be made compatible with the processes that characterize L2 acquisition and thereby overcome persistent developmental errors. Given that learners have a limited capacity to process the second language (L2) and have difficulty in simultaneously attending to meaning and form they are likely to prioritize meaning over form when performing a communicative activity (VanPatten, 1990a). Thus, it is necessary to draw their attention to form during a communicative activity. As Doughty (2001) noted 'the factor that distinguishes focus on form from other pedagogical approaches is the requirement that focus on form involves learners' briefly and perhaps simultaneously attending to form, meaning and use during one cognitive event' (p. 211).

Table 7.9 (taken from Ellis, Basturkmen and Loewen, 2002) describes the various ways in which focus on form can be accomplished. A basic distinction is drawn between 'reactive focus on form' (where attention to form arises out of some problem in a participant's utterance) and 'pre-emptive focus on form' (where the participants make a particular form the topic of the conversation even though no actual problem has arisen).

Studies have investigated focus on form in both lockstep task-based lessons and in small group work. Ellis, Loewen and Basturkmen (1999) reported a total of 448 focus-on-form episodes (FFEs) in 12 hours of adult ESL task-based lessons – a rate

Table 7.9 Principal focus-on-form options (Ellis, Basturkmen and Loewen, 2002)

Options	Description
A. Reactive focus on form	The teacher or another student responds to an error that a student makes in the context of a communicative activity.
1. Negotiation	
a. Conversational	The response to the error is triggered by a failure to understand what the student meant. It involves 'negotiation of meaning'.
b. Didactic	The response occurs even though no breakdown in communication has taken place; it constitutes a 'time-out' from communicating. It involves 'negotiation of form'.
2. Feedback	
a. Implicit feedback	The teacher or another student responds to a student's error without directly indicating an error has been made, e.g. by means of a recast.
b. Explicit feedback	The teacher or another student responds to a student's error by directly indicating that an error has been made, e.g. by formally correcting the error or by using metalanguage to draw attention to it.
B. Pre-emptive focus on form	The teacher or a student makes a linguistic form the topic of the discourse even though no error has been committed.
1. Student initiated	A student asks a question about a linguistic form.
2. Teacher-initiated	The teacher gives advice about a linguistic form he/she thinks might be problematic or asks the students a question about the form.

Source: Ellis, R., H. Basturkmen, and S. Loewen. 2002. "Doing Focus on Form." *System*, 30: 419–32.

of one FFE every 1.6 minutes. There was an almost equal number of reactive and preemptive FFEs. 60 per cent of the FFEs were initiated by the teacher and 40 per cent by the students. The majority of the FFEs were directed at grammar or vocabulary (i.e. discourse and pronunciation received much less attention). Interestingly, 75 per cent of the FFEs involved the negotiation of form rather than the negotiation of meaning. That is, they originated in perceived linguistic difficulty rather than in a communicative problem. Recasts were by far the most common strategy employed in reactive FFEs, accounting for 75 per cent of the total. Ellis, Basturkmen and Loewen (2001) also investigated learner uptake in relation to the different types of FFEs. The results of this study were reported in Chapter 6.

This study by Ellis et al. has spawned a number of other studies of incidental focus on form in task-based lessons (e.g. Baleghizadeh, 2010; Farrokhi et al., 2008;

Loewen, 2003). These have reported varying rates of FFEs. For example, Loewen examined 12 different adult ESL classes and found marked differences in the rate of FFEs (i.e. a high of 1.24 per minute and low of .24 per minute). Baleghizadeh found only 41 FFEs in 10 hrs of meaning-focused instruction involving adult EFL learners in Iran (a rate of one FFE every 15 minutes). These differences probably reflect how the classroom participants orientate to tasks – i.e. whether as purely meaning-and-fluency activities or as providing affordances for developing their interlanguages. In the next chapter, we will consider studies that have investigated to what extent focus on form results in learning.

Williams (1999) investigated learner-initiated focus on form in the context of collaborative group work. She found that the learners did initiate focus on form but not very often, that more proficient learners paid more attention to form than less proficient, that focus on form arose most frequently in learner-generated requests to the teacher about language, and that the type of form that the learners focused on was 'overwhelmingly lexical'. Zhao and Bitchener (2007) reported a much higher incidence of FFEs in interactions involving adult migrants in New Zealand performing ten two-way information gap tasks. These FFEs were both reactive and pre-emptive. The extent to which focus on form occurs in learner–learner interactions is likely to depend on a whole range of social and psychological factors that influence how learners orient to the task (i.e. whether they see the task as simply an opportunity to communicate or as also affording opportunities for language learning).

In the case of CR tasks, of course, there is a requirement that learners will attend to form and so are more likely to do so[10]. Interestingly learners do not only participate in language-related episodes directed at the specific structure(s) targeted by the task but also at a range of other linguistic features. Eckerth (2008b), in the same study referred to previously, reported that 'collaborative task completion made a sizable contribution to the articulation, reasoning and negotiation of hypotheses that lay outside the actual structural focus of the task' (p. 109). All in all he identified a total of 127 'individual learner hypotheses' directed at such features although not all these were correct. Again, there are likely to be individual differences that influence the extent to which learners attend to form in CR tasks. Leeser (2004), for example, found that learner proficiency was a factor; the higher the proficiency of the dyads completing a dictogloss task, the more they attended to form, the more likely they were to attend to grammar rather than vocabulary, and the more likely they were to solve their linguistic problems correctly.

There is now ample evidence to show that when learners perform tasks they do not focus exclusively on meaning but also take 'time out' to attend to form. When a task is performed in a whole-class context, the teacher has the opportunity to direct learners' attention to form both preemptively and reactively. Also, in such a context, students also initiate attention to form. In small group work, the extent to which learners attend to form may be more variable depending on their orientation to the task and the nature of the task (i.e. CR tasks are likely to elicit more extensive or more consistent attention to form than structure-related production tasks).

Evaluating Tasks

The evaluation of tasks is directed at establishing to what extent they constitute effective devices for planning and teaching a language course. 'Evaluation' is not the same as 'research' as they have somewhat different aims. The aim of researching tasks is to arrive at generalizations about tasks and their implementation. The aim of evaluating tasks is to establish whether and to what extent a particular task is effective in a particular instructional context.

Evaluation can be of two kinds: micro or macro. In a micro-evaluation the implementation of specific tasks is studied. It involves a consideration of what transpires when a specific task is performed in a specific instructional context. In a macro-evaluation whole courses based on tasks are investigated. Both types of evaluation can be directed at 'accountability' (i.e. the extent to which the task/course achieves its goals) or 'improvement' (i.e. how the task/course can be improved).

Micro-evaluations of tasks

In Ellis (1997b) I distinguished three different approaches for conducting a micro-evaluation of a task; (1) a student-based evaluation, (2) a response-based evaluation (where the evaluator seeks to determine whether the task elicited the performance and outcomes intended), and (3) a learning-based evaluation (where the evaluator investigates whether the task has resulted in any learning). Each of these approaches requires different types of data. A student-based evaluation can be conducted using self-report instruments such as questionnaires, interviews and focus group discussions. A response-based evaluation requires observation/recording of learners' performance of a task and also the analysis of any product that results from the outcome of the task. A learning-based evaluation ideally requires some kind of pre- and post-test to determine when any changes in learners' ability to use the L2 have occurred. However, it might also be possible to demonstrate learning microgenetically through the detailed analysis of learners' performance of the task.

Micro-evaluations of tasks are rarely published. However, over the years I have asked students in my masters-level classes at various institutions to carry out micro evaluations of tasks (see Ellis, 2011). I will report on one of these here.

Freeman (2007) set out to evaluate a dictogloss task. This required students to listen to a listening text nine sentences long on the subject of obesity. They listened three times. On the first occasion they were asked to answer a multiple-choice question designed to establish whether they had understood the general content of the text. On the second occasion, the students were told to note down the key content words while on the third occasion different students were required to focus and take notes on the use of different linguistic forms (i.e. relative clauses, passive verb forms and transition signals). The students then worked in groups of three to reconstruct the text and write it out. Freeman's evaluation was designed to establish both accountability (i.e. whether the task met its objectives) and to provide information about how to improve the task. To this end she collected a variety of data – the notes the students made during the third listening (i.e. the extent to which they noticed and noted the target forms they were directed to attend to), the reconstructed text, a questionnaire to elicit the students' opinions of the task, a transcript of the discussion that took place while the students were reconstructing, notes made by observers of the lesson and a summative reflective report by the teacher.

The analyses of these data sets demonstrated that the students were successful in noticing and noting the target structures, that they attempted to use the target forms in their reconstructed text, that they engaged in a number of language-related episodes as they discussed their reconstruction (most of which led to correct language use), and that they reported the task had enabled them to communicate freely and that the interactions they engaged in during the discussion helped them with grammar. Freeman concluded that the students were largely successful in achieving the outcome of the task (the reconstruction of the text), that the task was successful in inducing noticing of the target forms, also encouraged attendance to other aspects of language, and led to active engagement (although not equally for all students). By and large then she felt that the task had achieved its objectives. However, she also identified a number of ways in which it could be improved. For example, she suggested that allowing the student to share the notes they had taken reduced the amount and quality of the interaction and that a better procedure would be to have asked the students to put away their notes before they started to reconstruct the text. Another suggestion was to assign the task of scribe of the reconstructed text to the least proficient of the students to encourage greater participation by this student.

Micro-evaluations are designed to inform practice rather than theory. They are local in nature. They can be seen as a form of practitioner-research (see Chapter 2). They help teachers to examine the assumptions that lie behind the design of a task and the procedures used to implement it. They require them to go beyond impressionistic evaluation by examining empirically whether a task 'works' in the way they intended and how it can be improved for future use. However, micro-evaluations – like other forms of practitioner research – are very time-consuming and it is unlikely that teachers will be able to conduct them on a regular basis.

Macro-evaluations of task-based programmes

The first published macro-evaluation of task-based teaching was of Prabhu's Communicational Language Teaching Project (see Prabhu, 1987). This was a project designed to introduce task-based teaching into a number of secondary school classrooms in southern India. An evaluation of this project was carried out by Beretta and Davies (1985) – see Chapter 3 for a summary of their findings.

Since then a number of other evaluations of task-based courses/programmes have been published (e.g. Carless, 2004; Li, 1998; McDonough and Chaikitmongkol, 2007). The main concern of these macro-evaluations was the extent to which task-based teaching was implementable in different teaching contexts. They focused on the problems that teachers experienced in making the switch from a traditional to a task-based approach. For example, Carless (2004) reported that the Hong Kong primary school teachers he investigated had mixed and sometimes confused notions of what a 'task' involved. One of the teachers he investigated defined tasks as activities involving 'active participation, real-life relationship, learning by doing, putting language and learning to use' (p. 647) while another teacher defined a task as an activity that 'mainly has objectives and it can link the pupil ability of understanding, conceptualizing, that kind of communication' (p. 648). While the first definition bears a reasonably close resemblance to the standard definition of a task, the latter is vague and, as Carless pointed out fails to distinguish 'task' from other types of activities. Carless also identified a number of other problems the teachers experienced – overuse of the L1, a challenge to discipline from the noise that resulted when students performed tasks, and their very limited use of English.

It is not surprising that teachers experience problems in implementing a task-based programme. Such an approach to teaching calls for a radically different view about the relationship between teaching and learning and neither teachers nor learners can be expected to fully understand this unless they receive training. Mackey, Polio and McDonough (2004) found that experienced teachers were much more likely than inexperienced teachers to engage in incidental focus on form (a key feature of task-based teaching) and that training developed a greater sense of awareness of the importance of focus on form in the inexperienced teachers.

Task-based evaluations constitute an important approach to investigating tasks as they draw attention to the role that 'context' plays in the ways in which tasks are implemented and the local problems that arise. Arguably, task-based evaluations are more useful than theoretically-driven research on tasks when it comes to advising teachers how to plan and implement both individual tasks and a task-based course.

Conclusion

'Task' is a construct that has proven of great interest to both researchers and teachers. It is, in fact, a construct that mediates between research and teaching. Researchers are interested in testing theoretical claims about the relationship between task design and implementation features on the one hand and interaction and L2 production on the other. Many of the studies that have been carried out by researchers have taken place in a laboratory setting for this reason but a number are classroom-based and, for this reason, potentially of greater relevance to teaching. There is now a broad body of classroom-based research and evaluation studies that can inform task-based teaching. The primary aim of this chapter has been to introduce readers to this.

There are, of course, problems (and misunderstandings) about both tasks and task-based teaching. I identified and addressed a number of these in Ellis (2009). I will conclude this chapter by mentioning a number of them here.

1. Definition of 'task'

Widdowson (2003) argued that 'the criteria that are proposed as defining features of tasks are ... so loosely formulated ... that they do not distinguish tasks from other more traditional classroom activities' (p. 126). However, to my mind the problem is not so much with the definition of 'task' but rather with the application of the definition. Some so-called 'tasks' do not convincingly satisfy the definitional criteria I have provided. For example, I am not really convinced that a 'cloze passage' constitutes a task as there is no obvious outcome other than the display of correct language.

2. Impoverished interaction

Some commentators have argued that tasks will result only in samples of impoverished language use that are of little acquisitional value. Seedhouse (1999), for example, claimed that the performance of tasks is characterized by indexicalized and pidginized language as a result of the learners' over-reliance on context and the limitations of their linguistic resources. Clearly, this may arise if learners with very limited L2 proficiency are asked to perform production tasks. However, there is plenty of evidence to suggest that tasks can induce rich interaction and complex language use. Indeed, one of the purposes of much of the research examined in this chapter has been to identify the task characteristics likely to promote the kinds of language use hypothesized to facilitate acquisition.

3. Attention to form

R. Sheen (2003) claimed 'the only grammar to be dealt with (in TBLT) is that which causes a problem in communication'. This view derives from Long's view that attention to form should ideally arise incidentally as a result of a communication problem. However, as I have shown in this chapter, focus on form can occur in a variety of ways – preemptively and reactively - and in the case of the latter through the negotiation of form as well as meaning. Studies have shown that a wide range of grammatical and lexical features are attended to in the course of performing tasks.

4. Learner-centredness

Learner-centredness is generally considered an ideal to strive for in language teaching. However, Swan (2005), argued that task-based language teaching promotes learner-centredness at the expense of teacher-directed instruction. He commented 'the thrust of TBLT is to cast the teacher in the role of manager and facilitator of communicative activity rather than an important source of new language'. Tasks do cater to learner-centredness as they are frequently performed by students working pairs or small groups. But they can also be employed in lockstep teaching. Indeed, a number of studies I have considered in this chapter examined the role that teachers can play when they perform tasks with students in a whole-class context. Task-based teaching is both teacher- and learner-centred.

Of course, there are real problems with implementing tasks in the classroom. The evaluation studies I considered in the previous section point to these. But, arguably, these are not problems with tasks or task-based teaching per se but rather with managing an innovation. Innovation of any kind poses difficulties (see Kravas-Doukas, 1998). The conditions that need to be satisfied for an innovation to be successful apply no more and no less to task-based teaching than to any other kind of innovation.

The focus of this chapter has been on research that has investigated tasks from the perspective of how they are performed in language classrooms. The key question, of course, is whether performing tasks in a classroom actually results in language learning. I will address this question in the next chapter.

Notes

1. In distinguishing between a 'task' and an 'exercise' I do not wish to claim that one is more beneficial for language learning than another. My purpose is simply to provide a basis for the focus of this chapter – research that has investigated 'tasks'.
2. In a few studies – arguably too few – the dependent variable is 'learning'. That is, the researcher investigated to what extent the learners' performance of the task results in language development. These studies are considered in the following chapter.
3. Identifying 'clauses' is relatively unproblematic in written texts but can be difficult in oral interaction given that many utterances are sub-clausal. For this reason, researchers first divide a learner's oral production into speech units, such as AS-units (Foster, Tonkyn and Wigglesworth, 2000). An AS-unit is 'a single speaker's utterance consisting either of an independent clause, or sub-clausal unit, together with any subordinate clause(s) associated with either'. They then measure the amount of subordination in terms of the proportion of AS-units that contain a subordinate clause.
4. A problem with this measure is that it is influenced by text length; that is, it is easier to obtain a high type–token ratio in a short text than in a long one. An alternative measure is Mean Segmental Type–Token Ratio. This requires dividing a learner's text into segments (for example, 50 words each) and calculating the type–token ratio of each segment and then calculating the mean score for all the segments.
5. A subsequent study by De la Fuente (2002) also looked at listen-and-do tasks. However this study, which produced similar results to Ellis, Tanaka and Yamazaki (1994), was conducted in a laboratory.
6. The results of Kim's (2009) study are in quite marked contrast to those of Robinson's (2007) laboratory-based study. Robinson found that 'task complexity, along the resource-directing dimension . . . clearly *progressively* and *positively* affects the amount of interaction and attention to input' (p. 209).
7. In some cases (e.g. Robinson, 2001) there is insufficient information to be able to tell whether the study was classroom – or laboratory-based. Also, a number of studies (e.g. Wigglesworth, 2001) were conducted in a testing context. Studies that could not be clearly identified as classroom-based and testing studies have been excluded from consideration.

8. See Pienemann and Doughty (1991) for a set of structure-focused tasks designed to elicit different grammatical structures in a laboratory context.

9. It should be noted that learners have been observed to use target features that are entirely new to them when performing a task. A number of sociocultural studies (e.g. Donato, 1994) have shown this becomes possible when production of the new feature is successfully scaffolded through interaction.

10. Swain and Lapkin (2001) compared the number of LREs resulting from performance of a jigsaw task (a kind of opinion-gap task) and a dictogloss. Although they found no statistically significant differences in the number of LREs generated by each task they did find that the dictogloss resulted in less variance in LREs produced by pairs of learners.

8

Interaction and L2 Learning in the Classroom

Introduction

In the previous chapters I focused on the nature of second language (L2) classroom discourse by examining its general characteristics (Chapter 4), the teacher's contribution (Chapter 5), the learner's contribution (Chapter 6) and the role that tasks play as devices for eliciting talk in the classroom (Chapter 7). My aim has been primarily descriptive. That is, I have tried to document the key characteristics of L2 classroom discourse and, to some extent to examine why these are as they are. Of course, researchers who have explored talk in the L2 classroom have done so because they see interaction as 'the fundamental fact of language pedagogy' (Allwright, 1984: 156) in the sense that it is the crucible in which acquisition is forged. Thus, the features of talk that have been investigated have been chosen because of the 'affordances' for learning that they create.

In this chapter I will explore these 'affordances' in greater depth. In accordance with the theoretical perspectives of sociocultural theory I will examine to what extent participation in interaction demonstrates that 'development' is taking place. In accordance with the theoretical perspectives of interactionist-cognitive theories, I will examine what evidence there is that classroom input and interaction facilitate 'acquisition' (i.e. effect changes in learners' L2 systems). Given the fundamental differences in how learning is conceptualized – and therefore investigated – in these two paradigms, I will begin with a fuller discussion of them.

Language Teaching Research & Language Pedagogy, First Edition. Rod Ellis.
© 2012 John Wiley & Sons, Ltd. Published 2012 by John Wiley & Sons, Ltd.

'Development' versus 'Acquisition'

In sociocultural theory, language learning is viewed as a process rather than as a product. It originates in 'other-regulated' activity through the mediation afforded by social interaction and progresses over time to 'self-regulated' activity through the mediation of private speech and, eventually, to activity that is fully automatized. This reflects Vygotsky's general genetic law of development according to which higher forms of thinking appear first on the intermental plain (i.e. in social interaction) and secondly on the intramental plain as learners gain control over them and are able to employ them independently. Learning a language, like any other form of higher-order thinking, entails mediated development. As Swain (2000) pointed out 'dialogue serves second language learning by mediating its own construction, and the construction of knowledge about itself' (p. 11).

Implicit in this view of how a language is learned is that when two or more people are speaking they create their own linguistic resources (which may or may not correspond to target-language norms) and in so doing demonstrate acquisition taking place in flight. From this perspective, use is acquisition and acquisition is use and it is not possible to draw a clear distinction between 'acquisition' and 'participation' (Sfard, 1998). In other words, the 'language acquisition device' is not situated inside the learner's head but is located in the social interactions in which the learner participates (Artigal, 1992).

Interactionist-cognitive theories also emphasize the important role played by interaction in L2 learning. However, they do not view learning as taking place within interaction but rather see interaction as providing the learner with 'input' which is then processed internally by means of the cognitive mechanisms responsible for attention, rehearsal and restructuring of existing knowledge systems. The learner 'acquires' features not *in* but *from* the input. Interaction, however, does more than simply expose learners to input. It also serves to focus their attention on specific linguistic forms. In other words, it is more than just an input-machine; it helps to activate cognitive processes that are responsible for acquisition. For example, the negotiation of meaning and the negotiation of form induce attention to linguistic forms and provide opportunities for learners to modify their own output and in so doing create the conditions for acquisition to take place. Acquisition itself, however, is a mental phenomenon; it takes place inside the learner's head. As Van Lier (2000a) put it, 'activity and interaction . . . relate to learning in indirect ways by feeding into cognitive processes that are going on in the brain and mind of the learner' (p. 246).

Interactionist-cognitive theories have spawned a number of hypotheses and constructs that have informed the research we will consider in this chapter and which I have explained in previous chapters. The key constructs are: (1) negotiation of meaning, (2) negotiation of form, (3) focus on form, (4) uptake, (5) modified output, (6) noticing and (7) noticing the gap.

The essential differences between a sociocultural and interactionist-cognitive account of learning are summed up in the following two quotations.

In situated social practices, use and learning are inseparable parts of the interaction. They appear to be afforded by topics and tasks and they seem to be related to specific people, with particularized identities, with whom new ways of behaving occur as the unfolding talk demands (Firth and Wagner, 2007: 812).

A cognitive theory of second language acquisition seeks to explicate the psychological mechanisms that underlie comprehension and production and are the means by which competence develops in the mind of the learner (Harrington, 2002: 124).

These two theoretical perspectives have been evident throughout the previous chapters. But they become central in this chapter, where we seek to investigate the relationship between the interactions that take place in a classroom and L2 learning. Each perspective operationalizes and investigates learning in a different way.

Learning necessarily involves change (Ellis, 2010b). From a sociocultural perspective change can take a number of different forms that reflect different levels of development. These are shown in Table 8.1.

Sociocultural studies have, by and large, been content to investigate the role played by classroom interaction in learning in terms of (1) and, to a lesser extent, (2). (1) requires only a cross-sectional study; the researcher analyzes a sample of interactions to pinpoint occasions where the use of a new linguistic form is mediated. A weakness of much of this research, however, is that it has often failed to demonstrate that the learners were unable to use the feature previously (i.e. there was no pre-test). Thus, it is difficult to know whether the use of the linguistic feature represents development or simply the use of a feature that has already been (partially) internalized. (2) and (3) are unique to sociocultural studies. They require a longitudinal study in order to investigate changes in the degree of assistance that the learner requires in order to use a specific feature. (4), however, requires that a new context for the use of the feature is created and this typically involves some kind of test of the learner's ability to use the feature. Only a few sociocultural studies have investigated learning in terms of (4).

Change from an interactionist-cognitive perspective is operationalized somewhat differently. It is measured in three main ways (see Table 8.2). (1) and (3) adopt an

Table 8.1 Types of 'development' in sociocultural theory

1. The learner is unable to produce a specific target form even with assistance.
2. The learner demonstrates that with substantial assistance he/she can use a specific linguistic feature (x), which previously he/she could not use.
3. The learner demonstrates that subsequently he/she can use x in the same or similar context but now requires less assistance than on the previous occasion.
4. The learner subsequently demonstrates that he/she can now use x in the same or very similar context in which he/she had used it previously without any assistance.
5. The learner is now able to employ x on different occasions in new contexts and with different interlocutors without any assistance (i.e. 'transfer of learning' has taken place).

Table 8.2 Operationalizing 'acquisition' in interactionist-cognitive theories

1. Emergence – i.e. showing that the learner is able to use a specific linguistic feature, which he/she could not use previously.
2. Accuracy – i.e. showing that the learner is able to use a specific linguistic feature more accurately at time a than at time b.
3. Developmental route – i.e. showing that the learner has progressed from an early transitional stage to a later stage in the ability to use a specific linguistic feature.

'interlanguage perspective'. That is, emergence or progress along a developmental route need not imply the ability to use the target-language form. In contrast, (2), which is by far the most popular way, measures learning in relation to target-language norms.

From an interactionist-cognitive perspective it is not sufficient to simply demonstrate that learners can use a particular linguistic form. It is necessary to show that some change has taken place in the learner's interlanguage system and, also, ideally, that this change is durable (i.e. it is not just a temporary phenomenon). While this can be achieved through longitudinal studies of a descriptive nature, the preferred method is experimental, involving a pre-test, a treatment (consisting of the opportunity to participate in some form of interaction), an immediate post-test and a delayed-post. In such a design, evidence for learning does not come from the interaction itself but, independently, from the tests or tasks that precede and follow the interaction, reflecting the fact that interaction is seen as the source, not the context, of learning. It is in this respect that studies in the interactionist-cognitive tradition differ most clearly from those in the sociocultural tradition.

In the sections that follow, I will review the research that has investigated the relationship between interaction and learning first from a sociocultural perspective and second from an interactionist-cognitive perspective. In this chapter, I will consider only the incidental learning that arises in or out of interaction. That is, I will not include studies that report the effects of deliberate attempts to teach learners specific L2 features. These will be considered in Chapter 9.

Sociocultural Studies of Classroom Interaction and L2 Learning

In this section, I will limit myself to a consideration of studies that have investigated change in terms of (2), (3) and 4) in Table 8.1. That is, I will exclude studies that have simply examined 'development' in purely cross-sectional studies. I have made this decision for two reasons. First, a number of such studies have been considered in previous chapters. Second, I remain sceptical as to whether these studies do convincingly demonstrate that 'change' has taken place. The studies that do produce clear evidence of change are of two kinds. One type utilizes microgenetic analyses of interactions that take place over a period of time or of a sequence of interactions that take place in a single lesson. This type of study is directed at investigating whether the interactional assistance provided at one point is reflected in some kind of improved performance at a later point. The second type employs a quasi-experimental design involving tests to measure to what extent the other-regulated learning evident in interaction leads to self-regulated learning. What all of these studies have in common is the use of some kind of task designed to stimulate talk about language (what Swain, 2006 has called 'languaging about language').

Some of the studies I will consider in this section were not classroom-based. Learners were withdrawn from their normal classroom to complete the various tasks in order to facilitate data collection, which often involved both audio- and video-recordings. However, I have elected to include these studies in the review of the research as there are relatively few sociocultural studies that have investigated learning (as opposed to 'participation') inside the classroom. Also, the researchers and tutors that figured in these studies generally played a 'teacher-like role' (see, for example, Swain and Lapkin, 2007). Nevertheless, the results of these studies need to be treated with caution. Sociocultural theory explicitly acknowledges that the setting in which a 'task' is performed is an inherent component of the 'activity' that results.

Microgenetic analyses

Two influential studies that paved the way for the later research were Aljaafreh and Lantolf (1994) and Donato (1994). These two studies differ in an important way. Whereas Aljaafreh and Lantolf investigated the learning that arises in expert-novice interactions, Donato focused on scaffolded learning in novice-novice interactions. An important finding of socioculturally oriented studies is that the joint activity in which learning originates does not require the presence of an 'expert' (i.e. the teacher).

Aljaafreh and Lantolf (1994) examined the one-to-one interactions between three L2 learners and a tutor who provided oral corrective feedback on essays they had written. The feedback that they received on their linguistic errors manifested the 'regulatory scale' shown in Table 5.7 in Chapter 5. This scale described a range of corrective feedback strategies that differed in their degree of explicitness. In detailed analyses of selected protocols, Aljaafreh and Lantolf showed how the degree of scaffolding provided by the tutor for a particular learner diminished over time (i.e. whereas at one time the instructor needed to correct quite explicitly to enable a learner to self-correct, at a later time more implicit correction sufficed). Aljaafreh and Lantolf argued that this demonstrated that learning was taking place. In other words, the fact that learners needed less assistance to self-correct their errors served as evidence that self-regulation was taking place.

Aljaafreh and Lantolf identified a number of general principles governing the effectiveness of feedback: (1) it must be graduated (i.e. no more help than is necessary is provided at any single time), (2) it must be contingent (i.e. it must reflect actual need and be removed when the learner demonstrates an ability to function independently), and (3) it is dialogic (i.e. it involves dynamic assessment of a learner's zone of proximal development). Clearly, in the interactions that this study investigated, the expert (i.e. the tutor) needed considerable skill to determine the appropriate level of scaffolding. Interestingly, Lantolf and Aljaafreh (1995) noted that the tutor was not always successful in fine-tuning his assistance to the learner's level of development. Sometimes he provided more scaffolding than was required, thereby failing to push the learner towards greater autonomy.

Donato (1994) described the collective scaffolding employed by groups of university students of French performing an oral activity that required them to plan a conclusion to a scenario in which a man was discovered by his wife to have bought a fur coat for another woman (based on Di Pietro, 1987). In a detailed analysis of an exchange involving the negotiation of the form '*tu t'es souvenu*', Donato showed how the learners jointly managed components of the problem, distinguished between what they had produced and what they perceived as the ideal solution, and used their collective resources to minimize frustration and risk. This collective scaffolding enabled the learners to construct the correct form of the verb even though no single learner knew this prior to the task. This was an important finding as it showed that the presence of an 'expert' was not needed for other-regulated learning to take place. As Wells (1999) pointed out:

> ... in tackling a difficult task as a group, although no member has expertise beyond his or her peers, the group as a whole, by working on the problem together, is able to construct a solution that none could have achieved alone (p. 10).

Altogether Donato identified 32 instances of such collective scaffolding. However, these only provided evidence of other-regulated learning. They did not show that internalization of the new forms had taken place. However, one week later Donato asked the same students to participate in an oral activity. He inspected their oral performances to see whether individual learners were now able to produce those structures that had figured in their collective scaffolding independently. He reported that in 75 per cent of the cases (including the '*tu t'es souvenu*' structure) they did. This study provides clear support for the central claim of sociocultural theory, namely that the genesis of language learning can be observed in the interactions that learners engage in when addressing a problem-solving task.

Subsequent studies have followed in the path of these two studies. Poehner's work on 'dynamic assessment' (see Chapter 5) draws on Aljaafreh and Lantolf's idea that a reduction in the other-regulation that learners need to perform a specific linguistic feature constitutes evidence of development. However, both Alajaafreh and Lantolf's original study and Poehner's later work on dynamic assessment assume an instructional context where an expert (the tutor) works with a single learner. Interesting as this research is, its practical application to most classrooms is doubtful. Of greater interest, are studies that draw on Donato's approach by examining how collaborative scaffolding assists learning in classrooms involving small group work.

Ohta (2000) reported such a study. She investigated a second-year university-level Japanese language class, analyzing the interactions between pairs of students with a view to identifying the 'mechanisms of assistance' (i.e. what triggers suppliance of assistance), 'appropriate assistance' (i.e. assistance that led to language development) and 'internalization processes' (i.e. the appropriation of a language structure for individual use). Ohta focused on one particular pair of students – Becky and Hal. In detailed analyses of the interactions of this pair, she showed how Hal was able to provide Becky with help by responding to Becky's subtle cues that she needed assistance and also by withdrawing support as Becky's ability to function more independently increased. Ohta also provided evidence of Becky's transition from intermental to intramental functioning. Thus, whereas initially Becky was entirely reliant on Hal's help, she was ultimately able to spot her own errors and correct them without assistance. However, Ohta also pointed that Becky's self-regulation was not complete as she did not demonstrate the ability to use the target structure correctly in a broad range of contexts. This study is significant because it provides evidence of development within a single lesson.

These studies have all examined grammatical development. Other studies that have adopted a microgenetic approach have investigated the development of pragmatic knowledge. In Chapter 6, we considered the study by Belz and Kinginger (2003), which examined the acquisition of German informal address forms in a computer-mediated classroom. Gonzalez-Lloret (2008) also focused on addressivity in a study of second-year Spanish language students in the University of Hawaii. She reported a case study of the repair sequences involving one of the students (Vero) as she worked on a 10-week project with her project mate (Jeff) and her chat-pal in Spain (A. m). Gonzalez-Lloret used the techniques of conversational analysis to plot the gradual development that took place in Vero's use of informal pronouns and verb forms. She showed that that the collaborative repair work that Vero experienced did not lead to immediate use of the appropriate forms but that over several weeks, during which Vero participated in a number of repair sequences initiated by A_m, and displayed considerable variability in the use of address forms, she eventually learned to use the target forms.

These studies reveal a number of essential aspects of L2 'development' as this is understood in sociocultural theory:

1. Learning originates in joint activity, which serves to co-construct knowledge.
2. For the joint activity to be effective for language learning it has to be 'collaborative'.
3. Development arises not just in the joint activity of expert-novice pairs but also in that of novice-novice pairs.
4. Learning is emergent reflecting the process of internalization as learners shift gradually from the intermental to intramental plane.
5. Variability in the use of target forms (whether grammatical or pragmatic in nature) is inherent in the developmental process.

6. Learning is not only evident in the correct/appropriate use of target forms but also in the reduced amount of scaffolding that a learner needs from his/her partner in order to produce the target forms.

Quasi-experimental studies

A limitation of the studies I considered in the previous section is that they examine development entirely in terms of the learner performance in which the development is taking place. It is therefore impossible to say whether they have reached the final level of development (Level 5 in Table 8.1). To show that full internalization has taken place, some kind of experimental design involving pre- and post-tests is needed. In this section I will review a number of experimental-type studies that have been informed by sociocultural theory.

Nassaji and Swain (2000) sought to replicate and extend Alajjafreh and Lantolf's study. They compared the effectiveness of two kinds of oral feedback on the article errors made by two Korean learners of English in their written composition. The assistance to one learner was provided within her Zone of Proximal Development (ZPD) (i.e. the tutor systematically worked through Aljaafreh and Lantolf's scale to negotiate the feedback she supplied) while the assistance to the other learner was random (i.e. the tutor was supplied with a random list of correcting strategies drawn from the scale). This study included post-tests to investigate to what extent the two types of feedback enabled learners to use English articles accurately. The results showed that providing feedback within the learner's ZPD was effective in (1) helping the learner to arrive at the correct form during the feedback session, (2) enabling the learner to arrive at the correct form with much less explicit assistance in subsequent sessions, and (3) enabling the learner to use the correct form unassisted in a post-test consisting of a cloze version of the compositions she had written previously. In contrast, random feedback did not always succeed in enabling the learner to identify the correct article form in the feedback sessions and was much less effective in promoting unassisted use of the correct forms in the post-test.

In a series of studies Swain and her co-researchers investigated the extent to which the 'language-related episodes (LREs)' (see Chapter 7) that occurred when learners were performing a task in pairs or small groups led to development as measured by post-tests. The typical design of these studies was as follows:

1. Learners complete a task (e.g. a dictogloss) in pairs of groups.
2. Their performance of the task is recorded and transcribed and all the language-related episodes identified.
3. These episodes were coded as successfully resolved, unsuccessfully resolved or unresolved.
4. Individual learners take tailor-made post-tests to ascertain whether they are able to use the features targetted in the LREs correctly.

In some of the studies, pre-tests were also administered.

In an early study by La Pierre (reported in Swain, 1995), eight early-French immersion students completed a dictogloss task in pairs and one week later took tailor-made dyad-specific post-tests. The results showed that out of the 140 LREs that were successfully resolved, 80 per cent of the corresponding post-test items were correct. In the 21 episodes that were unsuccessfully resolved, 70 per cent of the corresponding post-test answers were also wrong. In other words, there was a strong correlation between the successful resolution of language problems and scores on the post-tests.

Swain and Lapkin (1998) reported a study of one pair of Grade 8 immersion learners (Kim and Rick) who completed two picture jigsaw tasks. They first took a pre-test designed to test their knowledge of the grammatical structures that a trial run of the task had shown were likely to be used when performing the task. The learners were first given a mini-lesson to focus attention on a specific grammatical feature (agreement of adjectives). They then completed the first task by generating the story told by the pictures and jointly preparing a written version. This was recorded. The following week they watched a pre-recorded mini-lesson on French reflexive verbs and repeated the second task. This was also recorded. The tapes were then transcribed and tailor-made post-tests developed. Finally, a post-test was administered that included the pre-test items and also additional items derived from the LREs observed in the task performances. The analysis included qualitative descriptions of the LREs that the two learners generated, illustrating the mental processes that mediated L2 learning (e.g. generating alternatives, assessing alternatives through hypothesis testing, and applying rules to new L2 contexts). These descriptions were then related to pre- and post-test scores to show how the dialogic activity of the two learners enabled them move from incorrect to correct responses. Swain and Lapkin argued that the dialogue these learners engaged in served as 'both a means of communicating and a cognitive tool' (p. 333). They noted, however, that both of these learners were 'strong students' and that other students in the class were much less collaborative, producing far fewer LREs.

In another study, this time of Grade 7 French immersion learners, Swain and Lapkin (2002) examined the effects of languaging on two learners' (Dara and Nina) rewriting of a story. They first viewed a video-tape of a mini-lesson on French reflexive verbs and watched two learners modelling writing a story. They were then asked to write a story collaboratively based on a picture jigsaw task. Next their text was reformulated by a native speaker and the learners were asked to notice the differences. This was followed by a stimulated recall interview where they were asked to comment on the features they had noticed. Finally, they were given a copy of their original story and asked to rewrite it. Swain and Lapkin examined the LREs that arose when the learners were writing the initial story and during the noticing activity. They then compared the learners' initial and final texts, treating them as a pre-test and a post-test. 80 per cent of the changes that Dara and Nina made were correct. What is especially interesting is that not all the correct changes corresponded to the changes in the reformulated text they had been given (i.e. they were able to make a number of correct changes on their own account). These

Table 8.3 Design of study by Swain et al. (2009)

1. Warm-up stage	2. Pre-test stage	3. Languaging stage	4. Break	5. Immediate post-test stage	6. Interview stage	7. Delayed post-test stage
Participants explain aloud a text containing several bolded determiners.	Pre-test: Participants talk about the form and meaning of bolded verbs in a text. Conceptual definition 1: Participants define the concept of voice using metalanguage provided.	Participants engage in a languaging activity based on cards that presented information about voice bit-by-bit and required the participants to think aloud and explain each bit.		Immediate post-test: Participants repeat the pre-test. Conceptual definition 2: Same as previously.	Participants talk about their backgrounds and perceptions of the activities.	Conceptual definition 3: Same as previously. Delayed post-test: Participants complete a cloze test using the same text as in previous tests. Stimulated recall: Based on the cloze test.

correct changes were directly traceable to the languaging that had taken place in the LREs.

Tocalli-Beller and Swain (2007), investigated the extent to which adult English as a second language (ESL) learners were able to collaboratively work out the meanings of jokes and puns, such as 'Waiter, I'd like a corned beef sandwich, and make it lean. Yes, sir! In which direction?' They were able to show that the learners were able to jointly interpret the jokes (even when both of them were novices and neither of them initially knew the meaning of the key lexical item in the joke) and, importantly, that, as a result of this collaborative activity, they internalized the meanings of the items as demonstrated in subsequent post-tests. In addition to demonstrating the role that collaborative dialoguing can play in language learning, this study provided support for Vygotsky's (1987) claims regarding the importance of play (in this case involving language) in 'stretching' learners (see also section on 'language play' in Chapter 6).

Clearly, there are individual differences in the quality of 'languaging' that learners engage in and these can be expected to affect the 'affordances' for learning that arise. Watanabe and Swain (2007), drawing on Storch's (2002) research on collaboration in small group work (see Chapter 6), investigated the patterns of interaction that took place in pairs of learners and the relationship of these to learning. The pairs of learners differed in their L2 (English) proficiency. In a similar design to Swain's previous studies, the learners wrote an essay in pairs (the pre-test), were given a reformulated version of it which, together, they compared with their own text, and then individually rewrote their initial essay (the post-test). Learning was again operationalized as the correct changes that the learners made to their original text. The results indicated that proficiency differences in the pairings made little difference in post-test performance but that the extent to which the pairs engaged in collaborative patterns of interaction did.

Swain and Lapkin (2007) used a similar design to their earlier studies but this time investigated the role played by 'interaction with the self' (p. 82) in language learning. The key difference between this study and Swain and Lapkin (2002) was that a single learner (Neil) performed the writing tasks independently. The focus of this study was on the differences that Neil reported noticing between his original text and the reformulated text and how these related to the changes he made to his original text in the 'post-test'. Swain and Lapkin used the results of the study to argue that 'Neil's learning is mediated by his own languaging' because 'languaging focused his attention, drew on and constructed new understandings, and consolidated existing knowledge' (p. 83). This can be seen as a study of the mediating role played by private speech.

Continuing in the same vein, Swain et al. (2009) investigated the relationship between the quality and quantity of languaging by intermediate learners of French at a Canadian university and their performance in an immediate and a delayed post-test. The focus of this study was a specific grammatical concept – voice in L2 French. I have outlined the complete design of this study in Table 8.3 to provide readers with a picture of the intricacy of Swain's studies and how they enabled her to examine the emergence and consolidation of L2 knowledge. This study, like the previous, one focused not on the role of dialoguing but on self-verbalization. Swain et al. provided detailed analyses of the learners' responses at each stage of the study. They also reported correlations between the various measures they calculated from the data they had collected. There were significant correlations between the number of 'language units' produced in the languaging stage and both the learners' immediate post-test scores and their stimulated recall scores (based on their explanation of their answers in the cloze test). While all the learners learned something about the concept of voice, it was the 'high languagers' who demonstrated greater depth of understanding. High languagers not only produced more 'language units' during stage 3 but also better quality units (i.e. they demonstrated a higher rate of self-assessment and inferencing).

Two related constructs underlie the quasi-experimental studies I have considered in this section – scaffolding and languaging. What links these two constructs is the idea of 'mediation' – the central notion in sociocultural theory (see Lantolf, 2000). All of the studies involved learners in grappling with language problems, working towards a conceptual understanding in order to solve them, and thereby learning to use linguistic forms in a target-like way. The studies show that both the mediation that occurs when learners work dialogically to solve a problem and when they work individually to verbalize solutions assists development. The strength of these studies is that 'development' is not just operationalized in terms of the 'language-related episodes' that arise in social interaction or in the 'language units' observed in interaction with the self but also in subsequent performance in tests. However, these studies do not convincingly demonstrate that complete transfer of learning has taken place as the post-tests typically involved performance of the same kind as the pre-test. Thus, we cannot be certain that the learners were able to generalize their learning to new tasks and new contexts. In particular, the tasks used to measure learning were of the kind likely to encourage the use of explicit L2 knowledge. Lantolf and Thorne (2006) argued for the importance of 'conceptually organized grammatical knowledge' (p. 303) and this provides a theoretical basis for measuring development in terms of explicit knowledge. But it is also important to establish whether learners have developed full procedural knowledge (i.e. have fully internalized the features they have acquired explicitly). This requires a different kind of evidence – for example, performance in free oral production tasks – but this has been lacking to date.

Interactionist-Cognitive Studies of Classroom Interaction and L2 Acquisition

Two types of research have investigated classroom interaction and L2 acquisition from an interactionist-cognitive perspective. The first type is descriptive and exploratory. It entails observing real-time language lessons, identifying specific interactional features, and relating these to measures of subsequent learning. In this type of research there is no attempt to intervene by directing the kinds of interactions that learners will participate in. The second type is experimental – or rather quasi-experimental as usually it is not possible to form groups of learners randomly in classroom research. In this type there is a pre-test, some form of interactional intervention (e.g. by means of corrective feedback) and one or more post-tests. In this chapter I will only consider experimental research that has investigated interaction (e.g. focus on form) derived from some kind of task. I will reserve consideration of research that has investigated the effects of form-focused instruction (FFI) involving explicit instruction and/or code-oriented practice (i.e. focus on forms) on learning to Chapter 9.

Descriptive/exploratory research

Descriptive/exploratory studies have examined the relationships between some type of focus on form (usually reactive), uptake, and language learning. They have asked three principal questions:

1. Does instructionally induced attention to form in the context of interaction result in learner uptake of linguistic features?
2. Does successful uptake (e.g. learner self-correction following corrective feedback) lead to acquisition?
3. Does instructionally induced attention to form in the context of interaction facilitate acquisition?

Figure 8.1 shows the relationships posited in these research questions. Interaction involves learner production, which leads to some form of interactionally induced attention to form and, possibly, uptake. Interactionally induced attention to form may be related directly to acquisition or may be indirectly related to it via uptake. The relationship between interactionally induced attention to form and uptake (Research Question 1) was considered in Chapter 7. Here I will focus on research that has investigated the relationships between uptake and acquisition (i.e. Research Question 2) and between interactionally induced attention to form and acquisition (i.e. Research Question 3). The studies I will consider divide into those that investigated foreign and second language contexts so I will consider them in this way.

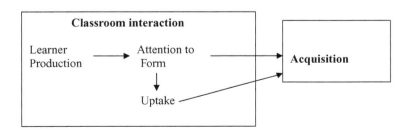

Figure 8.1 The relationships between focus on form, uptake and acquisition

Studies conducted in EFL contexts   Slimani (1989) investigated a series of lessons taught to a group of adult Algerian students. At the end of each lesson she asked the students to record on an 'uptake chart'[1] what they thought they had learnt. In the main, they listed vocabulary items. She then examined transcripts of the lessons to try to identify what it was in the classroom interactions that might have caused them to remember the items. In these classes it was the teacher who generally controlled the discourse. However, there were occasions when individual students nominated their own topics, i.e. learner topicalization occurred. Slimani found that 'whatever is topicalized by the learners rather than the teacher has a better chance of being claimed to have been learnt'. This suggests that when learners have the opportunity to initiate an exchange they are more likely to pay attention and that this holds true not just for the individual student doing the initiating but also for other students listening in.

In a similar study, Ellis (1995b) examined the uptake reported by groups of high school Japanese learners of L2 English who performed a listen-and-do task that exposed them to three kinds of input: baseline, premodified, and interactionally modified (see Chapter 7). The learners reported learning a mean of 2.71, 3.88, and 5.89 words respectively in these input conditions. In other words, reported uptake was highest in the interactionally modified input condition. However, the learners were exposed to considerably more input in the interactionally modified condition than in the other conditions simply as a result of the increased time it took to complete the task in this condition.

Havranek (2002) reported a large-scale exploratory study that investigated the effects of different types of correction on 207 German-speaking learners of English as a foreign language at different ages and proficiency levels. Eight consecutive lessons in 10 school and university classes were audio-recorded and transcribed. 1700 instances of corrective feedback were identified in the transcripts. At the conclusion of the observation period, each class completed a class-specific language test involving gapped texts, answering questions and correcting errors that had been underlined in a text. Ten different correction types were identified, the most frequent being recasts, similar to those reported in other studies (see Chapter 5). Havranek investigated the effect of the feedback on both those learners who had committed the specific errors (i.e. the perpetrators) and on the other students in the class (i.e. the auditors). She reported that the perpetrators used the structures they had received feedback on correctly in the language test 51.4 per cent of the time, while the auditors did so 61 per cent of the time[2]. The most successful type of corrective feedback was elicitation leading to the learners self-correcting. Feedback that explicitly rejected a deviant utterance and also provided the correct form was also successful. Havranek noted that both of these types of correction are only found in classrooms. In contrast recasts – the least successful type – is common to both classroom and naturalistic settings. The number of times a specific error was corrected also had an effect. For the perpetrators, there was hardly any difference for single, double or triple corrections while more than three corrections resulted in a markedly lower test score. The auditors, however, benefitted from a second and third correction. Perpetrators benefitted most from having their grammar errors corrected, especially when the errors involved relatively simple rules. They benefitted the least in the case of pronunciation errors. In contrast the auditors benefitted most by listening to pronunciation errors being corrected. Havranek's finding that corrective feedback was most effective when the learners were able to successfully uptake the correction is an important one and has a bearing on the debate about the role of uptake in language learning, which we will consider later.

Alcon (2007) investigated Spanish high school students. She collected data during a whole academic year from meaning-focused lessons. She asked the learners to keep diaries in which they recorded any new words they had learned after each conversational class. She also administered immediate and delayed translation tests, which were created on the basis of items the learners reported in their diaries. Form-focused episodes (FFEs) were identified and classified using a similar framework to that in Ellis, Basturkmen and Loewen (2001) – for example, Alcon distinguished preemptive FFES (teacher-initiated and learner-initiated) and reactive FFEs. Most of the FFEs were directed at vocabulary. The teachers' lexically oriented pre-emptive FFEs resulted in the learners recording the words in their diaries whereas the teachers' reactive FFEs did not. However, the teachers' reactive FFEs did have a positive effect on vocabulary learning as measured in the translation tests. In other words, although the teachers' reactive FFEs, most of which involved recasts, did not contribute to explicit noticing, they did have a positive effect on vocabulary learning. Alcon-Soler (2009) reported a similar study that found evidence of a relationship between noticing (as demonstrated in the learners' diaries) and immediate lexical gains but not with performance in delayed tests.

Studies conducted in ESL contexts   Lightbown and Spada (1990) examined the effects of corrective feedback in the context of communicative language teaching. This study investigated a number of classrooms, which were part of an intensive communicative ESL programme for francophone students in Quebec. Lightbown and Spada found that, although the teaching was mainly communicative in focus, some of the teachers paid more attention to the students' formal errors than others. They showed that the learners who received error correction achieved greater accuracy in the production of some structures (for example, the use of the correct 'There is . . .' in place of the L1-induced error 'It has . . .') but not of others (for example, adjectival placement).

Williams (2001) conducted a study in an intensive English programme in the USA. She examined the LREs initiated by teachers as well as by learners when reacting to some problem that arose in the course of trying to communicate. A tailor-made one-item test was designed for each LRE identified in 65 hours of audio-taping lessons. Test scores for four different proficiency groups ranged from 40 per cent to 94 per cent, indicating a close relationship between LREs and test scores, which grew stronger with proficiency. Test scores did not vary according to the initiator of the LREs; that is, whether the LRE began with the teacher providing feedback or the learner requesting assistance made no difference. The results also pointed to learners benefitting from solutions provided by other learners as their proficiency rises. At the most advanced level, information provided by other learners became more important than information from the teacher.

Loewen (2005) recorded teacher-led task-based lessons involving adult ESL learners and then identified the 'form-focused episodes' (FFEs) in the transcripts of the lessons (see Chapter 7). The FFEs were then coded for a number of characteristics – for example, uptake, successful uptake (i.e. repair), complexity (i.e. length of episode), and source (i.e. whether the episode was triggered by a communication breakdown or by the desire to attend to form for its own sake). Tailor-made tests were administered one or two days after the lessons or two weeks later. These were of three kinds – 'suppliance' (i.e. testing knowledge of lexical items), 'correction' (i.e. correcting grammatical errors in sentences) and 'pronunciation' (i.e. pronouncing words written on cards). The learners' responses were scored as correct, partially correct, or incorrect. Out of the 473 FFEs tested, 62.4 per cent were either correct or partially correct in the immediate tests and 49.1 per cent in the delayed tests. A logistic regression analysis showed that both uptake and successful uptake (i.e. uptake that repaired the original error) predicted the scores for the correction and suppliance tests, lending credence to the claim that uptake has a role to play in language acquisition. In the case of the pronunciation tests the predictor variables were complexity (short, simple FFEs), source (i.e. the FFE centred around a communication breakdown), and successful uptake. Loewen noted that these results suggest that different types of focus on form may be needed to treat different aspects of language.

Drawing on the same data, Loewen and Philp (2006) examined the effect of different characteristics of recasts (e.g. linguistic focus, length, number of changes, segmentation) on individual learners' uptake and acquisition, as measured by tailor-made tests. They found that those recasts with explicit linguistic characteristics were more likely to result in both uptake and learning.

Loewen (2006) extended the analysis of his data to investigate the extent to which the learners used the items targetted in the FFEs in subsequent classroom discourse, which can be considered another measure of acquisition. He reported that 20 per cent of the total forms targeted occurred subsequently in spontaneous communication. He also found that the accuracy of these forms in classroom use was greater after the FFE than before, suggesting the focus on form had had some effect.

General comments   These studies provide evidence of a clear relationship between discoursal attention to form that occurs both pre-emptively and reactively in classroom interaction and acquisition. Evidence of pre-emptive focus on form assisting learning is evident in the studies by Slimani, Alcon and Loewen. When pre-emptive focus on form is initiated by learners it provides an opportunity for them to control the discourse (see Chapter 6) and this may enhance the attention that they pay to problematic forms. Alcon, however, found that teacher-initiated lexical FFEs were also effective in this respect. Evidence of reactive focus on form assisting acquisition can be found in the studies by Lightbown and Spada, Williams, Havranek, Alcon and Loewen. These studies also show that a number of variables influence the extent to which focus on form impacts on acquisition, including (1) the nature of the target structure (Lightbown and Spada reported that corrective feedback assisted the acquisition of 'There is . . .' but not of adjectival placement), (2) the type of corrective feedback (Havranek reported that elicitations and explicit corrections had a notably stronger impact than recasts while Loewen and Philp showed that more explicit types of recasts promoted learning[3]), (3) the aspect of language that is focused on (e.g. grammar versus pronunciation), and (4) the learners' proficiency (Williams' study suggests that the benefit learners accrue from focus on form increases with proficiency). It is also worth pointing out that both those learners who instigate the attention to form and those who listen in are able to benefit. These studies also show that successful uptake has a role to play in acquisition. Both Havranek and Loewen reported that when learners self-corrected as a product of focus on form, learning was enhanced. Overall, then, the general answer to Research Questions (2) and (3) is a clear 'yes'.

Quasi-experimental studies of classroom interaction and L2 acquisition

The quasi-experimental studies I will consider here fall into three main groups; (1) those that investigated non-reciprocal tasks (i.e. listen-and-do tasks), (2) those that have investigated oral communication tasks (i.e. two-way tasks), and (3) those that have investigated consciousness-raising (CR) tasks. In the case of (1) and (2) the participatory structure was generally teacher-class. In the case of (3) the participatory structure was pair or small group work.

Studies involving non-reciprocal tasks   In Chapter 7, I reviewed a number of studies involving listen-and-do tasks that investigated the effect of different kinds of input on learners' comprehension. These studies also included post-tests designed to measure the learners' acquisition of the target items. I will revisit these studies here, this time examining the effect of the different kinds of input on acquisition. For convenience, Table 8.4 summarizes the results of each study.

The results are somewhat mixed. Loshcky (1994) found that the type of input had no effect on acquisition. Ellis and He (1999) also reported no difference between learners receiving premodified and interactionally modified input. However, Ellis, Tanaka and Yamazaki (1994) found that interactionally modified was superior to both baseline and premodified input. Two factors can explain these different results. First, in Loschky's study (but not in the other studies) the items were first presented to the learner before listening to the descriptions. This may have eliminated the need for modified input to make the items salient. Second, in Ellis and He the time taken to complete the task in the premodified and interactionally modified conditions was controlled and therefore the same whereas in Ellis, Tanaka and Yamazaki the interactionally modified input took longer. We might conclude, therefore, that interactionally modified input benefits acquisition when (1) the items are

Table 8.4 Effects of different kinds of input on L2 acquisition

Study	Design	Target features	Results
Loschky (1994)	Three experimental groups of adult learners. Teacher provides descriptions as (1) baseline input, (2) premodified input, (3) interactionally modified input.	Japanese locatives and vocabulary	No differential effect for type of input found for acquisition of either locatives or vocabulary.
Ellis, Tanaka and Yamazaki (1994)	Three experimental groups of Japanese HS students. Teacher provides descriptions as (1) baseline input, (2) premodified input, (3) interactionally modified input.	English Vocabulary	Groups (2) and (3) demonstrated receptive knowledge of more words than (1); (3) also acquired more words than (2) but only in the immediate post-test.
Ellis and Heimbach (1997)	Children work (1) in pairs and (2) in groups listening to teacher's descriptions. They are allowed to interact as much as they want to.	English Vocabulary	Both groups manifested receptive knowledge of about 25 per cent of the target items; very little productive knowledge evident.
Ellis and He (1999)	Three experimental groups of adult learners. Teacher provides descriptions as (1) premodified input and (2) interactionally modified input. In addition group (3) worked in pairs to provide opportunities for modified output.	English vocabulary	No statistically significant difference in scores on receptive and productive tests between groups (1) and (2). Group (3) acquired receptive and productive knowledge of more words than both (1) and (2).

not first presented to the learners and (2) it results in more time on task and more input – as would be the case, perhaps, when a task is performed naturally in this condition.

None of the studies in Table 8.4 investigated the specific properties of premodified and interactionally modified input that facilitated acquisition. However in Ellis (1995a) I analyzed the modified input used in Ellis, Tanaka and Yamazaki with a view to determining what it was in the input that enabled the learners to learn some new words more easily than others. In the case of premodified input, I found that learners remembered best those words that occurred in many different directions and in longer directions. In the case of interactionally modified input, the number of directions a word appeared in also proved important. However, length of direction no longer had an effect. In fact, the analysis showed that learners were less likely to remember words when the negotiation led to very long definitions of the target words (i.e. over-elaboration interfered with learning). I was also able to show that although interactionally modified input led to higher levels of vocabulary acquisition than premodified input, overall it was less efficient. That is, in terms of words acquired per minute of input (wpm), premodified input worked much better (e.g. 0.25 wpm as opposed to 0.13 wpm in the immediate post-test). Finally, I found that the number of negotiations that individual students took part in was not related to their vocabulary acquisition scores. There were learners who did not negotiate at all but who achieved relatively high levels of word acquisition. It should be noted, however, that the premodified input was still 'interactional' to some extent as the teacher engaged in one-way interaction with the students.

Only one of these studies (Ellis and He, 1999) involved a condition where learners needed to produce the target items. Interestingly, this study found the modified output condition where the learners interacted in pairs resulted in the highest level of vocabulary acquisition. Ellis and He explained this by drawing on sociocultural theory to propose that although the task was intended to be identical in all the conditions, the 'activity' that arose in the modified output condition was fundamentally different from that in the other two conditions. In the former, the learners treated the task as a collaborative problem-solving activity and scaffolded each other's understanding of the new words. In the latter, even in the interactionally modified condition, the teacher performed the task more as a test and thus engaged in relatively mechanical interactive work with the students.

These experimental studies all derived from the Interaction Hypothesis. They tested quite specific hypotheses about how interaction shapes the input that forges acquisition. They showed that performing listen-and-do tasks where attention is directed at target items engages the mental processes required for acquisition to take place. However, they did not lend unequivocal support to the early version of the Interaction Hypothesis (Long, 1983c) as interactionally modified input was not always found to be clearly superior to premodified input. More support was evident for the later version of the hypothesis (Long, 1996), which claims that it is not just comprehensible input but comprehensible output that facilitates acquisition, as shown in Ellis and He's study. In the following section we will examine other studies that have examined the effect of learner output when performing tasks in pairs or small groups.

Studies involving corrective feedback in oral tasks   Experimental studies that have investigated the acquisition that arises from the performance of a communicative task require the use of a focused task. This is because it is necessary to specify a specific feature as the target of the study in order to determine what the content of the pre- and post-tests will be. However, as we noted in Chapter 7, it is extremely difficult to design a focused task that makes the use of a specific feature essential[4]. For this reason, the studies that we will consider in this section all made use of methodological procedures to focus on the target feature during the performance of a task. By and large these procedures involved some kind of corrective feedback. Thus, readers may wish to familiarize themselves with the various options for providing corrective feedback that were described in Chapter 5.

The studies set out to answer three principal questions:

1.   Does corrective feedback in the context of performing a communicative task assist acquisition of specific target-language features?
2.   Do some corrective procedures in the context of performing a communicative task have a greater effect on acquisition than other procedures?
3.   Does 'noticing' mediate the effect that corrective feedback has on the acquisition of specific target-language features?

It should be noted that the studies I will consider here did not seek to compare the relative effects of 'focus on form' and 'focus on forms' (i.e. attempts to explicitly teach target features). Such comparative method studies are problematic for a number of reasons (see, for example, my discussion of R. Sheen's 2006 study in Chapter 3).

There are now a very large number of studies that have investigated the effects of corrective feedback on acquisition. A number of meta-analyses of these studies have appeared in the last few years (Li, 2010; Lyster and Saito, 2010; Mackey and Goo, 2007; Russell and Spada, 2006). Many of the studies were carried out in a laboratory setting and so will not be considered here. This decision can be justified by Li's (2010) finding that the effect of corrective feedback in laboratory and classroom settings differed, being notably greater in the former. Li suggested that this may be because 'in the classroom context, there is more distraction and feedback is not directed toward individual learners' (p. 345). Li's finding is further evidence of the need to consider laboratory-based and classroom-based studies separately (see discussion of this point in Chapter 7). The following review is based on a representative sample of the classroom-based studies.

I will begin by considering in some detail a study by Doughty and Varela (1998) that sought to address the first of the above research questions and that investigated just one feedback strategy – corrective recasts. These consisted of two moves, (1) a teacher's repetition of a learner's error, with emphasis placed on the erroneous word(s) and (2) a reformulation of the complete learner utterance, as in Extract 1.

Extract 1:
L: I think that the worm will go under the soil.
T: I think that the worm will go under the soil?
L: (no response)
T: I *thought* that the worm *would* go under the soil.
L: I thought that the worm would go under the soil.

The study took place in two intact science classes taught to 34 intermediate ESL students in a middle school in the United States. The task the students were asked to complete involved preparing oral and written reports of simple science experiments. As such, it required the use of past tense verbs, the focus of the study. During the oral reporting phase of the study, the learners received corrective recasts whenever they produced an utterance with an error in the use of a past verb form. Acquisition was measured in terms of both target-like use and progress along the acquisitional sequence for past time reference (i.e. by means of 'interlanguage analysis'). Both oral and written measures demonstrated significant and large gains from pre-test to the immediate post-test. In contrast, there was little evidence of any change in a control group, which did not receive the corrective feedback. The gains in the experimental group were maintained in the oral delayed post-test but the effects of the feedback were less evident in the delayed written test. The experimental group also attempted to use past-time reference more in the post-tests. This study provides clear evidence that corrective feedback is effective in assisting interlanguage development.

Doughty and Varela considered corrective recasts to be 'a relatively implicit focus-on-form technique' (p. 137) but this is doubtful. Corrective recasts are in fact quite explicit as the corrective force is very apparent from the repetition and the use of emphatic stress. A study that clearly did investigate the effects of implicit corrective feedback is Mackey (2006).

Mackey was interested in the relationships between implicit corrective feedback, noticing and acquisition. The target structures were questions, plurals and past tense. The task took the form of a game-show activity with the teacher acting as the game-show host. The feedback consisted of non-corrective recasts and clarification requests, as in Extract 2.

Extract 2:
1. Recast:
   Student: Why does the aliens attacked earth?
   Teacher: Right. Why did the aliens attack earth.
2. Request for clarification:
   Student: He have many spot in he have one.
   Teacher: Huh? One? Or many what? Quick.

(Mackey 2006: 413).

Data on noticing were collected by means of learning journals filled out during class time, oral-stimulated recall protocols, written responses in the learners' first language (L1) to a focused question about the nature of the classroom activities, and written responses in English to a questionnaire. Measures of learners' use of the target structures were obtained from oral tasks administered as a pre-test and a post-test. The results indicated a higher level of noticing in the experimental than in the control group. However, the level of noticing varied according to target structure, with higher levels evident for questions forms, much lower levels for past tense and intermediate levels for plurals. 83 per cent of the learners who reported noticing question forms also developed in their ability to form questions. However, the relationship between noticing and the other two target features was not established. Three points emerge from this study. The first point is that implicit corrective feedback is noticed by learners working on a task in a classroom context. The second is that the extent to which noticing occurs as a result of implicit corrective feedback varies according to the target feature. The third is that there is a relationship between noticing and acquisition for at least some structures. Thus, this study provides evidence that corrective feedback, in the context of the interaction that arises from performing a task, can assist acquisition even when the feedback is of the implicit kind. Other studies have investigated the relative effects of implicit and explicit feedback.

Ellis, Loewen and Erlam (2006) compared the effects of recasts (an implicit form of corrective feedback) and metalinguistic clues (an explicit form) on the acquisition of regular past tense *–ed*. The learners were 34 low-intermediate adult ESL students in a private language school in New Zealand. The two experimental groups performed two 30-minute tasks. Group (1) received recasts on verb *–ed* errors and Group (2) repetition of the wrong verb form followed by a metalinguistic clue. A control group (Group 3) just completed the three tests – (1) An oral elicitation test, (2) an untimed grammaticality judgement test, and (3) a metalinguistic knowledge test. Ellis et al. established that frequency of the feedback provided to the learners in the two experimental groups was roughly equivalent. The study found that there were no significant differences in any of the tests in the post-test, administered the day after the instruction, but that there were in the delayed post-test, which was completed 12 days later. The metalinguistic group outperformed the control group on both old and new verbs[5] in the oral imitation test. It also outperformed the recast group on new verbs in both the oral imitation test and the untimed grammaticality judgement test. There were no statistically significant differences between the recast group and the control group on any of the measures. This study then, points to the superiority over time of explicit corrective feedback. Furthermore, it suggests that explicit feedback assists the development of implicit knowledge if, as Ellis et al. argued, the oral imitation test is taken as a measure of this type of knowledge.

This study has been replicated by Fawbush (2010) in a different instructional context – in the ESL department of a suburban public middle school in the US. The learners in the study were classified as 'novice' and 'beginning'. They completed two picture story tasks and received feedback on their past tense errors exactly as in Ellis et al. Out of the six learners in the recast group, four demonstrated improvement in the use of regular past tense on the oral imitation test. The mean improvement for this group was 9.7 per cent. All five students in the metalinguistic group demonstrated improvement. The mean for this group was 28.6 per cent. No group differences were evident in a test of metalinguistic knowledge. Fawbush's study also suggests that explicit feedback is more effective than implicit.

These two studies, which were carried out using intact classrooms, point to a significant advantage for explicit feedback in tests that provide measures of both implicit and explicit L2 knowledge. In contrast, recasts were found to have little or no effect[6]. This may have been because the recasts lack salience in the classroom contexts and/or because the length of the treatments in these studies was relatively short. In this respect these studies differ from Doughty and Varela's and Mackey's studies, where the recasts may have been more salient and the treatments were longer. However, none of these studies examined whether the learners' proficiency mediated the effects of the feedback. It is very possible that the learners' developmental level influences the extent to which they both notice the correction in a recast and incorporate the target feature into their interlanguage systems. In the case of explicit feedback, however, the learners' proficiency may be less of a factor.

The other corrective feedback studies we will examine investigated another dimension of corrective feedback – the distinction between input-providing and output-prompting feedback. Prompts consist of a mixture of strategies, all which aim at eliciting self-correction from the learner. Table 8.5 summarizes a number of studies that have addressed the relative effects of these two types of feedback. These studies suggest the following:

1. Prompts result in gains in accuracy in a variety of target structures and these gains are durable (i.e. are evident in the delayed post-tests: Ammar and Spada, 2006; Lyster, 2004).
2. Prompts may also help to develop learners' automaticity (Ammar, 2008).
3. Recasts also lead to gains but to a lesser extent than prompts (Ammar and Spada, 2006; Lyster, 2004).
4. In some studies (Ammar, 2008; Yang and Lyster, 2010) no or few differences emerged between the effects of the recasts and prompts but those that did were in favour of the prompts.
5. A very short length of instruction may be insufficient for the positive effects of both prompts and recasts to become evident (Loewen and Nabei, 2007).
6. The learners' level of proficiency mediates the relative effects of prompts and recasts (e.g. low-proficiency learners may benefit more from prompts: Ammar and Spada, 2006).

Lyster and Saito's (2010) meta-analysis of classroom studies of corrective feedback[7] reported similar conclusions to those I have presented. That is, both recasts and prompts are effective in promoting acquisition but the effect size for prompts (0.83) is appreciably larger than that for recasts (0.53). However, the way in which the comparison between recasts and prompts has been carried out is not without its problems. First, recasts constitute a single corrective strategy whereas prompts include four different strategies (i.e. clarification requests, repetition of error, elicitation and metalinguistic clues). It is possible that the greater effect found for prompts

Table 8.5 Selected studies investigating the effects of recasts and prompts on L2 acquisition

Study	Participants	Target structure	Design	Tests	Results
Lyster (2004)	148 (Grade 5) 10–11-year-olds in a French immersion programme	French grammatical gender (articles + nouns).	Group 1 received FFI + recasts; Group 2 FFI + prompts (including explicit feedback); Group 3 FFI only. Control group.	Four tests; (1) binary choice test, (2) text completion test, (oral production tasks), (3) object identification test, (4) picture description test. Two post-tests (PT) with PT 2 administered eight weeks after PT1.	FFI-prompt group was only group to outperform control group on all eight measures (PT1 and PT2). FFI-recast group outperformed control group on 5 out of 8 measures. FFI-only group outperformed control group on four out eight measures. Statistically significant differences between FFI-prompt and FFI-only groups and also between FFI-prompt and FFI-recast group but only in the written tests.
Ammar and Spada (2006)	64 Grade 8 students in three classes in an ESL programme in Canada	Third-person singular English possessive pronouns	12 sessions each of 30–45 minutes over a four-week period. In session 1 the students were taught and practised possessive pronouns. In the following 11 sessions students completed tasks during which group (1) received recasts, group (2) prompts and group (3) no corrective feedback.	Two tests: (1) passage correction, (2) oral picture description. Two post-tests: (1) immediate post-test followed final task session and (2) delayed post-test four weeks later.	In the passage correction task, group (2) outperformed group (1) in both immediate and delayed post-tests. In the oral picture-description test, there was no difference between groups (1) and (2) on the immediate post test but (2) outperformed (1) on the delayed test while both groups (1) and (2) outperformed (3) on both post-tests. High proficiency learners benefitted from both prompts and recasts while low proficiency learners benefitted more from prompts.

Loewen and Nabei (2007)	66 Japanese university-level students	English question formation	Two intact classes; one class divided into groups of four and the other served as a test control. The experimental groups completed two tasks lasting 30 minutes. Different small groups received different feedback; (1) recasts, (2) classification requests, (3) metalinguistic feedback and (4) no feedback.	Three tests: (1) a timed grammaticality judgement test, (GJT) (2) an untimed GJT and (3) an oral production test. Only an immediate post-test was administered.	No significant group differences evident in the untimed GJT. All three groups improved in the timed GGT but the three feedback groups improved at a significantly higher rate than the no feedback group or the control group. There was no apparent increase in higher stage question forms in any of the groups.
Ammar (2008)	As in Ammar and Spada (2006)	Third person singular English possessive pronouns	As in Ammar and Spada (2006)	Two tests: (1) A computerized fill-in-the- blanks test + a measure of response time; (2) an oral picture-description test.	More learners in the prompt group than in the recast group moved up a developmental stage in both immediate and delayed oral production test. No group differences evident for accuracy in the computerized fill-in-the-blanks test; the prompt group was significantly faster than the recast group which was significantly slower than the control group.

(Continued)

Table 8.5 (*Continued*)

Study	Participants	Target structure	Design	Tests	Results
Yang and Lyster (2010)	72 undergraduate EFL students in China	Regular and irregular English past tense	Two hours of instruction based on four form-focused production activities. Three groups: (1) recasts, (2) prompts, and, (3) control.	Two tests; (1) oral production (story-retelling) and (2) written production (compose a story using 12 verbs). Immediate post-test administered immediately after instruction; delayed post-test two weeks later.	In the oral production test only group (2) made significant gains in regular past tense between pre-test and both post-tests; all three groups made significant gains in irregular past tense from pre-test to immediate post-test but only group (2) made gains from pre-test to delayed post-test. In the written production test all three groups made gains in regular past tense from pre- to immediate post-test but only (2) showed gains from pre- to delayed past tense; groups (1) and (2) but not (3) made significant gains in irregular past tense from pre-test to both post-tests. No statistically significant group differences in test scores were reported except for irregular past tense in the delayed written production test.

is simply because many strategies are more effective than one strategy. Also, prompts include a mixture of implicit and explicit strategies so it is possible that they are effective not because they elicit self-correction but because they are more salient (i.e. they work because they are explicit).

Ideally, what is needed is a comparison between recasts and a single, implicit output-prompting strategy. Mifka-Profozic (2011) carried out such a study, comparing the effects of recasts and requests for clarification on the acquisition of French *passé composé* and *imparfait* by 50 high school students in New Zealand. Her results differ markedly from those reported in Table 8.5. Recasts proved notably more effective than requests for clarification in both immediate and delayed post-tests and for both grammatical structures. The learners who received recasts demonstrated significantly greater levels of accuracy than the learners in the control group in all measures and in some of the comparisons were also significantly better than the learners receiving prompts. Mifka-Profozic also found that proficiency was a mediating factor. For example in the case of *passé composé*, recasts did lead learning but only for the high proficiency learners.

Finally, it should be noted that all the studies considered here involved corrective feedback provided by a teacher. Feedback also occurs in learner–learner interactions. One classroom-based study that investigated this is McDonough (2004). 16 university-level Thai English as a foreign language (EFL) learners engaged in task-based pair and small group activities that generated contexts for the use of conditional clauses. Out of 400 minutes of learner–learner interaction, there were 46 instances of corrective feedback directed at the target feature (34 involving requests for clarification and 12 involving recasts). McDonough reported that learners who participated more frequently in the corrective feedback were the ones who showed significant improvement in oral tests that elicited use of conditionals.

All of the studies considered in this section were based on oral tasks. In other words they investigated incidental acquisition (i.e. the acquisition that occurs when learners are not consciously attempting to learn). They provide clear evidence that the corrective feedback that learners receive in the context of performing such tasks, whether from a teacher or other learners, assists acquisition. Implicit, explicit, input-providing and output-prompting feedback are all effective in helping learners achieve greater accuracy in the use of grammatical features. The studies indicate, however, that explicit feedback is generally more effective than implicit feedback and prompts more effective than input-providing feedback. Nevertheless, caution is in order. These strategies are not as 'pure' as they are sometime presented in the literature. Recasts, in particular, occur in many different forms. Prompts are a mixture of implicit and explicit strategies. Also, it may be fundamentally mistaken to look for the most effective type of strategy – as these studies have attempted to do. First, as we have seen, from a sociocultural perspective, what is important is tailoring the choice of strategy to the learner's developmental level. Second, there are potentially a number of individual difference variables (proficiency being just one) that mediate the effect of the different strategies, a point we will return to in Chapter 10. Searching for the single 'best' strategy may be a chimera.

Studies involving consciousness-raising tasks   Many of the studies conducted within the compass of sociocultural theory made use of consciousness-raising tasks (see section on 'Sociocultural Studies of Classroom Interaction and L2 Acquisition' in this chapter). However, there are also studies that have examined such tasks from an interactionist-cognitive perspective. That is, they have investigated the extent to which performing consciousness-raising tasks enables learners to develop their explicit knowledge of the L2. These studies have been based on the theoretical assumption that explicit knowledge can prime processes such as noticing and noticing-the-gap that are hypothesized to be responsible for the development of implicit knowledge (Ellis, 1994).

A series of studies by Fotos (Fotos, 1993; Fotos, 1994; Fotos and Ellis, 1991) provided evidence that performing consciousness-raising (CR) tasks helps Japanese learners of English to understand grammatical structures as demonstrated in posttests. The studies constitute evidence that the CR tasks were effective in helping learners to develop explicit L2 knowledge. Also, Fotos (1993) was also able to show that the explicit knowledge the learners gained from the CR tasks may have aided the processes believed to be involved in the acquisition of implicit knowledge. That is, completing the CR tasks helped the learners' subsequent noticing of the targetted features. Several weeks after the completion of the CR tasks, the learners in her study completed a number of dictations that included exemplars of the target structures. They were then asked to underline any particular bit of language they had paid special attention to as they did the dictation. Fotos found that they frequently underlined the structures that had been targetted in the CR tasks whereas learners in a control group who had not completed the CR tasks did not. Overall, these studies show that CR tasks are effective in developing learners' understanding of grammatical structures and also that this understanding may promote subsequent acquisitional processes.

However, Fotos' studies made no attempt to investigate whether there was a relationship between the interactions that took place when learners performed the CR tasks and their increased understanding of the target structures. That is, they did not examine the role played by interaction in learning. A number of other studies, however, have set out to research this by probing the extent to which the language-related episodes that learners constructed while performing a CR task aided learning.

Kuiken and Vedder (2003) asked 34 Dutch high school students, divided into an experimental and control group to perform two dictogloss tasks. The experimental group reconstructed the text in groups while the control group did so individually. The target structure was English passives with one auxiliary verb (e.g. 'was owned'), two auxiliaries (e.g. 'had been stolen') and three auxiliaries (e.g. 'should have been given'). The learners completed a production pre-test, immediate post-test and delayed post-test. Both the experimental and control groups improved only minimally on the post-tests and there was no difference between them. Nor was there any evidence of any group difference in attempted use of passive forms when they performed the task. Kuiken and Vedder also provided a qualitative analysis of the language-related episodes that occurred when the experimental group performed the task. They distinguished between 'simple' and 'elaborate noticing', the former referring to occasions when the passive was mentioned but not discussed and the latter when it was discussed and alternative structures considered. There were numerous instances of interaction leading to 'elaborate noticing' but, crucially, there was considerable variation in the different small groups that comprized the experimental group. Kuiken and Vedder concluded that 'interaction leads to noticing, but not to acquisition' (p. 354). They suggested that this might be because the two dictogloss tasks did not afford sufficient opportunities for the learners to notice and work on the structure for the effects to become evident in production.

Eckerth (2008a; 2008b) investigated university-level learners of German who completed two CR tasks (a text-reconstruction task and a text-repair task), where the learners worked in pairs to agree on a correct version of a text given to them. One of his aims was to see whether CR tasks resulted in similar patterns of interaction to unfocused tasks. He found that the tasks he used were just as conducive to meaning negotiation as information-gap tasks and generated only slightly less output modification. He provided a number of examples to show that when performing the tasks 'learner–learner scaffolding features strongly' (p. 102) and that this led to the learners attending to the way in which form, meaning, function and context interrelate. He measured the task-specific gains in the specific structures targeted by the CR tasks by comparing pre- and post-test scores on sentence-assembly tests, arguing that these provided measures of the learners' explicit knowledge. He reported significant gains between both the pre-test and the immediate post-test and also between the immediate and delayed post-tests. In other words the learners showed incremental gains across the period of the study. Significant gains were evident in both lower and upper intermediate-level learners[8]. One of the most interesting findings of Eckerth's study is that non-predicted learning also took place. He identified occasions when 'controversial language-related episodes' occurred in the dyadic interactions (i.e. episodes where the students expressed differing opinions about linguistic forms other than those targeted by the tasks) and then administered tailor-made tests to investigate whether such episodes resulted in learning. He reported a close relationship between the solutions the learners arrived at in the controversial language-related episodes and their test responses.

These CR studies suggest the following:

1. CR tasks are effective in inducing learners to pay joint attention to the target structures and to instigate discussion of them.
2. CR tasks result in measurable gains in explicit knowledge of the target structures.
3. CR tasks can also result in unpredicted gains (i.e. in structures that were not targetted in the design of the task but that attracted joint attention by the learners when performing the tasks in groups).
4. The quality of learners' interaction when performing CR tasks appears to vary, with some studies reporting little negotiation of meaning and others much more extensive negotiation. However, most studies report that they result in a substantial number of language-related episodes.

5. The extent to which learners benefit from performing CR tasks varies. While some studies have reported substantial gains in explicit knowledge others report little. This may reflect the learning difficulty of the target structure.
6. It is not always the case that 'noticing' (even of the elaborate kind) results in learning.
7. There is considerable individual variation in learners' ability to benefit from performing CR tasks, suggesting a role for individual difference factors such as language aptitude.

These studies have all measured the learning that results from CR tasks using grammaticality judgement or controlled-response tests. Given that the aim of CR tasks is to facilitate explicit knowledge and that these tests are likely to tap this type of knowledge they can be seen as a valid method of assessing learning. However, the question arises as to whether the learning that results helps learners to use the structures in spontaneous communication. There is no evidence that it does. There is only limited evidence (e.g. Fotos, 1993) that it facilitates the processes responsible for the development of the implicit knowledge required for rapid communication. Here, then, is an important issue in need of further research.

Conclusion

If interaction is 'the fundamental fact of language pedagogy' then it is requisite of researchers to try to demonstrate how interaction fosters language acquisition. This has been the purpose of this chapter. The research reported stands in contrast to that examined in previous chapters where any link between interaction and learning was hypothesized on the basis of theory rather than demonstrated empirically.

As there are many different kinds of interaction that occur in the language class-room (see Chapter 4) the crucial question becomes 'What types of interaction are conducive of language acquisition?' Broadly speaking we can distinguish the interaction that arises in fluency-and-meaning contexts and that which arises in form-and-accuracy contexts (Seedhouse, 2004). This distinction also correlates loosely with the difference between incidental and intentional language learning. This chapter has been primarily concerned with how interaction shapes the incidental acquisition that occurs as a result of learners' performing tasks that lead to a focus on form in fluency-and-meaning contexts.

This chapter has drawn on two very different theoretical perspectives. Socio-cultural theory sees interaction as a site where learning takes place. It emphasizes acquisition-as-participation. Interactionist-cognitive theories view interaction as providing learners with input, feedback and opportunities to modify their own output, which connect with learner-internal processing to foster acquisition. They treat interaction as a source of acquisition. These theoretical orientations have led to different approaches to investigating interaction and its role in learning. Sociocul-tural researchers have focused on the genesis of learning by inspecting how learners' participation in interaction changes from one time to another as a result of collaborative scaffolding at the zone of proximal development. Alternatively, they have employed quasi-experimental designs to investigate how 'languaging' assists understanding of specific language features and their internalization. Interactionist-cognitive theories have informed both descriptive/exploratory research that has attempted to trace how learner involvement in the form-focused episodes that arise from time to time in fluency-and-accuracy contexts leads to learning and also quasi-experimental studies that have investigated the effects of corrective feedback on learning.

However, despite the differences in these theoretical perspectives there are a number of points of commonality. Both have explored the role played by interaction through research based on tasks. Both perspectives emphasize the importance of attention to linguistic features in the course of performing tasks. Both also recognize the value of talk directed at developing awareness at the level of understanding. Both acknowledge that both expert and novice interlocutors can help shape the kinds of interactions that promote learning. Both acknowledge the important role played by feedback (although they differ in how they see feedback contributing to learning). Both research traditions have explored the contribution to learning made by consciousness-raising tasks.

Perhaps the major difference is to be found in how the two theoretical perspectives view 'learning'. By and large, sociocultural studies have investigated learning in terms of either production of the target features during the performance of a task or some form of test that invites controlled use of the target features. In others words, learning is seen as involving conscious, explicit knowledge. Indeed sociocultural theories do not make a clear distinction between explicit and implicit knowledge. In contrast, interactionist-cognitive theories do see this distinction as important and, in some studies at least (e.g. the corrective feedback studies) have sought to establish whether participating in interaction leads to acquisition of implicit as well as explicit knowledge. To my mind, this constitutes a strength of the interactionist-cognitive studies and a weakness of the sociocultural studies. It simply does not follow that because a learner has engaged in a language-related episode and then demonstrated an ability to use a feature in a highly controlled tailor-made test item that the learner has 'acquired' the feature in the fullest sense of this term. It is surely also necessary to show that the learner has fully internalized the feature to the point where he/she can use it accurately in unmonitored communication in a new context. In other words, we want to know whether interaction leads to procedural ability[9].

Overall, the research provides ample evidence that focus on form – in its various guises – assists acquisition. The following is my attempt to synthesize the main findings of the research conducted within both the sociocultural and interactionist-cognitive theoretical frameworks.

1. Interaction assists acquisition in both teacher–class and student–student participatory structures. This is evident in both second and foreign language settings[10].

2. The acquisition that takes place is incidental in the sense that there was no de-
    liberate attempt to teach learners specific linguistic forms and (presumably) no
    deliberate attempt on the part of the learners to 'learn' them. Incidental acqui-
    sition occurs as a product of the interaction that arises out of the performance
    of tasks.
3. Evidence that interaction assists incidental acquisition can be found in both
    studies that have examined acquisition, in terms of a reduction in the scaffolded
    help that learners need in or order to perform a specific linguistic feature, and
    in studies that administered post-tests outside the interaction.
4. Interaction that involves 'languaging' (i.e. talk about specific linguistic features)
    is especially conducive of learning. The successful resolution of a linguistic
    problem that arises in the course of performing a task has been shown to be
    related to a subsequent gain in the accurate and independent use of the linguistic
    feature that was the source of the problem.
5. In this respect, consciousness-raising tasks performed in pairs or small groups
    appear to be especially effective in promoting interaction rich in language-related
    episodes.
6. Input-based tasks that allow learners access to premodified or interactionally
    modified input also result in acquisition (of vocabulary, at least). However,
    acquisition is better supported when learners have the opportunity to produce
    modified output containing the target structure.
7. There is a clear relationship between the attention to form that arises pre-
    emptively or reactively in teacher–class interaction and both learners' successful
    uptake of specific forms and their subsequent acquisition of them.
8. The effectiveness of different types of corrective feedback (i.e. reactive focus on
    form) in promoting acquisition varies. Explicit CF is more effective than implicit
    CF (i.e. recasts). However, the extent to which output-prompting CF is more
    effective than input-providing CF (as claimed by Lyster) is less clear.
9. The effectiveness of the different types of focus on form may ultimately depend
    on a variety of individual-learner factors such as the level of the learners' L2
    proficiency.

There are, of course, limitations to the research. One problem is that some of the
studies (e.g. Lyster, 2004) provided explicit instruction of the target feature, making
it impossible to determine whether it was this or the focus on form that took place
interactively that was the source of the acquisition they reported. From a pedagogic
perspective this may not matter – for, after all, teachers often do incorporate explicit instruction into communicative language teaching – but it would be useful to
know what the separate contributions of explicit instruction and focus on form to
acquisition are. I will examine research that has investigated the effects of explicit
instruction on intentional learning in the following chapter. Another limitation is
that there has been relatively little research examining the relationship between interaction and learning in younger learners (but see Philp, Oliver and Mackey, 2008).
It would seem reasonable to predict that learning-through-interaction is especially

well-suited to children because they are more likely to orient to language as a tool for communicating. But we need to see studies that show this. A greater limitation is the lack of studies that have investigated how individual learner factors mediate the benefits of interaction. We have seen a number of studies that report a high level of variation in group gains, which points to the fact that learners differ in their capacity to learn through interaction. One possible explanation for this is that factors such as language aptitude, anxiety, and motivation influence learners' ability and preparedness to 'notice' form when engaged in meaning-focused communication. If attention to form is crucial to learning – as both sociocultural and interactionist-cognitive theories claim – then this may explain why learners vary in how they engage in and what they take from interaction. In Chapter 10 we will examine research that has investigated the role of individual learner factors in classroom learning.

Notes

1. 'Uptake' in Slimani's study has a somewhat different meaning from the meaning of this term in most interactionist-cognitive studies. Slimani used it to refer to the items that learners reported learning after the lesson was over. Thus 'uptake' here really constitutes a measure of language acquisition.
2. Havranek pointed out that the better performance of the listeners on the test may have been due to the fact that they already knew the correct form. Only the perpetrators demonstrated an actual gap in their knowledge.
3. In general recasts have not been found to be a very effective form of corrective feedback in classroom studies. However, this is not the same as saying that they are without any effect. Alcon's study shows that where vocabulary learning is concerned reactive FFEs involving recasts are effective.
4. Newton (1995) reported an experimental study of one learner that overcame this problem. This study focused on vocabulary. The learner completed six communication tasks. He was pre-tested on the vocabulary contained in the task worksheets and then post-tested on the same vocabulary after completing the tasks. Results showed it was the use of the words in the process of completing the task rather than explicit negotiation of meaning that accounted best for the learner's gains in lexical knowledge. Such a design is less likely to work when the target features are grammatical or pragmatic.
5. 'Old verbs' were those that were used in the performance of the tasks. 'New verbs' were verbs that did not occur in the tasks. It was important to investigate whether corrective feedback had an effect on new verbs as this provided evidence that the learners had internalized a general rule for past tense *–ed* as opposed to just memorizing the past forms of specific verbs.
6. Whereas classroom-studies have found little and sometimes no effect for recasts, laboratory studies have shown that recasts can contribute to language learning. In laboratory studies learners interact intensively one-on-one with a researcher whereas in the classroom studies recasting occurs in a one-too-many context.
7. The other meta-analyses (e.g. Mackey and Goo, 2007) examined laboratory-based and classroom-based studies together.

8. Eckerth did not include a control group in his study. However, he did include control items in the test and showed that there were no gains in these.

9. A study by De Ridder, Vangehuchten and Gomez (2007) investigated whether task-based instruction enhanced automaticity of the language use of university-level learners of L2 English. This study compared a traditional communicative course and a course with a built-in task-based component. The results showed that the task-based group outperformed the traditional communicative group on measures of social adequacy and grammatical and lexical knowledge but not on a measure of fluency. The authors noted that the superior results of the task-based group may simply reflect their higher level of motivation.

10. Lyster and Saito's (2010) meta-analysis of classroom-based studies, for example, found no difference in the effect of corrective feedback in foreign and second language settings. This is an important finding because it suggests that the assumption of some commentators (e.g. Swan, 2005) that task-based teaching is not suited to foreign language settings is not justified.

9

Form-Focused Instruction and Second Language Learning

Introduction

In Ellis (2001a) I defined 'form-focused instruction' (FFI) as follows:

> "Form-focused instruction" is used to refer to any planned or incidental instructional activity that is intended to induce language learners to pay attention to linguistic form. It serves, therefore, as a cover term for a variety of other terms that figure in the current literature – "analytic teaching" (Stern, 1990), "focus on form" and "focus on forms" (Long, 1991), corrective feedback/error correction, 'negotiation of form' (Lyster and Ranta, 1997). Thus, FFI includes both traditional approaches to teaching forms based on structural syllabi and more communicative approaches where attention to form arises out of activities that are primarily meaning-focused (pp. 1–2).

As this definition makes clear, FFI incorporates two very different ways of viewing instruction directed at linguistic form. Long (1991) refers to these as 'focus on forms' (the traditional approach) and 'focus on form', which involves attempts to draw learners' attention to form while they are endeavoring to communicate.

There are other ways of conceptualizing FFI. Drawing on the psychological distinction between implicit and explicit learning, some applied linguistic researchers have investigated the differential effects of 'implicit' and 'explicit instruction'. This distinction rests on whether the instruction is designed to induce learning without or with awareness.

Both of these distinctions are problematic for a number of reasons. They are also psycholinguistic rather than pedagogic in nature. That is, they have been derived from theories of language learning. A third approach is to consider FFI in terms of

Language Teaching Research & Language Pedagogy, First Edition. Rod Ellis.
© 2012 John Wiley & Sons, Ltd. Published 2012 by John Wiley & Sons, Ltd.

the techniques and procedures that figure in pedagogical discussions of language teaching. I refer to this as the option-based approach to examining FFI.

I will begin this chapter with a discussion of these different ways of conceptualizing FFI.

Focus on Form versus Focus on Forms

The term 'focus on form' is used to refer to an approach that involves an attempt to induce incidental acquisition through instruction by drawing learners' attention to linguistic forms while they are communicating. This contrasts with 'focus on forms' – the 'traditional approach' – where the primary goal is to help learners master the structural features listed in the syllabus by making the linguistic target of each lesson quite explicit. Here 'the aim is to *direct* learner attention and to *exploit pedagogical grammar*' (Doughty and Williams, 1998: 232). Focus-on-forms instruction involves intentional learning on the part of the learners[1].

Table 9.1 summarizes the key differences between focus on form and focus on forms. A main difference lies in how the instruction orientates the learner to language – to either viewing language as a tool for communicating in the case of

Table 9.1 Focus on form versus focus on forms

Aspect	Focus on form	Focus on forms
Orientation	Language-as-tool	Language-as-object
Type of learning	Incidental	Intentional
Primary focus of attention	Message	Code
Secondary focus of attention	Code	Message
Acquisitional processes	Interpsychological mediation; intrapsychological mediation; noticing; noticing-the-gap; modified output.	Conscious rule-formation; proceduralization; automatization; monitoring
Syllabus type	Task-based	Structural
Target selection	Proactive and reactive	Proactive
Instructional processes	Tasks; scaffolded production; dynamic assessment; input-priming; negotiation of meaning; corrective feedback; consciousness-raising through tasks	Exercises; consciousness-raising through the provision of explicit rules; structured input; controlled production practice; free production practice; corrective feedback

focus on form or to treating it as an object to be studied and mastered in focus on forms. When language is treated as a tool for communicating, the language learning that occurs will be 'incidental'. That is, it will occur even though the learner was not consciously attempting to learn. When language is treated as an object, the learning that results will be intentional although there is always the possibility that some incidental acquisition of features that were not the explicit target of a lesson will occur. In focus-on-form instruction, learners are primarily concerned with trying to understand and produce messages that encode communicative meanings but, as we have seen in Chapter 8, there will be times when learners pay attention to the code. In focus on forms it is the other way round. Learners are primarily focused on using the code accurately but may also be given the opportunity to process messages. Focus-on-form instruction is supported by both sociocultural theory and interactionist-cognitive theories. In terms of sociocultural theory, focus on form mediates the intra- and interpsychological processes involved in learning. In terms of interactionist-cognitive theories it facilitates noticing, noticing-the-gap, and modified output. In contrast, focus-on-forms instruction views learning in terms of skill-learning, involving conscious rule-formation, proceduralization, automatization and monitoring.

The two types of FFI require different ways of organizing teaching. In focus on form the syllabus is task-based while focus on forms depends on a structural syllabus. Thus, the linguistic targets of focus-on-form instruction are typically determined reactively (i.e. as a response to a linguistic problem that a learner has experienced when performing a task) although when the tasks are of the focused kind the linguistic targets are determined proactively. In contrast, the linguistic targets of focus-on-forms instruction must necessarily be selected in advance. Finally, as might be expected, the instructional processes associated with each type of instruction differ. In focus on form the instructional processes are those associated with meaning-focused interaction (see Chapter 8) while focus on forms relies on explicit rule provision and practice exercises of various kinds. Corrective feedback, however, is common to both.

However, the distinction between focus on form and focus on forms is less clear cut than Table 9.1 indicates. For one thing, as Batstone (2002) noted, 'learners (like any discourse participants interpret and act on context in significantly different ways depending in particular on their sense of purpose' (p. 2). Teachers and students do not always share a common purpose. Thus it is possible that instruction that was designed as focus on form may be interpreted by students as focus on forms and vice versa. Further, Batstone emphasized that the instructional context is dynamic in nature; in other words, teachers and students are constantly orienting and re-orienting in a single lesson or even in a single activity. Thus, it does not follow that instruction intended as either focus on form or focus on forms will always end up as planned.

A good example of how instruction can be reconstituted as a lesson progresses is Samuda's (2001) account of a lesson designed to provide learners with communicative opportunities for using and learning epistemic modals (e.g. *might* and *must*). It began with an activity in which learners were told the contents of a mystery person's pocket and were asked to work together in groups, speculating about the person's possible identity. However, the students failed to use the target modal forms in this stage of the lesson. In the following class discussion the teacher attempted to shift the students' focus from meaning to form by interweaving the target forms into the interaction. However, the students still failed to use the target structures. The teacher then resorted to direct explanation – for example:

> When you when you're NOT 100 per cent certain, you can use must. OK? Not he *is* a businessman but he *must* be a businessman.

The students now began to use the target forms and the teacher employed corrective feedback when students failed to use them or used them erroneously. This lesson employed a focused task (as defined in Chapter 7) and was clearly intended as focus-on-form instruction. However, the students initially responded to the task as requiring them to focus on message (i.e. there was no secondary attention to form). This led the teacher to try to attract the learners' attention to the target structure (a focus-on-form technique) but when this failed she resorted to explicit explanation (a focus-on-forms technique), which was then followed by a further activity that afforded opportunity for free production practice. This lesson, which I have held up as exemplifying 'principled grammar teaching' (see Batstone and Ellis, 2008), cannot be easily classified as either focus on form or focus on forms. Rather it is a skillful amalgam of both.

A further reason for querying whether a clear distinction between focus on form and focus on forms can be made is the difficulty in classifying specific activities as one or the other. Doughty and Williams (1998) acknowledged this by proposing that focus-on-form techniques vary in terms of their obtrusiveness. For example, 'input flood' (i.e. materials that expose learners to multiple exemplars of the target feature) is 'unobtrusive' whereas 'input-processing' (i.e. materials that direct learners' attention to the target feature) is 'obtrusive'. In a similar vein, Sharwood-Smith (1981) distinguished different focus-on-forms techniques (which he referred to as 'explicit instruction') in terms of their degrees of explicitness and elaborateness. 'Brief indirect clues that hint at a regularity' is an example of a technique low in both explicitness and elaborateness while 'guidance in the form of an algorithm' is high in both. These two continua seem to overlap; activities at the obtrusive end of Doughty and William's list of focus-on-form techniques might well be included in activities that Sharwood-Smith would classify as low in explicitness and elaborateness.

The problem of classifying activities as either focus on form or focus on meaning is most clearly evident in the case of consciousness-raising (CR) tasks. Doughty and Williams included these in their list but given that they are clearly aimed at encouraging metalinguistic understanding of specific target structures they could be considered a focus-on-forms activity. Sharwood-Smith saw consciousness-raising as clearly belonging to explicit instruction. However, as noted in Chapter 7 and Chapter 8, consciousness-raising tasks serve a joint purpose. They aim to stimulate meaning-centred interaction where a linguistic feature simply serves as the content to be talked about (in which case they can be considered to belong to focus on form) but they also aim to develop explicit knowledge of a predetermined linguistic feature (in which case they constitute a focus-on-forms activity).

To my mind, then, while the distinction between focus on form and focus on forms is of theoretical interest as it encapsulates different positions regarding how FFI can contribute to second language (L2) acquisition, it cannot serve as a basis for examining the research that has investigated FFI, as it cannot really be rigorously defined operationally[2].

Implicit versus Explicit Instruction

In Ellis (2008) I explained the difference between explicit and implicit instruction as follows:

> Explicit instruction involves 'some sort of rule being thought about during the learning process' (DeKeyser, 1995). In other words, learners are encouraged to develop met-alinguistic awareness of the rule. This can be achieved deductively, as when a rule is given to the learners or inductively as when the learners are asked to work out a rule for themselves from an array of data illustrating the rule.

> Implicit instruction is directed at enabling learners to infer rules without awareness. Thus it contrasts with explicit instruction in that there is no intention to develop any understanding of what is being learned (p. 17).

It should be noted, however, that implicit instruction need not be entirely devoid of attempts to induce learners to attend to form. As de Graaf and Housen (2009) point out, the key difference lies in whether the instruction 'directs' or 'attracts' attention to form. Explicit instruction directs learners to not just attend to grammatical forms but also to develop conscious mental representations of them. Learners know what they are supposed to be learning. Implicit instruction aims to attract learners' attention to exemplars of linguistic forms as these occur in communicative input but does not seek to develop any awareness or understanding of the 'rules' that describe these forms. Housen and Pierrard also identify a number of other characteristics that differentiate implicit and explicit instruction, as shown in Table 9.2.

Readers may well be struck by the apparent similarity between this distinction and the previous one (i.e. focus on form versus focus on forms). Implicit FFI seemingly involves focus on form while explicit FFI involves focus on forms. In fact, though, these distinctions are not the same. Implicit FFI does not necessarily involve a task where there is a primary focus on meaning, as required in focus-on-form instruction. Indeed, one way in which some researchers have investigated implicit FFI is by simply asking students to read and memorize a set of discrete sentences – an activity that certainly would not count as a task. Also, explicit FFI does not exclude the possibility of using tasks. As we saw in Samuda's lesson, explicit instruction can be introduced

Table 9.2 Implicit and explicit forms of form-focused instruction (de Graaf and Housen, 2009: 737)

Implicit FFI	Explicit FFI
• attracts attention to language form	• directs attention to language form
• language serves primarily as a tool for communication	• language serves as an object of study
• delivered spontaneously and incidentally (e.g., in an otherwise communication-oriented activity)	• predetermined and planned (e.g. as the main focus and goal of a teaching activity)
• unobtrusive (minimal interruption of communication of meaning)	• obtrusive (interruption of communication of meaning)
• presents target forms in context	• presents target forms in isolation
• no rule explanation or directions to attend to forms to discover rules; no use of metalanguage	• use of rule explanation or directions to attend to forms to discover rules; use of metalinguistic terminology
• encourages free use of target form.	• involves controlled practice of target form.

Source: Based on de Graaff, R. and A. Housen, 2009. "Investigating the Effects and Effectiveness of L2 Instruction", in M. Long and C. Doughty (eds), *The Handbook of Language Teaching*. Oxford: Blackwell Publishing (pp. 726–755).

into a task-based lesson. Also, in Chapter 7 we saw that corrective feedback when students are performing a task can be explicit.

The same problems we noted with regard to the focus on form/focus on forms distinction apply to the implicit/explicit distinction. The external instructional perspective may not match the internal learner's perspective. Also, it is not easy to classify instructional techniques as implicit or explicit. In short, I am not convinced that the implicit/explicit distinction provides a viable way of examining the research on FFI although it may help to illuminate some of the research findings.

An Options-Based Approach

An alternative approach to investigating FFI – one that I have favoured (see Ellis 1997a; 1998a; 2002) – involves identifying the major methodological options available to teachers. I wrote:

> By methodological option I mean a design feature that results in some form of classroom activity which teachers recognize as distinctive . . . Options are identifiable with reference to the kinds of techniques and procedures commonly used to teach grammar, as evidenced, for example, in teachers' handbooks such as Ur (1996). They are pedagogical constructs (Ellis, 1997a: 77).

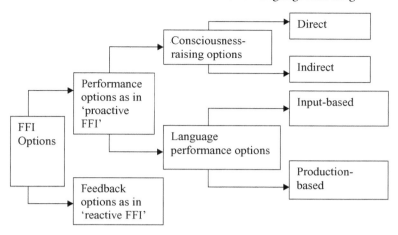

Figure 9.1 Key FFI methodological options

In other words, I proposed that FFI is best conceptualized not in terms of abstract constructs such as focus on form/focus on forms or implicit/explicit instruction but in terms of concrete instructional activities.

Figure 9.1 presents the main FFI options I have proposed. A broad distinction can be made between techniques and procedures that involve some kind of performance on the part of the learner and those that provide the learner with feedback on their performance. This distinction corresponds to the difference between 'proactive FFI' and 'reactive FFI'. The latter was examined in Chapter 5 and Chapter 8 so I will not discuss it further here. Instead, I will focus on the performance options involved in proactive FFI. These consist of two main types – consciousness-raising options and language-processing options. The former entail explicit grammar instruction (i.e. they are directed at developing learners' explicit knowledge of L2 features). They involve both direct instruction (i.e. learners are provided with an explicit explanation/description of L2 features either by the teacher or via instructional materials) and indirect instruction (i.e. learners are invited to develop their own explicit knowledge of L2 features by performing CR tasks). Language-processing options involve various kinds of activities designed to induce learners to process L2 features either by comprehending text or by producing text. More delicate subdivisions of this level of options are possible but not shown in Figure 9.1. For example, production-based options vary in terms of whether they are text-manipulating (i.e. involve activities that supply learners with the sentences that they are required to produce and ask them to operate on them in some limited way, as in a filling-in-the blank exercise) or text-creating (i.e. activities that require learners to produce their own sentences as in a structure-based production task). In Ellis (2002), I provided a more fine-grained classification of these methodological options. Readers might also like to consult Lyster (2007: Chapter 3) for a somewhat different account of the proactive FFI options applicable to content-based language teaching.

Different instructional approaches involve different combinations of options. For example, a typical focus-on-form lesson would involve a text-creating task combined with feedback options. A present–practice–produce (PPP) lesson would involve a consciousness-raising option (often of the direct type) followed by production-based practice involving both text-manipulating and text-creating activities and also feedback. Processing-instruction (VanPatten, 1996; see later section: Input-based versus production-based instruction) requires comprehension-based activities directed at inducing processing of the target feature[3].

My approach in the following sections of this chapter will be to examine research that has examined the relative effectiveness of different types of FFI on language learning in terms of the options shown in Figure 9.1. In so doing, however, I will also draw on the two other ways of conceptualizing FFI I have considered – focus on form versus focus on forms, and implicit instruction versus explicit instruction. I will only examine the various performance options, as feedback options were considered in depth in previous chapters. First, though, I will briefly report on some of the early FFI studies, which addressed a question that – at the time – was seen as fundamental: 'Does second language instruction make a difference?' (Long, 1983b).

Early FFI Research: The Effects of Instruction on L2 Acquisition

FFI has always been an area of enquiry of interest to both researchers and language teachers. Both researchers and teachers want to know whether FFI 'works' (i.e. whether it actually results in L2 acquisition). For L2 researchers this was a particularly important issue as research on naturalistic L2 learners in the 1960s and 1970s (see, for example, Hatch, 1978b) showed that learners followed a more or less universal order of acquisition and also progressed through a sequence of transitional stages when acquiring a specific grammatical structure. This led to questioning whether FFI was really necessary for learning and whether it had any effect on the order and sequence in which grammatical structures were naturally acquired.

The research addressed these questions in two main ways. First, a number of studies (reviewed in Long, 1983b) compared the ultimate level of achievement and rate of learning of groups of learners who had received instruction (which was assumed to consist of FFI) with groups who had not. Second, comparative and experimental studies were carried out to investigate whether learners who had received FFI manifested the same order and sequence of acquisition as naturalistic learners. For example, Pica (1983) compared groups of naturalistic learners, instructed learners and 'mixed' learners (i.e. learners who were receiving instruction but also had opportunities for naturalistic learning). She reported that although there were no statistically significant differences in the orders of acquisition of grammatical morphemes of the three groups, differences were evident in the groups' acquisition of specific morphemes (e.g. V*ing* and articles). Pienemann (1985; 1989) provided evidence to support the claim that instruction only 'worked' if it was directed at structures that were next in line to be acquired according to a well-defined developmental sequence.

On the basis of this, he advanced the Teachability Hypothesis, which stated that 'instruction can only promote language acquisition if the interlanguage is close to the point when the structure to be taught is acquired in a natural setting' (1985: 37).

The findings of these studies appeared to be contradictory. That is, while the majority of the studies indicated that instructed learners generally learned more rapidly and achieved higher levels of proficiency than non-instructed learners (suggesting that FFI assisted acquisition), other studies indicated that instructed learners followed the same order and sequence of acquisition as non-instructed learners (suggesting that the process of acquisition was not influenced by instruction). This apparent paradox had a major impact on theoretical thinking about the relationship between FFI and acquisition, leading to claims that FFI only works by promoting the processes involved in natural language acquisition, not by changing them. Some studies even indicated that FFI could impede the natural process of acquisition. As we saw in Chapter 6, Lightbown (1983)[4] suggested that the intensive teaching of V*ing* might have interfered with the learners' natural interlanguage development – a view supported by Pica's (1983) findings.

This early research was instrumental in leading commentators such as Long to propose that FFI was best implemented as focus on form rather than focus on forms. Given that learners had their own built-in syllabus and given the obvious difficulties of trying to match the instructional syllabus to the learner's syllabus (Lightbown, 1985b), it seemed unhelpful, if not impossible, to try to intervene directly in learners' interlanguage development by trying to implant specific grammatical features. The alternative was to try to enhance the natural processes of L2 acquisition by drawing 'students' attention to linguistic elements as they arose incidentally in lessons whose overriding focus was on meaning or communication (Long, 1991: 45–46). In other words, attention switched from asking whether FFI 'works' to asking what kind of FFI is most likely to impact on acquisition.

Doubts exist, however, as to the universality of the claim that instruction is powerless to affect the route of L2 grammatical development. Spada and Lightbown (1999) conducted a study that set out to explicitly test the claims of Pienemann's Teachability Hypothesis. They determined the precise developmental stage of 150 francophone children learning English question forms, establishing that most of them were at stage 2 (i.e. produced subject–verb–object – SVO – questions with rising intonation). The children were then exposed to hundreds of questions mainly at stage 4 (for example, 'yes/no' questions with auxiliary inversion) and stage 5 (i.e. WH questions with auxiliary second) in communicative activities over a two-week period. By and large, the learners moved up only one stage (i.e. those at stage 2 moved up to stage 3, while those at stage 3 moved up to stage 4). However, there were two learners at stage 2 who made the leap to stage 4 and also many of the students who were at the more advanced stages initially failed to progress at all. Spada and Lightbown concluded that these results failed to provide full support for the Teachability Hypothesis.

Also, some theoretical perspectives reject the existence of a natural and universal route of learning. Sociocultural theorists have argued that because learning originates in social interaction, individuals' experiences will necessarily vary and thus a predetermined universal route is simply not possible. Lantolf (2005), for example, commented:

> SCT . . . because of its fundamental theoretical assumption that development is rev-
> olutionary and therefore unpredictable, have [sic] a good deal of difficulty with the
> claims of universal predetermined developmental trajectories that are impervious to
> instructional intervention (p. 339).

Johnson (2004) also argued that the adoption of Vygotskian sociocultural theory 'would require that we . . . eradicate the assertion that L2 acquisition progresses along a predetermined mental path' (p. 172). Sociocultural theorists are not alone in taking this position. DeKeyser (1998: 2003) also challenged the existence of an incontrovertible route of acquisition from the perspective of skill-acquisition theory. He argued that automatized explicit knowledge is functionally indistinguishable from implicit knowledge and that declarative knowledge of any linguistic feature can be proceduralized providing there is sufficient and appropriate practice.

It always difficult to reconcile radically different theoretical perspectives but it may be possible if we distinguish the effects of instruction on implicit and explicit knowledge. The natural route of acquisition may only become evident in data that reflect learners' implicit knowledge of the L2. However, it seems perfectly possible for learners to develop explicit knowledge of grammatical features in any order and, if one accepts DeKeyser's arguments, such knowledge can be proceduralized. Thus, FFI may be powerless to change the course of acquisition of implicit knowledge (and, as Long has suggested, can only hope to facilitate the natural course of its development) but it can still be effective in developing functional control of specific features irrespective of learners' developmental level. This might explain why learners sometimes benefit from instruction even though they are not developmentally ready to do so. If this is the case, we can conclude that both focus on form and focus on forms have a place in FFI.

The early studies investigated FFI generically. However, the finding that learners receiving FFI did seem to benefit where rate of learning was concerned and the development of theoretical views about the nature of L2 acquisition led researchers to examine the effects of different types of FFI. I will now examine these by considering research that has investigated the various methodological options shown in Figure 9.1. My aim is not to provide a comprehensive survey of the FFI research but to identify key studies that have investigated each option.

Consciousness-Raising

Much of the research that has investigated the effects of consciousness-raising has been informed by the weak-interface position regarding the relationship between explicit and implicit L2 knowledge. This states that although explicit knowledge does not generally convert into implicit knowledge, explicit knowledge can assist the processes responsible for the development of implicit knowledge (see Ellis, 1994). Thus, consciousness-raising as a methodological option seeks to develop learners' explicit L2 knowledge on the grounds that, although this may not be available for immediate use in communication, it will facilitate noticing and noticing-the-gap and so lead to the development of the implicit knowledge needed for communication.

Sociocultural theory also recognizes the importance of consciousness-raising. Lantolf and Thorne (2006) argued that L2 communicative ability does not depend on implicit knowledge but can emerge from automatized explicit knowledge, a view also supported by skill-learning theory (DeKeyser, 1998). They went on to argue that advances in cognitive linguistics were making it possible to teach explicit knowledge more effectively, including knowledge of those grammatical features that DeKeyser considered 'too difficult to teach and practice explicitly' (p. 57). In short, sociocultural theory claims that learners not only benefit from the 'scientific knowledge' that explicit knowledge affords them but, in fact, need access to this knowledge for development to take place. However, while such a claim is tenable for adult learners, it is of doubtful validity where young learners are concerned.

I will begin by examining sociocultural-oriented research on consciousness-raising and then move on to consider research conducted within the framework of cognitive theory considering first a number of studies that have compared direct and indirect consciousness-raising and then studies that have investigated the possibility that explicitly teaching one feature may trigger the acquisition of related other features (as claimed by the Projection Hypothesis). It should be noted that although all the studies I will consider in this section included an explicit instruction option, many of them combined this with practice activities involving controlled production.

Conceptually organized grammatical knowledge

Sociocultural theory emphasizes the importance of developing 'conceptually organized grammatical knowledge' (i.e. accounts of grammatical features that explain in detail the link between form and semantic functional concepts). It disputes the usefulness of 'rules-of-thumb' on the grounds that these may actually impede effective development of the target language. Grammatical explanations need to be complete and accurate representations of knowledge.

Neguerela (2003; cited in Lantolf and Thorne, 2006) drew on systemic-theoretical instruction in a study designed to develop learners' scientific knowledge of three Spanish grammatical structures (aspect, use of articles, and verb tense). Systemic-functional instruction (Gal'perin, 1969) is based on three fundamental principles: (1) the instruction needs to be organized around coherent theoretical units, (2) it needs to provide a material instantiation of the target concepts by means of charts and diagrams, and (3) learners need to verbalize the concept-based explanation to foster full understanding and internalization of the concepts. In terms of

Sharwood-Smith's (1981) account of consciousness-raising, systematic-theoretical instruction is both highly explicit and elaborate.

Neguerela taught 12 students in a typical university foreign language course. The class met three times a week for 15 weeks and so, unlike many of the other studies we will consider in this chapter, was longitudinal in design. Neguerela embedded consciousness-raising activities into instruction based on the performance of scenarios (Di Pietro, 1987). The scenarios served to make the students aware of gaps in their grammatical knowledge of Spanish and led them to wishing to develop a better understanding of the three structural areas. The explicit instruction involved a 'Schema for the Complete Orienting Basis of an Action' for each grammatical area. For grammatical aspect, this consisted of a flow chart that led the learners through a series of questions to an understanding of when to use the preterit and imperfect tenses in Spanish. Neguerela asked students to verbalize the Schema while carrying out a number of oral and written activities both in class and for homework. The aim was to assist the students to internalize the information in the Schema so that they could use it automatically when communicating. Altogether the students completed six verbalizations of the aspect Schema. Neguerela collected verbal explanations of the grammatical structures at the beginning and end of the course. The learners' initial explanations were simplistic and incomplete, reflecting the rules of thumb that appear in student textbooks. Their explanations at the end of the course, although not always complete, were generally more coherent and accurate, reflecting the complex factors that determine choice of aspectual form in Spanish. Neguerela also showed that the learners were able to use the formal features associated with the target concepts more accurately at the end of the course and concluded that this was due to the development in their conceptual understanding.

Interestingly, however, the methods of testing learning in Neguerela's study and other similar studies (see Lantolf and Thorne, 2006) involved relatively controlled language. Tests consisting of written composition, fill-in-the-blank exercises, declining adjectives, translation, and multiple-choice tests are likely to have favoured the use of explicit knowledge. Neguerela found that the effects of the instruction were more clearly evident in students' written work, which allows for monitoring using explicit knowledge, than in their oral production. Thus, while the research suggests that conceptually organized instruction may help students develop clearer explicit knowledge, it does not, as yet, convincingly demonstrate that this knowledge is available for use in spontaneous oral communication. It is also doubtful whether such instruction is well-suited to learners other than university-level students of foreign languages – the type of learners investigated in all the studies.

Direct versus indirect consciousness-raising

In Chapter 7 and Chapter 8 we examined a number of studies that have investigated consciousness-raising tasks performed by learners working in pairs or small groups. We considered the extent to which learners engaged in negotiation of meaning and language-related episodes in the interactions that these tasks generated. We also considered the relationship between these interactions and L2 learning. These studies provided clear evidence that CR tasks were effective in developing learners' explicit L2 knowledge. In this section we will address a somewhat different question: Is there any difference in the learning that results from direct and indirect consciousness-raising? Direct consciousness-raising takes the form of explanations of linguistic features either provided by a teacher or by a textbook. Indirect-consciousness-raising is catered for by CR tasks that assist learners to discover for themselves how linguistic features work.

Fotos and Ellis (1991) found that both teacher-provided metalinguistic explanations and a CR task resulted in significant gains in understanding of the target structure (dative alternation), although the former seemed to produce the more durable gains. In a later study, Fotos (1994) found no statistically significant difference between direct explicit instruction and CR tasks in learners' development of explicit knowledge of adverb placement, dative alternation, and relative clauses. In other words, the CR tasks worked as well as direct teacher explanation.

Mohamed (2001) also compared CR tasks and direct grammar instruction. Her study involved 51 adult English as a second language (ESL) learners in a New Zealand tertiary institution. Direct grammar instruction took the form of handouts explaining the target structures and giving examples. Indirect instruction involved the performance of CR tasks in small groups. She found that the majority of learners were successful in performing the CR task. Both direct and indirect consciousness-raising led to gains in learning but the gains achieved through the indirect tasks were significantly greater. However, the lower-intermediate students experienced difficulty with both types of instruction. Mohammed concluded that CR tasks could serve as an effective way of teaching explicit knowledge and also provided learners with opportunities to communicate in the target language.

Pesce (2008) compared two groups' performance on two consciousness-raising tasks designed to develop German learners' explicit knowledge of Spanish past tenses (imperfect/preterit). In the teacher-instructed group, the students read a story told in the preterit tense. They then read an expanded version of the story that contained imperfect verb forms. This was followed by a teacher explanation of imperfect tense. The self-discovery group received the same texts but was asked to work out the rule for the imperfect tense in pairs. Both groups then completed two tasks – a fill-in-the gap cloze and a narrative task – and were asked to think aloud as they did so. In addition, both groups completed a pre-test, immediate post-test and delayed post-test. Results for both the written task solutions and the tests were reported. Overall, the teacher-instructed group performed the tasks better than the self-discovery group. However, in the immediate post-tests, the self-discovery group outperformed the teacher-instructed group in both morphology and syntax (but only in morphology in the delayed post-test). The results of this study also suggest that consciousness-raising tasks have much to offer.

These studies[5] all indicate that indirect conciousness-raising through CR tasks that invite learners to discover how grammatical features work are effective. They are generally as effective as direct consciousness-raising and sometimes more so. Again, though, the testing methods used to measure acquisition suggest that the instruction led to gains in explicit rather than implicit knowledge.

Projection studies

Projection studies have investigated the hypothesis that when a grammatically marked structure is taught, learners will not only learn this structure but also other implicated less-marked structures. This hypothesis has been investigated primarily with reference to relative pronoun functions, as described in the Accessibility Hierarchy. This claims that the functions of relative pronouns vary in markedness, with the subject function (e.g. 'I met the man *who* is marrying my sister.') being the least marked, the direct object function more marked (e.g. 'I met the man *whom* my sister is marrying.') and the object of preposition (e.g. 'I met the man *to whom* my sister is getting married.') still more marked.

All of the studies involved direct consciousness-raising. The learners received explanations of how to join two sentences using a relative pronoun and, in some studies, how to avoid pronoun retention (e.g. '*The man whom I bumped into *him* became very angry'). A number of early studies (e.g. Gass, 1982; Eckman, Bell, and Nelson, 1988) found that instruction directed at the object of preposition function triggered acquisition of the less-marked features than instruction directed at the subject or direct object functions. The reverse, however, did not occur to the same extent. For example, students taught the subject function did not show much gain on the object and object of preposition functions. Hamilton (1994), however, concluded that the evidence in support of the Projection Hypothesis was 'somewhat ambiguous' as there were clear cases of learners who generalized the instruction they received on an unmarked structure to a more marked structure, a result not predicted by the hypothesis. Ammar and Lightbown's (2006) study of Arabic learners of English also found evidence of generalization from both marked to unmarked and from unmarked to marked relative clauses.

Overall, the projection studies suggest that explicit instruction in one structure can sometimes aid acquisition of another structure but they do not uniformly support the directional claims of the Projection Hypothesis. Again, the tests used to measure acquisition involved grammaticality judgements, selected response or controlled production and cannot speak to whether the instruction resulted in learners' implicit knowledge.

Performance-Based Instruction

Performance-based instruction can be input-based or production-based. I will first consider studies that have examined various input-based options and production-based options separately and then examine studies that have sought to compare the relative effect of input-based and production-based instruction on L2 acquisition.

Input-based instruction

Input-based instruction involves the manipulation of the input that learners are exposed to or are required to process. It is directed at enabling learners to (1) notice the presence of a specific feature in the input, (2) comprehend the meaning of the feature, and (3) rehearse the feature in short-term memory. One of the assumptions of input-based FFI is that it is psycholinguistically easier to manipulate the processes involved in intake than it is to induce learners to restructure their production interlanguage systems. Pienemann (1985) noted that 'the input to the comprehension system does not need to be adjusted to the level of complexity of the production learning task since there are different types of processing procedures in the two systems' (p. 53).

Input-based instruction can take a number of different forms as shown in Figure 9.2. A first-level distinction can be made between options that are exposure-based (i.e. that involve simply exposing learners to oral or written text that contain exemplars of the target feature) or response-based (i.e. elicit some kind of response from the learner that demonstrates they have processed the meaning of the target feature). Exposure-based instruction consists of either enriched or enhanced input. Enriched input is input that contains a specific L2 feature with high frequency. It is often referred to as 'input flooding'. Enhanced input is input where the target feature has been emphasized in some way – through glossing, bolding or underlining. It seeks to increase the saliency of the feature so that it is more likely to be noticed. The response-based input takes the form of structured-input activities where learners are required to demonstrate that they have understood the meaning of the target feature through a response that is either non-verbal or minimally verbal. For example, they might be asked to listen to sentences like 'The dog was bitten by Mary' and choose which of two pictures (one showing Mary biting the dog and the other the dog

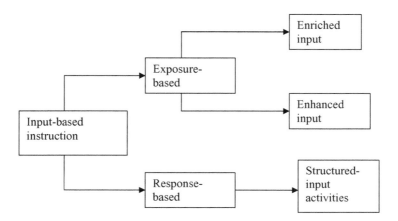

Figure 9.2 Input-based FFI options

biting Mary) represents the meaning of the sentence they heard. In this section I will mainly consider enriched and enhanced input studies, reserving consideration of studies involving structured input to a later section when I compare the effects of input-based and production-based instruction.

Input-based studies have investigated both whether the forms targetted in the enriched or enhanced input are noticed by learners, and whether enriched input promotes acquisition. I will review a number of key studies and then identify the main findings.

Enriched input studies   Trahey and White (1993) examined whether an 'input flood' was sufficient to enable francophone learners of L2 English to learn that English permits adverb placement between the subject and the verb (French does not) but does not permit placement between the verb and the object (French does). Exposure occurred one hour a day for 10 days. The target structure was not highlighted in any way. The learners succeeded in learning the subject–adverb–verb (SAV) position but failed to 'unlearn' the ungrammatical subject–verb–adverb–object (SVAO) position. In a follow-up test administered one year after the treatment, however, Trahey (1996) found that the beneficial effects of the input flood on the acquisition of SAV had disappeared. Overall, then, this study suggests that the effects of enriched input on acquisition are limited.

Loewen, Erlam and Ellis (2009) exposed adult ESL learners to input containing third person –s in the context of grammar lessons designed to teach them another grammatical structure (the use of the indefinite article to express generic reference). The idea was to investigate incidental acquisition of third person –s. Altogether, the instruction exposed learners to 51 examples of third person –s in written input and 23 in aural input in two one hour lessons taught over two days. Tests of both implicit and explicit knowledge showed that no acquisition had taken place in either the short or long term. Loewen et al. suggested that this failure might have been because of the low saliency of third person –s in the input, blocking (i.e. the tendency for learners to not attend to a feature when an alternative feature is well-established in their interlanguage) and the powerful distracting effect of the overt instruction on another structure.

Enhanced-input studies   Most other studies have investigated some form of en-hanced input and several compared the effects of enriched and enhanced input. Jourdenais et al. (1995) found that English-speaking learners of L2 Spanish were more likely to make explicit reference to preterit and imperfect verb forms when thinking aloud during a narrative writing task if they had previously read texts where the forms were typographically highlighted. They also found that the learners ex-posed to the enhanced text were more likely to use past tense forms than the learners who read the non-enhanced text even though both texts had been enriched.

J. White (1998) compared the effects of three types of input-based instruction: (1) typographically enhanced input flood plus extensive listening and reading,

(2) typographically enhanced input by itself, and (3) input flood. This study found that the three types of input worked equally effectively in assisting francophone learners to acquire the possessive pronouns 'his' and 'her', leading White to conclude that the target structure was equally salient in all three.

Reinders and Ellis (2009) exposed adult ESL learners to oral and written texts that had been seeded with sentences containing negative adverbials with subject-verb inversion (e.g. 'Seldom had he seen such a beautiful woman'). The nature of the exposure differed. In the enriched condition the learners were simply instructed to complete the tasks (a dictation, an individual text reconstruction task and a collaborative reconstruction task). In the enhanced input condition the learners were instructed to pay attention to where the auxiliary verb came in each sentence. Reinders and Ellis investigated both the uptake of the target structure in the various tasks, which they took as evidence of noticing, and acquisition as shown by scores in a timed and untimed grammaticality judgement test designed to provide measures of implicit and explicit knowledge respectively. They found no difference in noticing in the enriched and enhanced groups. The enriched input group outperformed the enhanced group on gain scores for the grammatical sentences in the timed grammaticality judgement test. There were no group differences in the scores for the untimed grammaticality judgement test (i.e. the measure of explicit knowledge). Reinders and Ellis suggested that the noticing instruction did not help learners because of the difficulty of the target structure in this study.

Input-based instruction with and without explicit instruction   Several studies have compared the effects of input-based instruction with and without explicit instruc- tion. Williams and Evans (1998) compared the effects of enriched input (consisting of an artificially increased incidence of the highlighted target forms) and the same input plus explicit instruction and corrective feedback on the acquisition of En- glish participial adjectives (for example, 'boring/bored') and present passive. For the participial adjectives, the enriched input + explicit instruction group did better than both the enriched input group and a control group on a grammaticality judge- ment test and a sentence completion test while the difference between the enriched group and the control did not reach statistical significance. For the passive, both the experimental groups outperformed the control group on a sentence completion test, but no group differences were evident on a narrative test. This study raises an important consideration – namely, that the effects of different types of instruction may vary depending on the target feature. I will return to this point later in the chapter.

Hernandez (2011) compared the effects of two types of instruction that involved input-based options. The target structure was Spanish discourse markers. One group received an input flood and communicative practice but without any corrective feedback. The other experimental group received explicit instruction, an input flood, communicative practice and corrective feedback. The results showed that both types of instruction had a positive effect on students' use of discourse markers in a speaking task. Although the transcripts of the communicative exchanges showed that the group that received explicit instruction used more discourse markers than the input flood group, overall there was no statistically significant difference between the two groups in the post-tests.

Input-based instruction versus explicit instruction   Finally, a number of studies carried out a direct comparison between explicit instruction and input-based instruction. Doughty (1991), for example, examined the effects of 'meaning-oriented instruction' and 'rule-oriented instruction' on the acquisition of relative clauses by 20 intermediate-level ESL students from different language backgrounds. The materials consisted of computer-presented reading passages, specially written to contain examples of clauses where the direct object had been relativized. All the subjects skimmed the texts first. The meaning-orientated group received support in the form of lexical and semantic rephrasings and sentence clarification strategies (i.e. input enhancement). The rule-orientated group received instruction in the form of explicit rule statements and on-screen sentence manipulation. A control group simply read the text again. The results showed that the meaning-orientated group and the rule-orientated group both outperformed the control group in their ability to relativize. There was no difference between the two experimental groups. The group that received input-enhancement, however, demonstrated an advantage with regard to comprehension of the content of the text.

Takimoto (2008) investigated the effects of explicit instruction and input-based instruction on the acquisition of the linguistic means for performing complex requests (e.g. 'I am wondering if you could . . .'). The explicit instruction took the form of indirect consciousness-raising. The input-based instruction consisted of structured input. There was also a third experimental group that received direct consciousness-raising and structured input. All three groups outperformed the control group on a battery of tests. There were no statistically significant differences between the experimental groups, except that the group that received explicit instruction plus structured input performed less well than the other two groups on the delayed-listening test. Takimoto suggested that this might have been because in this condition the students were given the explicit rules rather than having to work them out for themselves and the effect of this was less durable in a test that called for online processing.

Spada, Lightbown and J. White (2006) compared the effects of instruction consisting of direct consciousness-raising with input-based instruction involving both enriched and enhanced input on francophone learners' acquisition of English possessive determiners (i.e. 'his' and 'her'). The results indicated an advantage for the explicit instruction. However, it should be noted that the explicit instruction was accompanied with text-manipulation production practice (i.e. the learners were asked to refer to an explicit explanation of the use of possessive determiners while completing a cloze passage and discussed their answers in class). Thus the comparison between explicit instruction and input-based instruction was not a 'pure' one.

Conclusions   The results of these studies are quite mixed, which is not surprising given that FFI was operationalized in different ways, often involving several different options in addition to an input-based option. They suggest the following tentative conclusions:

1. Enriched input in the form of an input flood can help L2 learners acquire a new grammatical feature but it may not enable learners to eradicate erroneous rules from their interlanguage (Trahey and White) and the beneficial effects of the instruction may wear off over time if learners do not continue to receive exposure to the target feature (Trahey). Also, enriched input may be ineffective in helping learners acquire non-salient features such as English third person-*s* (Loewen, Erlam and Ellis).
2. Enhanced input involving text highlighting of features has also been found to promote noticing and to assist acquisition (Jourdanais et al.).
3. Enhanced input involving noticing instructions may not help to enhance learning if the target feature is complex (Reinders and Ellis).
4. There is no clear evidence that one type of input-based instruction is more effective than another (White).
5. Combining input-based and explicit instruction sometimes results in better learning than input-based instruction alone (Williams and Evans) but sometimes does not (Hernandez).
6. If the input-based instruction makes the meaning of the target structure clear, it is as effective as explicit instruction (Doughty) and in some cases more effective (Takimoto). However, input-based FFI appears to be less effective than explicit instruction when this is accompanied by production practice.

If the treatments that consisted of just input-based options are taken as involving implicit instruction, it is clear that such instruction can succeed in helping learners to acquire grammar – at least sometimes. Overall, the studies do not demonstrate that explicit instruction is superior to input-based instruction[6]. However, they do suggest that input-based instruction may work better if it is accompanied by explicit instruction. It is clear from these studies that there are a number of variables other than the type of instruction that affect learning outcomes. It is difficult to reach clear conclusions because of differences in such factors as the length of the instruction, the inherent difficulty of the target structures, and the methods used to measure learning.

Production-based instruction

In this section I will review studies that have investigated the effects of production-practice on L2 learning. 'Production practice' can take many different forms. I have attempted to capture the various possibilities in terms of a general distinction between text-manipulation and text-creation activities. This distinction reflects a continuum rather than a dichotomy but it constitutes a useful way of investigating the effects of different kinds of practice. It is also theoretically grounded. Drawing on skill-acquisition theory, DeKeyser has argued that text-manipulation activities serve a very limited purpose 'because they do not make the learner engage in what is the essence of language processing, i.e. establishing form-meaning connections' (2007: 11). DeKeyser views text-creation activities (such as tasks) as more important for learning both because they help to establish form-meaning connections and because they provide the 'real operating conditions' that foster 'transfer appropriate processing'[7] (i.e. enable learners to use what they practiced inside the classroom in communicative language use outside). I will first consider studies that have investigated text-manipulation activities and then those that have examined text-creation practice activities.

Text-manipulation practice   Does language practice consisting solely of text-manipulation activities lead to gains in L2 knowledge? In Ellis (1984b), I investigated whether there was any relationship between the number of times a group of ESL learners practised producing 'when' questions in a controlled teacher-led activity and their development of this structure. Somewhat surprisingly those students who had the fewest practice opportunities manifested greater development than those who received the most. Sciarone and Meijer (1995) investigated the effects of students' engaging in computer-based controlled-practice exercises on acquisition. They found no difference in the test results of students who completed the exercises and those who did not. They noted that even the 'good' students in their sample did not appear to benefit from the practice. These two studies involved primarily text-manipulation activities. They suggest that learning is not dependent on the sheer quantity of such practice.

Overall, then, mechanical practice of target structures does not seem be very effective in promoting acquisition. In fact, there is some evidence that purely mechanical practice can actually interfere with learning. Lightbown's (1983) study (see Chapter 6) suggested that it can result in 'overlearning' of some structures. Weinert (1987) and VanPatten (1990b) also provided evidence to suggest that instruction can impede acquisition of grammatical structures (i.e. negatives in L2 German and clitic pronouns in L2 Spanish). In all these studies the reason given for the failure of the formal instruction was that it distorted the input made available to the learner and thus prevented the normal processes of acquisition from operating smoothly.

However, there is one approach involving text-manipulation practice that has been shown to be effective. Most production practice is directed at enabling learners to produce the correct target-language forms (i.e. to avoid making errors). Tomasello and Herron (1988; 1989) investigated what they called 'garden path' instruction. This involved deliberately eliciting errors in production and then correcting them. They found this type of production practice more effective than simply providing learners with explanations of the target structures (i.e. direct consciousness-raising). However, arguably it was not really the production practice that led to learning but the corrective feedback that learners received. This induced the learners to carry out a 'cognitive comparison' between their own deviant utterances and the correct target-language utterances.

Text-creation practice   To investigate the effects of production practice involving text-creation we need to turn again to studies that have employed focused tasks. I considered a number of these in Chapter 8. These demonstrated that when tasks led to learners directing attention to form they facilitated acquisition. Here I will consider a number of further studies that set out to teach specific target structures by providing learners with opportunities to engage in text-creation activities.

Immersion programs have been shown to be effective in developing learners' confidence in using the L2, their oral fluency, and their general comprehension but less effective in ensuring high levels of grammatical accuracy or sociolinguistic-appropriate use of the L2[8]. This has led some researchers (e.g. Swain, 1993) to propose that more attention to language form is needed. I begin, therefore, by examining two studies that investigated the effects of 'functional-analytic teaching' on the acquisition of grammatical forms that constituted continuing problems for learners in French immersion programmes in Canada.

Harley (1989) devized a set of functional-grammar materials to teach French immersion students the distinction between *passé composé* and *imparfait*. An introduction to the materials provided the learners with a description of the linguistic functions of the two verb tenses. There followed eight weeks of mainly text-creation activities designed to focus attention on the uses of the tenses. Examples of these activities are:

> *Proverbes.* The activities . . . provided an opportunity to learn French proverbs along with opportunities for sustained oral production in referring to the past (p. 341).

> *Souvenirs de mon enfance.* A series of activities designed to draw on students' personal experience in the creation of albums of childhood memories and in tape-recorded interviews (p. 342).

Harley found that the eight weeks of instruction resulted in significant improvement in the accuracy with which the two verb tenses were used in a written composition, in a rational cloze test, and in an oral interview. However, a control group subsequently caught up with the experimental group. Harley suggested that this might have been because this group also subsequently received FFI directed at this feature.

The target feature in Lyster's (1994) study was a sociopragmatic one – French address forms ('*tu*' and '*vous*'). As in the previous studies, the choice was motivated by the fact that even after several years in an immersion programme, the Grade 8 learners were unable to use these forms appropriately. The instructional options included explicit techniques (e.g. comparing speech acts in formal and informal contexts), text-manipulation exercises, and (primarily) text-creation activities such as role-plays and letter writing. The effect of the instruction was measured by means of a written production test, an oral production test and a multiple-choice test. The immediate and delayed post-tests showed clear gains in oral and written production and also in awareness of socio-stylistic differences in the use of the two pronouns.

A number of other studies have examined the effects of FFI based largely on text-creation activities on the acquisition of various grammatical features by learners in intensive ESL classes in Canada. In these programmes the students received about five hours of instruction every day for five months. The ESL instruction was communicatively-based and focused on 'the provision of opportunities for learners to use language in meaningful and creative ways' (White et al., 1991: 420).

White et al. (1991) studied the effects of instruction on question formation (WH and 'yes/no') on the same groups of learners as those used in the adverb study referred to earlier. Five hours of instruction over a two-week period were provided. The first week consisted of explicit instruction on question formation. In the second week they engaged in various communicative activities. The teachers were also encouraged to provide corrective feedback. Acquisition was measured by means of a cartoon task, a preference grammaticality judgement task, and an oral communication task. In comparison to a control group, the experimental group showed substantial gains in accuracy in all three tasks. The instructed learners in this case demonstrated that they had learnt how to use inversion in questions.

In Spada and Lightbown (1993), francophone ESL learners received approximately nine hours of instruction and corrective feedback. The instruction involved explicit instruction, exercises (e.g. unscrambling interrogative sentences) and communicative activities (e.g. guessing games where the learners were required to ask a series of questions to discover the identity of an object or person). There was also a comparison group that did not receive the instruction directed at question forms. The experimental groups demonstrated acquisition in terms of both accuracy and developmental progression (i.e. movement along the acquisitional sequence for question forms over time). However, a surprise finding of this study was that the comparison group also improved. Lightbown and Spada explained this by noting that the teacher of this group frequently corrected the students' use of question forms (along with other errors) and also provided metalinguistic information.

While these studies involved text-creation activities, they also included other instructional options (including explicit instruction) and thus do not demonstrate what effect text-creation activities themselves have on learning. The results for the control group in Spada and Lightbown's (1993) study, however, is interesting because it suggests that instruction consisting of text-creation activities alone suffices as an instructional platform for acquisition providing it is supported by corrective feedback. In other words, focus-on-form instruction consisting of text-creation activities and corrective feedback constitutes an effective strategy – a conclusion supported by the research on corrective feedback I looked at in Chapter 8.

But can text-creation activities work without corrective feedback? This takes us back to a problem we noted in Chapter 7, namely that focused tasks, even when cleverly designed, do not always elicit the linguistic features they were intended to elicit. This is why they often require corrective feedback (and/or metalinguistic explanation) to induce students to use the target features. Sometimes, however, text-creation activities do work as designed. Does the practice afforded by such activities result in measurable gains in learning even when they are not accompanied by instructional options that raise learners' awareness of the target features? In other words, does text-creation practice by itself foster incidental acquisition?

The studies we looked at in Chapter 8 suggest that the answer to this question is 'yes'. An interesting study by Muranoi (2000) provides further support for the effectiveness of text-creation activities when these are conducted without any explicit instruction. Muranoi investigated Japanese university students' acquisition of English articles. She made use of Di Pietro's strategic interaction tasks. These involved the students in (1) a rehearsal stage where they worked in pairs to plan a role play, (2) a performance stage where they performed the tasks with the teacher, and (3) a debriefing stage where the teacher commented on the students' performance. There were three groups. They all carried out the rehearsal stage in the same way. Differences occurred in the performance and debriefing stages. One experimental group received interactional enhancement through requests for repetitions and recasts when performing the task followed by a formal debriefing where the teacher explained the functions of the indefinite article (i.e. explicit instruction was provided). The second experimental group also received interactional enhancement during the performance stage but the debriefing was meaning-focused (i.e. the teacher only provided comments on overall communicative effectiveness). The control group performed the scenarios without any interactional enhancement and the debriefing was meaning-focused – in other words, there was no instructional focus on form. Acquisition was measured by means of a grammaticality judgement test, an oral production test and a written production test. Those groups that received interactional enhancement and debriefing outperformed the control group but the latter did demonstrate some learning of articles.

In an interesting study, Griggs (2006) investigated what effect performing communicative tasks had on adult French learner's use of English present perfect and past tense. This learner (Sandrine) completed six communicative tasks at two weekly intervals. A quantitative and qualitative analysis of Sandrine's use of the two verb tenses showed that there was a gradual progression from production based on her first language (L1) to production conforming to target language use. Importantly, however, it was the metalinguistic activity that Sandrine engaged in and her conscious attempt to apply rules (not always target rules) when performing the tasks that Griggs saw as important for her development. Griggs commented 'the effectiveness of communication tasks resides not so much in the natural communicative and acquisitional processes they trigger as in the way learners use them to construct production rules appropriate to communicative needs while adjusting these rules to target language requirements' (p. 427–428). This study, then, provides evidence that when text-creation activities are accompanied by learner-generated attempts to manipulate output interlanguage development takes place. It supports the importance of 'languaging' in the performance of communicative tasks (see Chapter 8).

All of these studies investigated grammar learning. In contrast, De la Fuente (2006) addressed whether text-creation practice by itself resulted in the learning of vocabulary. She compared the effects of three types of instruction on the acquisition of new vocabulary by learners in an elementary-level university Spanish class. The three types of instruction were: (1) present–practice–produce (PPP), (2) task-based with no explicit focus on form, and (3) task-based with explicit focus on form that involved clarification of phonological, morphological and spelling issues. Acquisition was measured in terms of elicited production of the target words. In the immediate post-test no group differences were evident. However, in the delayed test, the two task-based groups outperformed the PPP group. There was no difference between the two task-based groups suggesting that it was the task-related activity rather than the explicit focus on form that was important[9].

To conclude, there is evidence that text-creation practice alone assists learning. However, in many cases, some kind of explicit instruction is needed for, as we have seen, focused tasks do not always make the use of the target structure essential. In Samuda's (2001) study, for example, the students only started to use the target structure after the teacher had explained it to them. In general, it seems that text-creation activities work best if they are accompanied by some kind of instruction (i.e. direct/indirect consciousness-raising or corrective feedback). This was the case in the immersion studies we considered earlier in this section, in Muranoi's study and in Griggs' study. In all of them there was either an explicit instruction component or learners voluntarily chose to focus on form.

Input-based versus production-based instruction

In this section I will consider a number of FFI studies that have compared the effects of input-based and production-based instruction. In these studies input-based in-struction consisted of structured input. This differs from enriched/enhanced input in that it presents learners with input in a context that requires them to demonstrate that they have correctly processed the target structure for meaning. The demonstra-tion takes the form of a learner response to an input stimulus, with the response being either non-verbal (for example, choosing the picture that matches the stimulus) or minimally verbal (for example, indicating whether they agree/disagree with some statement). The production-based instruction varied, sometimes consisting entirely of text-manipulation activities and sometimes of a mixture of text-manipulation and text-creation activities.

A number of the studies involved 'processing instruction'. VanPatten (1996) de-fined this as 'a type of grammar instruction whose purpose is to affect the ways in which learners attend to input data' (p. 2). The structural targets of process-ing instruction are chosen with reference to a set of principles that is hypothe-sized to govern how L2 learners process input. VanPatten argued that it is difficult for learners to attend concurrently to different stimuli in the input and so need to decide how to prioritize their attentional resources during online processing.

They do this in accordance with processing principles, examples of which are shown here (VanPatten, 1996: 14–15).

P1 Learners process input for meaning before they process it for form.

P1 (a) Learners process content words in the input before anything else.

P1 (b) Learners prefer processing lexical items to grammatical items (for example, morphological markings) for semantic information.

P1 (c) Learners prefer processing 'more meaningful' morphology before 'less or non-meaningful morphology'.

P2 For learners to process form that is not meaningful, they must be able to process informational or communicative content at no (or little) cost to attention.

VanPatten continued to work on these principles over time, modifying and extending them (see, for example, VanPatten, 2004a). Only grammatical features that are governed by these principles are deemed suitable targets for investigating input-processing instruction.

VanPatten argued that instruction that draws attention to form–meaning mappings and thus helps learners to overcome their natural ways of processing input will prove more effective than traditional production practice (i.e. practice involving text-manipulation activities). This claim has been tested in a series of studies. In an early study, VanPatten and Cadierno (1993) compared the effects of two instructional treatments, one directed at manipulating learners' output to effect change in their developing interlanguage systems (i.e. production practice), and the other aimed at changing the way the learners perceived and processed input. Learners of Spanish at university level who received input-processing training relating to Spanish word order rules and the use of clitic pronouns performed better in comprehension tests than a group of similar learners who received production training. This result is not perhaps surprising, as it can be argued that the comprehension test favoured the input-based group. However, this group also performed at the same level as the traditional practice group in a production task that favoured the latter. This study, then, provided evidence that processing instruction was superior to traditional production practice.

One of the problems with this study was that both the experimental groups received explicit instruction. However, VanPatten argued that explicit instruction is not an essential element of processing instruction. Accordingly, VanPatten and Oikennon (1996) compared three groups: (1) received explicit information about the target structure followed by structured-input activities, (2) received only explicit information, and (3) just completed the structured-input activities. Acquisition was measured by means of both comprehension and production tests. In the comprehension test, significant gains were evident in groups (1) and (3), but not in (2). In the production test, group (1) did better than group (2). VanPatten and Oikennon interpreted these results as showing that it was the structured input rather than the explicit information that was important for acquisition. Other studies (for example, Sanz and Morgan-Short, 2004 and Benati, 2004) have since replicated these results.

However, two other computer-based studies suggest that such a conclusion might be premature. Fernandez (2008) conducted a study that compared the effects of structured input with and without explicit instruction on college-level learners' acquisition of two L2 Spanish grammatical features – object-verb-subject word order and subjunctive. She measured learning in terms of how rapidly learners were able to process input containing the target structures online successfully (i.e. in a computer program). The main finding was that the effects of the two kinds of FFI differed according to the target structure. As in previous studies, no difference was found between the structured-input-only group and the structured-input plus explicit instruction group for object-verb-subject. However, the group receiving explicit instruction processed the subjunctive forms sooner and faster than the group that just received structured input. Fernandez suggested that explicit instruction may benefit acquisition when the target structure is redundant and therefore less noticeable in the input as was the case for the subjunctive but not for object-verb-subject. Henry, Culman and VanPatten (2009) carried out a similar study involving two German structures and also found an advantage for the group that received structured input and explicit instruction. They concluded:

> . . . not all explicit instruction is the same, not all structures are the same, and the interaction of explicit instruction, structure, and processing problem may yield different results in different studies (p. 573).

In short, explicit instruction does appear to enhance the effects of structured input for at least some structures and when the measure of acquisition is processing time.

While there is clear support for processing instruction and the theoretical principles on which it is based, there are a number of limitations in the research conducted to date that need to be considered. First, most of the studies have not examined whether input-processing instruction results in the ability to use the target structure in unplanned language use. VanPatten and Sanz (1995) addressed this issue but found no statistically significant difference between the input-based and production-based instructional groups on a free production test. Marsden (2006) found that processing instruction did result in statistically significant gains in measures obtained from oral narratives and guided conversation tasks in the first of the two studies she reported but not in the other. Also, even in the first study the gains were marginal and much weaker than those evident in the discrete-point tests. Overall, then, there is still no convincing evidence that input-processing instruction is effective (or more effective than production-based techniques) in developing the implicit knowledge needed for oral communication.

Some studies have also failed to find any advantage whatsoever for structured input over production practice (for example, DeKeyser and Sokalski, 1996). In fact, in some studies (for example, Allen, 2000) production-based practice was shown to result in higher scores in the production tests). However, VanPatten (2002) argued that input-processing instruction is only effective for those target structures that involve learners overcoming default-processing strategies (i.e. structures governed by his input-processing principles). He claimed that studies where no advantage was found for input-based practice had selected inappropriate target structures.

There is another possibility, however. The relative failure of the production practice in many of the studies may have been because it consisted only of text-manipulation activities. Studies that have included text-creation activities (e.g. Allen 2000; Erlam 2003) that help learners to map meaning onto form found that the production practice was more effective than the structured input practice. This second explanation is supported by the results of Toth's (2006) study, which found no advantage for structured input over production-based practice even though the target structure was clearly one that VanPatten would consider amenable to processing instruction. In this study the production-based instruction included text-creation activities.

Input-processing instruction continues to attract the attention of researchers (see the collection of studies in Lee and Benati, 2009; and in VanPatten, 2004b). It has also aroused considerable debate (see for example, the commentary in DeKeyser et al., 2002, on VanPatten's 2002 defence of input-processing instruction).

Not all studies that have compared input-based and output-based FFI have drawn on processing instruction. In Chapter 3, for example we considered a study by Shintani and Ellis (2010) that investigated the effects of the two types of instruction on the acquisition of plural –*s* by young Japanese children who were beginner learners of English. This study demonstrated an advantage for input-based instruction. It differed from the processing instruction studies in two key ways. First, whereas the grammatical target in the processing instruction studies was made apparent to the learners and thus invited intentional learning, the target of Shintani and Ellis' study was masked (i.e. the primary focus was on vocabulary) and thus catered to incidental acquisition. Second, whereas most of the processing instruction studies are product-oriented (i.e. only the effects of the instruction on tests of comprehension and production were considered), Shintani and Ellis' (like Toth's study) was a process-product study (i.e. it sought to explain the results with reference to qualitative differences in the interactions that occurred when the two types of instruction were implemented).

All of these studies investigated the effects of input-based and production-based instruction on grammar. Shintani (2011a), however, carried out a meta-analysis of studies that compared the effects of the two types of instruction on vocabulary acquisition. Her main finding was clear. Production-based instruction resulted in higher levels of acquisition. Shintani also investigated the mediating effect of a number of different instructional variables – whether or not there was explicit instruction, whether learning was measured receptively or productively, and whether the post-test was immediate or delayed. In each case, production-based instruction led to significantly higher levels of vocabulary acquisition than comprehension-based instruction.

It would seem, then, that effects of the two types of instruction on these different aspects of language (grammar and vocabulary) are very different. However, a close look at the comprehension-based instruction in many of the studies Shintani included in her meta-analysis revealed that it often failed to establish a *need* for learners to learn the target words (i.e. the tasks did not force attention to form-meaning mapping) whereas the production-based instruction generally did create such a need. It is possible, therefore, that comprehension-based instruction that creates such a need will prove as effective as production-based instruction (and perhaps more so) for vocabulary.

Shintani (2011b) reported a study that suggests that this may indeed be the case. She compared the effects of input-based instruction consisting of comprehension tasks and production-based instruction consisting of present-practice-produce on the acquisition of English vocabulary. As in Shintani and Ellis, the learners were young Japanese beginners. The results of four vocabulary tests measuring both receptive and productive knowledge of the target words showed that both types of instruction led to significant gains in word knowledge. However, the input-based instruction led to greater gains in a task-based comprehension test, a result that Shintani explained by showing that this type of instruction provided the learners with greater discourse control and more opportunity to negotiate the meanings of the words. In other words, it created a need for the learners to attend to form-meaning mapping.

To conclude this section, the results of the studies that have compared input-based and output-based instruction are quite mixed. There is evidence that input-based instruction may be more effective in the case of grammar but production-based instruction is more effective in the case of vocabulary. Perhaps, though, the main conclusion to be drawn is that either type of instruction will prove effective providing it helps learners to see how form and meaning map onto each. Ultimately, as the studies by Shintani, Shintani and Ellis, and Toth illustrate (and as argued in Chapter 8) whatever effect instruction has on learning is dependent on the interactions that arise in the instruction. The key issue, then, might be how the interactions that take place when implementing input-based or production-based FFI foster acquisition. This has hardly been examined as most of the studies were 'product' based rather than 'process-product'.

Some Outstanding Issues

As should be apparent from the preceding survey of research that has investigated FFI options it is not easy to reach clear generalizations. In part this is because of the complex nature of FFI itself (i.e. it can involve different options and combinations of options) and in part because of a number of methodological issues that need to be considered to ensure the external and internal validity of FFI studies. In this section I will briefly consider a number of these issues.

Durability

When teachers elect to teach learners a linguistic feature they do so not just in the assumption that they will learn to use it correctly in the short term but also that it will be remembered and available for use over time. Thus, to achieve external validity an FFI study needs to demonstrate that the effects of instruction are durable. This requires the inclusion of a delayed post-test.

Several studies have found that the effects of instruction are durable. Harley (1989), for example, retested her subjects three months after the instruction and found that the learners' improved ability to use French *imparfait* and *passé composé*, in an immediate post-test had been extended even further. White et al. (1991) found that their learners demonstrated increased accuracy in question formation when tested some six months after the instruction was over. Norris and Ortega's (2000) meta-analysis of twelve FFI studies that reported results for both immediate and delayed post-tests showed there was a decrease but that this was relatively small. They also noted that the decrease was less in studies with longer-term treatments (i.e. three hours or more in duration) than in studies where the instruction lasted less than two hours. Clearly, then, the effects of instruction are often durable[10].

However, other studies have found that effects of instruction atrophy over time. For example, White (1991) found that gains in the correct positioning of adverbs were largely lost five months after the instruction. Lightbown (1992a) explained why this might be:

> ... when form-focused instruction is introduced in a way which is divorced from the communicative needs and activities of the students, only short-term effects are obtained.

In other words, for the effects to be lasting, the instruction needs to be embedded in communicative activities. Also, learners need continued exposure to the target feature in communication after the instruction is over.

The durability of the effects of FFI may also depend on other factors. One possibility is the saliency of the target feature. Some grammatical features – for example, English copula *be* and third person *–s* are not very salient. Thus, although they occur frequently in communicative input, they may not easily be perceived in continuous speech. These features may also not be seen as very important for message conveyance. If learners are motivated primarily by communicative need, then they will probably retain only those features that they perceive to be important for communication. Another possibility is that the effects of FFI might be lost if learners receive subsequent instruction in a related structure and are unable to sort out the two structures in their interlanguage systems (Tode, 2007).

Some studies have found that the effects of instruction are delayed (i.e. they fail to appear in an immediate post-test only to emerge in a delayed post-test). In Ellis (2007), for example, I reported that whereas explicit corrective feedback had an immediate effect on the acquisition of comparative adjectives, it only had a delayed effect on the acquisition of past tense *–ed*. This suggests that both the immediate and long-term effects of instruction may depend on the specific targets of the instruction, an issue discussed in the following section.

It is clearly essential to establish whether the learning that results from instruction persists (or only emerges later); a positive feature of most recent FFI studies is that they include one or more delayed post-tests.

Instructional target

One reason for the mixed findings of FFI studies might be that the effect of instruction varies according to the learnability of the target features. For example, in the case of vocabulary, research has shown that learners find it more difficult to remember a set of words when these belong to a lexical set (e.g. they are all colour words or the names of animals) than when the target words are not paradigmatically related (Nation, 2000). In the case of grammar, two points need to be considered. First, some grammatical structures are inherently more difficult to learn than others (e.g. English third person –s is more difficult than plural –s). Second, the learnability of a specific grammatical structure will depend on the learners' developmental stage. For example, teaching beginner learners subject verb inversion in WH questions is not likely to be successful if they are not developmentally ready to acquire this feature (Ellis, 1984b).

It is also possible that interactions between the type of instruction and the choice of target feature will occur. Spada and Tomita (2010) addressed this possibility in a meta-analysis of FFI studies that investigated the effects of instruction on simple and complex grammatical forms. They distinguished grammatical forms in terms of the number of transformation rules a structure involved. Table 9.3 provides examples of simple and complex features determined in this way. They distinguished instruction in terms of whether it was explicit or implicit. Explicit instruction was found to produce a clear effect on acquisition on both controlled and free measures for both simple and complex features, with the largest effect evident for complex forms

Table 9.3 Simple and complex features (Spada and Tomita, 2010: 273)

Simple features	Complex features
Tense	Dative alternation
Articles	Question formation
Plurals	Relativization
Prepositions	Passives
Subject-verb inversion	Pseudo-cleft sentences
Possessive determiners	
Participial adjectives	

Source: Spada, N, and Y. Tomita. 2010. "Interactions between Type of Instruction and Type of Language Feature: A Meta-Analysis." *Language Learning*, 60 (2): 263–308.

in measures based on free construction. Implicit instruction was also effective for both simple and complex features albeit less so than explicit instruction. Spada and Tomita pointed out, 'overall these findings do not appear to support the hypothesis that type of language feature interacts with type of instruction' (p. 289). This result is somewhat surprising. However, as Spada and Tomita noted, it may reflect the way in which they defined simple and complex features. Arguably, the method they used relates more to explicit rather than implicit knowledge as it was based on explicit grammatical descriptions of the features. For example, articles may be 'simple' from the standpoint of grammatical description but are certainly 'complex' for many learners whose L1 does not include articles (e.g. Japanese).

One of my own studies (Ellis, 2007) suggests that there may be an interaction between type of instruction and choice of target feature. This study investigated the effects of two types of corrective feedback (recasts and metalinguistic comments) on two grammatical structures (past tense *–ed* and comparative *–er*). The recasts had no effect on the acquisition of either structure. However, the effect of the metalinguistic feedback did differ according to structure. Whereas it had an immediate effect on the acquisition of comparative adjectives, it only had a delayed effect on the acquisition of past tense *–ed*. I suggested that this might be due to two factors; (1) the extent to which explicit knowledge of the target features is already established prior to the instruction and (2) the availability of exemplars of the target features in the input that learners are exposed to subsequent to the instruction. With regard to (1), explicit knowledge of past tense *–ed* was more established than that of comparative *–er*. With regard to (2), learners were more likely to be exposed to exemplars of past tense *–ed* than comparative *–er*.

Clearly, though, this is an area where more research is required.

Measuring the effects of instruction

Throughout the preceding sections there has been frequent reference to the effects of instruction on implicit and explicit knowledge. There are no direct measures of these two types of knowledge. The question, therefore, is how one determines which type of knowledge instruction influences. This is a key question because ultimately the purpose of FFI is to help learners' develop implicit knowledge. Explicit knowledge is, by and large, only of value to the extent that it assists the acquisition of implicit knowledge or, from a sociocultural or skill-learning perspective, when it has been fully proceduralized.

In Chapter 2, I referred to Norris and Ortega's (2000) classification of the different kinds of instruments that can be used to collect data to measure acquisition:

1. metalinguistic judgements,
2. selected responses,
3. constrained-constructed responses,
4. free-constructed responses.

Norris and Ortega argued that the best measure of acquisition – the one most likely to tap learners' implicit knowledge – is that obtained from 'free-constructed responses' as, for example, by using tasks that elicit spontaneous oral production. In Ellis (2002) I set out to examine to what extent various types of FFI led to measurable gains in implicit knowledge by examining 11 studies that included this type of instrument. Seven of these studies reported results showing that instruction led to improvements in the accurate use of the targetted grammatical features in free oral or free written production. The effectiveness of instruction was evident in both immediate and delayed tests of free production and also for older as well young learners. However, none of the learners in these studies were true beginners. Also, by and large the effect of the instruction was greater if the target structure was simple and the instruction extensive (i.e. longer than three hours). Overall, this analysis, then, indicates that the effects of FFI are clearly evident not just on measures of explicit knowledge but also of implicit knowledge, at least for intermediate plus learners and for simple grammatical structures.

One problem with using free production as the basis for measuring acquisition is that learners frequently fail to create obligatory occasions for using the target feature. As we noted in Chapter 7, it is very difficult to design tasks that make the use of specific linguistic features 'essential' as opposed to just 'useful' or 'natural'. To overcome this problem researchers have turned to other ways of measuring the effects of FFI on implicit knowledge. Erlam (2006) produced arguments and statistical evidence to support her claim that oral-elicited imitation tests successfully tap learners' implicit knowledge. A number of studies (e.g. Ellis, Loewen and Erlam, 2006; Erlam, Loewen and Philp, 2009; Loewen, Erlam and Ellis, 2009) have made use of such tests. In some of these studies the FFI resulted in significant gains in accurate use of the target feature.

Work still remains to be done on how to measure implicit knowledge. In Ellis (2005a), I proposed that timed grammaticality judgement tests may provide an alternative means. However, even when performed under pressure such tests still elicit a metalinguistic response. In particular, work needs to be done on how to measure implicit knowledge through comprehension tests (see de Jong 2005 for an attempt – not entirely successful – to develop such a test). One way might be to measure not just learners' responses to input stimuli but also their response times.

Implementation of FFI

The vast majority of FFI studies we have considered in this chapter have been purely product-based. That is, they have investigated the effects of externally defined instructional treatments on learning outcomes as measured in tests. This must be seen as a limitation of the research to date. As we saw in Chapter 3 when we examined the comparative method studies, instruction that differs in clear ways in terms of how it has been externally defined may not in fact be so different in terms of actual classroom processes. Ideally, we need to know how the instruction is implemented both to assure its internal validity and because, as we saw in Chapter 8, all instruction – including FFI – must ultimately be viewed as interaction.

Some studies have examined the instructional processes by recording and transcribing lessons and analyzing the interactions that took place. Spada and Lightbown (1993), for example, investigated the interactions that occurred in the control group of their study in order to provide a post hoc explanation for why this group outperformed the experimental groups. Toth's (2006) comparative study of processing and production-based instruction also included a detailed analysis of one lesson. This showed how the teacher implemented a structured-input activity. It also suggested that output played a role in acquisition as the learners were shown to use their metalinguistic knowledge to help them reformulate output, thus demonstrating a potential role for mental processes other than input-processing in acquisition. A study by Shintani and Ellis (2010) likewise used an analysis of classroom processes to look for why the comprehension-based instruction resulted in greater incidental acquisition of plural –*s* than the production-based instruction.

It is to be hoped that future FFI studies will include analyses of the classroom interaction that arise when different types of instruction are executed. Such analyses can be used a priori to demonstrate the validity of instructional distinctions and post hoc to provide an explanation of the quantitative outcomes.

Conclusion

Ideally, this section should provide a set of research-based proposals for FFI. This is probably what most teachers would expect. The problem, however, is that FFI is a highly complex phenomenon and the instructional contexts in which it occurs are extremely varied. Generalizations are not easily arrived at. Most studies have involved different combinations of instructional options, which have been operationalized in different ways. This makes it difficult to compare results across studies. Thus, it is dangerous to commit to specific recommendations that are universally applicable to all contexts. Nevertheless, at some risk, I will attempt a set of tentative generalizations that reflect my own understanding of the research and what it suggests about FFI. In so doing I will draw on and extend a set of statements that I published in Ellis (2006).

1. FFI needs to assist learners to understand the connection between specific linguistic forms (lexical, grammatical or pragmalinguistic) and their ideational and interpersonal meanings. FFI that focuses simply on form is unlikely to have any substantial effect on learners' interlanguage development.
2. The linguistic targets of instruction should be those linguistic features that are known to be problematic to the learners being taught. It is clear from studies of both naturalistic and classroom learners that some linguistic features can

be acquired incidentally. That is, no intentional effort to learn these forms is necessary. The challenge, then, is to identify those linguistic features that will not develop at all or will develop only very slowly without some kind of FFI.

3. Possibly, FFI will prove most effective if it is directed at grammatical features that learners have already partially acquired and only need to gain greater control over. Attempts to teach entirely new grammatical features may founder unless the learners are developmentally ready to acquire them.

4. Both a focus on forms and a focus-on-form approach are effective. While there are theoretical grounds for claiming that focus on form is more likely to facilitate interlanguage development, the research evidence does not show a clear advantage for this type of instruction. Planned FFI lessons directed at specific grammatical structures result in acquisition providing that they include text-creation activities.

5. Although both implicit and explicit types of FFI have been found to be effective, it is clear that explicit types are more effective. Furthermore, FFI that includes an explicit component appears to assist the development of implicit L2 knowledge as well as explicit knowledge. That is, in the long term it can help learners to achieve greater accuracy in free oral production.

6. Where the aim of the instruction is simply to develop explicit L2 knowledge (as a 'hook' on which subsequent acquisition can be attached), indirect consciousness-raising by means of CR tasks that assist learners to discover facts about the L2 for themselves have been shown to be effective.

7. Both input-based and output-based FFI are effective. Learners do not need to produce a grammatical structure to acquire it. Input-based instruction may hold an advantage where the aim is to teach new linguistic features. Output-based instruction may be beneficial where the aim is to increase control over partially acquired features.

8. Instruction consisting solely of input- or output-based activities can promote acquisition but, by and large, the research indicates that including an explicit consciousness-raising option enhances the effect.

9. Incorporating corrective feedback (especially if this is explicit and output-prompting) enhances the effect of output-based FFI.

10. Purely mechanical practice consisting of text-manipulation exercises is unlikely to have much impact on learners' acquisition of the target features. Learners need to practise the use of the features under real operating conditions (i.e. in text-creation activities).

11. The effects of FFI are varied. In some cases, it has been found to have an immediate effect on acquisition but in other cases the effect may be delayed. Overall, however, the effects of FFI have been found to be durable.

12. Ultimately FFI is 'interaction'. That is, externally defined instructional options only have reality for learners through the interactions that occur in the classroom. Thus, what is important is for teachers (and researchers) to attend to whether these interactions create the conditions that assist acquisition.

One point needs to be made emphatically. As Spada and Lightbown (2008) pointed out:

> Language acquisition is not an event that occurs in an instant or as a result of exposure to a language form, a language lesson, or corrective feedback. It is an evolving and dynamic phenomenon ... (p. 182).

Thus, teachers should not expect direct and immediate results from teaching a linguistic or sociolinguistic feature. Rather they should recognize that FFI 'facilitates' rather than 'teaches'. Even when the instruction sometimes appears to have been entirely successful there is always the likelihood that learners will backslide at some point in the future.

Notes

1. A somewhat similar distinction to 'focus on form' and focus on forms' is that between 'integrated' and 'isolated' FFI (Spada and Lightbown, 2008). However, as Spada and Lighbown pointed out, both focus on form and focus-on-forms instruction can be integrated into a programme that is primarily communicative. Isolated FFI can constitute a separate strand from a communicative strand in the overall curriculum. Typically, this consists of focus on forms.
2. The problem of classifying specific instructional activities as focus on form or focus on forms is clearly apparent in Norris and Ortega's (2000) meta-analysis of FFI studies. They used as the key criterion 'integration of form and meaning' but clearly found this difficult to apply. They noted 'the essential features that supposedly distinguish FonF and FonFS instructional approaches have been inconsistently operationalized'. Not surprisingly, they reported no overall difference in the effect of these two types on L2 acquisition.
3. Processing instruction can also include a consciousness-raising activity. A number of studies have compared the effects of processing instruction with and without any consciousness-raising on L2 acquisition.
4. Lightbown's (1983) study is interesting because of how it conceptualized instruction. Lightbown did not consider instruction in terms of its external objectives but internally in terms of the frequency with which specific grammatical morphemes appeared in the input to the learners. Of course, up to a point, the features that have been selected as targets are likely to occur frequently in the input.
5. Robinson (1996) also investigated direct and indirect consciousness-raising, albeit from a very different epistemological base (i.e. experimental manipulations of implicit and explicit learning) and in a laboratory setting. For these reasons, I have not considered his study here. It is interesting to note, however, that Robinson found that the direct consciousness-raising condition was superior to the indirect one. One clear difference between Robinson's study and the studies of direct and indirect consciousness-raising I have included in this section was that the indirect condition did not involve any collaborative work on the part of the learners. Rosa and O'Neill (1999) carried out a similar laboratory-based study and found no differences between their direct and

      indirect consciousness-raising conditions, possibly because they engaged learners much more extensively (through solving a series of puzzles) than in Robinson's study.

6.   This conclusion is contrary to Norris and Ortega's (2000) finding that overall explicit treatments were more effective than implicit. The problem with their analysis is that the treatments they classified as 'explicit' were not 'purely' so (i.e. they included a production option).

7.   The grammatical problems of immersion learners may be more morphological than syntactic. The studies considered in this section all addressed problems relating to morphology. Jarvinen (2006) investigated an English immersion programme in Finland and reported that the students achieved 'complete access to relativization' after five years without any formal instruction.

8.   Lightbown (2006) proposed the transfer appropriate processing principle:

> ... according to the principle of transfer appropriate processing, the learning environment that best promotes rapid, accurate retrieval of what has been learnt is that in which the psychological demands placed on the learner resemble those that will be encountered later in natural settings.

9.   Readers might like to look back at Chapter 3 where a study by Laufer was discussed. This compared a task-based approach to teaching vocabulary with a traditional memorization approach. Laufer reported the traditional approach resulted in better learning. However, Laufer only tested receptive knowledge of the new words. De la Fuente tested productive knowledge. Also, the task-based instruction in the two studies differed considerably, being much more extensive in De la Fuente's study.

10.   Further evidence of the long-term effect of FFI can be found in Lyster and Saito's (2010) meta-analysis of classroom studies investigating the effects of oral corrective feedback. Interestingly, in this case – and in contrast to Norris and Ortega's meta-analysis – the effects of instruction were greater in the delayed than in the immediate post-tests.

10

Instruction, Individual Differences and L2 Learning

Introduction

In the previous chapters we examined how instructional instruments impact on (1) the interactions that take place in the classroom and (2) learning outcomes. My basic claim has been that instruction induces learning through the cognitive and social processes that interaction gives rise to. However, quite clearly, there is another factor that influences these processes – the learner him/herself. In other words, individual learner factors mediate the effect that instruction has on the cognitive and social processes and via these on second language (L2) learning. Figure 10.1 shows how this takes place. It assumes that the processes and the resulting learning are influenced by how individual learners respond to the instruction.

The study of individual differences in learning is well-established (see, for example, Dörnyei, 2005 and 2009; Robinson, 2002a; Skehan, 1989). By and large, however, researchers have sought to establish direct relationships between various individual difference factors and measures of L2 learning (i.e. they have explored the relationship between (B) and (D) in Figure 10.1). For example they have examined to what extent measures of classroom learners' motivation correlate with measures of L2 proficiency or achievement. I will not be concerned with such studies in this chapter. Instead my focus will be on the role played by individual learner factors (B) in mediating the effects of instruction (A) on both the cognitive and interactional processes that occur through interaction (C) and, through these, on learning outcomes (D).

Language Teaching Research & Language Pedagogy, First Edition. Rod Ellis.
© 2012 John Wiley & Sons, Ltd. Published 2012 by John Wiley & Sons, Ltd.

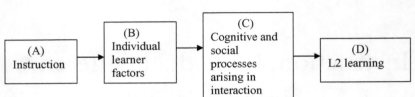

Figure 10.1 The mediating role of individual learner factors in instructed L2 learning

Individual learner factors

There are a well-established set of individual learner factors that have been found to influence learning outcomes. These have been traditionally divided into cognitive, affective and motivational factors. Dörnyei (2009) pointed out that it is in fact difficult to make such a clear division especially if one takes a neuropsychological approach as there is no evidence of their separation in neural functioning. Nevertheless – as Dörnyei also acknowledged – it is still useful to view these learner factors as separate because they 'feel' different. Doing so provides a schematic means for systematically examining how individual learner factors mediate L2 learning. Thus I will adhere to the tripartite distinction. Table 10.1 provides brief definitions of those factors which have figured most prominently in the classroom research and which I will consider in this chapter.

Processes

Figure 10.1 distinguishes cognitive processes (i.e. processes such as attention and rehearsal that go on inside the learner's head) and social processes (i.e. the specific interactions that result from different kinds of instruction). It must be acknowledged, however, that this distinction is not one that some researchers would accept as it involves separating the social and cognitive dimensions of L2 learning. Sociocognitive theories of L2 learning for example argue that social and cognitive aspects of learning are inseparable. For Atkinson (2002) language is simultaneously in the world and in the learner's head and thus is neither 'social' nor 'cognitive' but both simultaneously. Likewise sociocultural theorists see 'acquisition' as inherent in 'participation' rather than something that happens solely inside the learner's head. While recognizing the strength of these positions, I find it convenient to maintain the distinction between the cognitive and social – if only because the research that I will address has tended to focus on one or the other.

The key cognitive processes that have been hypothesized to be involved in language learning are set out below – instruction can be seen as a means of activating these processes:

1. Noticing (the learner consciously attends to a linguistic form in the input).
2. Rehearsing (the learner rehearses the form in working memory).

Table 10.1 Key individual difference factors mediating instructed L2 learning

Components	Learner factors	Definitions
Cognitive[1]	1. Language aptitude	This is the special ability that people have for learning an L2. It is considered to be separate from the general ability to master academic skills, often referred to as 'intelligence'. Various tests have been designed to measure language-learning aptitude, for example, the Modern Language Aptitude Test. Different components of language aptitude can be distinguished; phonemic discrimination ability, language analytical ability and memory.
	2. Working memory	Working memory is a psychological term that refers to those mental functions responsible for storing and manipulating information temporarily. A popular model of working memory (Baddeley, 2003) distinguishes four sub-components; (1) the central executive that controls attention, (2) the visuospatial sketchpad that stores and rehearses visual information, (3) the phonological loop that stores and rehearses oral information, and (4) the episodic buffer that combines information from different sources[2].
Affective	1. Language anxiety	Different types of anxiety have been identified: (1) trait anxiety (a characteristic of a learner's personality), (2) state anxiety (apprehension that is experienced at a particular moment in response to a definite situation), and (3) situation-specific anxiety (the anxiety aroused by a particular type of situation). Anxiety may be both facilitating (i.e. it has a positive effect on L2 acquisition), or debilitating (i.e. it has a negative effect).
	2. Willingness to communicate	This is the extent to which learners are prepared to initiate communication when they have a choice. In part it can be seen as a personality factor.
Motivational	1. Motivation	In general terms, motivation refers to the effort that learners put into learning an L2 as a result of their need or desire to learn it. Motivation can be extrinsic (i.e. either 'instrumental' as when a learner has a functional goal such as to get a job or pass an examination or 'integrative' as when a learner wishes to identify with the culture of the L2 group). It can also be intrinsic (e.g. the interest that is generated by participating in instructional processes).

3. Semantic processing (the learner constructs a form-function mapping by as-
    signing meaning to a linguistic form).
4. Comparing (the learner compares the form noticed in the input with her own
    mental grammar, registering to what extent there is a 'gap' between the input
    and her grammar).
5. Rule-formation (the learner constructs an explicit rule to account for the new
    information derived from the above processes).
6. Integrating (the learner integrates a representation of the new linguistic fea-
    ture into implicit memory and, if necessary, restructures the existing mental
    grammar).

The key social processes in language classrooms were examined in Chapter 4,
Chapter 5, Chapter 6 and Chapter 7. They include the patterns of turn-taking that
have been observed to occur in different participatory structures (e.g. whole-class
or small group work), scaffolding, the negotiation of meaning and of form, the
interactional strategies for conducting corrective feedback, language play, and the
metalinguistic exchanges that arise from the performance of consciousness-raising
tasks. As we have seen, social processes differ markedly depending on whether the
instruction results in a form-and-accuracy context or a meaning-and-fluency context
(Seedhouse, 2004).

The mediating role of individual difference factors

One way of characterizing the role played by individual difference factors in mediating the effects of instruction is in terms of learners' 'receptivity' to instruction
Allwright and Bailey (1991) define this as 'openness' to instruction and suggest that
it contrasts with 'defensiveness'. They identify a number of ways in which learners
can be receptive. For example, they can be receptive to their teacher as a person.
Allwright and Bailey note that within the same class of students there can be very
varied responses to the teacher. Students also vary in how open they are to different participatory-structures, with some learners preferring group work and others
resistant to it. Students differ in how receptive they are to the teacher's way of
teaching and to the teaching materials. Whereas some learners are open to being
'successful' others become disenchanted and foresee no real possibility of achieving
a high level of proficiency in the L2. Finally, learners vary in their 'communication apprehension' and thus respond differently to interactive methods of language
learning.

As a construct, 'receptivity' evokes the importance of affective factors in explaining how learners' respond to instruction. Allwright and Bailey discuss receptivity
primarily in terms of learners' 'anxiety' and 'competitiveness'. However, as the list of
individual difference factors in Table 10.1 shows, learners do not just vary in terms

of their affective dispositions but also in their cognitive abilities. A complete account of the mediating role of individual difference factors, therefore, needs to consider both affective and cognitive factors.

The role of cognitive factors in mediating instruction has traditionally been discussed in terms of 'aptitude-treatment interaction' (Cronbach and Snow, 1977), with 'aptitude' here referring to the various ways in which learners differ cognitively (e.g. it includes language aptitude, working memory and learning style). The most ambitious attempt to account for the role that cognitive factors play in instructed learning is Robinson's (2002b) proposal for how learners' might be matched to instructional tasks. Robinson distinguishes 'primary abilities' (which roughly correspond to language aptitude and working memory) and 'second order abilities' (which broadly correspond to the cognitive processes listed in this section). He groups these abilities into 'complexes' (i.e. combinations of aptitude variables) that influence the learning that occurs in response to specific instructional conditions. By way of example, he suggests that learners who are 'high' in both 'memory for contingent speech' and 'noticing-the-gap' may be better able to benefit from corrective feedback in the form of recasts than those who are 'low' in such abilities.

As we will see, there are three ways in which researchers have set about investigating the interaction between instruction and individual learner factors. One way is by trying to match learners with specific abilities to a particular instructional treatment (such as corrective feedback involving recasts), which is hypothesized to draw on those abilities. In a classical aptitude-treatment-interaction study, a factorial design is used where two different instructional conditions are investigated (e.g. recasts versus metalinguistic explanation) in terms of whether they are matched or complementary to two different learner types (e.g. learners with low and high working memory), as shown in Figure 10.2. Such studies are premised on the hypothesis that learners in the matching conditions will outperform those in the complementary conditions. They are difficult to design, however, especially if intact classes are used, so most studies have adopted the second way. This involves examining how learners who differ in some way (e.g. their type of language aptitude) respond to a specific type of instruction (e.g. processing instruction). Both of these research designs involve the collection of quantitative data that is analyzed statistically (see Chapter 2). In contrast, a third way involves the examination of data collected qualitatively (e.g. through diaries) and aims to investigate how learners manifest specific characteristics (e.g. high anxiety) as a result of their instructional experiences.

In the rest of this chapter I will examine research that has investigated how different learner factors mediate the effects of instruction. I will then conclude the chapter with a brief look at attempts to enhance learners' ability to benefit from instruction through learner training. In effect, then, we will be looking at two different ways of matching the learner to the instruction; (1) examining the fit between the instruction and the learner and (2) assisting the learner to make the best of the available instruction.

Instructional conditions

Learner factors	Matching * Recasts * High phonemic discrimination ability	Matching * Metalinguistic explanation * High language analytical ability
	Complementary * Recasts * High language analytical ability	Complementary condition * Metalinguistic explanation * High phonemic discrimination ability

Figure 10.2   Design of an aptitude-treatment-interaction study

Cognitive Factors

The main cognitive factors that have figured in classroom research are language aptitude and working memory. However, it is not clear that these two factors are really separate, with some researchers (e.g. Miyake and Friedman, 1998) arguing that working memory is in fact an essential component of language aptitude. I have treated them separately because they have been investigated by means of different instruments.

Language aptitude

Language aptitude can be viewed holistically with learners characterized as varying in their overall aptitude (i.e. as high or low in this ability). In this case scores on the different components of a language aptitude test such as the Modern Language Aptitude Test (Carroll and Sapon, 1959) are aggregated to provide an overall measure of a learner's aptitude. Alternatively, aptitude can be viewed as multi-faceted. In this case, separate measures of the different abilities that comprise language aptitude are used to differentiate learners in terms of their type of aptitude. This latter approach is preferable because, as Skehan (2002) argued, different aspects of language aptitude are potentially relevant to different aspects of L2 learning. He proposed that different components of aptitude are related to the four macro-stages of the acquisition process as shown in Table 10.2. Skehan (1998b) also suggested that language aptitude operates differently during the course of adult language learning. Whereas language analytic ability, which he saw as closely related to general intelligence, is involved throughout, phonemic-coding ability plays a major role only in the early stages. Memory ability is involved in all stages but in the case of exceptional learners it is enhanced, allowing them to achieve a more or less native-like level of proficiency. Skehan's proposals have obvious implications for the role played by language aptitude in mediating the effects of instruction on learning. For example, it can be hypothesized that learners strong in phonemic-coding ability will benefit from input-based forms of instruction whereas those strong in language analytic ability will fare better in consciousness-raising instruction.

Table 10.2 Role of language aptitude in L2 acquisition (based on Skehan, 2002)

Aptitude component	Macro-stages of L2 acquisition
Phonemic-coding; working memory	Input-processing (noticing)
Language analytic ability	Pattern detection
Memory retrieval	Output (control)
Memory ability	Lexicalizing

Support for Skehan's claims can be found in an early aptitude–treatment–interaction (ATI) study. Wesche (1981) examined the relationship between language aptitude and instruction. She started with the assumption that aptitude tests could be used to identify the special abilities and weaknesses of individual learners. She distinguished two types of student. Type A learners had a high overall score on aptitude tests. Type B learners manifested a high level of analytical ability but demonstrated problems with phonemic-coding and listening. There were two types of instruction in her study: (1) an audiovisual, inductive approach organized around the presentation of linguistic structures sequenced according to order of difficulty and (2) a more deductive, analytical approach, which taught oral and literacy skills together and provided explanations of grammatical points and of how to produce specific sounds. Type A students were taught by approach (1), and Type B students by approach (2). The results were encouraging. There were no significant differences in achievement between A and B students, suggesting that the matched condition led to equal achievement. In a follow up study, Wesche employed a standard ATI design, assigning students of both types to matched and complementary conditions. Students in the matched conditions gained higher scores in an achievement test. Also, when interviewed, they reported greater interest in foreign language study, more initiative in practising French outside the classroom, and less anxiety in class.

An issue of both theoretical and practical interest is whether learners' language aptitude (or, more specifically, their language analytic ability) is only relevant in instruction of the focus-on-forms kind or whether it also plays a role in more communicative classrooms. Ranta (2002) investigated intensive Grade 6 English as a second language (ESL) classrooms in Canada, where the instruction primarily consisted of a variety of oral activities such as games, puzzles, surveys, interviews and discussions. Observation of classroom teaching using the Communicative Orientation of Language Teaching (COLT – see Chapter 3) indicated that the teaching was 'experiential' in nature. 135 students completed a test of language analytic ability in their first language (L1) (French) and also a battery of language tests. Ranta reported weak but significant correlations between language analytic ability and scores on all the language tests except a listening test. The strongest relationships were found on tests that invited a focus on form. More interestingly, Ranta found that the role of language analytic ability varied among the students. Using cluster analysis, she identified four clusters of learners. In the first cluster, L1 language analytic ability was strongly associated with superior performance on the L2 measures. The second cluster was characterized by average levels of L1 analytical ability but weak test performance, and the third group by below average L1 analytical ability and below average performance on the cloze test and an L2 metalinguistic task. The learners in the fourth cluster were weak in L1 analytical ability and had poor test results. Ranta concluded that her study suggested that language analytic ability is an important factor in communicative classrooms[3].

Erlam (2005) examined the interactions between two aspects of language aptitude (phonemic-coding ability and language analytic ability) and three types of instruction (deductive instruction, inductive instruction and structured-input instruction) directed at French direct object pronouns. Phonemic-coding ability did not play a major role in any of the instructional groups. Interestingly, language analytic ability was not related to gains on a battery of tests in the deductive instructional group but it was to gains made by the inductive and structured-input groups. Erlam suggested that the structured presentation, which the learners in the deductive group received, enabled those learners with weaker language analytic abilities to perform at a similar level to those with stronger abilities. In other words, language analytical ability comes into play more strongly when the instruction is of a kind that requires learners to work out grammatical rules for themselves.

Two studies have investigated the role played by language aptitude in the learning that results from corrective feedback. Y. Sheen (2007) investigated the role played by language analytical ability in ESL learners' processing of two types of corrective feedback – recasts and direct correction accompanied with metalinguistic explanation – while learners were performing an oral narrative task. She calculated gain scores on tests of English articles (the grammatical feature targetted by the corrective feedback) and reported correlations between these scores and a measure of language analytical ability. A moderately strong relationship was found in the case of both immediate- and delayed-gain scores for the learners that received direct correction plus metalinguistic explanations. In contrast, language analytical ability played no part in the gains resulting from recasts[4]. On the face of it Sheen's findings contradict Erlam's. However, Erlam investigated proactive explicit instruction (i.e. learners were presented with a rule in the deductive condition) while Sheen investigated reactive explicit instruction (in the form of metalinguistic corrective feedback). It is quite possible that role played by language analytic ability varies according to the different kinds of explicit instruction. That is, it may be important for processing explicit feedback but not where proactive explicit instruction is concerned.

The second corrective feedback study examined the relationship between language aptitude and an implicit form of corrective feedback – recasts. Robinson and Yamaguchi (1999) (cited in Robinson, 2005) found 'high significant correlations' between measures of Japanese university students' phonetic sensitivity and rote memory and the learning that resulted from recasts provided during five weeks of task-based interaction.

Taken together these corrective feedback studies suggest that different aspects of language aptitude are involved in the processing of different kinds of feedback, with language analytical ability involved in the more explicit kind and phonetic sensitivity and rote memory in the more implicit kind.

Further evidence that different aspects of language aptitude may be implicated in different kinds of input-processing can be found in Nagata, Aline, and Ellis (1999). They examined learners' aptitude in relation to the premodified input they received in a one-way information-gap task. This task involved listening to and carrying out instructions that contained new L2 words. They reported moderate but statistically significant correlations between measures of sound–symbol association, grammatical–semantic sensitivity and memory for words on the one hand and comprehension of the instructions on the other. In contrast, only memory for words was systematically related to post-test measures of the acquisition of the new words. These results bear out the general claim that listening-for-comprehension and listening-to-learn involve different processes and suggest that they draw on different cognitive abilities.

Any conclusions reached from these studies must be tentative both because there are, as yet, relatively few studies that have examined the interactions between language aptitude and instruction and because the studies have employed different ways of measuring both aptitude and language learning. It would seem, however, that differences in language aptitude affect learners' ability to benefit from different kinds of instruction. This raises the intriguing possibility that it may be possible to match the type of instruction to particular learner types as Wesche's study suggested.

Working memory

Second language acquisition (SLA) researchers have been interested in working memory because they believe that 'short-term memory is an online capacity for processing and analyzing new information (words, grammatical structures and so on) ... and that the bigger the online capacity an individual has for new information, the more information will pass into off-line long-term memory' (Juffs, 2007: 105). In other words, working memory capacity determines the extent to which learners are able to (1) attend to and rehearse elements from the input they are exposed to and (2) access L2 resources from long-term memory to process both input and output.

Two main approaches to investigating working memory are evident in the psychological literature. Baddeley and associates (e.g. Baddeley, 2003) have developed a model of 'phonological working memory' consisting of four components; (1) the phonological loop which temporarily stores acoustic and verbal information, (2) the visuospatial spacepad which temporarily stores spatial, visual and kinaesthetic information, (3) the central executive which allocates attention resources and regulates encoding, storing and retrieval processes, and (most recently) (4) the episodic buffer, which combines information from different sources and stores them as a single 'episode'. The second approach is based on 'reading span memory' (Daneman and Carpenter, 1980). This differs from phonological working memory in that it views working memory as involving the simultaneous processing and storing of information. These two approaches have involved different measurement instruments. Phonological working memory has been investigated by asking participants to repeat polysyllabic words, nonce words or strings of unrelated words correctly. Reading span memory is measured by asking participants to read aloud increasingly long strings of words and then recall the final word in each string without any overt rehearsal. The differences in these two approaches needs to be taken into account in interpreting the results of the L2 research reported here.

Most of the studies that have investigated the relationship between working memory and L2 learning have been laboratory-based, reflecting the approach adopted in cognitive psychology. I will focus primarily on the classroom-based studies in accordance with the general purpose of this book but I was also draw on the findings of a number of laboratory-based studies where these help to amplify possible ways in which working memory affects instructed learning. The studies are of two basic kinds. Some have examined how working memory affects learners' ability to benefit from different instructional treatments. Others have investigated the role of working memory in processing input and output.

Erlam's (2005) study examined working memory as well as language aptitude. Students viewed lists of five-syllable words on an overhead projector for 7.5 seconds and were then asked to write down each list. They received one mark for each correctly remembered word. This measure was related only weakly and non-significantly to measures of learning in the deductive and inductive instructional groups. However, for learners in the structured-input group there were sizable positive correlations between working memory and gain scores (especially delayed) that were derived from tests of written production. Erlam suggested that learners with better working memory capacity were able to process the input more deeply in this instructional condition. This study, then, lends some credence to the possibility that the role played by working memory depends on the nature of the instruction.

Ando et al. (1992) investigated the mediating effects of working memory on groups of Japanese fifth graders taught by a traditional grammatical approach and a communicative approach. They used both listening and reading span tests to measure their working memory. In the case of those learners taught by the explicit grammar method, working memory scores predicted their level of success but only in a delayed test of grammar learning. In the case of those learners taught by the communicative approach, those with lower working memory scores benefitted more in an immediate post-test. Interestingly, this finding was replicated in a laboratory-based study by Mackey et al. (2002). They also found that lower working memory benefitted immediate learning from communicative interactions. In this study, however, the benefit disappeared in delayed tests. In contrast, higher working memory had no immediate mediating effect but did emerge as a positive factor later on. These studies suggest there are interactions between working memory, type of instruction, and whether the effects of the instruction are immediate or delayed.

Mackey et al. (2010) reviewed research that had investigated working memory in relation to input and output processing. Drawing on Payne and Whitney (2002) they proposed that 'as learners attempt to understand and produce language, their internal processing involves holding representations of the input in short-term memory while retrieving information about L2 grammar from long-term memory' (p. 505).

Two of the studies Mackey et al. reviewed were classroom-based (both of them involving computer-mediated instruction). In Sagarra's (2007) study, university students in a first-semester Spanish course received online feedback in the form of recasts on their responses to fill-in-the-blank exercises. Working memory was measured by a reading span test. Scores predicted both their linguistic accuracy in written post-tests and also the extent to which they modified their output following feedback in later face-to-face interactions. Payne and Whitney (2002) compared the mediating effect of working memory on university-level third-semester learners of Spanish, some of whom received face-to-face instruction and others computer-mediated instruction. The effects of working memory were much stronger for the face-to-face group but the improvement in proficiency was greater in the computer-mediated group. This led Payne and Whitney to suggest that differences in working memory are less important in an instructional context where learners do not need to maintain verbal information in memory. They argued that the computer-mediated learning environment allowed for delayed processing of input and output and thus was less demanding on working memory. Mackey at al.'s own study was laboratory-based. It showed that scores on a listening span test predicted the extent to which learners modified their output in response to corrective feedback consisting of prompts (see Chapter 5) when performing communicative tasks.

There is sufficient evidence in all of this to indicate that working memory capacity influences the extent to which students benefit from instruction. Indeed other studies (see, for example, reviews in Juffs 2007; and N. Ellis 2001) that have examined the relationship between working memory and L2 proficiency point to this conclusion. It is not easy, however, to come to clear conclusions regarding how working memory interacts with instruction. There is some evidence that learners with higher working-memory capacity benefit from instruction in the long term rather than the short-term (Ando et al., 1992; Erlam, 2005; Mackey et al., 2002). This might be because they have processed the input at a deeper level but that learning needs time to be consolidated. It also seems reasonable to conclude that working memory is likely to play a more significant role in instruction that requires learners to process oral input – as suggested in the studies by Erlam (2005) and Mackey et al. (2010) – rather than written input as in Payne and Whitney. However, there is also some evidence (Ando et al., 1992; Mackey et al., 2002) to suggest that learners with lower working-memory capacity benefit more from instruction based on oral communication, at least where short-term learning effects are concerned.

One problem is that these studies have measured working memory, input- processing and learning outcomes in very different ways, making cross-study comparisons difficult. A potentially useful way of further exploring the role played by working memory might be to explore how it mediates learners' responses to and learning from different kinds of corrective feedback. As N. Ellis (2001) observed it would seem very likely that working memory capacity influences learners' ability to process the different kinds of feedback (i.e. explicit versus implicit; input-providing versus output-prompting) quite differently.

Affective factors

The two factors to be considered here are language anxiety and willingness to communicate. It is, of course, quite likely that these factors are related as the extent to which learners are prepared to make efforts to communicate in an L2 is in part a matter of their personality, which also influences their level of classroom anxiety. Both factors can also be seen as having a motivational element. That is, anxious learners may lose motivation to learn and so be less willing to try to communicate. Both constructs are 'situational' (i.e. will vary according to the specific instructional context) and both are of obvious significance to language teaching.

Anxiety

There is plenty of evidence to show that learners experience anxiety when learning an L2. As Pavlenko (2002) noted, language learning is an inherently emotional affair. Classroom learners face special difficulty in that they are often required to try to speak in the L2 in front of their classmates and to undertake tests. Public performance in an L2 is inherently threatening as a number of diary studies of language learners have shown (see, for example, Bailey, 1983) and language tests are an obvious threat. It should be noted however, that anxiety need not always be a negative factor. Scovel (1978) pointed out that anxiety can be facilitative as well as debilitative. For example, a learner who is anxious about a test may revise harder. Nevertheless, the research on anxiety in SLA has generally shown it to have a negative effect on learning (see Dörnyei, 2005).

Different types of anxiety have been distinguished – trait anxiety (a personality variable), state anxiety (the apprehension experienced at a particular moment) and situation-specific anxiety (the anxiety that derives from experience of a particular type of situation). Language anxiety is an example of the last type. It has been studied through the diaries kept by language learners and also by means of questionnaires such as the Foreign Language Classroom Anxiety Scale (FLCAS) (Horwitz, Horwitz, and Cope, 1986).

Much of the research has been directed at identifying the sources of learners' classroom anxiety. Bailey's (1983) analysis of the diaries of 11 classroom learners showed that they tended to become anxious when they compared themselves with other learners in the class and found themselves less proficient. She also identified other sources of anxiety, including tests and learners' perceived relationship with their teacher. A common finding of many studies is that learners feel apprehension when they are required to communicate spontaneously in the L2 in front of their peers (Horwitz, Horwitz, and Cope, 1986). Woodrow (2006), for example, reported that the three most prominent 'stressors' in 47 advanced EAP students in Australia were 'performing English in front of classmates', 'giving an oral presentation', and 'speaking in English to native speakers' (p. 39). Woodrow found evidence of two types of anxious learner: those who experienced retrieval interference and those with a skills deficit.

How does anxiety affect learners' ability to benefit from instruction? This question has been addressed in two ways. One way is by investigating whether language anxiety influences the quantity and quality of learner participation in classroom interaction (a social process). The second way is by examining how language anxiety affects learners' ability to process input and output (a cognitive process). MacIntyre and Gardner (1991) pointed out anxiety can affect the different stages of the learning process. When learners are feeling anxious, they may be less able to attend to input, experience difficulty in making connections between new information and existing knowledge, and experience problems in accessing their knowledge in oral production. Anxiety may interfere with the smooth operation of working memory leading to reduced capacity to process L2 forms, especially if these have not been fully automatized.

Two studies have examined the relationship between language anxiety and classroom participation. Robson (1994) reported significant negative correlations between scores on the FLCAS and measures of the quantity of Japanese college students' voluntary oral participation in free discussion classes (i.e. the greater the learners' anxiety, the fewer words or C-units they produced in their speech). However, no significant correlations were found between anxiety and fluency measures of participation. Thus Robson concluded that although anxiety affected the quantity of participation it had no affect on the quality. Robson also reported significant correlations between the learners' quantity of participation and their scores on two proficiency tests (the TOEFL and SPEAK Test). However, this relationship was evident in the pre-tests as well as the post-tests suggesting that it was proficiency that triggered participation rather than vice versa.

Delaney (2009) carried out a similar study with intact groups of Japanese college students. He also found that foreign language anxiety was negatively related to the quantity of voluntary participation in free discussion classes but not to measures of fluency, accuracy and complexity (i.e. qualitative measures of participation). Like Robson, Delaney also investigated the relationship between participation and proficiency. Unlike Robson he found no significant relationships between the students' initial L2 proficiency and their participation but did find a relationship between participation and gains in proficiency as a result of the instruction. Interestingly, however it was the quality rather than the quantity of participation that was important. Delaney concluded that the assumption that some teachers make that 'talking a lot' is beneficial to learners' development may not be justified as what counts is the quality not the quantity of their talk.

These two studies suggest that language anxiety does influence how learners respond to instructional activities involving voluntary participation but mainly in terms of how much they participate and that this may not be what is important for L2 learning. If language anxiety does not affect the quality of participation, and this is what matters for learning, then it would seem language anxiety may play a less significant role in the classroom than has been claimed by some researchers (e.g. Horwitz, 2001). However, it would be dangerous to generalize from these studies as they involved only one type of learner (Japanese college-level students) and, also, both studies provided the learners with opportunities to plan prior to engaging in oral discussion and this may have helped the more anxious learners to engage qualitatively in the discussions.

In Robson and Delaney's studies the mediating effect of language anxiety on instruction was examined in terms of 'participation' – at best, a rather crude construct. More interesting perhaps are studies that have examined how anxiety affects learners' ability to respond to specific instructional features. Such a study is Y. Sheen (2008). She examined the effect that anxiety had on intermediate ESL learners' responses to recasts directed at utterances containing errors in article usage. Sheen administered a short questionnaire designed to measure the learners' language anxiety and used their responses to divide the learners into 'low-anxiety' and 'high-anxiety' groups. She administered a pre-test, immediate post-test and delayed post-test to measure the accuracy of their use of articles. The recast treatment took place in two intact classes where the learners reconstructed oral narratives, taking it in turn to speak in front of the whole class. When a learner made an article error, the teacher corrected it using a recast and then paused to give the learner the chance to uptake the correction and repair the error. A control group completed the anxiety questionnaire and the tests but did not receive the instructional treatment. There were two major findings of this study. First, the low-anxiety learners who received recasts produced higher levels of modified output (i.e. uptake with repair) than the high-anxiety learners. Second, the low-anxiety recasts group outperformed both the high-anxiety recasts group and the high-anxiety control group in the post-tests while there was no difference between the high-anxiety recasts and control group. Sheen suggested that the high-anxiety learners experienced difficulty in both attending to the recasts and also in producing 'pushed output' in response to the recasts and that, as a result, they were unable to benefit from them acquisitionally.

All of these studies examined the effect of anxiety on learners' oral production in whole-class discourse. It is possible however, that production is less threatening if students are working in small groups or in computer-mediated environments where they are under less pressure to produce spontaneously in the L2. Evidence that small group work reduces anxiety can be found in Young (1990), who reported that American secondary language students felt more comfortable speaking in the L2 in small groups than in front of the whole class. It is less clear that computer-mediated classrooms reduce the anxiety that learners feel. Baralt and Gurzynski-Weiss (2011) compared the state of anxiety experienced by university learners of L2 Spanish when performing communicative tasks in a computer-mediated and a face-to-face classroom. In this case, the comparison involved 'written speech' in a chat room versus oral production. They found no difference. Why might this be? One possibility is that it is the requirement to perform in public (something common to both face-to-face and computer-mediated classrooms) that creates anxiety rather than the requirement to perform spontaneously.

A question of considerable interest is what helps to reduce learners' anxiety in the classroom. One possibility is that teachers desist from pressurizing learners to speak in front of the whole class. Teachers might consider allowing students to volunteer rather than nominating specific individuals as in the studies by Robson and Delaney. In this way, high-anxiety learners could opt to stay silent in class. Of course, this would mean that participation opportunities were unequal but this need not matter given that there is no convincing evidence that sheer quantity of participation is related to language learning. More generally, teachers could aim to enhance receptivity and reduce defensiveness by ensuring a positive classroom atmosphere. Palacios (1998; cited in Horwitz, 2001), for example, found that the level of support students perceive their teacher was providing had the greatest impact in reducing anxiety. Students saw support as evident when the teacher talked openly to them, trusted them and showed interest in their ideas.

Willingness to communicate

Anxiety is likely to affect students' willingness to communicate in the L2 classroom. However, anxiety is not the only factor that influences willingness to communicate (WTC). MacIntyre, Clement, Dörnyei, and Noels (1998) presented a schematic model of the WTC construct showing multiple layers of variables (such as communication anxiety, perceived communication competence, and perceived behavioural control) feeding into it. WTC, then, is best seen as a final-order variable that is determined by other individual learner factors and is the immediate antecedent of actual communication behaviour. Like anxiety, WTC can also be viewed as a trait (i.e. a general tendency) or as a situational variable, influenced by specific instructional factors. Like anxiety also it can be viewed as s relatively stable factor or as dynamic, varying according to ongoing changes in the instructional environment.

There have been three major studies investigating WTC in classroom contexts. Dörnyei and Kormos (2000) found that the WTC of Hungarian secondary school students' was influenced by their attitudes to the instructional tasks – in this case oral argumentative tasks. They measured WTC using a questionnaire that asked them to rate their readiness to enter into discourse in different social situations (e.g. 'Standing at the bus stop with friends'). Strong, positive correlations were found between the measure of WTC and both the number of words produced and the number of turns taken while performing the communicative tasks but only in the case of learners who expressed positive attitudes to the task. In the case of learners with low-task attitudes near zero, correlations were reported. It would seem then that learners' willingness to communicate depends in part on their personality and in part on their intrinsic motivation to perform specific classroom activities. Dörnyei and Kormos also noted that WTC was influenced by the learners' disposition towards the whole course as well as their attitudes towards the specific tasks they were asked to perform, with the former neutralizing their negative responses to the latter to some extent.

When learners work in pairs – as in Dörnyei and Kormos' study – WTC is likely to be co-constructed. That is the extent to which a learner is willing to communicate will depend in part on the extent to which his/her partner is also willing. In recognition of this, Dörnyei (2002) calculated the joint WTC of the dyads in the Dörnyei and Kormos' study. The resulting correlation between WTC and number of turns each dyad produced was much higher than that for individual students (i.e. r = . 59 as opposed to r = . 35).

Cao and Philp (2006) and Cao (2009) reported on the WTC of adult L2 learners taking an EAP course in a university-based language school. These studies triangulated data collection procedures by conducting observations of the learners in their normal classrooms and obtaining self-reports through a questionnaire, learner diaries and stimulated-recall interviews. Cao and Philp (2006) found no clear correlation between the learners' self-reported WTC in a questionnaire and their WTC as demonstrated in their actual classroom behaviours. However, this study did find a strong association between context and WTC behaviour with the learners more reticent when required to communicate in a whole-class context than in pair work or group work. There were also marked individual differences in the learners' WTC behaviour. The main factors that the learners identified as affecting their WTC were group size (smaller seen as better than larger), self-confidence, interlocutor familiarity and the extent to which other members of a group participated actively. Cao (2009) identified three sets of factors that influenced the situated level of WTC: (1) individual characteristics of learners (i.e. their self-confidence, their personality, their emotion and their perception of opportunities to communicate), (2) linguistic aspects (i.e. the learners' L2 proficiency and their reliance on their L1), and (3) classroom aspects (i.e. discourse topic, task type, interlocutor, the teacher, and class interactional patterns). She noted, however, that it was difficult to predict how these factors combined to determine classroom WTC at any given moment and also reported considerable variation in individual learners' responsiveness to classroom factors with some very sensitive to them and others relatively immune. Table 10.3 illustrates the fluid nature of WTC evident in two of the learners Cao studied.

The most extensive study of WTC to date is that of Peng and Woodrow (2010). This involved a pilot study of 330 university students recruited from a single Chinese University and a main study of 579 students from eight different Chinese universities. The method used was to administer a number of questionnaires designed to measure variables hypothesized to impact directly or indirectly on WTC. These variables were:

1. communication anxiety in English;
2. perceived communication competence in English;
3. motivation to learn English;
4. learner beliefs;
5. classroom environment.

Table 10.3 Factors influencing two L2 learners' WTC (based on Cao, 2009)

Mu-cheng

He reports that he felt relaxed and interested in participating in the afternoon class because he liked the teacher, who never pushed him to express opinions, and he found the project work provided a basis for concrete discussions; however, he felt reluctant to participate in the morning class in which the teacher often called on him to answer questions, and he considered the academic content of the course tedious.

Cai-wei

She considered her self-confidence and personality quite fluid as far as her WTC was concerned. She reported that she felt more confident and appeared more outgoing when she was talking to family members and friends but she seemed to be a quiet and less confident person and felt shy about talking to people she was not familiar with.

Source: Cao, Y. 2009. "Understanding the Notion of Interdependence, and the Dynamics of Willingness to Communicate". Unpublished PhD Thesis, University of Auckland.

The study was premised on the theoretically-based assumption that WTC is a final-order variable that is influenced by both learner internal factors and external factors. Peng and Woodrow used a statistical technique known as structural equational modelling to investigate the inter-relationships among the variables. Figure 10.3 shows the results of this analysis. Communication confidence and classroom environment (comprised of 'teacher support', 'student cohesiveness' and 'task orientation') were found to be directly related to the learners' WTC. The other variables were indirectly related. In other words, WTC was enhanced by a combination of an engaging classroom environment (where the students viewed the learning tasks as useful, the teacher as supportive and the student body as cohesive) and the students' own evaluation of their confidence in communicating in English. Interestingly, motivation was only indirectly related to WTC. In other words, it did not necessarily follow that a highly motivated student would be willing to communicate. Peng and Woodrow explained this as follows: ' . . . if students believe they can learn little by engaging in classroom communication or believe that class time should be given to grammar lectures, they may reduce their motivational effort in a communication-oriented class' (p. 855–856). It should also be noted that the classroom environment had an indirect effect on WTC through the influence it exerted on students' communication confidence. Overall, this study indicates that the extent to which students are willing to communicate in a classroom depends on a variety of factors.

WTC is of obvious interest for communicative language teaching (CLT); learners with a strong willingness to communicate may be able to benefit from CLT while those who are not so willing may learn better from more traditional instructional approaches. However, a caveat is in order. First, researchers interested in WTC have tended to assume blindly that students will benefit by communicating actively in the classroom. MacIntyre et al. (1998) went so far as to argue that the creation of WTC should be the 'primary goal of language instruction' (p. 545). There is, however, no

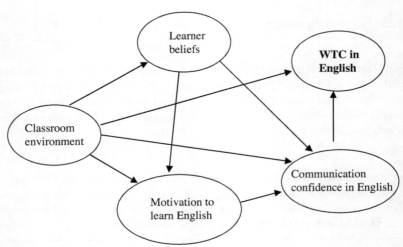

Figure 10.3 Structural model of willingness to communicate in English in the Chinese EFL classroom (Peng and Woodrow, 2010: 853; simplified)
Source: Based on Peng, J., and L. Woodrow. 2010. "Willingness to Communicate in English: A Model in the Chinese EFL Classroom Context." *Language Learning*, 60: 834–876.

clear evidence as yet that willingness to communicate translates into better learning. Speaking in an L2 may well assist learning, but so may listening. We have seen plenty of evidence in Chapter 8 and Chapter 9 to suggest that greater participation does not necessarily translate into more learning and that input-based instruction can be as effective as production-based approaches. Perhaps what is crucial for learning inside the classroom is not so much willingness to communicate as willingness to listen closely.

Motivational Factors

Current theories of motivation emphasize the dynamic nature of motivation (i.e. its temporal and situational nature). For example, Dörnyei's (2001) process model of learning motivation for the L2 classroom distinguished a 'pre-actional stage' involving 'choice motivation', which relates closely to how learners orientate to the instruction, an 'actional stage' involving 'executive motivation', which concerns the effort learners are prepared to invest to achieve their overall goal and which is heavily influenced by the quality of their learning experience, and a 'post-actional stage' involving 'motivational retrospection', where learners evaluate their learning experience and progress to date and determine their preparedness to continue. While instruction may initially have only a limited role to play in the pre-actional stage as learners will have their own reasons for learning the L2 (or for not wanting to learn it), it is likely to have a much stronger role in the 'actional stage' and may also figure in the post-actional stage through the feedback that teachers provide on learners' efforts to learn. Over time the motivation derived from the actional and post-actional stages may lead to changes in pre-actional motivation.

There is a large literature on the role played by motivation in language learning. While the research has produced mixed results there is overwhelming evidence that more motivated learners learn more. Thus, arguably, motivation is one of the most important factors influencing the success of instruction. However, surprisingly, there are remarkably few studies that have specifically examined how motivation affects the way learners respond to instruction or how instruction affects learners' motivation.

Motivation and learners' response to instruction

A reasonable assumption is that more motivated learners will respond more positively to instruction. In Figure 10.3 'motivation to learn English' is shown to be related indirectly to 'willingness to communicate' via the effect it exerts on learners' 'communication confidence'. Thus one can expect motivated learners to be more active in the classroom. Two early studies provide evidence of this. Gliksman, Gardner and Smythe (1982) investigated students studying French in Canadian high schools. They reported positive correlations between the learners' integrative motivation (i.e. the motivation that derives from a 'sincere and personal interest in the people and culture represented by the other language group' (Lambert, 1974: 98) and both their volunteered responses and their correct answers. Naiman et al. (1978) reported a relationship between instrumental motivation (i.e. the motivation that derives from a desire to achieve some functional goal such as passing a test) and learners' hand-raising. Dörnyei (2002) reported that Hungarian high school students who held positive attitudes towards a communicative task were more likely to produce more words and take more turns when they performed the task. Also, teachers seem to be more responsive to highly motivated learners. Gliskman et al. also reported that teachers directed more questions and gave more positive reinforcement to the more integratedly motivated learners. These studies suggest that motivated learners engage more fully in the learning process both because they make greater efforts to do so and because teachers favour them.

It is also reasonable to assume that more motivated learners pay more attention to input and process it more deeply. Manolopoulo-Sergi (2004), for example, argued that extrinsically motivated learners are likely to attend only to the surface characteristics of the input, whereas intrinsically motivated learners will process input in a more elaborated, deeper manner. Evidence that motivation influences how learners process instructional input comes from a study by Takahashi (2005). Drawing on Schmidt's (1994) claim that integratively motivated learners are more likely to pay close attention to the pragmatic aspects of input, Takahashi examined the relationship between Japanese English as a foreign language (EFL) learners' motivation and their noticing of the pragmalinguistic features of complex request forms (e.g. 'Would it be possible for you to . . . ?'). She administered a motivation questionnaire to the learners who then completed two awareness-raising tasks that directed their attention to the linguistic features needed to perform polite requests in English. The learners also completed an Awareness Retrospection Questionnaire, which asked them to rate the extent to which they had become aware of the linguistic features as they performed the tasks. The results supported Manolopoulo-Sergi's claim about the importance of intrinsic motivation. There was a positive correlation between a measure of this aspect of motivation and the learners' reported awareness of a number of pragmalinguistic features. There was also evidence that 'different motivational profiles are concerned with awareness of different aspects of pragmalinguistic features'.

Effect of instruction on motivation

There has been considerably more research that has investigated how instruction affects learners' motivation. There has also been considerable interest among teacher educators about how teachers can motivate their students.

One line of enquiry has focused on investigating demotivation in the L2 classroom. Dörnyei (2001) defined a demotivated learner as 'someone who was once motivated but has lost his or her commitment/interest for some reason' (p. 142). Dörnyei made the point that demotivation does not imply that all the positive factors that once constituted a learner's motivation have been lost as some positive motives may remain. He also distinguished demotivation from 'amotivation' (Deci and Ryan, 1985), which refers to a 'lack of motivation'. The whole point about demotivation is that it is traceable to specific external causes.

What then are the instructional factors that lead to demotivation? Dörnyei (2001) reviews a number of studies that have sought answers to this question (Chambers, 1993; Dörnyei, 1998; Oxford, 1998; Ushioda, 1998). Table 10.4 summarizes the main demotivating factors that the classroom learners in these studies identified. However, the studies also show that individual learners vary considerably in what they find demotivating. For example, Ushioda's learners (university learners of L2 French) identified 'negative aspects of the institutionalized learning framework rather than negative self-perceptions of ability' (p. 86) as the main factors, whereas Oxford's (1998) study of American students learning foreign languages in both schools and universities emphasized the teacher's role in their demotivation.

Interestingly, teachers appear to have a different view of why their students appear unmotivated. Chambers, for example, reported that the teachers he interviewed tended to identify factors external to the instruction (e.g. the fact that learners were forced to learn a foreign language against their will or their lack of language aptitude) as responsible. Sakui (2004) also found that the Japanese high school teachers she interviewed tended to explain their students' poor motivation to learn English in terms of social and community factors that were beyond their control. In effect, then, teachers seem to focus on students' 'amotivation' rather than their demotivation.

Only one of these studies (Oxford) identified differences between the teacher's teaching style and learners' preferred learning style as the source of demotivation.

Table 10.4 Summary of main demotivating factors

General factors	Specific causes of demotivation
Teacher factors	• poor relationship with students (e.g. through criticizing them) • failure to give clear instruction and explanations
Learner factors	• reduced self-confidence (lack of belief in one's own capability) • experience of failure • negative attitudes towards L2/L2 community • negative attitudes towards fellow students
Facilities	• class size (i.e. class too big) • frequent change of teachers
Classroom activities	• activities perceived by students as irrelevant • overload • repetitiveness • dislike of the course book

Learners do have distinct beliefs about how they can best learn an L2 and these often conflict with the type of instruction they are experiencing (see, for example, Sakui and Gaies' 1999 study of Japanese high school students' beliefs). Bialystok (1985) argued that there needs to be 'minimal congruity' between the learners' preferred approach to learning and the type of instruction. Where there are disparities, learning will be adversely affected and one reason for this is that learners lose motivation.

An alternative research approach to investigating how instruction affects motivation is to try to identify the specific teaching strategies that promote motivation. Dörnyei and Csizer (1998) conducted a study of 200 high school teachers in Hungary. They asked the teachers to evaluate the importance of 51 motivational strategies and also to say how frequently they used each strategy. They then grouped strategies that were closely related and ranked them in terms of the mean importance scores, ending up with 'ten commandments for motivating language learners' (see list). The results for reported frequency of use of these strategies showed that some commandments were frequently overlooked (e.g. (9) and (1)). Two points need to be made about this study. First, while there may be some motivating strategies that have universal applicability, it is likely that there are others that are relevant to the specific instructional context that Dörnyei and Csizer were investigating. Second, we cannot take for granted that those strategies teachers *think* are motivating actually are so. The ten commandments for motivating language learners (Dörnyei and Csizer, 1998: 215) are:

1. Set a personal example with your own behaviour.
2. Create a pleasant, relaxed atmosphere in the classroom.
3. Present the tasks properly.

4.   Develop a good relationship with the learners.
5.   Increase the learners' self-confidence.
6.   Make the language classes interesting.
7.   Promote learner autonomy.
8.   Personalize the learning process.
9.   Increase the learners' goal-orientedness.
10. Familiarize learners' with the target culture.

Clearly what is needed is a study that examines the relationship between teachers' motivating strategies and learners' motivation. Guilloteaux and Dörnyei (2008) reported the results of just such a study (see Table 2.5 in Chapter 2 for a summary of this study). They investigated 40 EFL classrooms involving 27 different teachers in Korea. The used a classroom observation scheme consisting of 25 strategy variables to measure the teachers' motivational practice. Examples of these variables are:

Having an informal (often humorous) chat with the students on matters unrelated to the lesson.
Setting up a cooperative learning activity.
Offering students a choice of activities.
Offering praise for effort or achievement that is sincere, specific and commensurate with the student's achievement.

They carried out real-time observation of lessons, recording whether a strategy was used in every one-minute time segment. They then calculated the mean amount of time for each strategy. The students' situation-specific motivational dispositions were investigated by means of a Student Motivational State Questionnaire and also a Post-Lesson Teacher Evaluation Scale. The results showed a significant positive correlation between the teacher's motivational practice and the learners' motivated behaviour. Overall, the teachers' motivational practice accounted for 37 per cent of the variance in the students' motivated behaviour. There is, of course, a problem is interpreting such correlations as it is not clear how to interpret the direction of the relationship. Is it the teachers' motivated practices that enhance the students' situated motivation or is it the students' motivated behaviour that motivates the teachers? Guilloteaux and Dörnyei were aware of this problem but favoured the first interpretation of the results. My own interpretation is that the relationship between teachers' motivating practices and students' motivation is an interactive one. They feed off each other.

Another way of examining how instruction affects learners' motivation is by exploring how learners react to specific instructional tasks. Egbert (2003) investigated fourth-semester university Spanish learners' performance of a number of communicative tasks focusing on what she called 'flow'. She defined this as 'an experiential state characterized by intense focus and involvement that leads to improved performance on a task' (p. 499). Clearly, 'flow' is a motivational construct. Multiple sources of data were collected (i.e. a perceptions survey, observations of the learners performing the tasks, the task products, and post-task interviews). One of the main findings was that the nature of the task influenced flow. The task that elicited the greatest flow was one that required the students to engage in an electronic chat about artists while the one that produced the least flow was reading out loud in Spanish and asking questions. Egbert concluded that because the patterns of flow across tasks were very similar it was possible to 'talk about tasks that support flow' (p. 514). This study, then, indicates that the specific activities that learners are asked to perform affect the learners' levels of motivation.

All of these approaches to investigating the impact that instruction has on motivation are premised on the assumption that teaching can enhance learning if the teachers' practices are motivational. This is a very reasonable assumption as there is ample evidence that motivated learners learn more than amotivated or demotivated learners but it is important to acknowledge that the role of motivation in mediating the effects of instruction has not actually been demonstrated. Ideally we need studies that show how specific instructional practices (for example, the choice of tasks in Egbert's study) affect learners' motivation and how, as a result, specific learning processes (for example, attention and awareness) are enhanced leading to specific learning outcomes (for example, increased fluency, accuracy or complexity of L2 use). Such studies have not yet been conducted.

Strategy Training

So far I have focused on how the attributes and states of individual learners affect the way they respond to instruction. Instruction cannot be treated as a monolithic phenomenon because learners clearly respond to it in very different ways. One way of dealing with this is to ensure that the instruction matches the cognitive abilities and affective dispositions of individual learners. However, given the myriad ways in which learners differ, it is doubtful whether such matching can be achieved in a rigorous manner in most instructional contexts. Instead teachers are likely to try to accommodate learner diversity by varying the instructional activities and the specific methodological procedures for implementing them. That is, they try to ensure there is something to suit everyone, drawing largely on their own experience of teaching (rather than on research) to work out ways of achieving this.

However, there is an alternative approach. Teachers can try to equip students with the learner strategies that will enable them to benefit from the type of instruction they provide. Such an approach requires first identifying those strategies that have been shown to facilitate learning and second devising ways of training students to employ these strategies effectively.

Background to the study of learner strategies

Oxford (1989) defined 'learning strategies' as 'behaviours or actions which learners use to make language learning more successful, self-directed and enjoyable'. However, such a definition is not entirely unproblematic. There is uncertainty about the precise nature of the behaviours that count as learning strategies. Stern (1983) distinguished 'strategies' and 'techniques', defining the former as general and more or less deliberate 'approaches' to learning (for example, 'an active task approach') and the latter as observable forms of language learning behaviour evident in particular areas of language learning such as grammar (for example, 'inferring grammar rules from texts') and vocabulary (for example, 'using a dictionary when necessary'). More typically, however, researchers have preferred to use the term 'strategies' for what Stern called techniques. They have identified two general characteristics of strategies: they are problem-oriented and they are applied consciously.

Two of the most common typologies of learner strategies are those of Oxford (1990) and O'Malley and Chamot (1990). The typology that appears to have figured most prominently in strategy training research is O'Malley and Chamot's. This distinguishes three basic categories of strategies:

1. Metacognitive strategies, e.g. 'selective attention' (deciding in advance to attend to specific aspects of language input).
2. Cognitive strategies, e.g. 'inferencing' (using available information to guess meanings of new items, predict outcomes, or fill in missing information).
3. Social/affective strategies, e.g. 'question for clarification' (asking a teacher or another native speaker for repetition, paraphrasing, explanation).

Researchers have been concerned with both investigating what strategies learners report using and, more importantly, which strategies are important for successful language learning. A number of early studies identified learners who were demonstrably 'good' at learning an L2 and then explored the strategies that they used. The idea underlying this kind of research was to identify the strategies linked to successful learning so that these could serve as the strategies to be targetted in learner training. A recent example of this kind of study is Gan, Humphreys, and Hamp-Lyons (2004). They compared successful and unsuccessful learners of English in Chinese universities in terms of both standard test scores and their teachers' perceptions of their proficiency. They reported clear differences in the ways in which the successful and unsuccessful learners went about learning vocabulary; whereas the unsuccessful students relied on rote-memorization, the successful students supplemented rote-learning with strategies for reinforcing what they had learnt (for example, doing vocabulary exercises or reading). Also, the successful students set particular objectives for themselves and identified systematic ways of achieving these. In contrast, the unsuccessful learners did not appear to have a clear agenda and experienced difficulty in identifying their learning problems. A general finding of such studies is that good language learners have a range of strategies at their disposal and select strategies in accordance with both their long-term goals for learning the L2 and the particular task to hand. In other words, they use clusters of strategies and adjust their strategy use flexibly.

Other studies have explored the relationship between reported strategy use and L2 learning. These correlational studies are difficult to interpret as it is not clear whether it is strategy use that contributes to L2 proficiency or L2 proficiency that determines what strategies learners are able to use. The main finding was learners elect to use different strategies at different stages of L2 development. For example, at elementary levels they prioritize strategies that relate to the functional use of language and to processing chunks of language while at later stages they employ strategies that involve close attention to form. Also, metacognitive strategies are more commonly-used by advanced learners.

While a number of general observations relating to the efficacy of strategy use are possible (e.g. 'be flexible'; 'use metacognitive strategies to plan, monitor and evaluate your progress'; 'combine strategies' – see Macaro, 2006) there is little evidence to show which specific strategies foster learning especially where general proficiency is concerned[5]. This raises a problem for strategy training: it is not very clear what strategies the training should focus on. Perhaps, therefore, we should not expect too much of strategy training.

There are other reasons for not expecting too much of learner training studies. Macaro (2006) pointed out that the lack of standardization in both the intervention packages and the manner in which learning was assessed make it difficult to reach any firm conclusions regarding the effectiveness of strategy training.

Studies of strategy training

A number of surveys of training studies (Chamot, 2001; McDonough, 1999; Hassan et al., 2005) have been published. I will draw on the last of these as it is the most comprehensive.

Hassan et al. defined strategy training as 'any intervention which focuses on the strategies to be regularly adopted and used by language learners to develop their proficiency, improve particular task performance or both' (p. 1). They undertook a survey of all strategy training studies conducted since 1960 with a view to determining whether strategy training was effective, whether it was effective with different languages, different learners (i.e. school, university and adult) and different language skills. They also hoped to be able to identify which particular types of strategy training worked best. After an extensive search of published studies, they identified 25 for an in depth review.

The main findings of this survey were as follows:

1. The evidence generally points to the effectiveness of strategy training at least in the short term. Out of the 25 studies, 17 reported positive results, five mixed results and only two negative results. However, there was inadequate evidence to say whether the effects were long-lasting.
2. The effectiveness of the training varies according to the different language skills. Its effect is most robust in improving reading comprehension and writing skills. Training directed at improving overall language ability produced mixed results.

3. It was not possible to determine which types of strategy training or which
    particular training techniques were effective. It was impossible to differentiate the
    effect of training based on awareness-raising as opposed to behaviour modelling.
    Nor was it possible to determine whether training based on discrete strategies
    or packages of strategies worked best.
4. The studies investigated mainly non-school populations so little can be said
    about the effectiveness of strategy training with school-based learners.
5. The survey did not shed light on whether the learners' stage of development was
    a significant factor influencing the success of learner training.

Not surprisingly, Hassan et al. are quite cautious in the recommendation with
which they concluded their review. In short, while there are strong theoretical
grounds for believing that strategy training will help learners, the empirical evidence in support of it remains slender:

> The evidence needs to be interpreted carefully by practitioners, policy-makers and
> researchers for specific contexts (e.g. schools versus tertiary sector, beginner versus
> advanced learner, etc.), and the findings are not immediately transferable to all language
> learning situations (2005: p. 8).

One of the points that Hassan et al. make is the need for better-designed studies. A
good model for strategy training studies is Holunga (1995). This experimental study
investigated the effects of metacognitive strategy training on the accurate use of verb
forms by advanced learners of English. It involved three instructional conditions:
(1) metacognitive strategy training plus communicative practice, (2) metacognitive
strategy training plus a requirement to verbalize the strategies plus communicative
practice, and (3) communicative practice only. During the instructional period the
learners performed a focused task (i.e. a communicative task designed to elicit a
specific linguistic feature). Whereas groups (1) and (3) attended predominantly to
message content, producing interaction typical of a 'negotiation of meaning' task,
group (2) focused on both message content and the conditional verb form that the
task required. Group (2) demonstrated significantly greater gains in the ability to use
complex verb forms accurately than the other groups. This suggests that for strategy
training to be effective, learners need to verbalize while they are practising the use of a
strategy as suggested by the socioculturally framed studies we considered in Chapter
8. One of the strengths of Holunga's study is that it examined the effects of strategy
training on the acquisition of a specific linguistic feature (rather than on general
language proficiency) and also collected process data that showed to what extent
the learner interactions in the different groups reflected the training requirements.
Another strength was the testing regime. There were both closed and open-ended
tests and these were administered both immediately following the training session
and later.

Learner training is popular. It has been endorsed by a number of researchers (e.g.
Macaro, 2006). Many textbooks now include some form of strategy training and

there are also whole books given over to strategy training activities. Nevertheless, there is also considerable scepticism. Few of the strategies proposed in these books have been submitted to empirical scrutiny. Dörnyei (2005) concluded his account of strategy training with this comment:

> Although the available strategy and training materials are generally creative and impressive, it is not clear whether the benefits of their explicit employment warrant the time and effort spent on them in comparison to spending the same amount of creative energy designing 'ordinary' learning activities (pp. 176–7).

He noted that whereas research into learning strategies was popular in general educational research in the 1980s, it declined dramatically in the 1990s, with researchers turning their attention to a related concept, self-regulation (i.e. 'the degree to which individuals are active participants in their own learning', p. 191) and suggested that researchers should do the same. Holanga's study is a good example of how this can be accomplished.

Conclusion

No book on language teaching research and language pedagogy is complete without a consideration of individual learner factors. My concern in this chapter has not been with the bountiful research that has examined the relationship between specific individual learner factors and language proficiency or achievement, but with the much smaller body of research that has explored the relationship between individual learner factors and instruction. We have seen that this is two-directional. The benefit that learners can obtain from instruction depends on their particular cognitive abilities and their initial affective and motivational states. Also, the type of instruction learners experience can impact on their initial affective states (and, less clearly, on their cognitive abilities), modifying them[6]. Thus the relationship between instruction and individual learner factors is an interactive and dynamic one. It is subject to shifts not just from lesson to lesson but within a single lesson and even within a single learning activity.

There are two lessons to be learned from this view of how individual learner factors interrelate with instruction. The first is that it may be a mistake to emphasize the initial abilities and states of learners. While these do impact on what learners are able to take from instruction, there is always the potential of the instruction to modify what learners bring to the classroom. Thus, for example, while high-aptitude, low-anxiety and highly motivated learners may be in the best position to benefit from instruction, it also possible – given the right instructional conditions – for low-aptitude, high-anxiety and weakly-motivated learners to benefit too. The greatest danger in individual difference research is characterizing learners as 'types' who are either able or not able to take advantage of language instruction. The second lesson to be learned is that the interplay between individual learner factors and instruction is a highly complex one. Different kinds of instruction favour different abilities and affective states. Thus different learners benefit from different kinds of instruction. This raises the key question of how to ensure an appropriate match between learner and instruction.

There are two possible answers to this question. One is to adapt the instruction to the learner. However, it is neither theoretically desirable nor practically possible to match instruction to specific learner groups (e.g. to restrict input-based instruction to learners with strong phonemic discrimination abilities or to direct recasts only at low-anxiety learners). It is probably useful for teachers to be aware of the kinds of factors that constrain some learners' responses to certain types of instruction but learner-instruction matching assumes that it is possible to identify types of learners, which I have questioned, and, in any case, it is asking too much of teachers to design instruction in such a way that it takes account of learners who differ on a whole range of cognitive abilities, affective dispositions and motivational states. The only way that teachers can take account of learner differences is through getting to know the individual learners in their classroom – itself a process that occurs gradually through interaction with the learners – and through experimenting with varied types of instructional activities and observing how learners respond to them. Adapting instruction to learners in real classrooms (as opposed to laboratory settings) can never be undertaken scientifically as in aptitude-treatment-interaction studies. It is necessarily a dynamic and experiential process.

The other way of answering the question is by finding ways of adapting the learner to the instruction. This can be undertaken by seeking to modify learners' belief systems to make students more receptive to a particular type of instruction – for example, assisting students to recognize that language learning can take place incidentally through task-based instruction as well as intentionally through more traditional forms of instruction. The problem here is that it is very difficult to change learners' belief systems and, in any case, there is no guarantee that learners will consistently act on their beliefs even if teachers do succeed in modifying them. Another way is strategy training by identifying those strategies that have been shown to promote successful language learning. As we have seen, this approach also has problems not least because the relationship between strategy use and language learning still remains unclear. We need much firmer evidence that belief-modification and strategy training are capable of enhancing the effects of different kinds of instruction before we can spend time on trying to adapt the learner to the instruction.

To my mind, the most promising research is that which explores how IDs affect the interactional and learning processes that take place when learners grapple with different kinds of instructional activities. We have seen a number of examples of such research – for example, Y. Sheen's (2008) study of how language anxiety impacts on the processing of corrective feedback or Dörnyei and Csizer's (1998) study of the relationship between willingness to communicate and performance of a communicative task – but such studies are still relatively rare. We need, too, rich case studies of how learners react to instruction in the course of a single lesson (or when performing a single task) as only in this way will we begin to understand the complex and dynamic interplay between learner factors and instruction.

Notes

1. 'Cognitive style' constitutes another cognitive factor. However, although there is a substantial literature that has investigated the relationship between field dependence/independence (one type of cognitive style) and L2 proficiency/achievement, there has been little research that has examined how cognitive style affects the way learners respond to instruction. For this reason, I have not considered it in this chapter.
2. An alternative model of working memory is that of Daneman and Carpenter (1980) based on the notion of 'reading span memory'. However, as Juffs (2007) pointed out, this model is much less well-investigated with L2 learners.
3. White and Ranta's (2002) study also reported that some students in an intensive, communicative ESL programme were able to acquire the grammatical rule for the use of 'his' and her' without any direct explicit instruction and that this could be explained by the fact that they had higher levels of language analytical ability.
4. In fact the gains resulting for the recast treatment in Sheen's study were minimal and not statistically significant. This is a possible explanation for her failure to find any correlation between metalinguistic ability and gains.
5. It is somewhat easier to identify the specific strategies that promote the acquisition of vocabulary (see, for example, Brown and Perry, 1991) or specific skills such as reading.
6. The extent to which cognitive abilities such as language aptitude and working memory are modifiable as a result of learning experiences is a controversial issue. Carroll (1981) argued that language aptitude is more or less fixed. However, there are laboratory-based studies (e.g. Nation and McLaughlin, 1986) that demonstrate quite clearly that experienced language learners are cognitively advantaged.

11

Conclusion: Research and Language Teaching

Introduction

Ideally, the concluding chapter for a book such as this would summarize the main findings of the research that it has examined. However, the research is now so extensive and so disparate in terms of the questions it has addressed and its methodology, and its theoretical orientation so diverse, that I baulk at trying to produce an overall summary. Instead, readers are referred to the summaries of the key findings at the end of each of the preceding chapters.

I have two goals for this chapter. First, I will address a number of key methodological issues in language teaching research, reviewing the issues that Chaudron (1988) considered in the concluding chapter to his own survey of the research. Second, I will examine the relationship between research and teaching and advance my own proposals for how research about language teaching can best inform the practice of language teaching.

Methodological Issues

Chaudron was justifiably critical of the research that he reviewed. He commented:

> It has been shown that research is (a) lacking in consistent measures of classroom processes and products, (b) sometimes inadequate in design to address critical research issues, (c) inexplicit or incomplete in quantitative or qualitative analysis, and (d) in need of greater theoretical specification of the constructs, and relationships to be investigated (p. 180).

Language Teaching Research & Language Pedagogy, First Edition. Rod Ellis.
© 2012 John Wiley & Sons, Ltd. Published 2012 by John Wiley & Sons, Ltd.

To what extent are his criticisms still valid some 20 years later? I will consider each of his criticisms in turn.

Measures of classroom processes and products

There have been considerable advances in ways of measuring classroom processes since Chaudron's review. As Chaudron pointed out, 'the ultimate issue is one of validity of the constructs used to describe and interpret classroom interaction' (p. 181). For Chaudron validity could be achieved only by developing constructs that were theoretically motivated and could be shown to be related to learning outcomes. To what extent has this now been achieved?

We have seen that researchers draw on very different constructs to describe classroom interaction. On the one hand the kind of quantitative measures that were Chaudron's primary concern have continued to figure in much of the research. These have continued to be purely descriptive rather than explanatory, involving both low- and high-inference categories. However, increasingly, they have been theoretically motivated. For example, such constructs as initiate–respond–follow-up or 'IRF' exchanges, 'teacher questions', 'use of the first language (L1)', 'metalanguage' and 'language play' were all motivated by theoretical positions regarding the role these played in second language (L2) learning. However, as I frequently noted in the preceding chapters, there have been few attempts to validate these by demonstrating what impact they have on actual learning. In this respect it would appear that there has not been much progress since Chaudron's review.

Importantly though, there have been attempts to develop explanatory categories by investigating the relationship between specific categories and learning. This is perhaps most clearly evident in the ongoing research that has investigated corrective feedback. This research constitutes an excellent example of how categories derived from purely descriptive research (as in Lyster and Ranta's 1997 taxonomy of corrective strategies) were subsequently used to devise experimental studies that tested specific hypotheses about the effect of different strategies on learning (as in Lyster, 2004). The fact that it has been possible to carry out a number of meta-analyses of studies that examined the effects of different kinds of instruction (see, for example, Norris and Ortega, 2006) on learning is clear evidence that classroom research has advanced considerably since Chaudron's review. Thus, the situation today is markedly different from that in 1988.

Arguably, too, second language classroom research has been greatly enriched by a line of enquiry that did not figure at all in Chaudron's review – namely, research based on sociocultural theory. This has provided rich and rigorous descriptions of classroom interaction by drawing on the techniques of microgenetic analysis and conversational analysis (see Chapter 2 and Chapter 4). It has been based on a very different view of what 'learning' entails. For Chaudron 'learning' meant 'measurable outcomes' established by means of post-tests. Sociocultural theory sees learning not as 'outcomes' but as inherent in the very processes that arise when learners interact with a teacher or among themselves. To my mind this is both a strength and a weakness. Its strength is that it has led researchers to investigate the interactive conditions that enable learners to construct utterances that were beyond them independently – in other words, it has shown us the genesis of learning. Its weakness is that it has not always attempted to show how scaffolded use evolves into independent use. However, in recent years there has been an attempt to rectify this weakness both by means of longitudinal studies that examine how what is accomplished through interaction at one time leads to more independent use at a later time (as in Aljaafreh and Lantolf, 1994; and Donato, 1994) and by experimental studies that include post-tests (as in the research by Swain and her co-researchers – see Chapter 8).

All in all, then, it can be claimed that there have been considerable advances in developing 'descriptively adequate categories of classroom behaviors and events' (Chaudron 1988: 181).

The design of classroom studies

Chaudron was critical of the design of many of the studies he reviewed. He noted that classroom researchers are rarely in a position to conduct true experimental studies as more often than not they are obliged to use intact classes often with a quite small sample of learners. These sampling problems continue. For example, researchers continue to experience difficulty in ensuring the equivalence of experimental and control groups. However, most studies now include a pre-test and, where lack of equivalence becomes evident, are in a position to use appropriate statistical measures (e.g. analysis of co-variance) to take account of any pre-test group differences. Also, increasingly studies have included a delayed post-test that makes it possible to investigate the durability of the effects of the experimental treatment. A number of studies have also endeavoured to investigate the instructional processes that arise during the experimental treatment so making it possible to analyze process-product relationships. In these respects, there have been advances in the design of experimental studies since Chaudron's review.

Chaudron commented on the 'pronounced unavailability of appropriate measures of L2 progress' (p. 183). This problem is also still evident with many studies still over-reliant on discrete-point testing of learning outcomes which may not be indicative of acquisition if this is conceptualized as the development of implicit knowledge of the L2. However, again, there has been progress. Researchers (e.g. Norris and Ortega, 2000) have shown increasing awareness of the need to investigate the effects of instruction using measures of learning derived from tasks that elicit learners' freely constructed responses'. Some studies (e.g. Doughty and Varela, 1998) have also employed measures of interlanguage development. These avoid the 'comparative fallacy' (Bley Vroman, 1983) inherent in the use of measures based on compliance to target language norms. Other studies (e.g. Ellis, Loewen and Erlam, 2006) have made use of elicitation techniques such as oral imitation tests that can claim to measure implicit knowledge.

Issues to do with how learning is measured remain, however. All too often class-room researchers do not give due consideration to establishing the validity and the reliability of the instruments they have used to measure learning. In part, this is because there is still no consensus about how 'learning' should be theorized. Not all theories accept the distinction between implicit and explicit L2 knowledge and are content to use measures that are likely to tap controlled rather than automatic processes of language use. Some sociocultural researchers (e.g. Poehner, 2008) have argued that learning is best measured not by means of some kind of test but 'dynam-ically' by investigating changes in the extent to which learners require interactional mediation in order to perform some specific linguistic feature. Validity issues to do with the measurement of learning, then, continue to plague L2 classroom research. There is much less excuse for the continued failure to examine the reliability of whatever measures of learning are employed. Reliability is an issue no matter how learning is theorized.

Data analysis

According to Chaudron, the research he reviewed was characterized by 'marked misuse, frequent underuse, and occasional unwarranted overuse of various statistical procedures' (p. 183). In addition, Chaudron noted that some studies failed to report the critical statistics needed for a proper interpretation of statistical tests. It is in this respect, perhaps, that classroom research has witnessed the greatest improvement. Journals publishing classroom research are now much more demanding about the use of statistical procedures, requiring that the appropriate descriptive statistics are provided and that the conditions for the use of specific inferential statistics are established. Researchers are also now asked to report effect sizes – in addition to measures of statistical significance – to show the strength of the relationship between variables. This is especially important in classroom studies as we need to know not just that the difference between two instructional treatments is statistically significant but also the extent of this difference. Better reporting of results has also made it possible for researchers to carry out meta-analyses of relatively large numbers of studies and thus to investigate the generalizability of the effect of specific instructional variables on learning.

Qualitative studies of L2 classrooms have faced different problems of data analysis. Nevertheless rigour is still important if the trustworthiness of the analysis is to be demonstrated. Studies that have made use of conversational analysis (CA) have been able to draw on a set of well-defined procedures based on clearly delineated principles (see Seedhouse, 2004; and Chapter 2) that allow for confidence in how data is interpreted. However, learning cannot be demonstrated conclusively through cross-sectional studies no matter how sophisticated the CA analyses are and there have been very few qualitative longitudinal studies. Sociocultural researchers have argued that cross-sectional studies can examine learning if this is defined in terms of the assisted performance of some linguistic feature that a learner cannot handle independently but such an approach is only valid if it can also be shown that the learner is in fact incapable of independent performance of the feature and this has rarely been attempted. Thus, to my mind, many of the qualitative data analyses I have reported in this book only address 'language use', not 'learning'.

Theoretical issues

Chaudron advanced a plea for greater theoretical specification of the constructs and the relationships between them. Arguably, as the discussion in the preceding sections of this chapter indicates, constructs and relationships are now more clearly theorized. Constructs such as the negotiation of meaning, language-related episodes and focus-on-form episodes (see Chapter 7), for example, have been defined in both theoretical and operational terms. However, other constructs such as 'scaffolding' while theoretically grounded, remain somewhat opaque. Thus there is room for further progress here.

Chaudron observed that there was no general theory of L2 acquisition that could inform classroom research but also noted that 'efforts were well underway' (p. 184) to develop such a theory. In this respect, he was overly optimistic. There still is no general theory of L2 acquisition – indeed, theoretical pluralism is even more evident now than at the time Chaudron was writing, with no agreed set of criteria for evaluating and 'culling' weak theories (see Ellis, 2010a). However, this need not be seen as problematic. Theoretical pluralism is in fact advantageous as it affords multiple perspectives on what is a highly complex phenomenon – language teaching and learning.

This has been very much my own perspective in this book. In particular, I have tried to interweave reports of experimental studies based on interactionist-cognitive theory and interpretative studies based on sociocultural theory on the grounds that they both provide valuable insights about the processes and products of language instruction. There is a tendency to view these theories as incommensurate and for researchers to stake out claims in favour of their own paradigm through criticizing the theoretical foundations and limitations of the other paradigm. This seems to me an unprofitable way to proceed. A better stance is to accept that classroom research – of any kind – affords only insights that can inform language teaching and that what is needed is a set of principles that can guide the way these insights are used by teacher educators and teachers. In the next section of this chapter I turn to an examination of what these principles might look like.

From Research to Teaching

Research and teaching are very different activities. Research aims to systematically examine specific phenomena with a view to describing and/or explaining them and then publishing the findings. It contributes to *technical knowledge* about language teaching and learning. Teaching involves curriculum planning, designing lessons and then implementing and evaluating them. This is shaped less by teachers' technical knowledge than by their practical knowledge of what is likely to work in their specific contexts. In this respect, teaching is no different from other professional activities that are conducted through interpersonal interaction. Friedson's (1977, cited in Eraut, 1994: 53) account of how a medical practitioner operates is equally applicable to teachers:

> One whose work requires practical application to concrete cases simply cannot maintain the same frame of mind as the scholar or scientist . . . Dealing with individual cases, he cannot rely solely on probabilities or on general concepts or principles: he must also rely on his own senses. By the nature of his work the clinician must assume responsibility for practical action, and in so doing he must rely on his concrete, clinical experience.

The key question becomes 'How can the technical knowledge that research provides assist teachers who, given the fundamental nature of teaching, are bound to rely primarily on the practical knowledge that they have gained through experience?' To answer this question we need to distinguish two general aspects of teaching – the planning of a lesson and the actual teaching of the lesson through interaction with learners in a classroom.

Planning teaching

Technical knowledge is perhaps more readily applied when planning language teaching. Many second language teacher education texts are premised on a technical–rational model of curriculum development. That is, they emphasize the importance of planning teaching using 'combinations of systematic procedures such as assessing the teaching context and learners' needs, developing general aims and specific objectives, describing entry and exit levels, selecting syllabus frameworks and developing units of instruction' (Wette, 2009: 339). Language teaching handbooks such as those by Ur (1996), Hedge, (2000) and Harmer (2001) aim to equip teachers with the technical knowledge they need to undertake these planning activities. They mediate between researchers and teachers, making the empirical and theoretical information provided by research accessible to teachers and showing how it can be applied to the practical requirements of teaching. The research I have examined in this book assists planning most obviously in two of the 'systematic procedures' that Wette mentions – namely 'developing general aims and specific objectives' and 'developing units of instruction'.

Fundamental to developing specific aims and objectives is the distinction between synthetic and analytic approaches to teaching (Wilkins, 1986). The former involves a structural approach to teaching that has as its goal the creation of 'form and accuracy contexts', while the latter involves a task-based approach that seeks to create 'meaning-and-fluency contexts'. There is now plenty of evidence to show that both approaches can contribute to learning. Chapter 8 examined how tasks can foster the kinds of interaction that lead to incidental acquisition. Chapter 9 examined a number of form-focused options that have been shown to cater successfully to intentional language learning. There is, however, insufficient evidence to show that one approach is superior to another (see Chapter 3). Where then does this leave the teacher (or the teacher educator)? I would argue that the only response that is appropriate is one that involves (1) teachers developing an awareness of the theoretical rationale for the two approaches and, in a selective way, knowledge of the empirical evidence that provides support for each approach and (2) teachers acquiring the technical knowledge they need to make explicit decisions about aims and objectives for the specific instructional context in which their operate. However, although technical knowledge will enable a teacher to make informed decisions about how to plan a course of action, it will have to be filtered through the teacher's personal understanding of the instructional context, and this, to a large extent, will depend on experience.

Research is perhaps of clearest value when it comes to 'developing units of instruction' – i.e. in lesson planning. Teacher education texts are replete with suggestions for specific workplans that teachers can draw on when planning a lesson. It makes sense that to ensure that these reflect what is currently known about the kinds of activity that arise when different workplans are implemented and about the learning that is likely to result from them. Sociocultural theory claims that classroom participants always interpret a workplan in accordance with their own goals and motives. But, as I pointed out in Ellis (2000) – and showed in Chapter 7 – there is plenty of evidence to show that carefully designed workplans often do result in the activity intended. Classroom research, then, contributes in three major ways. First, it has enriched the store of workplans available for lesson planning. Researchers have been creative in developing workplans for a whole range of task types (see, for example, Yule's (1997) *Referential Communication Tasks*). Second, it has codified the various workplans that have been investigated (see, for example, Chapter 9 where I discussed various options for form-focused instruction). Research-based taxonomies of workplan types are surely of greater value to teachers than lists of 'tips for teaching' based purely on experience of teaching. Third, it has contributed empirical evidence about the actual use of these workplans in classrooms. Thus, teachers can see what is likely to transpire when a workplan is implemented. Again, though, teachers will need to make their own decisions – based in part on their practical knowledge – regarding which workplans to include in the lesson plans for their own learners. Research is best seen as providing 'tools', the use of which individual teachers must determine for themselves.

The process of teaching

Much of the research reported in this book has focused on the process features of teaching. That is, it has examined the face-to-face interactions that arise as a result of the countless online decisions that teachers make as they teach. Like Allwright, I have treated interaction as 'the fundamental fact of language pedagogy'; lessons are accomplished interactionally. Chapter 4, Chapter 5, Chapter 6 and Chapter 7 all reported research that view language teaching as the 'discourse' that is constructed moment-by-moment as a lesson unfolds. Language learning – whether of the incidental or intentional kind – takes place through 'discourse'. Teachers, however, do not always view teaching in this way. Understandably, they focus more on the 'what' (i.e. the workplans) than on the 'how' (i.e. the interactional processes) of teaching as the former is more amenable to conscious decision-making. One use of research, then, might be to make teachers more aware of the processes that teaching entails. Teacher educators, for example, might make use of the transcriptions of parts of actual lessons to help teachers explore the processes involved when they attempt to implement particular workplans. This, it seems to me, is just as important in initial pre-service training programmes as in more advanced post-service programmes where the use of such transcriptions is perhaps more common. Teachers need an understanding of what is involved when they allocate turns, ask certain types of questions, resort to the use of the L1 (or allow their students to do so), make use of metalanguage, correct their students' errors and so on. They also need an understanding of how the interactions that take place during group work can promote or impede learning. These all involve 'process' features.

However, It is difficult to see how technical knowledge about such processes can be applied during actual teaching. Online decision-making is instant, continuous and dynamic. Teachers do not usually have the time to consult their fund of technical knowledge and thus rely instead on 'fluid interactive thinking and extensive repertoires of routines, curriculum scripts and contingency plans for coping with the complex and unpredictable world of the classroom' (Wette, 2009: 338). In other words, they draw on their practical knowledge of how to interact in the classroom. How then can research about classroom processes assist teachers' teaching?

There are three possible ways. One is to 'train' teachers to utilize specific methodological techniques that have been shown to lead to processes conducive to learning. For example, teachers might be trained to use referential rather than display questions or to allow time for learner uptake after they have corrected an error. There is, however, a fundamental problem with such an approach. Much of the research on discourse processes such as teacher questions has not demonstrated whether or how they enhance learning. Often, there is no agreement among researchers about the learning potential of specific discourse features. See for example the discussion of the initiate–respond–follow up (IRF) pattern of discourse – so common in many classrooms – in Chapter 4. While there is clear evidence that this can restrict learners' opportunity to use the L2, researchers have also made a case for its effectiveness, especially when the follow-up move is conducted in a way that elicits active contributions from the learner. Also, as sociocultural researchers have convincingly argued, it is not possible to identify a set of universal discourse processes that promote learning; interactional support needs to be context-sensitive and tailored to the development of individual learners. In short, training teachers to utilize specific interactional devices holds little promise.

The second approach is to raise teachers' awareness' about the various options available to them in order to encourage reflective practice. This approach seeks to challenge teachers' 'espoused theory' of language teaching (Argyris and Schön, 1974) by presenting them with technical knowledge about teaching and learning. The aim is not immediate behavioural change in the way teachers' teach but the initiation of change in teachers' belief systems by encouraging them to question their existing conceptions of how to teach. The assumption here is that teachers will subsequently seek to adjust their actual practice to bring it in line with their revised beliefs. Technical knowledge from research has a valuable role to play in such awareness-raising.

Here are a set of principles (based on Ellis, 2010c) that can guide such an approach to the use of research for awareness-raising:

Principle 1: The overall goal in teacher education is to assist teachers to develop/modify their own theory of how language teaching can assist learners to learn an L2.

Principle 2: The issues addressed in awareness-raising activities should be those that are perceived by teachers as relevant. Relevant issues are issues that teachers find problematic.

Principle 3: It is preferable to confront teachers with issues raised by the research (e.g. What constitutes appropriate use of the L1 or how to correct learner errors) than present 'models' of how to teach based on theories of language teaching or learning.

Principle 4: The issues should be presented in such a way that they are accessible to teachers (i.e. any readings used should be readable by teachers).

Principle 5: Any research evidence presented to teachers should be derived from classroom-based rather than laboratory-based studies. Such evidence has greater face-validity and is more likely to convince teachers of its practical value.

Principal 6: Teachers can be encouraged to reflect on their own experiences of learning a new language. One way of achieving this is through exposing teachers to mini-lessons designed to expose them to specific pedagogical practices.

Principle 7: Data consisting of transcriptions of classroom interaction illustrating specific process features can be used to develop awareness-raising tasks.

Principle 8: Teachers need opportunities to become researchers in their own classroom as well as consumers of research. This can be achieved in a variety of ways – through collaborative research with a researcher or through action research and exploratory practice.

An example of how these principles can be applied to develop learners' awareness of one particular issue – oral corrective feedback – can be found in the teacher education unit outlined Table 11.1. The aim of such a unit is not 'training' but 'development'. That is, the unit draws on a reflective model of teacher education

Table 11.1 **Example of a teacher education unit designed to raise awareness about a critical issue in language pedagogy**

Topic:	Oral corrective feedback (CF) in the classroom
Aim:	To assist the teachers to examine their own beliefs about oral CF and to develop an explicit theory of CF relevant to their own teaching contexts.
Questionnaire	The teachers complete a questionnaire on CF. The purpose of this is to enable them to state their own beliefs about CF. A secondary purpose is to provide a basis for a final evaluation of the unit by asking the students to complete it a second time after completing the unit.
Text:	Lightbown and Spada (2006) – students complete the teacher questionnaire in this as a preliminary to work on the topic.
Research articles	The teachers read two articles and evaluate the arguments presented in relation to their own classroom. Nobuyoshi, J. and R. Ellis. 1993. Focused communication tasks and second language acquisition. *English Language Teaching Journal* 47: 203–210. Hopkins, D. and M. Nettle. 1994. Second language acquisition research: a response to Rod Ellis. *English Language Teaching Journal* 48: 157–161.
Evaluating 'ideas' about CF	The teachers are presented with guidelines about how to conduct CF in the form of a set of 'ideas' about CF. Each idea is discussed and the teachers are invited to agree, disagree with it or modify it. Examples of the 'ideas': 1. CF works and so teachers should not be afraid to correct students' errors. This is true for both accuracy and fluency work so CF has a place in both. 2. Teachers should ensure that learners know they are being corrected (i.e. they should not attempt to hide the corrective force of their CF moves from the learners).
Awareness-raising task	The teachers are given a number of corrective feedback episodes taken from a communicative language lesson for young adults and are asked to discuss each episode in terms of whether teacher and student appear to have shared goals in each episode, whether the students show awareness they are being corrected, whether the teacher is able to adapt the CF strategies she employs to the needs of the students, whether the students uptake the correction, whether the teacher allows time for this to happen, and whether the students appear anxious or negatively disposed to the correction. They then assess the overall effectiveness of each CF episode.

Table 11.1 (*Continued*)

	Example of CF episode:
	S: I have an ali[bi]
	T: you have what?
	S: an ali[bi]
	T: an alib-? (.2.) An alib[ay]
	S: ali [bay]
	T: okay, listen, listen, alibi
Research project	Teachers are asked to work in groups to plan a proposal for a small action-research project for investigating an aspect of CF of their own choice. They are encouraged to reflect on their own practice as well as researching the literature on CF in order to identify an aspect to investigate.
Evaluation	The teachers complete the questionnaire a second time. The teacher collects in the questionnaires and compares the teachers' responses with their initial responses. Students are shown their initial and final questionnaire and invited to examine whether and how their beliefs about CF have changed. Finally, the students are asked to identify any issues about CF about which they remain uncertain or would like to learn more.

(Wallace, 1991) – the model that I see as best suited for making effective use of research.

There is some evidence of the effectiveness of an awareness-raising approach. Angelova (2005), for example, taught a group of teachers a mini-lesson in Bulgarian – a language they had no prior knowledge of. She reported that although there were no dramatic changes in their beliefs they did modify their views about the role of imitation, which was viewed favourably initially but generally rejected later. The teachers also demonstrated an increased awareness of how learners *feel* when they are learning a new language, in particular the high level of frustration they experience. Angelova noted that the trainees found the mini-lessons more useful than traditional transmission methods of teacher education. Busch (2010) asked teachers to undertake 10 hours of tutoring an English as a second language (ESL) student as part of a course on second language acquisition. She reported clear evidence of changes in the students' beliefs about how an L2 is learned – in particular, with regard to the role that errors play in learning and the length of time it takes to learn an L2. These and other studies suggest that the strategies for awareness-raising referred to in the list of principles in Table 11.1 are effective. However, there are no studies that have investigated whether the changes in teachers' beliefs that result from awareness-raising techniques such as those employed by Angelova and Busch are subsequently reflected in actual practice.

The unit in Table 11.1 also illustrates the third approach for utilizing research in language teaching – the promotion of practitioner research. Practitioner research was discussed in Chapter 2 where I presented two models for conducting such research – the action research model and exploratory practice. As noted in Chapter 2, the key point about practitioner research is that it makes a direct connection between research and practice by encouraging teachers to submit their own practices to critical inspection and in so doing establish technical knowledge of their own.

But teachers do not always find it easy to come up with researchable issues (Nunan, 1990b). One solution to this problem might be for teachers to undertake partial replications of published classroom studies. Vasquez and Harvey (2010), for example, asked teachers enrolled in an applied linguistics course to replicate Lyster and Ranta's (1997) study of corrective feedback (CF). They reported that the replication resulted in changes in the teachers' beliefs about corrective feedback (e.g. they placed less emphasis on the affective dimension of CF) and a greater appreciation of the relationship between CF and uptake. Interestingly, too, the teachers reported that conducting the replication helped them gain access to useful technical knowledge and the terminology for talking about it. They saw it as contributing to their professional development. Replication is, of course, not the only way of engaging in practitioner research. In Chapter 8, I discussed how the micro-evaluation of tasks provided an excellent way for teachers to investigate their own classrooms. Both replication and micro-evaluations of tasks, it should be noted, are based on an awareness-model of teacher development.

Conclusion

Hatch (1978a), in an early article, questioned whether the findings of research were sufficiently robust to warrant application to language teaching and advised 'apply with caution'. Chaudron was less sanguine, despite his reservations about the quality of much of the research. He claimed that 'second language classroom research has an important role to play' and was confident that 'further study of second language classrooms will lead to more concrete knowledge about how to help learners' (p. 192). The classroom research since Chaudron's (1988) book has continued to flourish and has undoubtedly led to 'more concrete knowledge'. However, it is not so much a question of whether the knowledge is 'concrete' enough to apply to language teaching and more a question of how the technical knowledge that research provides can be used to enhance teachers' practical knowledge. As Lightbown (1985a; 2000) noted, research can help teachers develop reasonable expectations about what they can achieve in their teaching, but it cannot be used to tell them how to teach. Classroom research, then, is valuable not because it tells teachers how to teach but because it serves as a resource for raising awareness about teaching and, thereby, for developing reflective practice. In this chapter, I have attempted to outline some of the ways in which classroom research might be used in this way to help teachers.

References

Abbs, B., and I. Freebairn. 1982. *Studying Strategies.* London: Longman.

Abelson, R. 1979. "Differences between Belief Systems and Knowledge Systems." *Cognitive Science* 3: 255–366.

Achiba, M. 2003. *Learning to Request in a Second Language.* Bristol: Multilingual Matters.

Ajzen, I. 1991. "The Theory of Planned Behaviour." *Organizational Behavior and Human Decision Processes.* 50: 179–211.

Alcon, E. 2007. "Incidental Focus On Form, Noticing and Vocabulary Learning in the EFL Classroom." *IRAL* 7: 41–60.

Alcon-Soler, E. 2009. "Focus On Form, Learner Uptake and Subsequent Lexical Gains in Learners' Oral Production." *IRAL* 47: 347–365.

Alderson, J. 1997. "Models of Language? Whose? What For? What Use?" In *Evolving Models of Language*, edited by A. Ryan and A. Wray, 1–22. British Association for Applied Linguistics/Multilingual Matters.

Alderson, J., C. Clapham, and D. Steel. 1997. "Metalinguistic Knowledge, Language Aptitude and Language Proficiency." *Language Teaching Research*, 1: 93–121.

Aljaafreh, A., and J. Lantolf. 1994. "Negative Feedback as Regulation and Second Language Learning in the Zone of Proximal Development." *The Modern Language Journal*, 78: 465–83.

Allen, J. P., M. Fröhlich, and N. Spada. 1984. "The Communicative Orientation of Language Teaching: An Observation Scheme." In *On TESOL '83: The Question of Control*, edited by J. Handscombe, R. Orem, and B. Taylor. Washington DC: TESOL.

Allen, J. P., M. Swain, B. Harley, and J. Cummins. 1990. "Aspects of Classroom Treatment: Toward a More Comprehensive View of Second Language Education." In *The Development of Second Language Proficiency*, edited by B. Harley, J. P. Allen, J. Cummins, and M. Swain. Cambridge: Cambridge University Press.

Allen, L. 2000. "Form-Meaning Connections and the French Causative: An Experiment in Input Processing." *Studies in Second Language Acquisition*, 22: 69–84.

Language Teaching Research & Language Pedagogy, First Edition. Rod Ellis.

Allwright, D. 1988. *Observation in the Language Classroom.* London: Longman.

Allwright, D. 2003. "Exploratory Practice: Rethinking Practitioner Research in Language Teaching." *Language Teaching Research*, 7: 113–141.

Allwright, D. 2005. "From Teaching Points to Learning Opportunities and Beyond." *TESOL Quarterly*, 39: 9–31.

Allwright, D. 2007. "Introduction: Practitioner Research." *Language Teaching Research*, 11: 223.

Allwright, D., and K. Bailey. 1991. *Focus on the Language Classroom: An Introduction to Classroom Research for Language Teachers.* Cambridge: Cambridge University Press.

Allwright, R. 1975. "Problems in the Study of the Language Teacher's Treatment of Learner Error." In *On TESOL '75: New Directions in Language Learning, Teaching, and Bilingual Education*, edited by M. Burt and H. Dulay, 96–109. Washington, DC: TESOL.

Allwright, R. 1980. "Turns, Topics and Tasks: Patterns of Participation in Language Teaching and Learning." In *Discourse Analysis in Second Language Research*, edited by D. Larsen-Freeman. Rowley, MA: Newbury House.

Allwright, R. 1983. "Classroom-Centered Research on Language Teaching and Learning: A Brief Historical Overview." *TESOL Quarterly*, 17: 191–204.

Allwright, R. 1984. "The Importance of Interaction in Classroom Language Learning." *Applied Linguistics*, 5: 156–71.

Ammar, A. 2008. "Prompts and Recasts: Differential Effects on Second Language Morphosyntax." *Language Teaching Research*, 12: 183–210.

Ammar, A., and P. Lightbown. 2006. "Teaching Marked Linguistic Structures – More about the Acquisition of Relative Clauses by Arab Learners of English." In *Investigations in Instructed Second Language Acquisition*, edited by A. Housen and M. Pierrard, 168–198. Berlin: Mouton de Gruyter.

Ammar, A., and N. Spada. 2006. "One Size Fits All? Recasts, Prompts, and L2 Learning." *Studies in Second Language Acquisition*, 28: 543–74.

Ando, J., N. Fukanaga, J. Kurahashi et al. 1992. "A Comparative Study of the Two EFL Methods: The Communicative and the Grammatical Approach." *Japanese Journal of Educational Psychology*, 40: 247–256.

Andrews, S. 1999. "'All These Like Little Name Things': A Comparative Study of Language Teachers' Explicit Knowledge of Grammar and Grammatical Terminology." *Language Awareness*, 8: 143–59.

Angelova, M. 2005. Using Bulgarian Mini-Lessons in an SLA Course to Improve the KAL of American ESL Teachers. In *Applied Linguistics and Teacher Education: Vol. 4 Educational Linguistics*, edited by N. Bartels. New York: Springer.

Anton, M. 1999. "The Discourse of a Learner-Centred Classroom: Sociocultural Perspectives on Teacher-Learner Interaction in the Second-Language Classroom." *The Modern Language Journal*, 83: 303–318.

Anton, M., and F. DiCamilla. 1998. "Socio-Cognitive Functions of Ll Collaborative Interaction in the L2 Classroom". *The Canadian Modern Language Review*, 54: 314–42.

Anton, M., and F. DiCamilla. 1999. "Socio-Cognitive Functions of L1 Collaborative Interaction in the L2 Classroom." *Modern Language Journal*, 83: 233–247.

Argyris, C., and D. Schön. 1974. *Theory in Practice: Increasing Professional Effectiveness.* San Francisco: Jossey-Bass.

Arslanyilmaz, A., and S. Pedersen. 2010. "Improving Language Production Using Subtitled Similar Task Videos." *Language Teaching Research*, 14, 4.

Artigal, J. 1992. "Some Considerations on Why a New Language is Acquired by Being Used." *International Journal of Applied Linguistics*, 2: 221–40.

Asher, J. 1972. "Children's First Language as a Model for Second Language Learning." *The Modern Language Journal* 56, 3: 133–39.

Asher, J. 1977. *Learning Another Language Through Actions: The Complete Teachers' Guidebook*. Los Gatos, CA: Sky Oaks Publications.

Asher, J. 1981. "The Total Physical Response: Theory and Practice." *Annals of the New York Academy of Sciences*, 379: 324–331.

Asher, J., J. Kusado, and R. de la Torre. 1974. "Learning a Second Language through Commands: The Second Field Test." *The Modern Language Journal*, 35: 27–30.

Atkinson, D. 1987. "The Mother Tongue in the Classroom: A Neglected Resource." *ELT Journal* 41: 241–47.

Atkinson, D. 2002. "Toward a Sociocognitive Approach to Second Language Acquisition." *The Modern Language Journal*, 86: 525–45.

Auerbach, E. 1993. "Reexamining English Only in the ESL Classroom." *TESOL Quarterly*, 27: 9–32.

Baddeley, A. D. 2003. "Working Memory and Language: An Overview." *Journal of Communication Disorders*, 36: 189–208.

Bailey, K. 1983. "Competitiveness and Anxiety in Adult Second Language Learning: Looking at and Through the Diary Studies." In *Classroom-Oriented Research in Second Language Acquisition*, edited by H. Seliger and M. Long. Rowley, MA: Newbury House.

Baleghizadeh, S. 2010. "Focus on Form in an EFL Communicative Classroom." *Novitas-ROYAL (Research on Youth and Language)*, 4: 119–128.

Banbrook, L. 1987. "Questions About Questions: An Inquiry Into The Study Of Teachers' Questioning Behaviour In ESL Classrooms." *TESOL Quarterly*, 20: 47–59.

Banbrook, L., and P. Skehan. 1990. "Classroom and Display Questions." In *Research in the Language Classroom. ELT Documents 133*, edited by C. Brumfit and R. Mitchell. London: Modern English Publications.

Baralt, M., and L. Gurzynski-Weiss. 2011. "Comparing Learners' State Anxiety during Task-Based Interaction in Computer-Mediated and Face-to-Face Communication." *Language Teaching Research*, 15, 2.

Barkhuizen, G. 2009. "Topics, Aims and Constraints in English Teacher Research: A Chinese Case Study." *TESOL Quarterly*, 43: 113–125.

Barnes, D. 1969. "Language in the Secondary Classroom. In *Language, the Learner and the School*, edited by D. Barnes, J. Britton, and M. Torbe. Harmondsworth: Penguin.

Barnes, D. 1976. *From Communication to Curriculum*. Harmondsworth: Penguin.

Basturkmen, H., S. Loewen, and R. Ellis. 2002. "Metalanguage in Focus on Form in the Communicative Classroom." *Language Awareness*, 11: 1–13.

Basturkmen, H., S. Loewen, and R. Ellis. 2004. "Teachers' Stated Beliefs about Incidental Focus on Form and their Classroom Practices." *Applied Linguistics*, 25: 243–272.

Batstone, R. 2002. "Contexts of Engagement: A Discourse Perspective on "Intake" and "Pushed Output"." *System*, 30: 1–14.

Batstone, R., and R. Ellis. 2008. Principled Grammar Teaching. *System,* 37: 194–204.

Beck, T. 1951. "An Experiment in Teaching French by the Oral-Cultural Approach Method." *The Modern Language Journal,* 35: 595–601.

Bell, N. 2009. "Learning about and through Humor in the Second Language Classroom." *Language Teaching Research*, 13: 241–258.

Bellack, A., A. Herbert, M. Kliebard et al. 1966. *The Language of the Classroom*. New York: Teachers College Press.

Belz, J., and C. Kinginger. 2003. "Discourse Options and the Development of Pragmatic Competence by Classroom Learners of German: The Case of Address Forms." *Language Learning*, 53: 591–657.

Benati, A. 2004. "The Effects of Structured Input Activities And Explicit Information on The Acquisition of Italian Future Tense." In *Processing Instruction: Theory, Research, and Commentary*, edited by B. VanPatten. Mahwah, NJ: Lawrence Erlbaum.

Bennett, F. 1917. "Translation Study and Immediate Study of German, A Comparison." *Modern Language Journal*, 2: 114–131.

Beretta, A. 1986. "Program-Fair Language Teaching Evaluation." *TESOL Quarterly*, 20: 431–444.

Beretta, A., and A. Davies. 1985. Evaluation of the Bangalore Project. *ELT Journal*, 39: 121–7.

Berry, M. 1981. "Systemic Linguistics and Discourse Analysis: A Multi-Layered Approach to Exchange Structure." In *Studies in Discourse Analysis*, edited by M. Coulthard and M. Montgomery. London: Routledge and Kegan Paul.

Berry, R. 2005. "Making the Most of Interlanguage." *Language Awareness*, 14: 3–20.

Berry, R. 2009. "EFL Majors' Knowledge of Metalinguistic Terminology: A Comparative Study." *Language Awareness*, 18: 113–128.

Bialystok, E. 1985. "The Compatibility of Teaching and Learning Strategies." *Applied Linguistics*, 6, 3: 255–62.

Bitchener, J., and U. Knoch. 2008. "The Value of Written Corrective Feedback for Migrant And International Students." *Language Teaching Research*, 3: 409–31.

Bley-Vroman, R. 1983. "The Comparative Fallacy in Interlanguage Studies: The Case of Systematicity." *Language Learning* 33: 1–17.

Blickenstaff, C., and E. Woerdehoff. 1967. "A Comparison of Monostructural and Dialogue Approaches to the Teaching of College Spanish." *Modern Language Journal*, 51: 14–23.

Bloom, M. 2007. "Tensions in a Non-Traditional Classroom." *Language Teaching Research*, 11: 85–102.

Borg, S. 1998. "Teachers' Pedagogical Systems and Grammar Teaching; A Qualitative Study." *TESOL Quarterly*, 32: 9–38.

Borg, S. 1999. "The Use of Grammatical Terminology in the Second Language Classroom." *Applied Linguistics*, 20: 95–126.

Borg, S. 2003. "Teacher Cognition in Grammar Teaching: A Literature Review." *Language Awareness*, 2: 96–108.

Borg, S. 2009a. "English Language Teachers' Conceptions of Research." *Applied Linguistics*, 30: 358–88.

Borg, S. 2009b. "Introducing Language Teacher Cognition." http://wwww.education.leeds.ac.uk/people/staff.php?staff=29 (accessed 1 August, 2010).

Boston, J. 2010. "Pre-Task Syntactic Priming and Focused Task Design." *ELT Journal*, 64: 165–174.

Boyd, M. and V. Maloof. 2000. "How Teachers Can Build on Student-Proposed Intertextual Links to Facilitate Student Talk in the ESL Classroom." In *Second and Foreign Language Learning through Classroom Interaction*, edited by J. Hall and L. Verplaetse. Mahwah, NJ: Lawrence Erlbaum.

Boyd-Bowman, P., B. Flickinger, A. Papalia, and K. Rasmusen. 1973. A Comparative Study in the Teaching of Spanish through Team-Teaching and Supervised Independent Study." *Modern Language Journal*, 57: 199–201.

Breen, M. 1989. "The Evaluation Cycle for Language Learning Tasks." In *The Second Language Curriculum*, edited by R. K. Johnson. Cambridge: Cambridge University Press.

Breen, M., ed. 2001. *Learner Contributions to Language Learning: New Directions in Research*. Harlow: Pearson Education.

Brock, C. 1986. "The Effects of Referential Questions on ESL Classroom Discourse." *TESOL Quarterly*, 20: 47–8.

Broner, M. 2001. "Impact of Interlocutor and Task on First and Second Language Use in a Spanish Immersion Program." *CARLA Working Paper #18*. Minneapolis, MN: Center for Advanced Research on Language Acquisition.

Broner, M., and E. Tarone. 2001. "Is It Fun? Language Play in a Fifth-Grade Spanish Immersion Classroom." *Modern Language Journal*, 85: 363–79.

Brooks, F., and R. Donato. 1994. "Vygotskyan Approaches to Understanding Foreign Language Learner Discourse during Communicative Tasks." *Hispania*, 77: 262–74.

Brown, J. 1988. *Understanding Research in Second Language*. Cambridge: Cambridge University Press.

Brown, J., and T. Rogers. 2002. *Doing Second Language Research*. New York: Oxford.

Brown, R. 1991. "Group Work, Task Difference, and Second Language Acquisition." *Applied Linguistics*, 21: 1–12.

Brown, T., and F. Perry. 1991. "A Comparison of Three Learning Strategies for ESL Vocabulary Acquisition." *TESOL Quarterly*, 25: 655–70.

Brumfit, C., and K. Johnson. 1979. *The Communicative Approach to Language Teaching*. Oxford: Oxford University Press.

Brumfit, C., and R. Mitchell, eds. 1990. *Research in the Language Classroom. ELT Documents 133*. Modern English Publications.

Brumfit, C., R. Mitchell, and J. Hooper. 1996. "'Grammar', 'Language' and 'Practice'." In *Teaching and Learning in Changing Times*, edited by M. Hughes. Oxford: Blackwell.

Burns, A. 2005. "Action Research." In *Handbook of Research in Second Language Teaching and Learning*, edited by E. Hinkel, 241–250. Mahwah, NJ: Lawrence Erlbaum.

Burns, A. 2009. *Doing Action Research in English Language Teaching. A Guide for Practitioners*. New York: Routledge.

Busch, D. 2010. "Pre-Service Teacher Beliefs about Language Learning: The Second Language Acquisition Course as an Agent for Change." *Language Teaching Research*, 14, 3.

Bushnell. C. 2008. "'Lego my Keego!': An Analysis of Language Play in a Beginning Japanese as a Foreign Language Classroom." *Applied Linguistics*, 30: 49–69.

Butler, Y. G. 2002. "Second Language Learners' Theories on the use of English Articles: An Analysis of the Metalinguistic Knowledge used by Japanese Students in Acquiring the English Article System." *Studies in Second Language Acquisition*, 24, 451–480.

Bye, A. 1991. "Classroom Research: Message-Oriented and Medium-Oriented Discourse." *LSU Bulletin*, 2: 7–19.

Bygate, M. 1988. "Units of Oral Expression and Language Learning in Small Group Interaction." *Applied Linguistics*, 9: 59–82.

Bygate, M., P. Skehan, and M. Swain, eds. 2001. *Researching Pedagogic Tasks, Second Language Learning, Teaching and Testing*. Harlow: Longman.

Canale, M., and M. Swain. 1980. "Theoretical Bases of Communicative Approaches to Second Language Teaching and Testing." *Applied Linguistics*, 1: 1-47.

Cancino, H., E. Rosansky, and J. Schumann. 1978. "The Acquisition of English Negatives and Interrogatives by Native Spanish Speakers." In *Second Language Acquisition*, edited by E. Hatch. Rowley, MA: Newbury House.

Cao, Y. 2009. *Understanding the Notion of Interdependence, and the Dynamics of Willingness to Communicate*. Unpublished PhD Thesis, University of Auckland.

Cao, Y., and J. Philp. 2006. "Interactional Context and Willingness to Communicate: A Comparison of Behaviour in Whole Class, Group and Dyadic Interaction." *System*, 34: 480–93.

Carless, D. 2004. "Issues in Teachers' Reinterpretation of a Task-Based Innovation in Primary Schools." *TESOL Quarterly*, 38: 639–662.

Carr, W., and S. Kemmis. 1986. *Becoming Critical: Education, Knowledge and Action Research*. London: The Falmer Press.

Carroll, J. 1981. "Twenty-Five Years in Foreign Language Aptitude." In *Individual Differences and Universals in Language Learning Aptitude*, edited by K. Diller. Rowley, MA: Newbury House.

Carroll, J., and S. Sapon. 1959. *Modern Language Aptitude Test – Form A*. New York: The Psychological Corporation.

Cathcart, R. 1986. "Situational Differences and the Sampling of Young Children's School Language." In *Talking to Learn: Conversation in Second Language Acquisition* edited by R. Day. Rowley, MA: Newbury House.

Cekaite, A. 2007. "A Child's Development of Interactional Competence in a Swedish L2 Classroom." *Modern Language Journal*, 91: 45–62.

Centano-Cortes, B., and A. Jimenez-Jimenez. 2004. "Problem-Solving Tasks in a Foreign Language: The Importance of the L1 in Private Verbal Thinking." *International Journal of Applied Linguistics*, 14: 7–35.

Chambers, G. 1993. "Taking the 'De' Out of De-Motivation." *Language Learning Journal*, 7: 13–16.

Chamot, A. 2001. "The Role of Learning Strategies in Second Language Acquisition." In *Learner Contributions to Language Learning: New Directions in Research*, edited by M. Breen. Harlow: Longman.

Chaudron, C. 1977. "A Descriptive Model of Discourse in the Corrective Treatment of Learners' Errors." *Language Learning*, 27: 29–46.

Chaudron, C. 1988. *Second Language Classrooms: Research on Teaching and Learning*. Cambridge: Cambridge University Press.

Chaudron, C. 2001. "Progress in Language Classroom Research: Evidence from the *Modern Language Journal*, 1916–2000." *Modern Language Journal*, 85: 57–76.

Clapham, C. 2001. "The Assessment Of Metalinguistic Knowledge." In *Experiencing with uncertainty: Essays in honour of Alan Davies*, edited by C. Elder, A. Brown, E. Grove et al. 31–41. Cambridge: Cambridge University Press.

Clark J. 1969. "The Pennsylvania Project and the 'Audio-Lingual vs. Traditional' Question." *Modern Language Journal*, 53: 388–96.

Cochran-Smith, M., and S. L. Lytle. 1999. "Relationships of Knowledge of Practice: Teacher Learning in Communities." *Review of Research in Education*, 24: 249–305.

Cohen, A. 1982. "Writing Like a Native: The Process of Reformulation." *ERIC ED*, 224–338.

Collentine, K. 2009. "Learner Use of Holistic Language Units in Multimodal, Task-Based Synchronous Computer-Mediated Communication." *Language Learning and Technology*, 13: 68–87.

Coniam, D., and P. Falvey. 2002. "Selecting Models and Setting Standards for Teachers of English in Hong Kong." *Journal of Asian Pacific Communication*, 12, 1: 13–38.

Consolo, A. 2000. "Teachers' Action and Student Oral Participation in Classroom Interaction." In *Second and Foreign Language Learning Through Classroom Interaction*, edited by J. Hall and L. Verplaetse. Mahwah, NJ: Lawrence Erbaum.

Cook, G. 1997. "Language Play, Language Learning." *ELT Journal*, 51: 224–231.

Cook, V. 2001. "Using the First Language in the Classroom." *Canadian Modern Language Review*, 57: 402–23.

Corder, S. P. 1967. "The Significance of Learners' Errors." *International Review of Applied Linguistics*, 5: 161–9.

Corder, S. P. 1976. "The Study of Interlanguage." In Proceedings of the Fourth International Conference of Applied Linguistics. Munich, Hochschulverlag.

Coughlan, P., and P. A. Duff. 1994. "Same Task, Different Activities: Analysis of a SLA Task from an Activity Theory Perspective." In *Vygotskian Approaches to Second Language Research*. edited by J. Lantolf and G. Appel, 173–194. Norwood, NJ: Ablex.

Coulthard, M. 1977. *An Introduction to Discourse Analysis*. Harlow: Longman.

Creese, A., and A. Blackledge. 2010. "Translanguaging in the Bilingual Classroom: A Pedagogy for Learning and Teaching." *Modern Language Journal*, 94: 103–115.

Cronbach, L., and R. Snow. 1977. *Aptitudes and Instructional Methods: A Handbook for Research on Interactions*. New York: Irvington.

Crookes, G. 1993. "Action Research for Second Language Teachers: Going Beyond Teacher Research." *Applied Linguistics*, 14: 130–144.

Cullen, R. 1998. "Teacher-Talk and the Classroom Context." *ELT Journal*, 52: 179–87.

Cummins, J. 2005. "A Proposal for Action: Strategies for Recognizing Heritage Language Competence as a Learning Resource within the Mainstream Classroom." *Modern Language Journal*, 89: 585–592.

Daneman, M., and P. Carpenter. 1980. "Individual Differences in Working Memory and Reading." *Journal of Verbal Learning and Verbal Behavior*, 19: 450–466.

de Graaff, R. and Housen, A. (2009) "Investigating the Effects and Effectiveness of L2 Instruction." In *The Handbook of Language Teaching*, edited by M. Long and C. Doughty. Oxford: Blackwell Publishing, 726–55.

De Jong, N. 2005. "Can Second Language Grammar be Learned through Listening? An Experimental Study." *Studies in Second Language Acquisition* 27: 205–234.

De la Colina, A., and P. Mayo. 2009. "Oral Interaction in Task-Based RFL Learning: The Use of the L1 as a Cognitive Tool." *IRAL*, 47: 325–45.

De la Fuente, M. 2002. "Negotiation and Oral Acquisition of L2 Vocabulary: The Roles of Input and Output in the Receptive and Productive Acquisition of Words." *Studies in Second Language Acquisition*, 24: 81–112.

De la Fuente, M. 2006. "Classroom L2 Vocabulary Acquisition: Investigating the Role of Pedagogical Tasks and Form-Focused Instruction." *Language Teaching Research*, 10: 263–95.

De Ridder, I., L. Vangehuchten, and M. Gomez. 2007. "Enhancing Automaticity through Task-Based Language Learning." *Applied Linguistics*, 28: 309–15.

Deci, E. L., and R. M. Ryan. 1985. *Intrinsic Motivation and Self-Determination in Human Behavior*. New York: Plenum Press.

DeKeyser, R. 1995. "Learning Second Language Grammar Rules: An Experiment with a Miniature Linguistic System." *Studies in Second Language Acquisition*, 17: 379–410.

DeKeyser, R. 1998. "Beyond Focus on Form: Cognitive Perspectives on Learning and Practicing Second Language Grammar." In *Focus on Form in Classroom Second Language Acquisition* edited by C. Doughty and J. Williams. Cambridge: Cambridge University Press.

DeKeyser, R. 2003. "Implicit and Explicit Learning. In *Handbook of Second Language Acquisition*, edited by C. Doughty and M. Long. Malden, MA: Blackwell.

DeKeyser, R. 2007. "Introduction: Situating the Concept of Practice." In *Practice in a Second Language*, edited by R. DeKeyser. Cambridge: Cambridge University Press.

DeKeyser, R., and K. Sokalski. 1996. "The Differential Role of Comprehension and Production Practice." *Language Learning*, 46: 613–42.

DeKeyser, R., R. Salaberry, P. Robinson, and M. Robinson. 2002. "What Gets Processed in Processing Instruction? A Commentary on Bill VanPatten's 'Processing Instruction: An Update'". *Language Learning*, 52: 805–24.

Delaney, T. 2009. *Individual Differences, Participation, and Language Acquisition in Communicative EFL Classes in a Japanese University*. Unpublished PhD Thesis, University of Auckland, Auckland.

Di Pietro, R. J. 1987. *Strategic Interaction*. Cambridge: Cambridge University Press.

DiCamilla, F., and M. Anton. 1997. "The Function of Repetition in the Collaborative Discourse of L2 Learners." *The Canadian Modern Language Review*, 53: 609–33.

Diller, K. 1978. *The Language Teaching Controversy*. Rowley, MA: Newbury House.

Dillon, J. 1997. "Questions." In *The Handbook of Communication Skills: Second Edition*, edited by O. Hargie, 103–133. New York: Routledge.

Dipano, B., and R. Job. 1991. "A Methodological Review of Studies of SALT (Suggestive-Accelerative Learning and Teaching) Techniques." *Australian Journal of Educational Technology* 7: 127–43.

Donato, R. 1994. "Collective Scaffolding in Second Language Learning." In *Vygotskian Approaches to Second Language Research*, edited by J. Lantolf and G. Appel. Norwood, NJ: Ablex.

Donato, R. 2000. "Sociocultural Contributions to Understanding the Foreign and Second Language Classroom." In *Sociocultural Theory and Second Language Learning*, edited by J. Lantolf. Oxford: Oxford University Press.

Dörnyei Z. 1998. "De-Motivation in Foreign Language Learning." Paper presented at the TESOL '98 Congress, Seattle, USA.

Dörnyei, Z. 2001. *Motivational Strategies in the Language Classroom*. Cambridge: Cambridge University Press.

Dörnyei, Z. 2002. "The Motivational Basis of Language Learning Tasks." In *Individual Differences in L2 Learning*, edited by P. Robinson, 137–158. Amsterdam: John Benjamins.

Dörnyei, Z. 2005. *The Psychology of the Language Learner: Individual Differences in Second Language Acquisition*. Mahwah, NJ: Lawrence Erlbaum.

Dörnyei, Z. 2007. *Research Methods in Applied Linguistics*. Oxford: Oxford University Press.

Dörnyei, Z. 2009. *The Psychology of Second Language Acquisition*. Oxford: Oxford University Press.

Dörnyei, Z., and J. Kormos. 2000. "The Role of Individual and Social Variables in Oral Task Performance." *Language Teaching Research*, 4: 275–300.

Dörnyei, Z., and K. Csizér. 1998. "Ten Commandments for Motivating Language Learners: Results of an Empirical Study." *Language Teaching Research* 2, 3: 203–29.

Doughty, C. 1991. "Second Language Instruction Does Make a Difference: Evidence from an Empirical Study on SL Relativization." *Studies in Second Language Acquisition*, 13: 431–69.

Doughty, C. 2001. "Cognitive Underpinnings of Focus on Form." In *Cognition and Second Language Instruction*, edited by P. Robinson. Cambridge: Cambridge University Press.

Doughty, C., and E. Varela. 1998. "Communicative Focus-on-Form." In *Focus-on-Form in Classroom Second Language Acquisition*, edited by C. Doughty and J. Williams. Cambridge: Cambridge University Press.

Doughty, C., and J. Williams, eds. 1998. *Focus-on-Form in Classroom Second Language Acquisition*. Cambridge: Cambridge University Press.

Duff, P. 2000. "Repetition in Foreign Language Classroom Interaction." In *Second and Foreign Language Learning through Classroom Interaction*, edited by J. Hall and L. Verplaetse. Mahwah, NJ: Lawrence Erlbaum.

Duff, P. 2002. "The Discursive Co-Costruction of Knowledge, Identity, and Difference: An Ethnography of Communication in the High School Mainstream." *Applied Linguistics*, 22: 289–322.

Duff, P. 2003. "New Directions in Second Language Socialization Research." In Proceedings of the 2003 KASELL International Conference, Seoul, Korea.

Duff, P. 2007. "Qualitative Approaches to Classroom Research with English Language Learners." In *International Handbook of English Language Teaching*, edited by J. Cummins and C. Davison. Philadelphia: Kluwer.

Duff, P., and C. Polio. 1990. "How Much Foreign Language Is There in the Foreign Language Classroom?" *Modern Language Journal*, 74: 154–66.

Dulay, H., and M. Burt. 1973. "Should We Teach Children Syntax?" *Language Learning*, 23: 245–58.

Duran, G., and G. Ramaut. 2006. "Tasks for Absolute Beginners and Beyond: Developing and Sequencing Tasks at Basic Proficiency Levels." In *Task-Based Language Education: From Theory to Practice*, edited by K. Van den Branden, 47–75. Cambridge: Cambridge University Press.

Early, M. 1985. *Input and Interaction in Content Classrooms: Foreigner Talk and Teacher Talk in Classroom Discourse*. Unpublished PhD dissertation, University of California at Los Angeles. (Cited in Chaudron, 1988.)

Eckerth, J. 2008a. "Task-Based Language Learning and Teaching – Old Wine in New Bottles?" In *Task-Based Language Learning and Teaching: Theoretical, Methodological, and Pedagogical Perspectives*, edited by J. Eckerth and S. Siekmann, 13–46. Frankfurt am Main: Peter Lang.

Eckerth, J. 2008b. "Task-Based Learner Interaction: Investigating Learning Opportunities, Learning Processes, and Learning Outcomes." In *Task-Based Language Learning and Teaching: Theoretical, Methodological, and Pedagogical Perspectives*, edited by J. Eckerth and S. Siekmann. Frankfurt am Main, Peter Lang.

Eckman, F., L. Bell, and D. Nelson. 1988. "On the Generalization of Relative Clause Instruction in The Acquisition of English as a Second Language." *Applied Linguistics*, 9: 1–20.

Edge, J. (1989). *Mistakes and Correction*. Harlow: Longman.

Edmondson, W. 1985. "Discourse Worlds in the Classroom and in Foreign Language." *Studies in Second Language Acquisition*, 7: 159–68.

Edstrom, A. 2006. "L1 Use in the L2 Classroom: One Teacher's Self-Evaluation." *Canadian Modern Language Review*, 63: 275–92.

Edstrom, A. 2009. "Teacher Reflection as a Strategy for Evaluating L1/L2 Use in the Classroom." *Babylonia*, 1: 12–15.

Edwards, C., and J. Willis, eds. 2005. *Teachers Exploring Tasks in English Language Teaching*. Basingstoke, Palgrave Macmillan.

Egbert, J. 2003. "A Study of Flow Theory in the Foreign Language Classroom." *Modern Language Journal*, 87: 499–518.

Ehrlich, S., P. Avery, and C. Yorio. 1989. "Discourse Structure and the Negotiation of Comprehensible Input." *Studies in Second Language Acquisition*, 11: 397–414.

Elder, C. 2009. "Validating a Test of Metalinguistic Knowledge." In *Implicit and Explicit Knowledge in Second Language Learning, Testing and Teaching*, edited by R. Ellis, S. Loewen, C. Elder et al., 113–138. Bristol: Multilingual Matters.

Elder, C., J. Warren, J. Hajek et al. 1999. "Metalinguistic Knowledge: How Important is it in Studying at University?" *Australian Review of Applied Linguistics*, 22: 81–95.

Ellis, N. 1996. "Sequencing in SLA: Phonological Memory, Chunking, and Points of Order" *Studies in Second Language Acquisition*, 18: 91–126.

Ellis, N. 2001. "Memory for Language." In *Cognition and Second Language Instruction*, edited by P. Robinson. Cambridge: Cambridge University Press.

Ellis, N. 2002. "Frequency Effects in Language Processing: A Review with Implications for Theories of Implicit and Explicit Language Acquisition." *Studies in Second Language Acquisition*, 24: 143–88.

Ellis, R. 1984a. *Classroom Second Language Development*. Oxford: Pergamon.

Ellis, R. 1984b. "Can Syntax Be Taught? A Study of the Effects of Formal Instruction on the Acquisition of WH Questions by Children." *Applied Linguistics*, 5: 138–55.

Ellis, R. 1984c. "Formulaic Speech in Early Classroom Second Language Development." In *On TESOL '83: The Question of Control*, edited by J. Handscombe, R. Orem, and B. Taylor. Washington DC: TESOL.

Ellis, R. 1985. "Teacher–Pupil Interaction in Second Language Development" In *Input in Second Language Acquisition*, edited by S. Gass and C. Madden. Rowley, MA: Newbury House.

Ellis, R. 1988. "The Role of Practice in Classroom Language Learning." *AILA Review*, 5: 20–39.

Ellis, R. 1990. *Instructed Second Language Acquisition*. Oxford: Blackwell.

Ellis, R. 1992. "Learning to Communicate in the Classroom." *Studies in Second Language Acquisition*, 14: 1–23.

Ellis, R. 1994. "A Theory of Instructed Second Language Acquisition." In *Implicit and Explicit Learning of Languages*, edited by N. Ellis. San Diego: Academic Press.

Ellis, R. 1995a. "Modified Input and the Acquisition of Word Meanings." *Applied Linguistics*, 16: 409–41.

Ellis, R. 1995b. "Uptake as Language Awareness." *Language Awareness*, 4: 147–60.

Ellis, R. 1997a. *SLA Research and Language Teaching*. Oxford: Oxford University Press.

Ellis, R. 1997b. "The Empirical Evaluation of Language Teaching Materials." *ELT Journal*, 51: 36-42.

Ellis, R. 1998a. "Teaching and Research: Options in Grammar Teaching." *TESOL Quarterly*, 32: 39–60.

Ellis, R. 1998b. "The Evaluation of Communicative Tasks." In *Materials Development in Language Teaching*, edited by B. Tomlinson, 217–38. Cambridge: Cambridge University Press.

Ellis, R. 1999. *Learning a Second Language through Interaction*. Amsterdam: John Benjamin.

Ellis, R. 2000. "Task-based Research and Language Pedagogy." *Language Teaching Research*, 4: 193–220.

Ellis, R. 2001a. "Investigating Form-Focused Instruction." In *Form-Focused Instruction and Second Language Learning*, edited by R. Ellis. Malden, MA: Blackwell.

Ellis, R. 2001b. "Non-Reciprocal Tasks, Comprehension and Second Language Acquisition." In *Researching Pedagogic Tasks, Second Language Learning, Teaching and Testing*, edited by M. Bygate, P. Skehan, and M. Swain, 49–74. Harlow: Longman.

Ellis, R. 2002. "Does Form-Focused Instruction Affect the Acquisition of Implicit Knowledge? A Review of The Research." *Studies in Second Language Acquisition*, 24: 223–36.

Ellis, R. 2003. *Task-based Language Learning and Teaching*. Oxford: Oxford University Press.

Ellis, R. 2004. "The Definition and Measurement of L2 Explicit Knowledge." *Language Learning*, 54: 227–75.

Ellis, R. 2005a. "Measuring Implicit and Explicit Knowledge of a Second Language: A Psychometric Study." *Studies in Second Language Acquisition*, 27: 141–72.

Ellis, R. 2005b. *Planning and Task-Performance in a Second Language*. Amsterdam: John Benjamins.

Ellis, R. 2006. "Current Issues in the Teaching of Grammar: An SLA Perspective." *TESOL Quarterly*, 40: 83–108.

Ellis, R. 2007. "The Differential Effects of Corrective Feedback on Two Grammatical Structures." In *Conversational interaction and Second Language Acquisition: A Series of Empirical Studies*, edited by A. Mackey. Oxford: Oxford University Press.

Ellis, R. 2008. *The Study of Second Language Acquisition*. Second Edition. Oxford: Oxford University Press.

Ellis, R. 2009. "Task-Based Language Teaching: Sorting Out the Misunderstandings." *International Journal of Applied Linguistics*, 19, 3: 222–46.

Ellis, R. 2010a. "Second Language Acquisition Research and Language Teaching Materials." In *Materials in ELT: Theory and Practice*, edited by N. Harwood, 33–57. Cambridge: Cambridge University Press.

Ellis, R. 2010b. "Theoretical Pluralism in SLA: Is There a Way Forward?" In *Conceptualising 'Learning' In Applied Linguistics*, edited by P. Seedhouse, S. Walsh and C. Jenks. Basingstoke: Palgrave Macmillan.

Ellis, R. 2010c. "Second Language Acquisition, Teacher Education and Language Pedagogy." *Language Teaching*, 43, 2: 182–201.

Ellis, R. 2011. "Macro- and Micro-Evaluations of Task-Based Teaching." In *Materials Development in Language Teaching*, edited by B. Tomlinson, 212–35. Cambridge: Cambridge University Press.

Ellis, R., and G. Barkhuizen. 2005. *Analyzing Learner Language*. Oxford: Oxford University Press.

Ellis, R., and G. Wells. 1980. "Enabling Factors in Adult-Child Discourse." *First Language*, 1: 46–82.

Ellis, R., and M. Rathbone. (1987). The Acquisition of German in a Classroom Context. Mimeograph, London: Ealing College of Higher Education.

Ellis, R., and R. Heimbach. 1997. "Bugs and Birds: Children's Acquisition of Second Language Vocabulary through Interaction." *System*, 25: 247–59.

Ellis, R., and X. He. 1999. "The Roles of Modified Input and Output in the Incidental Acquisition of Word Meanings." *Studies in Second Language Acquisition*, 21: 285–301.

Ellis, R., H. Basturkmen, and S. Loewen. 2001. "Learner Uptake in Communicative ESL Lessons." *Language Learning*, 51: 281–318.

Ellis, R., H. Basturkmen, and S. Loewen. 2002. "Doing Focus on Form." *System*, 30: 419–32.

Ellis, R., S. Loewen, and H. Basturkmen. 1999. "Focusing on Form in the Classroom." *Occasional Paper 13*. Institute of Language Learning and Teaching, University of Auckland.

Ellis, R., S. Loewen, and R. Erlam. 2006. "Implicit and Explicit Corrective Feedback and the Acquisition of L2 Grammar." *Studies in Second Language Acquisition*, 28: 339–68.

Ellis, R., Y. Tanaka, and A. Yamazaki. 1994. "Classroom Interaction, Comprehension and the Acquisition of Word Meanings." *Language Learning*, 44: 449–91.

Eraut, M. 1994. *Developing Professional Knowledge and Competence*. London: Falmer.

Erickson, F., and G. Mohatt. 1982. "Cultural Organization of Participation Structures in Two Classrooms of Indian Students." In *Doing the Ethnography of Schooling*, edited by G. Spindler, 132–74. New York: CBS College Publishing.

Erlam, R. 2003. "Evaluating the Relative Effectiveness of Structured-Input and Output-Based Instruction in Foreign Language Learning: Results from an Experimental Study." *Studies in Second Language Acquisition*, 25: 559–82.

Erlam, R. 2005. "Language Aptitude and Its Relationship to Instructional Effectiveness in Second Language Acquisition." *Language Teaching Research*, 9: 147–72.

Erlam, R. 2006. "Elicited Imitation as a Measure of L2 Implicit Knowledge: An Empirical Validation Study." *Applied Linguistics*, 27: 464–91.

Erlam, R., S. Loewen, and J. Philp. 2009. "The Role of Output-Based and Input-Based Instruction in the Acquisition of L2 Implicit and Explicit Knowledge." In *Implicit and Explicit Knowledge in Second Language Learning, Testing and Teaching*, edited by R. Ellis, S. Loewen, C. Elder et al., 241–60. Bristol: Multilingual Matters.

Ernst, S. 1994. "'Talking Circle': Conversation, Negotiation in the ESL Classroom." *TESOL Quarterly*, 28: 293–322.

Eskildsen, S. 2009. "Constructing Another Language – Usage-Based Linguistics in Second Language Acquisition." *Applied Linguistics*, 30: 335–357.

Ewald, J. 2004. "A Classroom Forum on Small Group Work: Learners See and Change Themselves." *Language Awareness*, 12: 163–79.

Fanselow, J. 1977. "Beyond 'Rashomon' – Conceptualizing and Describing the Teaching Act." *TESOL Quarterly*, 10: 17–39.

Farrokhi, F., A. Ansarin, and Z. Mohammadnia. 2008. Preemptive Focus on Form: Teachers' Practices across Proficiencies." *The Linguistics Journal*, 3, 2.

Fawbush, B. 2010. *Implicit and Explicit Corrective Feedback for Middle School ESL Learners*. Unpublished MA Thesis, Hamline University, Saint Paul, Minn.

Felix, S. 1981. "The Effect of Formal Instruction on Second Language Acquisition." *Language Learning*, 31: 87–112.

Fernandez, C. 2008. "Reexamining the Role of Explicit Information in Processing Instruction." *Studies in Second Language Acquisition*, 30: 277–305.

Feryok, A. 2010. "Language Teacher Cognitions: Complex Dynamic Systems?" *System*, 38: 272–79.

Firth, A., and J. Wagner. 2007. "Second/Foreign Language Learning as a Social Accomplishment: Elaborations on a Reconceptualized SLA." *Modern Language Journal*, 91: 798–817.

Flanders, N. 1970. *Analyzing Teaching Behavior*. Reading, MA: Addison Wesley.

Flanigan, B. 1991. "Peer Tutoring and Second Language Acquisition in the Elementary School." *Applied Linguistics*, 12: 141–58.

Fortune, A. 2005. "Learners' Use of Metalanguage in Collaborative Form-Focused L2 Output Tasks." *Language Awareness,* 14: 21–38.

Foster, P. 1996. "Doing the Task Better: How Planning Time Influences Students' Performance." In *Challenge and Change in Language Teaching,* edited by J. Willis and D. Willis. Oxford: Heinemann.

Foster, P. 1998. "A Classroom Perspective on the Negotiation of Meaning." *Applied Linguistics,* 19: 1–23.

Foster P., and P. Skehan. 1996. "The Influence of Planning on Performance in Task-Based Learning." *Studies in Second Language Acquisition,* 18, 3: 299–324.

Foster, P., A. Tonkyn and G. Wigglesworth. 2000. "Measuring Spoken Language: A Unit for All Reasons." *Applied Linguistics,* 21: 354–75.

Fotos, S. 1993. "Consciousness-Raising and Noticing through Focus-on-Form: Grammar Task Performance vs. Formal Instruction." *Applied Linguistics,* 14: 385–407.

Fotos, S. 1994. "Integrating Grammar Instruction and Communicative Language Use through Grammar Consciousness-Raising Tasks." *TESOL Quarterly,* 28: 323–51.

Fotos, S., and R. Ellis. 1991. "Communicating about Grammar: A Task-Based Approach." *TESOL Quarterly,* 25: 605–28.

Freeman, D. 1996. "Redefining the Relationship between Research and What Teachers Know." In *Voices from the Language Classroom: Qualitative Research,* edited by K. Bailey and D. Nunan, 88–115. New York: Cambridge University Press.

Freeman, J. 2007. *A Task Evaluation.* Unpublished MA paper, University of Auckland, Auckland.

Freidson, E. 1977. *Profession of Medicine: A Study of Sociology of Applied Knowledge.* New York: Dodd, Mead and Co.

Fries, C. 1952. *The Structure of English: An Introduction to the Structure of English Sentences.* New York: Harcourt Brace.

Fujii, A., and A. Mackey. 2009. "Interactional Feedback in Learner-Learner Interactions. In A Task-Based EFL Classroom." *IRAL,* 47: 267–301.

Gal'perin, P. 1969. "Stages in the Development of Mental Acts." In *A Handbook of Contemporary Soviet Psychology,* edited by M. Cole and I. Matlzman, 248–273. New York: Basic Books.

Gan, Z., G. Humphreys, and L. Hamp-Lyons. 2004. "Understanding Successful and Unsuccessful EFL Students in Chinese Universities." *Modern Language Journal,* 88: 229–44.

Gary, J. 1978. "Why Speak If You Don't Need To? The Case for a Listening Approach to Beginning Foreign Language Learning." In *Second Language Research,* edited by W. Ritchie, 185–199. New York: Academic Press.

Gary, J., and N. Gary. 1981. "Comprehension-Based Language Instruction: Theory." *Annals of the New York Academy of Sciences,* 379: 332–42.

Gass, S. 1982. "From Theory to Practice. In *On TESOL '81,* edited by M. Hines and W. Rutherford, 129–39. Washington DC: TESOL.

Gass, S., A. Mackey, and L. Ross-Feldman. 2005. "Task-Based Interactions in Classroom and Laboratory Settings." *Language Learning,* 55: 575–611.

Gass, S., and A. Mackey. 2000. *Stimulated Recall Methodology in Second Language Research.* Mahwah, NJ: Lawrence Erlbaum.

Gibbons, J. 1985. "The Silent Period: An Examination." *Language Learning,* 35: 255–67.

Gibbons, P. 2007. "Mediating Academic Language Learning through Classroom Discourse." In *International Handbook of English Language Teaching,* edited by J. Cummins and C. Davison, 701–18. New York: Springer.

Gilabert, R. 2007. "The Simultaneous Manipulation of Task Complexity along Planning Time and (+/− Here-and-Now): Effects on L2 Oral Production." In *Investigating Tasks in Formal Language Learning*, edited by M. Garcia Mayo, 44–68. Bristol: Multilingual Matters.

Gilabert, R., J. Baron, and A. Llanes. 2009. "Manipulating Cognitive Complexity across Task Types and Its Impact on Learners' Interaction during Oral Performance." *IRAL*, 47: 367–95.

Girard, M., and C. Sionis. 2004. "The Functions of Formulaic Speech in the L2 Class." *Pragmatics*, 14: 31–53.

Gliksman, L., R. Gardner, and P. Smythe. 1982. "The Role of Integrative Motivation on Students' Participation in the French Classroom." *Canadian Modern Language Review*, 38: 625–47.

Golombek, P. 1998. "A Study of Language Teachers' Personal Practical Knowledge." *TESOL Quarterly*, 32: 447–64.

Gonzalez-Lloret, M. 2008. "Computer-Mediated Learning of L2 Pragmatics." In *Investigating Pragmatics in Foreign Language Learning, Teaching and Testing*, edited by E. Alcon-Scoler and A. Martinze-Flor, 114–32. Bristol: Multilingal Matters.

Gourlay, L. 2005. "OK, Who's Got Number One? Permeable Triadic Dialogue, Covert Participation and the Co-Construction of Checking Episodes." *Language Teaching Research*, 9: 403–22.

Green, P., and K. Hecht. 1992. "Implicit and Explicit Grammar: An Empirical Study." *Applied Linguistics*, 13: 168–84.

Grew, J. 1958. "An Experiment in Oral French in Grade III." *Modern Language Journal*, 42: 186–95.

Griggs, P. 2006. "Assessment of the Role of Communicative Tasks in the Development of Second Language Oral Production Skills." In *Investigations in Instructed Second Language Acquisition*, edited by A. Housen and M. Pierrard, 407–32. Berlin: Mouton de Gruyter.

Grotjahn, R., 1987. "On the Methodological Basis of Introspective Methods." In *Introspection in Second Language Research*, edited by C. Faerch and G. Kasper, 54–81. Bristol: Multilingual Matters.

Guilloteaux, M., and Z. Dörnyei. 2008. "Motivating Language Learners: A Classroom-Oriented Investigation of the Effects of Motivational Strategies on Student Motivation." *TESOL Quarterly*, 42: 55–77.

Guk, I., and D. Kellogg. 2007. "The ZPD and Whole Class Teaching: Teacher-Led and Student-Led Interactional Mediation of Tasks." *Language Teaching Research*, 11, 281–99.

Håkansson, G., and I. Lindberg. 1988. "What's the Question? Investigating Questions in Second Language Classrooms." *AILA Review*, 5.

Hall, J. 1998. "Differential Teacher Attention to Student Utterances: The Construction of Different Opportunities for Learning in the IRF." *Linguistics and Education*, 9: 287–311.

Hall, J., and M. Walsh. 2002. "Teacher-Student Interaction and Language Learning." *Annual Review of Applied Linguistics*, 22: 186–203.

Halliday, M. 1961. "Categories of the Theory of Grammar." *Word*, 17: 241–292.

Halliday, M. 1973. *Explorations in the Functions of Language*. London: Edward Arnold.

Hamilton, R. 1994. "Is Implicational Generalization Unidirectional and Maximal? Evidence from Relativization Instruction in a Second Language." *Language Learning*, 44: 123–57.

Hammond, R. 1988. "Accuracy versus Communicative Competency: The Acquisition of Grammar in the Second Language Classroom." *Hispania*, 71: 408–17.

Han, Y., and R. Ellis. 1998. "Implicit Knowledge, Explicit Knowledge and General Language Proficiency." *Language Teaching Research*, 2: 1–23.

Harbord, J. 1992. "The Use of the Mother Tongue in the Classroom." *ELT Journal*, 46: 350–55.

Hardy, I., and J. Moore. 2004. "Foreign Language Students' Conversational Negotiations in Different Task Environments." *Applied Linguistics*, 25: 340–70.

Hargie, O. 1978. "The Importance of Teacher Questions in the Classroom." *Educational Research*, 20: 99-102.

Harklau, L. 1994. "ESL versus Mainstream Classes: Contrasting L2 Learning Environments." *TESOL Quarterly*, 28: 241–72.

Harley, B. 1989. "Functional Grammar in French Immersion: A Classroom Experiment." *Applied Linguistics*, 19: 331–59.

Harmer, J. 1983. *The Practice of English Language Teaching*. London: Longman.

Harmer, J. 2001. *The Practice of Language Teaching*. Harlow: Longman.

Harrington, M. 2002. "Cognitive Perspectives on Second Language Acquisition." In *The Oxford Handbook of Applied Linguistics,* edited by R. Kaplan, 124–40. New York: Oxford University Press.

Hasan, R. 1988. "Language in the Processes of Socialization: Home and School." In *Language and Socialization: Home and School. Proceedings from the Working Conference on Language in Education,* edited by L. Gerot, J. Oldenburg and T. Van Leeuwen. Sydney: Macquarie University.

Hassan, X., E. Macaro, D. Mason et al. 2005. *Strategy Training in Language Learning – A Systematic Review of Available Research. In Research Evidence in Education Library.* London: EPPI-Centre, Social Science Research Unit, Institute of Education, University of London.

Hatch, E. 1978a. "Apply with Caution." *Studies in Second Language Acquisition*, 2: 123–43.

Hatch, E., ed. 1978b. *Second Language Acquisition*. Rowley, MA: Newbury House.

Havranek, G. 2002. "When is Corrective Feedback Most Likely to Succeed? *International Journal of Educational Research,* 37: 255–70.

Hayn, N. 1967. "After Colorado, What?" *Hispania*, 50: 104–07.

Hedge, T. 2000. *Teaching and Learning in the Language Classroom*. Oxford: Oxford University Press.

Hendrickson, J. 1978. "Error Correction in Foreign Language Teaching: Recent Theory, Research and Practice." *Modern Language Journal*, 62: 387–398.

Henry, N., H. Culman, and B. VanPatten. 2009. "More of the Effects of Explicit Information in Instructed SLA: A Partial Replication and a Response to Fernandez (2008)" *Studies in Second Language Acquisition,* 31: 559–75.

Hernandez, T. 2011. "Re-Examining the Role of Explicit Instruction and Input Flood on the Acquisition of Spanish Discourse Markers." *Language Teaching Research*, 15, 2.

Hinkel, E., ed. 2005. *Handbook of Research in Second Language Teaching and Learning*. Mahwah, NJ: Lawrence Erlbaum.

Ho, D. 2005. "Why Do Teachers Ask the Questions They Ask?" *RELC Journal*, 36: 297–10.

Holunga, S. 1995. *The Effect of Metacognitive Strategy Training with Verbalization on the Oral Accuracy of Adult Second Language Learners*. Unpublished doctoral dissertation, University of Toronto (Ontario Institute for Studies in Education).

Hopkins, D., and M. Nettle. 1994. "Second Language Acquisition Research: A Response to Ellis." *ELT Journal*, 48: 157–61.

Horwitz, E. 2001. "Language Anxiety and Achievement." *Annual Review of Applied Linguistics*, 21: 112–26.

Horwitz, E., M. Horwitz, and J. Cope. 1986. "Foreign Language Classroom Anxiety." *The Modern Language Journal*, 70: 125–32.

House, J. 1986. "Learning to Talk: Talking to Learn. An Investigation of Learner Performance in Two Types of Discourse." In *Learning, Teaching and Communication in the Foreign Language Classroom*, edited by G. Kasper. Aarhus: Aarhus University Press.

Housen, A., and M. Pierrard. 2006. "Investigating Instructed Second Language Acquisition." In *Investigations in Instructed Second Language Acquisition*, edited by A. Housen and M. Pierrard. Berlin: Mouton de Gruyter.

Howatt, A. P. R. 1984. A History of English Language Teaching. Oxford: Oxford University Press.

Hu, G. 2010. "A Place for Metalanguage in the L2 Classroom." *ELT Journal.*

Hutchby, L., and R. Wooffitt. 1988. *Conversation Analysis.* Cambridge: Polity Press.

Hyland, K., and F. Hyland. 2006. "Contexts and issues in Feedback on L2 Writing: An Introduction." In *Investigations in Instructed Second Language Acquisition*, edited by K. Hyland and F. Hyland. Cambridge: Cambridge University Press.

Hymes, D. 1970. "On Communicative Competence." In *Directions in Sociolinguistics*, edited by J. J. Gumperz and D. Hymes. New York: Holt, Rinchart and Winston.

Iddings, A., and E. Jang. 2008. " The Meditational Role of Classroom Practices during the Silent Period: A New-Immigrant Student Learning the English Language in the Mainstream Classroom." *TESOL Quarterly*, 42: 567–90.

Itoh, H., and E. Hatch. 1978. "Second Language Acquisition: A Case Study." In *Second Language Acquisition*, edited by E. Hatch. Rowley, MA: Newbury House.

Jarvinen, H. 2006. "Language Learning in Content-Based Instruction." In *Investigations in Instructed Second Language Acquisition*, edited by A. Housen and M. Pierrard, 433–56. Berlin: Mouton de Gruyter.

Jarvis G. 1968. "A Behavioral Observation System for Classroom Foreign Language Learning." *Modern Language Journal*, 52: 335–41.

Johnson, K. 1988. "Mistake Correction." *ELT Journal*, 42: 89–101.

Johnson, K. 1995. *Understanding Communication in Second Language Classrooms.* Cambridge: Cambridge University Press.

Johnson, M. 2004. *A Philosophy of Second Language Acquisition.* New Haven, CT: Yale University Press.

Jourdenais, R., M. Ota, S. Stauffer et al. 1995. "Does Textual Enhancement Promote Noticing? A Think-Aloud Protocol Analysis." In *Attention and Awareness in Foreign Language Learning*, edited by R. Schmidt. Honolulu: University of Hawai'i Press.

Juffs, A. 2007. "Working Memory, Second Language Acquisition and Low-Educated Second Language and Literacy Learners." In *Low-Educated Second Language and Literacy Acquisition: Proceedings of the Inaugural Symposium – Tilburg 05*, edited by I. van de Craats, J. Kurvers, and M. Young-Scholten, 89–104. LOT Occasional Series.

Kanagy, R. 1999. "Interactional Routines as a Mechanism for L2 Acquisition and Socialization in an Immersion Context." *Journal of Pragmatics*, 31: 1467–1492.

Kang, D-M. 2008. "The Classroom Language Use of a Korean Elementary School EFL Teacher: Another Look at TETE. *System*, 36: 214–226.

Karavas-Doukas, E. 1998. "Evaluating the Implementation of Educational Innovations: Lessons from the Past." In *Managing Evaluation and Innovation in Language Teaching: Building Bridges*, edited by P. Rea-Dickins, and K. P. Germaine, 25–50. London: Longman.

Kasper, G. 1985. "Repair in Foreign Language Teaching." *Studies in Second Language Acquisition*, 7: 200–15.

Kasper, G. 2001. "Four Perspectives on L2 Pragmatic Development." *Applied Linguistics*, 22: 502–30.

Kearsley, G. 1976. "Questions and Question-Asking in Verbal Discourse: A Cross-Disciplinary Review." *Journal of Psycholinguistic Research*, 5: 355–75.

Kim, S., and C. Elder. 2005. "Language Choices and Pedagogic Functions in the Foreign Language Classroom: A Cross-Linguistic Functional Analysis of Teacher Talk." *Language Teaching Research*, 9: 335–80.

Kim, Y. 2009. "The Effects of Task Complexity on Learner-Learner Interactions." *System*, 37: 254–68.

Kim, Y., and K. McDonough. 2008. "The Effect of Interlocutor Proficiency on the Collaborative Dialogue between Korean as a Second Language Learners." *Language Teaching Research*, 12: 211–34.

Klapper, J., and J. Rees. 2003. "Reviewing the Case for Explicit Grammar Instruction in the University Foreign Language Learning Context." *Language Teaching Research*, 2003: 285–314.

Klein, W., and C. Perdue. 1997. "The Basic Variety (or: Couldn't Natural Languages Be Much Simpler?)." *Second Language Research*, 13: 301–48.

Ko, J., D. Schallert, and K. Walters. 2003. "Rethinking Scaffolding: Examining Negotiation of Meaning in an ESL Storytelling Task." *TESOL Quarterly*, 37: 303–24.

Koivukari, A. 1987. "Question Level and Cognitive Processing: Psycholinguistic Dimensions of Questions and Answers." *Applied Psycholinguistics*, 8: 101–20.

Kowal, M., and M. Swain. 1994. "Using Collaborative Language Production Tasks to Promote Students' Language Awareness." *Language Awareness*, 3, 2: 73–93.

Kowal, M., and M. Swain. 1997. "From Semantic To Syntactic Processing: How Can We Promote Metalinguistic Awareness in the French Immersion Classroom?" In *Immersion Education: International Perspectives*, edited by R. Johnson and M. Swain, 284–309. Cambridge: Cambridge University Press.

Kramsch, C. 1985. "Classroom Interaction and Discourse Options." *Studies in Second Language Acquisition*, 7: 169–83.

Krashen, S. 1981. *Second Language Acquisition and Second Language Learning*. Oxford: Pergamon.

Krashen, S. 1982. *Principles and Practice in Second Language Acquisition*. Oxford: Pergamon.

Krashen, S. 1985. *The Input Hypothesis: Issues and Implications*. London: Longman.

Krashen, S., and R. Scarcella. 1978. "On Routines and Patterns in Second Language Acquisition and Performance." *Language Learning*, 28: 283–300.

Krashen, S., and T. Terrell. 1983. *The Natural Approach: Language Acquisition in the Classroom*. Oxford: Pergamon.

Kravas-Doukas, K. 1998. "Evaluating the Implementation of Educational Evaluations: Lessons from the Past." In *Managing Evaluating and Innovation in Language Teaching*, edited by P. Rea-Dickens and K. Germaine, 25–50. London: Longman.

Krumm, H. J. 1973. "Interaction Analysis and Microteaching for the Training of Modern Language Teachers." *IRAL*, 11, 163–70.

Kuhl, P. 2000. "A New View of Language Acquisition." *Proceedings of the National Academy of the Sciences*, 92: 11850–7.

Kuiken, F., and I. Vedder. 2002. "The Effect of Interaction in Acquiring the Grammar of a Second Language." *International Journal of Educational Research*, 37: 343–58.

Kumaradivelu, B. 1994. "The Post-Method Condition: (E)merging Strategies for. Second/Foreign Language Teaching." *TESOL Quarterly*, 28: 27–48.

Kumaravadivelu. B. 2001. "Toward a Postmethod Pedagogy." *TESOL Quarterly*, 35, 4: 537–60.

Lado, R. 1964. *Language Teaching: A Scientific Approach*. New York: McGraw Hill.

Lambert, W. 1974. "Culture and Language and Factors in Learning and Education." In *Cultural Factors in Learning and Education*, edited by F. E. Aboud. and R. D. Meade. Washington: Fifth Western Washington Symposium on Learning.

Lange, M. 2000. *Factors Affecting Communication Task Performance in Small Groups*. Unpublished MA Thesis, University of Auckland.

Lantolf, J. 1997. "The Function of Language Play in the Acquisition of Spanish as a Second Language." In *Contemporary Perspectives on the Acquisition of Spanish*, edited by W. Glass and A. Perez-Leroux. Somerville, MA: Cascadilla Press.

Lantolf, J. 2000. "Introducing Sociocultural Theory." In *Sociocultural Theory and Second Language Learning*, edited by J. Lantolf. Oxford: Oxford University Press.

Lantolf, J. 2005. "Sociocultural and Second Language Learning Research: An Exegesis." In *Handbook of Research on Second Language Teaching and Learning*, edited by E. Hinkel. Mahweh, NJ: Lawrence Erlbaum.

Lantolf, J. 2006. "Sociocultural Theory and L2." *Studies in Second Language Acquisition*, 28: 67–109.

Lantolf, J. and A. Aljaafreh. 1995. "Second Language Learning in the Zone of Proximal Development: A Revolutionary Experience." *International Journal of Educational Research*, 23: 619–32.

Lantolf, J., and P. Genung. 2002. "'I'd Rather Switch Than Fight': An Activity-Theoretic Study of Power, Success and Failure in a Foreign Language." In *Language Acquisition and Language Socialization: Ecological Perspectives*, edited by C. Kramsch. London: Continuum.

Lantolf, J., and S. Thorne. 2006. *Sociocultural Theory and the Genesis of Second Language Development*. Oxford: Oxford University Press.

LaPierre, D. 1994. *Language Output in a Cooperative Learning Setting: Determining Its Effects on Second Language Learning*. Unpublished MA Thesis, Toronto, University of Toronto (OISE).

Lasagabaster, D., and J. Sierra. 2005. "Error Correction: Students' Versus Teachers' Perceptions." *Language Awareness*, 14: 112–127.

Laufer, B. 2006. "Comparing Focus on Form and Focus on Forms in Second-Language Vocabulary Learning." *The Canadian Modern Language Review*, 63, 1: 149–66.

Laufer, B., and J. Hulstijn. 2001. "Incidental Vocabulary Acquisition in a Second Language: the Construct of Task-Induced Involvement." *Applied Linguistics* 22: 1–26.

Lave, J., and Wenger, E. (1991). *Situated Learning: Legitimate Peripheral Participation*. Cambridge: Cambridge University Press.

Lazaraton, A. 2004. "Gesture and Speech in the Vocabulary Explanations of One ESL Teacher: A Microanalytic Inquiry." *Language Learning*, 54: 79–117.

Leaver, B., and J. Willis, eds. 2004. *Task-Based Instruction in Foreign Language Education*. Washington DC: Georgetown University Press.

LeCompte, M., and J. J. Schensul. 1999. *Analyzing and Interpreting Ethnographic Data*. Walnut Creek, CA: Sage Publications.

Lee, J., and A. Benati. 2009. *Research and Perspectives on Processing Instruction*. Berlin: Walter de Gruyter.

Lee, Y. 2006. "Respecifying Display Questions: Interactional Resources for Language Teaching." *TESOL Quarterly*, 40L 691–713.

Leeser, M. 2004. "Learner Proficiency and Focus on Form during Collaborative Dialogue." *Language Teaching Research*, 8: 55–81.

Lemke, J. 1990. *Talking Science: Language. Learning and Values (Language and Classroom Processes Volume 1)*. Norwood, NJ: Ablex Publishing.

Lerner, G. 1995. "Turn Design and the Organization of Participation in Instructional Activities." *Discourse Processes*, 19: 111–31.

Levin, L. 1972. *Comparative Studies in Foreign-Language Teaching*. Godteborg Studies in Educational Sciences 9.

Lewin, K. 1948. *Resolving Social Conflicts; Selected Papers on Group Dynamics*. New York: Harper and Row.

Li, D. 1998. "It's Always More Difficult than You Planned. Teachers' Perceived Difficulties in Introducing the Communicative Approach in South Korea." *TESOL Quarterly*, 32: 677–703.

Li, S. 2010. "The Effectiveness of Corrective Feedback in SLA: A Meta-Analysis." *Language Learning*, 60: 309–65.

Lightbown, P. 1983. "Exploring Relationships between Developmental and Instructional Sequences in L2 Acquisition." In *Classroom-Oriented Research in Second Language Acquisition*, edited by H. Seliger and M. Long. Rowley, MA Newbury House.

Lightbown, P. 1985a. "Great Expectations: Second Language Acquisition Research and Classroom Teaching." *Applied Linguistics*, 6: 173–89.

Lightbown, P. 1985b. "Can Language Acquisition Be Altered by Instruction?" In *Modelling and Assessing Second Language Acquisition*, edited by K. Hyltenstam and M. Pienemann. Bristol: Multilingual Matters.

Lightbown, P. 1992a. "Getting Quality Input in the Second/Foreign Language Classroom." In *Text and Context: Cross-Disciplinary Perspectives on Language Study*, edited by C. Kransch and S. McConnell-Ginet, 187–97. Lexington, MA: D.C. Heath and Company.

Lightbown, P. 1992b. "Can They Do It Themselves? A Comprehension-Based ESL Course for Young Children." In *Comprehension-Based Second Language Teaching*, edited by R. Courchene, J. Glidden, J. St John, and C. Therien. Ottowa: University of Ottawa Press.

Lightbown, P. 2000. "Anniversary Article: Classroom SLA Research and Language Teaching." *Applied Linguistics*, 21: 431–62.

Lightbown, P. 2006. "Perfecting Practice." Plenary talk given at the IRAAL/ BAAL Conference, Cork, Ireland.

Lightbown, P., and N. Spada. 1990. "Focus-on-Form and Corrective Feedback in Communicative Language Teaching: Effects on Second Language Learning." *Studies in Second Language Acquisition*, 12: 429–48.

Lightbown, P., and N. Spada. 2006. *How Languages are Learned*. Oxford: Oxford University Press.

Lightbown, P., R. Halter, J. White, and M. Horst. 2002. "Comprehension-Based Learning: the Limits of 'Do it Yourself'". *Canadian Modern Language Journal* 58: 427–64.

Loewen, S. 2003. "Variation in the Frequency and Focus of Incidental Focus on Form." *Language Teaching Research,* 7: 315–345.

Loewen, S. 2005. "Incidental Focus on Form and Second Language Learning." *Studies in Second Language Acquisition*, 27: 361–86.

Loewen, S. 2006. "The Prior and Subsequent Use of Forms Targeted in Incidental Focus on Form. In *Form-Focused Instruction and Teacher Education: Studies in Honour of Rod Ellis,* edited by S. Fotos and H. Nassaji. Oxford: Oxford University Press.

Loewen, S., and J. Philp. 2006. "Recasts in the Adult English L2 Classroom; Characteristics, Explicitness, and Effectiveness." *Modern Language Journal,* 90: 536–56.

Loewen, S., and T. Nabei. 2007. "Measuring the Effects of Oral Corrective Feedback on L2 Knowledge." In *Conversational Interaction in Second Language Acquisition,* edited by A. Mackey, 361–378. Oxford: Oxford University Press.

Loewen, S., R. Erlam, and R. Ellis. 2009. The Incidental Acquisition of 3rd Person *–s* as Implicit and Explicit Knowledge. In *Implicit and Explicit Knowledge in Second Language Learning, Testing and Teaching,* edited by R. Ellis, S. Loewen, C. Elder et al., 262–80. Bristol: Multilingual Matters.

Long, M. 1977. "Teacher Feedback on Learner Error: Mapping Cognitions." In *On TESOL '77,* edited by H. D. Brown, C. A. Yorio, and R. H. Crymes, 278–293. Washington, DC: TESOL.

Long, M. 1980. "Inside the 'Black Box': Methodological Issues in Classroom Research on Language Learning'. *Language Learning,* 30: 1–42.

Long, M. 1983a. "Native Speaker/Non-Native Speaker Conversation and the Negotiation of Comprehensible Input." *Applied Linguistics,* 4: 126–41.

Long, M. 1983b. "Does Second Language Instruction Make a Difference? A Review of the Research." *TESOL Quarterly,* 17: 359–82.

Long, M. 1983c. "Native Speaker/Non-Native Speaker Conversation in the Second Language Classroom." In *On TESOL '82,* edited by M. Clarke and J. Handscombe. Washington DC: TESOL.

Long, M. 1984. "Process and Product in ESL Program Evaluation." *TESOL Quarterly,* 18, 3: 409–25.

Long, M. 1985. "A Role for Instruction in Second Language Acquisition: Task-Based Language Teaching." In *Modelling and Assessing Second Language Acquisition,* edited by K. Hyltenstam and M. Pienemann. Bristol: Multilingual Matters.

Long, M. 1991. "Focus on Form: A Design Feature in Language Teaching Methodology." In *Foreign Language Research in Cross-Cultural Perspective,* edited by K. de Bot, R. Ginsberg, and C. Kramsch, 39–52. Amsterdam: John Benjamin.

Long, M. 1996. "The Role of the Linguistic Environment in Second Language Acquisition." In *Handbook of Second Language Acquisition,* edited by W. Ritchie and T. Bhatia. San Diego: Academic Press.

Long, M. 2007. "Recasts in SLA: The Story So Far." In *Problems in SLA,* edited by M. H. Long, 75–116. Mahwah, NJ: Laurence Erlbaum.

Long, M., and C. Sato. 1984. "Methodological Issues in Interlanguage Studies: An Interactionist Perspective." In *Interlanguage,* edited by A. Davies, C. Criper, and A. Howatt. Edinburgh: Edinburgh University Press.

Long, M., and G. Crookes. 1992. "Three Approaches to Task-Based Syllabus Design." *TESOL Quarterly,* 26: 27–56.

Long, M., and P. Porter. 1985. "Group Work, Interlanguage Talk, and Second Language Acquisition." *TESOL Quarterly,* 19: 207–28.

Long, M., L. Adams, M. Mclean, and F. Castanos. 1976. "Doing Things with Words: Verbal Interaction in Lockstep and Small Group Classroom Situations." In *On TESOL '76,* edited by J. Fanselow and R. Crymes. Washington DC: TESOL.

Lörscher, W. 1986. "Conversational Structures in the Foreign Language Classroom." In *Learning, Teaching and Communication in the Foreign Language Classroom*, edited by G. Kasper. Aarhus: Aarhus University Press.

Loschky, L. 1994. "Comprehensible Input and Second Language Acquisition: What Is the Relationship." *Studies in Second Language Acquisition*, 16: 303–23.

Loschky, L., and R. Bley-Vroman. 1993. "Grammar and Task-Based Methodology." In *Tasks and Language Learning: Integrating Theory and Practice*, edited by G. Crookes and S. Gass. Bristol: Multilingual Matters.

Lyster, R. 1994. "The Effect of Functional-Analytic Teaching on Aspects of French Immersion Students' Sociolinguistic Competence." *Applied Linguistics*, 15: 263–87.

Lyster, R. 1998a. "Negotiation of Form, Recasts, and Explicit Correction in Relation to Error Types and Learner Repair in Immersion Classrooms." *Language Learning*, 48: 183–218.

Lyster, R. 1998b. "Recasts, Repetition and Ambiguity in L2 Classroom Discourse." *Studies in Second Language Acquisition,* 20, 1: 51–81.

Lyster, R. 2004. "Differential Effects of Prompts and Recasts in Form-Focused Instruction." *Studies in Second Language Acquisition*, 26, 3: 399–432.

Lyster, R. 2007. *Learning and Teaching Languages through Content: A Counterbalanced Approach*. Amsterdam: John Benjamins.

Lyster, R., and H. Mori. 2006. "Interactional Feedback and Instructional Counterbalance." *Studies in Second Language Acquisition,* 28: 269–300.

Lyster, R., and K. Saito. 2010. "Oral Feedback in Classroom SLA: A Meta-Analysis." *Studies in Second Language Acquisition*, 32: 265–302.

Lyster, R., and L. Ranta. 1997. "Corrective Feedback and Learner Uptake: Negotiation of Form in Communicative Classrooms." *Studies in Second Language Acquisition*, 19: 37–66.

Macaro, E. 2001. "Analysing Student Teachers' Codeswitching in Foreign Language Classrooms: Theories and Decision Making." *Modern Language Journal*, 85: 531–48.

Macaro, E. 2006. "Strategies for Language Learning and for Language Use: Revising the Theoretical Framework." *Modern Language Journal*, 90: 320–37.

MacIntyre, P., and R. Gardner. 1991. "Language Anxiety: Its Relationship to other Anxieties and to Processing in Native and Second Languages." *Language Learning*, 41: 513–34.

MacIntyre, P., R. Clement, Z. Dörnyei, and K. Noels. 1998. "Conceptualizing Willingness to Communicate in a L2: A Situated Model of Confidence and Affiliation." *Modern Language Journal*, 82: 545–62.

Mackey, A. 2006. "Feedback, Noticing and Instructed Second Language Learning." *Applied Linguistics*, 27: 405–30.

Mackey. A. 2007. "Introduction" In *Conversational Interaction in Second Language Acquisition: A Collection of Empirical Studies,* edited by A. Mackey. Oxford: Oxford University Press.

Mackey, A., A. Kanganas, and R. Oliver. 2007. "Task Familiarity and Interactional Feedback in Child ESL Classrooms." *TESOL Quarterly*, 41: 285–312.

Mackey, A., and J. Goo. 2007. "Interaction Research in SLA: A Meta-Analysis and Research Synthesis." In *Conversational Interaction in Second Language Acquisition: A Collection of Empirical Studies,* edited by A. Mackey. Oxford: Oxford University Press.

Mackey, A., and S. Gass, eds. 2005. *Second Language Research: Methodology and* Design. Mahwah, NJ: Lawrence Erlbaum.

Mackey, A., C. Polio, and K. McDonough. 2004. "The Relationship between Experience, Education and Teachers' Use of Incidental Focus-on-Form Techniques." *Language Teaching Research*, 8: 301–27.

Mackey, A., J. Philp, T, Egi, J. Fujii et al. 2002. "Individual Differences in Working Memory, Noticing of Interactional Feedback and L2 Development." In *Individual Differences in L2 Learning*, edited by P. Robinson. Amsterdam: John Benjamins.

Mackey, A., R. Adams, C. Stafford, and P. Winke. 2010. "Exploring the Relationship between Modified Output and Working Memory Capacity." *Language Learning*, 60: 501–533.

Manolopoulo-Sergi, E. 2004. "Motivation within the Information Processing Model of Foreign Language Learning." *System*, 32: 427–42.

Markee, N. 2000. *Conversation Analysis*. Mahwah, NJ: Lawrence Erlbaum.

Markee, N. 2005. "Conversation Analysis for Second Language Acquisition." In *Handbook of Research in Second Language Teaching and Learning*, edited by E. Hinkel, 355–74. Mahwah, NJ: Erlbaum,

Markee, N. and G. Kasper. 2004. "Classroom Talks: an Introduction." *The Modern Language Journal*, 88: 491–500.

Marsden, E. 2006. "Exploring Input Processing in the Classroom: An Experimental Comparison of Processing Instruction and Enriched Input." *Language Learning*, 56, 3: 507–6.

McCormick, D., and R. Donato. 2000. "Teacher Questions as Scaffolding Assistance in an ESL Classroom." In *Second and Foreign Language Learning Through Classroom Interaction*, edited by J. Hall and L. Verplaetse. Mahwah, NJ: Lawrence Erlbaum.

McDonough, K. 2004. "Learner-Learner Interaction during Pair and Small Group Activities in a Thai EFL Context." *System*, 32: 2007–34.

McDonough, K. 2006. "Interaction and Syntactic Priming: English L2 Speakers' Production of Dative Constructions." *Studies in Second Language Acquisition*, 28: 179–207.

McDonough, K., and W. Chaikitmongkol. 2007. "Teachers' and Learners' Reactions to a Task Based EFL Course in Thailand." *TESOL Quarterly*, 41: 107–32.

McDonough, S. 1999. "Learner Strategies." *Language Teaching*, 32: 1–18.

McGrew, S. 2005. "Student Questions in an Intermediate Hebrew Classroom." *Working Papers in Educational Linguistics* 21: 61–78.

McHoul, A. 1978. "The Organization of Turns at Formal Talk in the Classroom." *Language and Society*, 7: 183–213.

McKay, S. 2006. *Researching Second Language Classrooms*. Mahwah, NJ: Lawrence Erlbaum.

McLaughlin, B. 1985. *Second-Language Acquisition in Childhood. Vol. 2: School-Age Children*. Mahwah, NJ: Lawrence Erlbaum.

McTear, M. 1975. "Structure and Categories of Foreign Language Teaching Sequences. In *Working Papers: Language Teaching Classroom Research*, edited by R. Allwright. University of Essex, Department of Language and Linguistics.

Mehan, H. 1979. *Learning Lessons: Social Organization in the Classroom*. Cambridge, MA: Harvard University Press.

Mellow, D., K. Reeder, and E. Forster. 1996. "Using Time-Series Research Designs to Investigate the Effects of Instruction on SLA." *Studies in Second Language Acquisition*, 18, 325–350.

Mifka-Profozic, N. 2011. *Corrective Feedback, Individual Differences and the L2 Acquisition of French Preterite and Imperfect Tenses*. Unpublished PhD Thesis, University of Auckland, Auckland.

Mishler, E. G. 1990. "Validation in Inquiry-Guided Research: The Role of Exemplars in Narrative Studies." *Harvard Educational Review*, 60, 415–442.

Miyake, A., and N. Friedman. 1998. "Individual Differences in Second Language Proficiency: Working Memory as Language Aptitude." In *Foreign Language Learning: Psycholinguistic*

Studies on Training and Retention, edited by A. Healy and L. Bourne. Mahwah, NJ: Lawrence Erlbaum.

Mochizuki, N., and L. Ortega. 2008. "Balancing Communication and Grammar in Beginning-Level Foreign Language Classroom: A Study of Guided Planning and Relativization." *Language Teaching Research,* 12: 11–37.

Mohamed, N. 2001. *Teaching Grammar through Consciousness-Raising Tasks.* Unpublished MA Thesis, University of Auckland, Auckland.

Mori, J. 2002. "Task Design, Plan, and Development of Talk-in-Interaction: An Analysis of a Small Group Activity in a Japanese Language Classroom." *Applied Linguistics,* 23: 323–47.

Morita, N. 2004. "Negotiating Participating and Identity in Second Language Communities." *TESOL Quarterly,* 38: 573–603.

Moskowitz, G. 1967. "The FLINT System: An Observational Tool for the Foreign Language Classroom." In *Mirrors for Behavior: An Anthology of Classroom Observation Instruments,* edited by A. Simon and E. Boyer. Philadelphia: Center for the Study of Teaching at Temple University.

Moskowitz, G. 1978. *Caring and Sharing in the Foreign Language Class a Sourcebook on Humanistic Techniques.* Boston, MA: Heinle and Heinle.

Moskowitz, G. and E. Amidon. 1962. "TV FLES vs. Live FLES." *Modern Language Journal,* 46: 213–19.

Muranoi, H. 2000. "Focus-on-Form through Interaction Enhancement: Integrating Formal Instruction into a Communicative Task in EFL Classrooms." *Language Learning,* 50: 617–73.

Myles, F. 2004. "From Data to Theory: The Over-Representation of Linguistic Knowledge in SLA." *Transactions of the Philological Society,* 102: 139–68.

Myles, F., J. Hooper, and R. Mitchell. 1998. "Rote or Rule? Exploring the Role of Formulaic Language in Classroom Foreign Language Learning." *Language Learning,* 48: 323–63.

Myles, F., R. Mitchell, and J. Hooper. 1999. "Interrogative Chunks in French L2: A Basis for Creative Construction?" *Studies in Second Language Acquisition,* 21: 49–80.

Nagata, H., D. Aline, and R. Ellis. 1999. "Modified Input, Language Aptitude and the Acquisition of Word Meanings." In *Learning a Second Language through Interaction,* edited by R. Ellis. Amsterdam: John Benjamins.

Naiman, N., M. Fröhlich, H. Stern, and A. Todesco. 1978. *The Good Language Learner. Research in Education Series No 7.* Toronto: The Ontario Institute for Studies in Education. Reprinted in 1996 by Multilingual Matters.

Nassaji, H., and G. Wells. 2000. "What's the Use of 'Triadic Dialogue'?: An Investigation of Teacher-Student Interaction." *Applied Linguistics,* 21, 376–406.

Nassaji, H., and M. Swain. 2000. "A Vygotskian Perspective on Corrective Feedback in L2: The Effect of Random Versus Negotiated Help in the Learning of English Articles." *Language Awareness,* 9: 34–51.

Nation, P. 2000. "Learning Vocabulary in Lexical Sets: Dangers and Guidelines." *TESOL Journal,* 9: 6–10.

Nation, R., and B. McLaughlin. 1986. "Experts and Novices: An Information-Processing Approach to the 'Good Language Learner' Problem." *Applied Psycholinguistics,* 7: 41–56.

Naughton, D. 2006. "Cooperative Strategy Training and Oral Interaction: Enhancing Small Group Communication in the Language Classroom." *The Modern Language Journal,* 90: 169–84.

Negueruela, E. 2003. "Systemic-Theoretical Instruction and L2 Development: A Sociocultural Approach to Teacher-Learnering and Researching L2 Learning." Unpublished doctoral dissertation, The Pennyslvania State University, University Park.

Nerenz, A., and C. Kopf. 1982. "A Time-Based Approach to the Study of Teacher Effectiveness." *Modern Language Journal*, 66: 253–264.

Newton, J. 1991. "Negotiation: Negotiating What?" Paper given at SEAMEO Conference on Language Acquisition and the Second/Foreign Language Classroom, RELC, Singapore.

Newton, J. 1995. "Task-Based Interaction and Incidental Vocabulary Learning: A Case Study." *Second Language Research*, 11: 159–77.

Newton, J., and G. Kennedy. 1996. "Effects of Communication Tasks on the Grammatical Relations Marked by Second Language Learners." *System*, 24: 309–322.

Nicholas, H., P. Lightbown, and N. Spada. 2001. "Recasts as Feedback to Language Learners." *Language Learning*, 51, 4: 719–58.

Nizegorodcew, A. 2007. *Input for Instructed L2 Learners*. Bristol: Multilingual matters.

Nobuyoshi, J., and R. Ellis. 1993. 'Focused Communication Tasks'. *ELT Journal*, 47: 203–10.

Norris, J., and L. Ortega. 2000. "Effectiveness of L2 Instruction: A Research Synthesis and Quantitative Meta-Analysis." *Language Learning*, 50: 417–528.

Norris, J., and L. Ortega. 2006. *Synthesizing Research on Language Teaching and Learning*. Amsterdam: John Benjamins.

Norris, J., J. D. Brown, and T. Hudson. 2000. "Assessing Performance on Complex L2 Tasks: Investigating Raters, Examinees and Tasks." Paper presented at the Language Testing Research Colloquium, Vancouver, March.

Norton, B. 1997. "Language, Identity, and the Ownership of English." *TESOL Quarterly* 31: 409–29.

Nunan, D. 1989. *Designing Tasks for the Communicative Classroom*. Cambridge: Cambridge University Press.

Nunan, D. 1990a. "The Questions Teachers Ask." *JALT Journal*, 12: 187–202.

Nunan, D. 1990b. "The Teacher as Researcher." In *Research in the Language Classroom. ELT Documents 133*, edited by C. Brumfit and R. Mitchell. Modern English Publications.

Nunan, D. 1991. "Methods in Second Language Classroom-Oriented Research: A Critical Review." *Studies in Second Language Acquisition*, 13: 249–74.

Nunan, D. 2004. *Task-Based Language Teaching*. Cambridge: Cambridge University Press.

Nunan, D., and K. Bailey. 2009. *Exploring Second Language Classroom Research*. Boston, MA: Heinle.

Nystrom, N. 1983. "Teacher–Student Interaction in Bilingual Classrooms: Four Approaches to Error Feedback." In *Classroom-Oriented Research in Second Language Acquisition*, edited by H. Seliger and M. Long. Rowley, MA: Newbury House.

O.Neill, R. 1994. "The Myth of the Silent Teacher." Talk given at Annual IATEFL Conference, April 1994, http://www.btinternet.com/~ted.power/esl0420.html (accessed 13 October, 2011).

O'Malley, J., and A. Chamot. 1990. *Learning Strategies in Second Language Acquisition*. Cambridge: Cambridge University Press.

Oh, S-Y. 2001. "Two Types of Input Modification and EFL Reading Comprehension: Simplification versus Elaboration." *TESOL Quarterly*, 35: 69–96.

Ohta, A. 2000. "Rethinking Interaction in SLA: Developmentally Appropriate Assistance in the Zone of Proximal Development and the Acquisition of L2 Grammar." In *Sociocultural Theory and Second Language Learning*, edited by J. Lantolf, 51–78. Oxford: Oxford University Press.

Ohta, A. 2001. *Second Language Acquisition Processes in the Classroom: Learning Japanese.* Mahwah, NJ: Lawrence Erlbaum.

Ohta, A., and T. Nakane. 2004. "When Students Ask Questions: Teacher and Peer Answers in the Foreign Language Classroom." *International Review of Applied Linguistics,* 42: 217–37.

Oliver, R. 2000. "Age Differences in Negotiation and Feedback in Classroom and Pairwork." *Language Learning,* 50: 119–51.

Oliver, R., and A. Mackey. 2003. "Interactional Context and Feedback in Child ESL Classrooms." *The Modern Language Journal,* 87: 519–33.

Ortega, L., and G. Iberri-Shea. 2005. "Longitudinal Research in Second Language Acquisition: Recent Trends and Future Directions." *Annual Review of Applied Linguistics,* 25: 26–45.

Oxford, R. 1989. "Use of Language Learning Strategies: A Synthesis of Studies with Implications for Teacher Training." *System,* 17: 235–47.

Oxford, R. 1990. *Language Learning Strategies: What Every Teacher Should Know.* Rowley, MA: Newbury House.

Oxford, R. 1998. "The Unravelling Tapestry: Teacher and Course Characteristics Associated with De-Motivation in the Language Classroom. Demotivation in Foreign Language Learning." Paper presented at TESOL '98 Congress, Seattle, USA.

Palacios, L. M. 1998. "Foreign Language Anxiety and Classroom Environment: A Study of Spanish University Students." Unpublished doctoral dissertation, The University of Texas, Austin.

Palmer, A. 1979. "Compartmentalized and Integrated Control: An Assessment of Some Evidence for Two Kinds of Competence and Implications for the Classroom." *Language Learning,* 29: 169–80.

Pavlenko, A. 2002. "Poststructuralist Approaches to the Study of Social Factors in Second Language Learning and Use." In *Portraits of the L2 User,* edited by V. Cook. Bristol, England: Multilingual Matters.

Payne, J., and P. Whitney. 2002. "Developing L2 Oral Proficiency Synchronous CMC: Output, Working Memory, and Interlanguage Development." *CALICO Journal,* 20: 7–32.

Peng, J., and L. Woodrow. 2010. "Willingness to Communicate in English: A Model in the Chinese EFL Classroom Context." *Language Learning,* 60: 834–76.

Penner, J. 1998. "A Balance or a Battle? L1 Use in the Classroom." In *Teaching in Action: Case Studies from Second Language Classrooms,* edited by J. Richards. Washington, DC: Teachers of English to Speakers of other Languages.

Perdue, C. 2000. "Introduction to Special Issue on the Structure of Learner Varieties." *Studies in Second Language Acquisition,* 22: 299–305.

Pesce, S. 2008. "Focused Tasks in L2 Spanish Grammar Learning and Teaching." In *Task-Based Language Learning and Teaching: Theoretical, Methodological, and Pedagogical Perspectives,* edited by J. Eckerth, 67–88. Frankfurt am Main, Peter Lang.

Philips, S. 1972. "Participant Structures and Communicative Competence; Warm Springs Children in Community and Classroom." In *Functions of Language in the Classroom,* edited by C. Cazden, V. John and D. Hymes, 370–94. Columbia University: Teachers College Columbia.

Philp, J., R. Oliver, and A. Mackey. 2008. *Child's Play: Second Language Acquisition and the Younger Learner.* Amsterdam: John Benjamins.

Phipps, S., and S. Borg. 2009. "Exploring Tensions between Teachers' Grammar Teaching Beliefs and Practices." *System,* 37: 380–90.

Pica, T. 1983. "Adult Acquisition of English as a Second Language under Different Conditions of Exposure." *Language Learning*, 33: 465–97.

Pica, T. 1991. "Classroom Interaction, Participation and Comprehension: Redefining Relationships." *System*, 19: 437–52.

Pica, T. 1994. "Questions from the Language Classroom: Research Perspectives." *TESOL Quarterly*, 28: 49–79.

Pica, T. 2002. "Subject-Matter Content: How Does It Assist the Interactional and Linguistic Needs of Classroom Language Learners?" *The Modern Language Journal*, 86: 1–19.

Pica, T., and C. Doughty. 1985a. "Input and Interaction in the Communicative Language Classroom: A Comparison of Teacher-Fronted and Group Activities." In *Input in Second Language Acquisition*, edited by S. Gass and C. Madden. Rowley, MA: Newbury House.

Pica, T., and C. Doughty. 1985b. "The Role of Group Work in Classroom Second Language Acquisition." *Studies in Second Language Acquisition* 7: 233–48.

Pica, T., and M. Long. 1986. "The Linguistic and Conversational Performance of Experienced and Inexperienced Teachers." In *Talking to Learn: Conversation in Second Language Acquisition*, edited by R. Day. Rowley, MA: Newbury House.

Pica, T., R. Kanagy, and J. Falodun. 1993. "Choosing and Using Communication Tasks for Second Language Research and Instruction." In *Task-based Learning in a Second Language*, edited by G. Crookes and S. Gass. Bristol: Multilingual Matters.

Pica, T., R. Young, and C. Doughty. 1987. "The Impact of Interaction on Comprehension." *TESOL Quarterly*, 21: 737–58.

Pienemann, M. 1984. "Psychological Constraints on the Teachability of Languages." *Studies in Second Language Acquisition*, 6: 186–214.

Pienemann, M. 1985. "Learnability and Syllabus Construction." In *Modelling and Assessing Second Language Acquisition*, edited by K. Hyltenstam and M. Pienemann. Bristol: Multilingual Matters.

Pienemann, M., and C. Doughty. 2001. "Task Analysis for Rapid Profiling." Paper published at the Second Language Research Forum, Los Angeles.

Pinter, A. 2007. "Some Benefits of Peer-Peer Interaction: 10-Year-Old Children Practising with a Communication Task." *Language Teaching Research*, 11: 187–207.

Platt, E., and F. Brooks. 1994. "The 'Acquisition-Rich Environment' Revisited." *The Modern Language Journal*, 78: 497–511.

Poehner, M. E. 2008. *Dynamic Assessment: A Vygotskian Approach to Understanding and Promoting Second Language Development*. Berlin: Springer.

Poehner, M., and J. Lantolf. 2005. "Dynamic Assessment in the Language Classroom." *Language Teaching Research*, 233–65.

Polio, C., and P. Duff. 1994. "Teachers' Language Use in University Foreign Language Classrooms: A Qualitative Analysis of English and Target Language Alternation." *The Modern Language Journal*, 78: 313–26.

Politzer, R. 1970. "Some Reflections on 'Good' and 'Bad' Language Teaching Behaviors." *Language Learning*, 20: 31–43.

Poole, D. 1992. "Language Socialization in the Second Language Classroom." *Language Learning*, 42: 593–616.

Porter, P. 1986. "How Learners Talk to Each Other: Input and Interaction in Task-Centred Discussions." In *Talking to Learn: Conversation in Second Language Acquisition*, edited by R. Day. Rowley, MA: Newbury House.

Prabhu, N. S. 1987. *Second Language Pedagogy*. Oxford: Oxford University Press.

Ranta, L. 2002. "Learning Conditions, Aptitude Complexes and SLA: A Framework for Research and Pedagogy." In *Individual Differences and Instructed Language Learning*, edited by P. Robinson, 113–35. Amsterdam: John Benjamins.

Raupach, M. 1983. "Analysis and Evaluation of Communication Strategies." In *Strategies in Interlanguage Comminication*, edited by C. Faerch and G. Kasper, 199–209. London: Longman.

Read, J., and P. Nation. 2004. "Measurement of Formulaic Sequences." In *Formulaic Sequences*, edited by N. Schmitt. Amsterdam: John Benjamins.

Reinders, H., and R. Ellis. 2009. "The Effects of Two Types of Input on Intake and the Acquisition of Implicit and Explicit Knowledge." In *Implicit and Explicit Knowledge in Second Language Learning, Testing and Teaching*, edited by R. Ellis, S. Loewen, C. Elder et al., 281–302. Bristol: Multilingual Matters.

Renout, J. 2001. "An Examination of the Relationship between Metalinguistic Awareness and Second-Language Proficiency of Adult Learners of French." *Language Awareness*, 10: 248–67.

Richards, J., and T. Rodgers. 1986. *Approaches and Methods in Language Teaching*. Second Edition. Cambridge: Cambridge University Press.

Richards, J., J. Platt, and H. Platt, eds. 1992. *Longman Dictionary of Language Teaching and Applied Linguistics*. London: Longman.

Richards, K. 2006. "'Being a Teacher': Identity and Classroom Conversation." *Applied Linguistics*, 27, 51–77.

Riley, P. 1977. *Discourse Networks in Classroom Interaction: Some Problems in Communicative Language Teaching*. Melanges Pedagogiques, University of Nancy: Crapel.

Robinson, P. 1996. "Learning Simple and Complex Rules under Implicit, Incidental Rule-Search Conditions, and Instructed Conditions." *Studies in Second Language Acquisition*, 18: 27–67.

Robinson P. 2001. "Task Complexity, Cognitive Resources, and Syllabus Design: A Triadic Framework for Examining Task Influences on SLA." In *Cognition and Second Language Instruction*, edited by P. Robinson. Cambridge: Cambridge University Press.

Robinson, P., ed. 2002a. *Individual Differences and Instructed Language Learning*. Amsterdam, John Benjamins.

Robinson, P. 2002b. "Learning Conditions, Aptitude Complexes and SLA: A Framework for Research and Pedagogy." In *Individual Differences and Instructed Language Learning*, edited by P. Robinson. Amsterdam, John Benjamins.

Robinson, P. 2005. "Aptitude and Second Language Acquisition." *Annual Review of Applied Linguistics*, 25: 46–73.

Robinson, P. 2007. "Task Complexity, Theory of Mind, and Intentional Reasoning: Effects on L2 Speech Production, Interaction, Uptake and Perceptions of Task Difficulty." *IRAL*, 45: 193–213.

Robinson, P., and Y. Yamaguchi. 1999. "Aptitude, Task Feedback and Generalizability of Focus on Form: A Classroom Study." Paper presented at the 12th AILA World Congress, Waseda University, Tokyo.

Robson, G. 1994. *Relationships between Personality, Anxiety, Proficiency and Participation*. Unpublished EDd Thesis, Temple University Japan, Tokyo.

Roebuck, R., and L. Wagner. 2004. "Teaching Repetition as a Communicative and Cognitive Tool: Evidence from a Spanish Conversation Class." *International Journal of Applied Linguistics*, 14: 70–89.

Roehr, K. 2008. "Metalinguistic Knowledge and Language Ability in University-Level L2 Learners." *Applied Linguistics*, 29: 173–99.

Roehr, K., and A. Ganem-Guttierrez. 2009. "The Status of Metalinguistic Knowledge in Instructed Adult L2 Learning." *Language Awareness*, 18: 165–81.

Rolin-Inzati, J. 2010. "The Organization of Delayed Second Language Correction." *Language Teaching Research*, 14: 183–206.

Rosa, E., and M. D. O'Neill. 1999. "Explicitness, Intake, and the Issue of Awareness." *Studies in Second Language Acquisition*, 21: 511–53.

Rulon, K., and J. McCreary. 1986. "Negotiation of Content: Teacher-Fronted and Small Group Interaction." In *Talking to Learn: Conversation in Second Language Acquisition*, edited by R. Day. Rowley, MA: Newbury House.

Russell, J., and N. Spada. 2006. "The Effectiveness of Corrective Feedback for the Acquisition of L2 Grammar: A Meta-Analysis of the Research." In *Synthesizing Research on Language Learning and Teaching*, edited by J. Norris and L. Ortega. Amsterdam: John Benjamins.

Rutherford, W. 1988. *Second Language Grammar: Learning and Teaching*. London: Longman.

Sacks, H., E. Schegloff, and G. Jefferson. 1974. "A Simplest Systematics for the Organization of Turn Taking in Conversation." *Language*, 50: 696–735.

Sagarra, N. 2007. "From CALL to Face-To-Face Interaction: The Effect of Computer-Delivered Recasts and Working Memory on L2 Development." In *Conversational Interaction in Second Language Acquisition*, edited by A. Mackey, 229–48. Oxford: Oxford University Press.

Sakui, K. 2004. *Caught in a Dilemma: The Beliefs and Practices of Japanese Teachers of English*. Unpublished PhD Thesis, University of Auckland, Auckland.

Sakui, K., and S. Gaies. 1999. "Investigating Japanese Learners' Beliefs about Language Learning." *System*, 27, 4: 473–92.

Samauda, V., and M. Bygate. 2008. *Tasks in Second Language Learning*. New York: Palgrave Macmillan.

Samuda, V. 2001. "Guiding Relationships between Form and Meaning during Task Performance: The Role of the Teacher." In *Researching Pedagogic Tasks, Second Language Learning, Teaching and Testing*, edited by M. Bygate, P. Skehan, and M. Swain, 119–14. Harlow: Longman.

Sanz, C., and K. Morgan-Short. 2004. "Positive Evidence versus Explicit Rule Presentation and Negative Feedback: A Computer-Assisted Study." *Language Learning*, 54: 35–78.

Savignon, S. 1972. *Communicative Competence: An Experiment in Foreign Language Teaching*. Philadelphia: Center for Curriculum Development.

Saville-Troike, M. 1988. "'Private Speech': Evidence for Second Language Learning Strategies during the 'Silent Period'." *Journal of Child Language*, 15: 567–90.

Saville-Troike, M. 1996. "The Ethnography of Communication." In *Sociolinguistics and Language Teaching*, edited by S. McKay and N. Hornberger. Cambridge: Cambridge University Press.

Scherer, A., and M. Wertheimer. 1964. *A Psycholinguistic Experiment in Foreign Language Teaching*. New York: McGraw Hill.

Schieffelin, B., and E. Ochs. 1986. "Language Socialization." *Annual Review of Anthropology*, 15: 163–91.

Schmidt, R. 1994. "Deconstructing Consciousness in Search of Useful Definitions for Applied Linguistics." *AILA Review*, 11: 11–26.

Schmidt, R. 2001. "Attention." In *Cognition and Second Language Instruction*, edited by P. Robinson. Cambridge: Cambridge University Press.

Schulz, R. 2001. "Cultural Differences in Student and Teacher Perceptions Concerning the Role of Grammar Instruction." *The Modern Language Journal*, 85: 244–58.

Sciarone, A., and P. Meijer. 1995. "Does Practice Make Perfect? On The Effect of Exercises on Second/Foreign Language Acquisition." *ITL Review of Applied Linguistics*, 107–108: 35–7.

Scott, V., and M. de la Fuente. 2008. "What's The Problem? Learners' Use of the L1 during Consciousness-Raising Form-Focused Tasks." *Modern Language Journal*, 92: 100–113.

Scovel, T. 1978. "The Effect of Affect on Foreign Language Learning: A Review of the Anxiety Research." *Language Learning*, 28: 129–42.

Seedhouse, P. 1996. "Classroom Interaction: Possibilities and Impossibilities." *ELT Journal*, 50: 17–24.

Seedhouse, P. 1999. "Task-Based Interaction." *ELT Journal*, 53: 149–56.

Seedhouse, P. 2004. *The Interactional Architecture of the Language Classroom: A Conversation Analysis Perspective*. Malden, MA: Blackwell.

Seedhouse, P. 2005a. "'Task' as Research Construct." *Language Learning*, 55, 3: 533–70.

Seedhouse, P. 2005b. "Conversation Analysis and Language Learning." *Language Teaching*, 38, 4: 165–87.

Selinker, L. 1972. "Interlanguage." *International Review of Applied Linguistics*, 10: 209–31.

Sfard, A. 1998. "On Two Metaphors for Learning and the Dangers of Choosing Just One." *Educational Researcher*, 27, 2: 4–13.

Sharwood-Smith, M. 1981. "Consciousness-Raising and the Second Language Learner." *Applied Linguistics*, 2: 159–69.

Sheen, R. 1994. "A Critical Analysis of the Advocacy of the Task-Based Syllabus." *TESOL Quarterly*, 28: 127–57.

Sheen, R. 2003. "Focus-on-Form – a Myth in the Making." *ELT Journal*, 57: 225–33.

Sheen, R. 2006. "Focus on Forms as a Means of Improving Accurate Oral Production." In *Investigations in Instructed Language Acquisition*, edited by A. Housen and M. Pierrard, 271–310. Berlin: Mouton de Gruyter.

Sheen, Y. 2007. "The Effects of Corrective Feedback, Language Aptitude, and Learner Attitudes on the Acquisition of English Articles." In *Conversational Interaction in Second Language Acquisition*, edited by A. Mackey, 301–322. Oxford: Oxford University Press.

Sheen, Y. 2008. "Recasts, Language Anxiety, Modified Output and L2 Learning." *Language Learning*, 58, 4: 835–74.

Shintani, N. 2011a. *A Comparison of the Effects of Comprehension-Based and Production-Based Instruction on the Acquisition of Vocabulary and Grammar by Young Japanese Learners of English*. Unpublished PhD Thesis. The University of Auckland, Auckland.

Shintani, N. 2011b. A comparative study of the effects of input-based and production-based instruction on vocabulary acquisition by young EFL learners. *Language Teaching Research*, 15, 137–58.

Shintani, N. 2011c. "Task-Based Language Teaching versus Traditional Production-Based Instruction: Do They Result in Different Classroom Processes?" *University of Sydney Papers in TESOL*, University of Sydney, Sydney.

Shintani, N., and R. Ellis. 2010. "The Incidental Acquisition of Plural-S by Japanese Children in Comprehension-Based Lessons: A Process-Product Study." *Studies in Second Language Acquisition*, 32, 4: 607–37.

Sinclair, J., and M. Coulthard. 1975. *Towards an Analysis of Discourse*. Oxford: Oxford University Press.

Skehan, P. 1989. *Individual Differences in Second-Language Learning*. London: Edward Arnold.

Skehan, P. 1996. "A Framework for the Implementation of Task-Based Instruction." *Applied Linguistics* 17: 38–62.

Skehan, P. 1998. *A Cognitive Approach to Language Learning*. Oxford: Oxford University Press.

Skehan, P. 2001. "Tasks and Language Performance Assessment." In *Researching Pedagogic Tasks, Second Language Learning, Teaching and Testing*, edited by M. Bygate, P. Skehan and M. Swain, 167–185. Harlow: Longman.

Skehan, P. 2002. "Theorising and Updating Aptitude." In *Individual Differences and Instructed Language Learning*, edited by P. Robinson. Amsterdam, John Benjamins.

Skehan, P., and P. Foster. 1997. "Task Type and Task Processing Conditions as Influences on Foreign Language Performance." *Language Teaching Research*, 1: 185–211.

Skehan, P., and P. Foster, 2005. "Strategic and Online Planning: the Influence of Surprise Information and Task Time on Second Language Performance." In *Planning and Task-Performance in a Second Language*, edited by R. Ellis, 193–208. Amsterdam: John Benjamins.

Slimani, A. 1989. "The Role of Topicalization in Classroom Language Learning." *System*, 17: 223–34.

Slimani-Rolls, A. 2005. "Rethinking Task-Based Language Learning: What We Can Learn from the Learners." *Language Teaching Research*, 9: 195–218.

Smith, P. 1970. *A Comparison of the Audiolingual and Cognitive Approaches to Foreign Language Instruction: the Pennsylvania Foreign Language Project*. Philadelphia, PA: Center for Curriculum Development.

Song, Y., and S. Andrews. 2008. "The L1 in L2 Learning – Teachers' Beliefs and Practices." *LINCOM Studies in Language Acquisition 24*. Lincom GmbH.

Spada, N. 1987. "Relationships between Instructional Differences and Learning Outcomes: A Process-Product Study of Communicative Language Teaching." *Applied Linguistics*, 8: 137–61.

Spada, N., and M. Fröhlich. 1995. *The Communicative Orientation of Language Teaching Observation Scheme (COLT)*. The National Centre for English Language Teaching, Australia.

Spada, N., and P. Lightbown. 1989. "Intensive ESL Programmes in Quebec Primary Schools." *TESL Canada*, 7: 11–32.

Spada, N., and P. Lightbown. 1993. "Instruction and the Development of Questions in the L2 Classroom." *Studies in Second Language Acquisition*, 15: 205–24.

Spada, N., and P. Lightbown. 1999. "First Language Influence and Developmental Readiness in Second Language Acquisition." *The Modern Language Journal*, 83: 1–21.

Spada, N., and P. Lightbown. 2008. "Form-Focused Instruction: Isolated or Integrated?" *TESOL Quarterly*, 42: 181–207.

Spada, N., and P. Lightbown. 2009. Interaction in Second/Foreign Language Classrooms. In *Multiple Perspectives on Interaction: Second Language Research in Honor of Susan M. Gass*, edited by A. Mackey and C. Polio, 157–74. New York: Routledge.

Spada, N., P. Lightbown, and J. White. 2006. "The Importance of Form/ Meaning Mappings in Explicit Form-Focussed Instruction." In *Investigations in Instructed Second Language Acquisition*, edited by A. Housen and M. Pierrard, 199–234. Berlin: Mouton de Gruyter.

Spada, N., and Y. Tomita. 2010. "Interactions between Type of Instruction and Type of Language Feature: A Meta-Analysis." *Language Learning*, 60, 2: 263–308.

Spolsky, B. 1968. "Recent Research in TESOL." *TESOL Quarterly*, 2, 4: 304.

Stapa, S., and Majid, A. 2009. "The Use of First Language in Developing Ideas in Second Language Writing." *European Journal of Social Sciences*, 7: 41–7.

Stenhouse, L. 1975. *An Introduction to Curriculum Research and Development*. London: Heinemann.

Sterlacci, P. 1996. "A Micro-Evaluation of a Focused-Communication Task for the ESL/EFL Classroom." Unpublished course paper. Tokyo: Temple University Japan.

Stern, H. 1983. *Fundamental Concepts of Language Teaching*. Oxford: Oxford University Press.

Stern, H. 1990. "Analysis and Experience as Variables in Second Language Pedagogy." In *The Development of Second Language Proficiency*, edited by B. Harley, J. P. Allen, J. Cummins, and M. Swain. Cambridge: Cambridge University Press.

Stewart, T. 2006. "Teacher-Researcher Collaboration or Teachers' Research?" *TESOL Quarterly*, 40: 421–30.

Stone, C. 1993. "What Is Missing in the Metaphor of Scaffolding?" In *Contexts for Learning: Sociocultural Dynamics in Children's Development*, edited by E. Forman, N. Minick, and C. Stone, 169–83. Oxford: Oxford University Press.

Storch, N. 2002. "Patterns of Interaction in ESL Pair Work." *Language Learning*, 52: 119–58.

Storch, N. 2007. "Investigating the Merits of Pair Work on a Text-Editing Task in ESL Classes." *Language Teaching Research*, 11: 143–59.

Storch, N., and A. Aldosari. 2010. "Learners' Use of L1 (Arabic) in Pair Work in An EFL Class." *Language Teaching Research*, 14, 4.

Storch, N., and G. Wigglesworth. 2003. "Is There a Role for the Use of the L1 in an L2 Setting?" *TESOL Quarterly*, 37: 760–70.

Swaffar, J., K. Arens, and M. Morgan. 1982. "Teacher Classroom Practices: Redefining Method as Task Hierarchy." *Modern Language Journal*, 66: 24–32.

Swain, M. 1993. "The Output Hypothesis: Just Speaking and Writing Aren't Enough." *Canadian Modern Language Review*, 50 158–64.

Swain, M. 1995. "Three Functions of Output in Second Language Learning." In *Principles and Practice in the Study of Language: Studies in Honour of H. G. Widdowson*, edited by G. Cook and B. Seidhofer. Oxford: Oxford University Press.

Swain, M. 1998. "Focus on Form through Conscious Reflection." In *Focus-on-Form in Classroom Second Language Acquisition*, edited by C. Doughty and J. Williams. Cambridge: Cambridge University Press.

Swain, M. 2000. "The Output Hypothesis and Beyond: Mediating Acquisition Through Collaborative Dialogue." In *Sociocultural Theory and Second Language Learning*, edited by J. Lantolf. Oxford: Oxford University Press.

Swain, M. 2006. "Languaging, Agency and Collaboration in Advanced Second Language Learning." In *Advanced Language Learning: The Contributions of Halliday and Vygotsky*, edited by H. Byrnes. London: Continuum.

Swain, M., and S. Lapkin. 1998. "Interaction and Second Language Learning: Two Adolescent French Immersion Students Working Together." *The Modern Language Journal*, 82: 320–37.

Swain, M., and S. Lapkin. 2000. "Task-Based Second Language Learning: The Use of the First Language." *Language Teaching Research*, 4: 251–74.

Swain, M., and S. Lapkin. 2001. "Focus on Form through Collaborative Dialogue: Exploring Task Effects." In *Researching Pedagogic Tasks, Second Language Learning, Teaching and Testing*, edited by M. Bygate, P. Skehan, and M. Swain. Harlow: Longman.

Swain. M., and S. Lapkin. 2002. "Talking it Through: Two French Immersion Learners' Response to Reformulation." *International Journal of Educational Research*, 37: 285–304.

Swain, M., and S. Lapkin. 2007. "The Distributed Nature of Second Language Learning: A Case Study." In *Focus on Form and Teacher Education: Studies in Honour of Rod Ellis*, edited by S. Fotos and H. Nassaji. Oxford: Oxford University Press.

Swain, M., S. Lapkin, I. Knouzi et al. 2009. "Languaging: University Students Learn The Grammatical Concept of Voice in French." *Modern Language Journal*, 93: 5–29.

Swan, M. 2005. "Legislating by Hypothesis: The Case of Task-Based Instruction." *Applied Linguistics*, 26: 376–401.

Takahashi, S. 2005. "Pragmalinguistic Awareness: Is It Related to Motivation and Proficiency." *Applied Linguistics*, 26: 90–120.

Takimoto, M. 2008. "The Effects of Various Kinds of Form-Focused Instruction on Learners' Ability to Comprehend and Produce Polite Requests in English." *TESL Canada Journal*, 26: 31–51.

Tarone, E., and M. Swain. 1995. "A Sociolinguistic Perspective on Second-Language Use in Immersion Classrooms." *Modern Language Journal*, 79: 166–78.

Tharp, R., and R. Gallimore. 1988. *Rousing Minds to Life. Teaching, Learning and Schooling in Social Context*. Cambridge: Cambridge University Press.

Thesen, J., and A. Kuzel. 1999. "Participatory Inquiry." In *Doing Qualitative Research*, edited by B. Crabtree and W. Miller, 269–290. Newbury Park CA: Sage Publications.

Thornbury, S. 1996. "Teachers Research Teacher Talk." *ELT Journal*, 50: 279–89.

Tocalli-Beller, A., and M. Swain, 2007. "Riddles and Puns in The ESL Classroom: Adults Talk to Learn." In *Conversational Interaction in Second Language Acquisition: A Series of Empirical Studies*, edited by A. Mackey, 143–67. Oxford: Oxford University Press.

Tode, T. 2007. "Durability Problems with Explicit Instruction in an EFL Context: The Learning of Copula Be Before and After the Introduction of Auxiliary Be." *Language Teaching Research*, 11: 11–30.

Tomasello, M., and C. Herron. 1988. "Down the Garden Path: Inducing And Correcting Overgeneralization Errors in the Foreign Language Classroom." *Applied Psycholinguistics*, 9: 237–46.

Tomasello, M., and C. Herron. 1989. "Feedback for Language Transfer Errors: The Garden Path Technique." *Studies in Second Language Acquisition*, 11: 385–95.

Tong-Fredericks, C. 1984. "Types of Oral Communication Activities and The Language They Generate: A Comparison." *System*, 12: 133–34.

Torr, J. 1993. "Classroom Discourse: Children From English-Speaking and Non-English Speaking Backgrounds." *Australian Review of Applied Linguistics*, 16: 37–56.

Toth, P. 2006. "Processing Instruction and a Role for Output in Second Language Acquisition." *Language Learning*, 56: 319–85.

Trahey, M. 1996. "Positive Evidence in Second Language Acquisition: Some Long Term Effects." *Second Language Research*, 12: 111–39.

Trahey, M., and L. White. 1993. "Positive Evidence and Preemption in the Second Language Classroom." *Studies in Second Language Acquisition*, 15: 181–204.

Turnbull, M. 2000. "Analyses of Core French Teachers' Language Use. A Summary." Proceedings of Bilingual Child, Global Citizen Colloquium. University of New Brunswick, Fredericton, New Brunswick. Retrieved from www.casalt.org (accessed 12 October, 2011).

Turnbull, M., and K. Arnett. 2002. "Teachers' Uses of the Target and First Languages in Second and Foreign Language Classrooms." *Annual Review of Applied Linguistics*, 22: 204–18.

Tuz, E. 1993. "From Controlled Practice to Communicative Activity: Does Training Transfer?" *Temple University Japan Research Studies in TESOL*, 1: 97–108.

Ur, P. 1996. *A Course in Language Teaching*. Cambridge: Cambridge University Press.

Urano, K. 2002. "Effects of Simplification and Elaboration on L2 Comprehension and Acquisition." Retrieved from http://www2.hawaii.edu/~urano/research/slrf (accessed August 20, 2005).

Ushioda, E. 1998. "Effective Motivation Thinking: A Cognitive Theoretical Approach to the Study of Language Learning Motivation." In *Current Issues in English Language Teaching Methodology*, edited by E. Soler and V. Espurs, 39–50. Plymouth: University of Plymouth.

Van den Branden, K., ed. 2006. *Task-based Language Teaching: From Theory to Practice*. Cambridge: Cambridge University Press.

Van den Branden, K., M. Bygate, and J. Norris. 2009. *Task-Based Language Teaching: A Reader*. Amsterdam: John Benjamins.

Van Lier, L. 1988. *The Classroom and the Language Learner*. London: Longman.

Van Lier, L. 1991. "Inside the Classroom: Learning Processes and Teaching Procedures." *Applied Language Learning*, 2: 29–69.

Van Lier, L. 1996. *Interaction in the Language Curriculum: Awareness, Autonomy and Authenticity*. London: Longman.

Van Lier, L. 2000a. "From Input to Affordance: Social-Interactive Learning from an Ecological Perspective." In *Sociocultural Theory and Second Language Learning*, edited by J. Lantolf. Oxford: Oxford University Press.

Van Lier, L. 2000b. "Constraints and Resources in Classroom Talk: Issues in Equality and Symmetry." In *English Language Teaching in its Social Context: A Reader*, edited by C. Candlin and N. Mercer, 90–107. New York: Routledge.

VanPatten, B. 1990a. "Attending to Form and Content in the Input." *Studies in Second Language Acquisition*, 12: 287–301.

VanPatten, B. 1990b. "The Acquisition of Clitic Pronouns in Spanish: Two Case Studies." In *Second Language Acquisition – Foreign Language Learning*, edited by B. VanPatten and J. Lee. Bristol: Multilingual Matters.

VanPatten, B. 1996. *Input Processing and Grammar Instruction in Second Language Acquisition*. Norwood, NJ: Ablex.

VanPatten, B. 2002. "Processing Instruction: an Update." *Language Learning*, 52: 755–804.

VanPatten, B. 2004a. *Processing Instruction: Theory, Research, and Commentary*. Mahwah, NJ: Lawrence Erlbaum.

VanPatten, B. 2004b. "Input-Processing in Second Language Acquisition." In *Processing Instruction: Theory, Research, and Commentary*, edited by B. VanPatten. Mahwah, NJ: Lawrence Erlbaum.

VanPatten, B., and C. Sanz. 1995. "From Input to Output: Processing Instruction and Communicative Tasks." In *Second Language Acquisition Theory and Pedagogy*, edited by F. Eckman, D. Highland, P. Lee et al. Mahwah. NJ: Lawrence Erlbaum.

VanPatten, B., and S. Oikennon. 1996. "Explanation vs. Structured Input in Processing Instruction." *Studies in Second Language Acquisition*, 18: 495–510.

VanPatten, B., and T. Cadierno. 1993. "SLA as Input Processing: A Role for Instruction." *Studies in Second Language Acquisition*, 15: 225–43.

Varonis, E., and S. Gass. 1985. "Non-Native/Non-Native Conversations: A Model for Negotiation of Meaning." *Applied Linguistics*, 6: 71–90.

Vasquez, C., and J. Harvey. 2010. "Raising Teachers' Awareness about Corrective Feedback through Replication." *Language Teaching Research*, 14: 421–43.

Von Elek, T., and M. Oskarsson. 1973. *Teaching Foreign Language Grammar to Adults: A Comparative Study*. Stockholm: Almqvist and Wiksell.

Vygotsky, L. 1978. *Mind in Society*. Cambridge: MA: MIT Press.

Vygotsky, L. 1987. *The Collected Works of L. S. Vygotsky Volume 1: Thinking and Speaking*. New York: Plenum Press.

Wagner, M., and G. Tilney. 1983. "The Effect of 'Superlearning Techniques' on the Vocabulary Acquisition and Alpha Brainwave Production of Language Learners." *TESOL Quarterly*, 17: 5–17.

Wajnryb, R. 1990. *Grammar Dictation*. Oxford: Oxford University Press.

Wallace, M. 1998. *Action Research for Language Teachers*. Cambridge: Cambridge University Press.

Walsh, S. 2002. "Construction or Obstruction: Teacher Talk and Learner Involvement in the EFL Classroom." *Language Teaching Research*, 6: 3–24.

Walsh, S. 2006. *Investigating classroom discourse*. London: Routledge.

Waring, H. 2008. "Using Explicit Positive Assessment in the Language Classroom: IRF, Feedback, and Learning Opportunities." *Modern Language Journal*, 92: 577–94.

Warren-Price, T. 2003. "Action Research: Investigating the Amount of Teacher Talk in My Classroom." Unpublished MA paper, University of Birmingham.

Watanabe, Y., and S. Swain. 2007. "Effects of Proficiency Differences and Patterns of Pair Interaction on Second Language Learning: Collaborative Dialogue between Adult ESL Learners." *Language Teaching Research*, 11: 121–42.

Watson-Gegeo, K. 1988. "Ethnography in ESL: Defining the Essentials." *TESOL Quarterly*, 22: 575–91.

Weinert, R. 1987. "Processes in Classroom Second Language Development: the Acquisition of Negation in German." In *Second Language Acquisition in Context*, edited by R. Ellis. London: Prentice Hall International.

Wells, G. 1999. *Dialogic Inquiry: Towards a Sociocultural Practice and Theory of Education*. Cambridge: Cambridge University Press.

Wesche, M. 1981. "Language Aptitude Measures in Streaming, Matching Students with Methods, and Diagnosis of Learning Problems." In *Individual Differences and Universals in Language Learning Aptitude*, edited by K. Diller. Rowley, MA: Newbury House.

Wesche, M., and D. Ready. 1985. "Foreigner Talk in the University Classroom." In *Input in Second Language Acquisition*, edited by S. Gass and C. Madden. Rowley, MA: Newbury House.

Wette, R. 2009. "Making the Instructional Curriculum as an Interactive, Contextualized Process: Case Studies of Seven ESOL Teachers." *Language Teaching Research*, 13: 337–65.

White, J. 1998. "Getting Learners' Attention: A Typographical Input Enhancement Study." In *Focus-on-Form in Classroom Second Language Acquisition*, edited by C. Doughty and J. Williams. Cambridge: Cambridge University Press.

White, J., and L. Ranta. 2002. "Examining the Interface between Metalinguistic Task Performance and Oral Production in a Second Language." *Language Awareness*, 11: 259–90.

White, J., and P. Lightbown. 1984. "Asking and Answering in ESL Classes." *Canadian Modern Language Review*, 40: 288–344.

White, L. 1987. "Against Comprehensible Input: The Input Hypothesis and the Development of Second Language Competence." *Applied Linguistics*, 8: 95–110.

White, L. 1991. "Adverb Placement in Second Language Acquisition: Some Effects of Negative and Positive Evidence in the Classroom." *Second Language Research*, 7: 133–61.

White, L., N. Spada, P. Lightbown, and L. Ranta. 1991. "Input Enhancement and Question Formation." *Applied Linguistics*, 12: 416–32.

White, M. 1992. "Teachers' Questions – Form, Function, and Interaction: A Study of Two Teachers." Unpublished paper, Temple University Japan.

Widdowson, H. 1978. *Teaching Language as Communication.* Oxford: Oxford University Press.

Widdowson, H. 2003. *Defining Issues in English Language Teaching.* Oxford: Oxford University Press.

Wigglesworth, G. 2001. "Influences on Performance in Task-Based Oral Assessments." In *Researching Pedagogic Tasks: Second Language Learning, Teaching and Testing*, edited by M. Bygate, P. Skehan, M. Swain et al., 186–209. London: Longman.

Wilkins, D. 1976. *Notional Syllabuses.* Oxford: Oxford University Press.

Williams, J. 1999. "Learner-Generated Attention to Form." *Language Learning*, 49: 583–625.

Williams, J. 2001. "The Effectiveness of Spontaneous Attention to Form." *System*, 29: 325–40.

Williams, J., and J. Evans. 1998. "What Kind of Focus and on Which Forms?" In *Focus-on-form in Classroom Second Language Acquisition*, edited by C. Doughty and J. Williams. Cambridge: Cambridge University Press.

Willis, J. 1996. *A Framework for Task-Based Learning.* Harlow: Longman.

Wong Fillmore, L. 1985. "When Does Teacher Talk Work as Input?" In *Input in Second Language Acquisition*, edited by S. Gass and C. Madden. Rowley, MA: Newbury House.

Wood, D., J. Bruner and G. Ross. 1976. "The Role of Tutoring in Problem-Solving." *Journal of Child Pyschology and Psychiatry*, 17: 89–1000.

Woodrow, L. 2006. "Anxiety and Speaking English as a Second Language." *RELC Journal*, 37: 308–28.

Woods, D. 1996. *Teacher Cognition in Language Teaching.* Cambridge: Cambridge University Press.

Wray, A. 2000. "Formulaic Sequences in Second Language Teaching: Principle and Practice." *Applied Linguistics*, 21: 463–89.

Wu, K. 1993. "Classroom Interaction and Teacher Questions Revisited." *RELC Journal*, 24: 49–68.

Yang, Y., and R. Lyster. 2010. "Effects of Form-Focused Practice and Feedback on Chinese EFL Learners' Acquisition of Regular and Irregular Past Tense Forms." *Studies in Second Language Acquisition*, 32: 235–63.

Yano, Y., M. H. Long. and S. Ross. 1994. "The Effects of Simplified and Elaborated Texts on Foreign Language Reading Comprehension." *Language Learning*, 44, 189–219.

Yoshida, R. 2008. "Teachers' Choice and Learners' Preference of Corrective-Feedback Types." *Language Awareness*, 17: 78–93.

Young, D. J. 1990. "An Investigation of Students' Perspectives on Anxiety and Speaking." *Foreign Language Annals*, 23, 539–53.

Yule, G. 1997. *Referential Communication Tasks.* Mahwah, New Jersey: Lawrence Erlbaum.

References

Yule, G., and D. McDonald. 1990. "Resolving Referential Conflicts in L2 Interaction: The Effect of Proficiency and Interactive Role." *Language Learning*, 40: 539–56.

Zhao S., and J. Bitchener. 2007. "Incidental Focus on Form in Teacher-Learner and Learner-Learner Interactions." *System*, 35: 431–47.

Zimmerman. D. 1998. "Discoursal Identities and Social Identities." In *Identities in Talk*, edited by C. Antaki and S. Widdicombe, 87–106. London: Sage.

Zuengler, J., and K. Cole. 2005. "Language Socialization and Second Language Learning.' In *Handbook of Second Language Teaching and Learning*, E. Hinkel. Mahwah, NJ: Lawrence Erlbaum.

Index

action research, 21, 27–30, 31, 48, 119, 345
analytic teaching, 62, 69, 271, 291
applied research, 3–4
aptitude-treatment-interaction (APT),
    311–12, 313, 334

classroom discourse, Chapter 4, 10–11, 42, 45,
    115–16, 175–84, 191
    of language use in, 95–6, 114
Cognition Hypothesis, 202, 208, 216
communicative language teaching, (CLT), 10,
    52, 60–4, 73, 85, 129, 196, 251, 268,
    323
    see also task-based language teaching
comparative method studies, Chapter 3, 9–10,
    35, 256, 302
comprehension-based language teaching, 17,
    24–5, 57–60, 65, 67, 70, 278, 297–8, 303
confirmatory research, 34–41, 48
    see also input-based instruction
consciousness-raising (CR), 272, 274–5,
    277–8, 281–4, 288, 289, 294, 304, 305–6
consciousness-raising tasks, 169, 226, 229,
    264–6, 274, 277, 283–4, 304
conversation analysis (CA), 11, 76, 79, 96–104,
    110, 203, 206, 243, 338, 340
corrective feedback (CF), 3, 8, 12, 13, 14, 16,
    17, 24, 36, 42, 46, 64, 100, 119, 120,

    135–43, 148, 149, 178, 180, 197, 201,
    241–2, 250–3, 256–63, 268, 269, 270,
    273, 274, 290, 292–3, 299, 301, 304, 306,
    311–12, 314–15, 317, 338, 345–6, 348
explicit correction/feedback, 16, 138, 139,
    140, 179, 180, 228, 253, 258–9, 263, 314
implicit correction/feedback, 16, 228,
    241–2, 263, 268
input-providing feedback, 17, 139, 143, 259,
    263, 268, 318
metalinguistic feedback, 138, 141, 261, 301
output-prompting feedback, 17, 22, 139,
    142, 263, 268, 318; *see also* prompts
prompts, 141, 180, 259–63, 317
recasts, 16, 17, 24, 26, 137, 138, 139, 140–1,
    143, 148, 180–1, 190, 204, 210, 228, 250,
    251, 252–3, 256–63, 269, 293, 301,
    311–12, 314, 317, 320, 334
regulatory scale, 140, 241
timing of corrective feedback, 142
uptake, 13, 23, 24, 87, 135, 178–81, 184–5,
    192, 206, 228, 249–52, 268, 269, 287, 320,
    344, 348
correlational research, 35, 37–9

definition of 'language teaching research', 1
definition of 'second language classroom
    research', 2

Language Teaching Research & Language Pedagogy, First Edition. Rod Ellis.
© 2012 John Wiley & Sons, Ltd. Published 2012 by John Wiley & Sons, Ltd.

demotivation, 18, 326–7
descriptive research, 25, 41–6, 47, 48, 75, 338
'development' versus 'acquisition', 238–40
discourse control, 92, 93, 122, 298

enhanced input, 17, 285, 286–7, 289, 294
enriched input, 285, 286, 287, 289
ethnographic research, 43–5, 46, 76
experimental research, 25, 35–8, 40, 53, 249
explicit instruction, 3, 17, 56, 67, 71, 249, 268, 271, 274, 275–6, 277, 278, 282, 283, 284, 288–9, 292, 293, 294, 295–6, 297, 300, 314
explicit L2 knowledge, 17, 18, 54, 148, 248, 264, 265, 266, 267, 275, 277, 280–4, 287, 301, 302, 304
exploratory practice, 4, 21, 30–2, 190, 345

focused tasks *see* tasks
FOCUS system, 80
focus on form, 14, 16, 17–18, 34, 62–4, 69, 70–1, 145–6, 175, 176, 180, 181, 197, 201, 205–6, 226, 227–9, 232, 233, 249, 252–3, 256, 266, 267, 271, 272–5, 278, 279, 280, 292, 294, 304, 305, 312, 341
focus on forms, 16, 18, 62, 63–4, 69, 70, 71, 249, 256, 271–5, 276, 277, 279, 280, 304, 305, 313
form-focused episodes (FFEs), 16, 48, 133–4, 145–6, 176, 181, 184–5, 205–6, 227–9, 229, 251–2, 267, 269
formal research, 21, 23–6, 31, 46
formulaic speech, 13, 153, 156, 162, 163–6, 176, 191
functional instruction, 281–2

group work, 13–14, 96, 107–9, 162, 175, 177, 184–91, 192, 197, 201, 214–15, 229, 242–3, 247, 310, 320, 322, 344

history of language teaching research, 4–9

immersion programmes, 2, 9, 24–5, 110, 115, 127, 139, 141, 161, 166, 167, 168, 169–70, 177, 180–1, 183, 188, 245, 291, 306
implicit instruction, 275–6, 278, 289, 301
implicit L2 knowledge, 18, 146, 258, 264, 266, 267, 280–1, 284, 296, 301–2, 339
individual learner factors, Chapter 10, 8, 18–19, 35, 38, 39, 40, 68, 201, 208, 268

initiate–respond–follow-up (IRF), 11, 88–92, 93, 95, 103, 104, 105, 107, 111, 112, 120, 124, 151, 177, 192, 338, 344
interaction analysis, 45, 62, 75, 77–86
Interaction Hypothesis, 23, 25, 255
interactional sequences, 95, 110, 112
interactionist-cognitive theories, 16, 135, 147, 181, 187, 192, 204, 238, 239–40, 264, 267, 269, 273, 341
interlanguage, 2, 14, 154, 156, 167, 186, 188, 192, 202, 207, 240, 257, 259, 279, 285, 286, 289, 295, 299, 339

L1 use, 127–31, 142, 143, 144, 145
language analytical ability, 309, 312, 314–15, 335
language aptitude, 9, 18, 40, 48, 56, 192, 266, 269, 309, 311, 312–15, 326, 335
language anxiety, 18, 35, 36, 40, 309, 318–21, 334
language play, 13, 169, 182–4, 191, 193, 310, 338
language-related episodes (LREs), 204–5, 210, 215, 218, 229, 231, 244, 264, 265, 268, 283, 341
languaging, 174, 175, 204, 226, 241, 245–8, 267, 268, 293
learner initiation, 13, 84, 88, 92, 94, 95, 111, 146, 176, 178, 179, 181, 185, 205–6, 210, 230, 250, 252, 309
  see also discourse control
learner questions, 176–7, 191
learner repetitions, 177–8
learners' grammatical development, 152–5
learners' pragmatic development, 155–7
learning strategies, 329–33

measures of L2 learning, 40, 72, 239, 240, 302
measures of L2 production, 206–8
measuring classroom processes, 338–9
metalanguage:
  learners' use of, 171–5, 184, 191
  teacher's use of, 12, 13, 131–4, 144, 148, 228, 276, 344
metatalk, 88, 169, 170, 171, 216
method comparisons *see* comparative method studies
micro-genetic analysis, 42, 43, 108, 157, 206, 230, 240, 242–4
modified input, 22, 23, 36, 212–13, 250, 253–5, 268, 315

modified output, 22, 36, 181, 187, 210, 211, 212, 214, 254, 255, 268, 273, 320

motivation, 18, 29, 37–9, 56, 73, 128, 270, 307, 308, 309, 318, 322, 323, 324–9

negotiation of meaning, 14, 15, 23, 91, 93–4, 100, 102, 112, 139, 181, 184, 185, 187, 189, 195, 204, 208, 209, 212, 215, 217, 226, 228, 238, 265, 269, 332

negotiation of form, 139, 180, 226, 228, 233, 238, 271

noticing, 135, 148, 212, 231, 238, 245, 247, 251, 256, 257–8, 264–5, 266, 273, 281, 287, 289, 308, 311, 313, 325

off-task talk, 97, 102

order of acquisition, 17, 52, 278

participant structure *see* classroom discourse

practical knowledge, 146, 342, 343, 344, 348

practitioner research, 5, 26–33, 231, 348

present-practice-produce (PPP), 59, 61, 63, 64, 68, 70, 197, 278, 294, 298

private speech, 13, 128, 158, 162–3, 169–71, 182, 238, 247

Processing Instruction, 39, 278, 294–8, 305, 311

process-product research, 47, 77, 81, 85

production-based instruction, 34, 35, 59, 60, 68, 278, 285, 286, 289–98, 303

recasts *see* corrective feedback

receptivity, 310–11, 321

repair, 12, 13, 98, 100–2, 110, 111–12, 134, 135, 141, 142, 148, 179, 180–1, 185, 190, 243, 252, 320

scaffolding, 90, 91, 104–8, 112, 126, 128, 136, 140, 141, 187, 188, 217, 241–2, 244, 248, 265, 267, 310, 341

sequence of acquisition, 13, 17, 152–3, 278

silent period, 13, 161–3, 191, 211

socialization of classroom learners, 76, 109–10, 152, 157, 158–60

sociocultural theory (SCT), 8, 11. 14, 16, 104–5, 128, 136, 140, 141, 143, 169, 170, 181, 183, 237, 238–9, 241, 242, 243, 248, 255, 264, 266, 273, 280, 281, 282, 338, 341, 343

structural and semantic simplification, 166–8, 191

superlearning methods, 57, 65, 67

task-based teaching (TBLT), 9, 15, 16, 60, 62, 71, 92, 111, 186, 191, 196–8, 201, 226, 231–2, 233–4, 270

tasks, Chapter 7:
  defining 'task', 198–9
  design variables, 14, 187, 200–1, 214–17, 219
  effects of setting on task performance, 209–11
  evaluation of, 230–2
  focused tasks, 16, 17, 141, 197, 200, 203–4, 208, 224–7, 235, 291, 292, 294
  implementation variables, 14, 187, 201–2, 203, 204, 214, 217–18, 219–23
  information-gap tasks, 14, 169, 187, 200, 201, 209–10, 265, 315
  input-based tasks, 14, 208, 211–14, 268
  learner interaction and, 214–18
  learner production and, 218–23
  opinion-gap tasks, 14, 187, 200, 209–10, 218, 219, 225, 235
  unfocused tasks, 197, 200, 203, 224, 225, 226, 227, 265

teacher cognitions/beliefs, 9, 12, 129, 133, 143–7, 148

teacher education, 9, 19, 119–20, 125, 134, 341–8

teacher-questions, 12, 90, 120–6, 147, 338, 344

teacher-talk, 7, 11–12, 61, 116–20, 147, 149, 186

technical knowledge, 134, 146, 342–3, 344, 345, 348

tests and testing, 36–7, 58, 59, 61, 62, 64, 72, 196, 205, 241, 248, 252, 258, 266, 282, 284, 302

text-creation activities, 289–90, 291–4, 297, 304

text-manipulation activities, 17, 288, 290, 291, 294, 295, 297, 304

Total Physical Response (TPR), 52, 58–9, 67

turn-taking, 11, 79, 87, 90, 98–100, 111, 176, 310

uptake *see* corrective feedback

willingness to communicate, 18, 309, 321–4, 325, 334

working memory, 18, 188, 208, 309, 311, 312, 315–18, 319, 335

Zone of Proximal Development (ZPD), 105, 107, 108, 136, 188, 242, 244, 267

CPSIA information can be obtained
at www.ICGtesting.com
Printed in the USA
BVHW08s1137130918
527376BV00007B/20/P